PERSPECTIVES ON MEDIA EFFECTS

COMMUNICATION

A series of volumes edited by:
Dolf Zillmann and Jennings Bryant

PERSPECTIVES ON MEDIA EFFECTS

Edited by

Jennings Bryant
University of Houston

Dolf Zillmann
Indiana University

LEA LAWRENCE ERLBAUM ASSOCIATES, PUBLISHERS
1986 Hillsdale, New Jersey   London

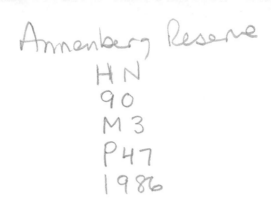
Lawrence Erlbaum Associates, Inc., Publishers
365 Broadway
Hillsdale, New Jersey 07642

Library of Congress Cataloging in Publication Data
Main entry under title

Perspectives on media effects.

   Includes index.
   1.   Mass media — Psychological aspects — United States —
Addresses, essays, lectures.   2. Mass media — Social
aspects — United States — Addresses, essays, lectures.
3. Television and children — United States — Addresses,
essays, lectures.   4. Television broadcasting — Influence
— United States — Addresses, essays, lectures.   I. Bryant,
Jennings.   II. Zillmann, Dolf.
HN90.M3P47   1986   302.2'34   85-13110
ISBN 0-89859-641-6

Printed in the United States of America
10 9 8 7 6 5 4 3 2

Contents

List of Contributors

Samuel Ball, Department of Education, The University of Sydney, Sydney, Australia

Leonard Berkowitz, Department of Psychology, University of Wisconsin, Madison, Wisconsin

Victoria Billings, Department of Sociology, University of California, Los Angeles, California

Jennings Bryant, School of Communication, University of Houston, Houston, Texas

James Ettema, School of Speech, Northwestern University, Evanston, Illinois

George Gerbner, The Annenberg School of Communication, University of Pennsylvania, Philadelphia, Pennsylvania

Sheldon Gilbert, S.I. Newhouse School of Public Communication, Syracuse University, Syracuse, New York

Bradley S. Greenberg, Department of Telecommunication, Michigan State University, East Lansing, Michigan

Larry Gross, The Annenberg School of Communication, University of Pennsylvania, Philadelphia, Pennsylvania

Robert P. Hawkins, School of Journalism and Mass Communication, University of Wisconsin, Madison, Wisconsin

Jerome Johnston, Institute for Social Research, The University of Michigan, Ann Arbor, Michigan

Neil M. Malamuth, Communication Studies, University of California, Los Angeles, California

Maxwell McCombs, Department of Journalism, University of Texas, Austin, Texas

Emelia Millward, Department of Education, The University of Sydney, Sydney, Australia

Michael Morgan, Department of Communication Studies, University of Massachusetts, Amherst, Massachusetts

Patricia Palmer, Department of Education, The University of Sydney, Sydney, Australia

Suzanne Pingree, Department of Agricultural Journalism, University of Wisconsin, Madison, Wisconsin

Byron Reeves, Mass Communication Research Center, University of Wisconsin, Madison, Wisconsin

Alan M. Rubin, School of Speech Communication, Kent State University, Kent, Ohio

Jerry Salvaggio, School of Communication, University of Houston, Houston, Texas

Joan Schleuder, Mass Communication Research Center, University of Wisconsin, Madison, Wisconsin

Nancy Signorielli, The Annenberg School of Communication, University of Pennsylvania, Philadelphia, Pennsylvania

Robin Smith, Institute of Child Development, University of Minnesota, Minneapolis, Minnesota

Alexis S. Tan, Department of Mass Communication, Texas Tech University, Lubbock, Texas

Percy H. Tannenbaum, Survey Research Center, University of California, Berkeley, California

Esther Thorson, School of Journalism and Mass Communication, University of Wisconsin, Madison, Wisconsin

J. Mallory Wober, Independent Broadcasting Authority, London, England

Dolf Zillmann, Institute for Communication Research, Indiana University, Bloomington, Indiana

Preface

An anomaly exists in the coverage of mass communication research. If the scholarly journals in this area were to be examined, it would be clear that a preponderance of the empirical research reported is and has been concerned with media effects—the social, cultural, and psychological impact of communicating via the mass media. Yet, very few general scholarly monographs or anthologies on this topic exist. In fact, the case could be made that this volume is the first such general and relatively comprehensive collection of scholarly "state of the art" reports on mass media effects since the 1954 publication of the classic anthology *The Process and Effects of Mass Communication* edited by Wilbur Schramm (somewhat revised edition in 1971, with Donald F. Roberts). Those books and numerous government documents that have appeared in the interim between that initial anthology and the present volume either have tended to focus exclusively on a single medium and/or on a single audience, or they have been targeted primarily toward undergraduate audiences.

There is a second reason why the time seems to be right for a book such as this one. In several domains of active media-effects research, that critical point has been reached where sufficient evidence has been aggregated to begin to generate or support theory (e.g., cultivation processes, entertainment theory) or at least to justify an informed critical appraisal (e.g., uses and gratifications, minorities and the media) or a reappraisal (e.g., educational effects, prosocial effects). At the same time, research on several relatively new but promising topics and perspectives has matured to a point where controlled speculation can become more constructive and can provide valuable heuristic guidance and momentum (e.g., television addiction, personality differences).

For better or for worse, the tradition of studying the social and psychological impact of mass communication seems to have "matured" to the level where certain domains of inquiry either have lost momentum or have outgrown feasible treatment in a single chapter. Therefore, a treatment of persuasion, advertising effects, or general aspects of political communication—topics that formed much of the heart of Schramm's anthology—are absent from the present volume. The reason for this is that specialized monographs and anthologies devoted to each topic are readily available.

We have been most fortunate in attaining the collaboration of investigators who have made notable contributions to the study of media effects. Their work spans a great variety of concerns with the various dimensions of media impact and of approaches to studying it. Unlike the authors whose works graced Schramm's earlier anthology, the majority of our contributors claim departments or schools of communication as their academic home. Yet the fact that the "state of the art" of certain areas of mass communication inquiry is most frequently associated with researchers whose primary affiliations are with departments of psychology, sociology, or education attests to the lingering interdisciplinary character of theory and research in media effects.

The first chapter of *Perspectives on Media Effects* reflects 25 years of investigation of the impact of delivering "news" via the mass media. As noted by Maxwell McCombs and Sheldon Gilbert, the impact questions they consider "signal a shift to research on the cognitive, long-term implications of daily journalism." In this chapter, the focal topic of media agenda-setting is conceptualized within the broader study of public opinion, and the studies that have contributed most substantially to this important area are examined for their primary contributions to the ways news influences our pictures of the world.

The cultivation process that the media serve and the potential of the predominant public medium of our current era—television—to influence our most important cultural conventions recently have received much scholarly and popular attention. George Gerbner, Larry Gross, Michael Morgan, and Nancy Signorielli have undertaken the task of synthesizing the massive body of research in this area. Their comprehensive report spans the several approaches to cultivation research. These authors describe cultivation research as "a complement to traditional approaches to media effects research."

Possibly no single media-effects tradition has received more scholarly or lay attention than the study of social learning of aggression from television. Alexis Tan presents the theoretical model that has generated such a large body of research and then summarizes many of the primary research findings in this area. As he reports, "the interest in television violence and aggression lingers, and with it the accompanying controversy."

One of the scholars whose research has contributed most substantially to the study of media violence and viewer aggression is Leonard Berkowitz. In his chapter with Karen Heimer Rogers, a perspective is introduced that should cause many scholars to rethink the conclusions that they have derived from research on media effects. Their "priming effect analysis" is thoughtfully applied both to antisocial and prosocial behaviors that may be promoted by the mass media.

Neil Malamuth and Victoria Billings examine a recurrent "hot" topic in media-effects research: the functions and effects of pornography. After introducing two theoretical models that have been proposed to account for such functions and effects, they critically evaluate a sizable body of empirical literature that has recently emerged in the study of pornography's impact.

For many years, the "addictive" power of the mass media, especially television, has been touted. Yet scholars have only just begun to study this process and these effects. Robin Smith reports on the uses and abuses of the term *television addiction,* questions the validity of using the term in light of psychological theories of addiction processes, and reports the first research evidence that seeks "to document the existence, nature, and prevalence of TV addiction." It seems quite likely that this work may represent the beginnings of an important new research tradition in media effects.

Samuel Ball, Patricia Palmer, and Emelia Millward examine another perennial issue in media effects: the educational impact of television. In their chapter they examine the direct influence of television viewing on IQ, school achievement, and reading; the indirect influence of television viewing in the development of social relationships; and the mediating factors of family context on learning from television. Finally, they promote the reconsideration of television and education, urging teachers to "recognize that television is a major part of our children's experiences" and "to share the pedagogical dais with television."

Among the probing questions asked by Jerome Johnston and James Ettema in considering how to use television to the best advantage are: "Can highly effective prosocial television be engineered?" "What role can social research play in its creation?" After providing a useful conceptualization to assist in answering these and related questions, the authors review the "large and growing body of research" that helps provide interesting answers to these questions.

Offering a stern indictment of research that is not there when it is needed, Bradley Greenberg summarizes the available research on minorities and the mass media. Included in this chapter are examinations of the kinds of portrayals of minorities found in a variety of media, trends in minority portrayal, and an analysis of studies examining social effects and effectiveness. His thought-provoking final section outlines "new research on what appear to us as missed opportunities and altogether new ones in a changing mass media environment."

Recent newspaper headlines reported "Networks Vow Not to Project Early Returns." To understand the whys, wherefores, and implications of this decision, or to consider alternative solutions to the problem of "how the media have influenced our natural political life," all one has to do is turn to Percy Tannenbaum's chapter on "Policy Options for Early Election Projections."

Until recently, personality studies in media effects were rare. J. M. Wober traces the development of personality theories that offer much in the way of clarifying media effects; then he reviews the literature concerning the possible role of personality in influencing the uses and effects of television messages. He concludes: "Television is now a principal channel or purveyor of culture and as such can be studied as one determinant of personality among the young, as well as something that interacts with personality among older people" (p. 227).

Robert Hawkins and Suzanne Pingree focus on a process that recently has been considered more frequently in the examination of media effects—the activity level of the child. They "elaborate on meanings of activity as this activity is applied to television use, and suggest how these different meanings imply different kinds of effects" (p. 233). A persistent theme of their chapter is that effective prediction of media effects requires the consideration of viewer sensitivity.

In recent years, cognitive psychology increasingly has been adopted by mass communication scholars who seek to explain media effects or their antecedent or concomitant conditions. Byron Reeves, Esther Thorson, and Joan Schleuder represent this tradition as they indicate how psychological theories and chronometric measures can be used in the study of attention to television. Their chapter reports pilot experimentation in the areas of information processing and neural functioning, areas that are crucial for the full consideration of media effects.

During the past decade, little could have been more rare than a mass communication conference without a paper or panel on "uses and gratifications" research. Alan Rubin reviews this popular perspective, critically analyzes its strengths and weaknesses, and explains its contribution to the study of media effects. As the author concludes, "the synthesis of media uses and effects still has a long way to go" (p. 298). This chapter provides a major effort toward a useful integration of these traditions.

Although many scholars have examined the side-effects of entertainment, Dolf Zillmann and Jennings Bryant argue that few have examined its intended, primary effect: entertainment. Their chapter provides one of the first comprehensive reports of behavioral research "exploring the entertainment experience."

Business and professional communicators were the primary early adopters of the new communication technologies. Then the entertainment industry began to adapt their messages to these new delivery systems. Now scholars have begun to assess the social and psychological side effects of consumers' commercial and entertainment uses of these information devices. In the final chapter, Jerry Salvaggio provides a valuable service for those seeking to do research in this area by "setting the parameters for information society research."

We are most grateful to our contributors for making this volume possible. We also owe a fond debt of gratitude to our spouses and children for showing us tolerance as our family time was effected by the study of media effects. Last but not least, we are greatly indebted to Jennings Bryant, Sr. and Elvira Bryant, devoted parents to one of us, and special friends to both of us, to whom we wish to dedicate this volume.

Jennings Bryant
Dolf Zillmann

1

News Influence on Our Pictures of the World

Maxwell McCombs
University of Texas

Sheldon Gilbert
Syracuse University

News impacts many facets of our daily lives! How we dress for work, sometimes the route we take to work, what we plan to do this weekend, our general feeling of well-being or insecurity, the focus of our attention toward the world beyond immediate experience, and our concerns about the issues of the day all are influenced by the daily news.

Occasionally, our total behavior is instantly and completely dictated by the news. Everyone old enough to remember at all remembers where they first heard the news of John F. Kennedy's assassination and how so much of the next 3 or 4 days was spent in absorption and discussion of the news. Even on less traumatic occasions, millions of Americans follow the national political conventions, watch the presidential candidates debate, or follow the tabulation and projection of the nation's vote on election night. And daily, millions of citizens dutifully glean their knowledge of politics and public affairs from the pages of their local newspaper.

For the vast majority of Americans, this use of the mass media, coupled with brief visits to the voting booth on election day, represents their total participation in politics. This is one of the reasons why the most enduring and sustained line of scholarly research on mass communication traces the influence of the news media on voter behavior. Beginning with the classic study of Erie County, Ohio, by Columbia University sociologists Lazarsfeld, Berelson, and Gaudet (1944) during the 1940 U.S. presidential election, there has been an ever widening array of studies exploring the impact of news media on voter behavior. But as sociologists Lang and Lang (1959) have noted, the influence of the news media extends far beyond the political campaigns:

1

All news that bears on political activity and beliefs—and not only campaign speeches and campaign propaganda—is somehow relevant to the vote. Not only during the campaign, *but also in the periods between*, the mass media provide perspectives, shape images of candidates and parties, help highlight issues around which a campaign will develop, and define the unique atmosphere and areas of sensitivity which mark any particular campaign. (p. 226)

Over a half century ago, Lippmann (1922) also noted this role of the news media in defining our world, not just the world of politics during and between elections, but almost all of our world beyond immediate personal and family concerns. The issues, personalities, and situations toward which we hold feelings of endorsement or rejection, those points of attention about which pollsters seek the public pulse, are things about which we depend on the media to inform us.

Lippmann made an important distinction between the *environment* (i.e., the world that is really out there) and the *pseudo-environment* (i.e., our private perceptions of that world.) Recall that the opening chapter of his book *Public Opinion* is entitled "The World Outside and the Pictures in Our Heads." And, as Lippmann eloquently argued, it is the news media that sketch so many of those pictures in our heads. This view of the impact of news was congruent with both scholarly and popular assessment in Lippmann's day of the power of mass communication, views growing out of experiences with mass communication and propaganda during World War I. But subsequent scholarly investigations, such as the Erie County study, led scholars down another path in later decades.

Focused squarely on the ability of the news media and mass communication to persuade and change voters' attitudes, early empirical studies of mass communication instead discovered the strength of the individual, secure in his or her personal values and social setting and inured from much social change. The result was the law of minimal consequences, a scientific statement of a limited effects model for mass communication. Although this law may have been the proper palliative for the sometimes near-hysterical ascription of super persuasive powers to mass communication, such a constrained view of mass communication overlooks many effects that are plausibly ascribed to the mass media, especially to the news media.

After all, it is not the goal of professional journalists to persuade anybody about anything. The canons of objectivity, which have dominated professional journalistic practice and thought for generations, explicitly disavow any effort at persuasion. This is not to say that the news stories of the day are not exactly that, news *stories*. They are indeed! And like all stories, they structure experience for us, filtering out many of the complexities of the environment and offering a polished, perhaps even literary, version. The importance of this narrative form per se has been noted by Schudson (1982):

the power of the media lies not only (and not even primarily) in its power to declare things to be true, but in the power to provide the form in which the declaration appears. News in a newspaper or on television has a relationship to the "real world," not only in content but in form; that is, in the way the world is incorporated into unquestionable and unnoticed conventions of narration, and then transfigured, no longer for discussion, but as a premise of any conversation at all. (p. 98)

Journalism provides a structured account of the environment, a background and setting in which a few objects and selected attributes are highlighted.

Many scholars of mass communication and journalism have abandoned any concern with persuasion and have begun to explore audience awareness and learning. Which stories are attended to? What do people actually learn and remember from the news? How does this construction of reality by journalists influence the news audience?

CHANGING PERSPECTIVES

These questions signal a shift to research on the cognitive, long-term implications of daily journalism, research that begins to test empirically the thoughts put forward by Lippmann in the 1920s. Rather than addressing mass communication from the perspective of a model of limited effects, research in the 1960s began to consider a variety of limited models of effects.

As the history of science repeatedly demonstrates, just changing the perspective—or dominant paradigm, as Kuhn (1970) terms it—changes the picture sketched by the empirical evidence. Consider, for example, the large body of evidence on knowledge of public affairs. From the perspective of a model of limited effects, Hyman and Sheatsley's (1947) portrait of low levels of knowledge about public affairs and the existence of a sizable group of "chronic know-nothings" is hardly surprising.

But shifting the perspective to limited models of media effects focuses attention to those situations in which the transfer of functional information of some sort from the mass media to individuals in the audience does take place. Part of the scientific puzzle, of course, is to identify exactly what is transferred—the denotative message and its "facts," the cultural and individual connotations associated with those facts and the style of their presentation, or some other attribute of the message.

Part of this new look at mass communications has been the discovery that the audience not only learns some facts about public affairs, but also learns how much importance to attach to those facts from the emphasis placed on them by the news media. Considerable evidence has accumulated since 1972 that journalists play a key role in shaping our pictures of the world as they go about their daily task of selecting and reporting the news.

Here may lie the most important effect of the mass media: their ability to structure and organize our world for us. As Cohen (1963) remarked, the press may not be very successful in telling us what to think, but it is stunningly successful in telling us what to think *about!* This ability of the mass media to structure audience cognitions and to effect change among existing cognitions has been labeled the agenda-setting function of mass communication.

AGENDA-SETTING ROLE OF NEWS

Initially studied in the traditional context of mass communication and voter behavior, the concept of agenda setting took its metaphorical name from the idea that the mass media have the ability to transfer the salience of items on their news agendas to the public agenda. Through their routine structuring of social and political reality, the news media influence the agenda of public issues around which political campaigns and voter decisions are organized.

Each day journalists deal with the news in several important ways. First, they decide which news to cover and report and which to ignore. Next, all these available reports must be assessed. On the typical daily newspaper, over 75% of the potential news of the day is rejected out of hand and never transmitted to the audience. These are the first steps in the gatekeeping routine. But the items that pass through the gate do not receive equal treatment when presented to the audience. Some are used at length and prominently displayed. Others receive only brief attention. Newspapers, for example, clearly state the journalistic salience of an item through its page placement, headline, and length.

Agenda setting asserts that audiences acquire these saliences from the news media, incorporating similar sets of weights into their own agendas. Even though the communication of these saliences is an incidental, and inevitable, byproduct of journalistic practice and tradition, these saliences are one of the attributes of the messages transmitted to the audience. Agenda setting singles out the transmission of these saliences as one of the most important aspects of mass communication. Not only do the news media largely determine our awareness of the world at large, supplying the major elements for our pictures of the world, they also influence the prominence of those elements in the picture!

The basic idea of an agenda-setting role of the news media can be traced at least as far back as Lippmann, and a variety of empirical evidence about mass communication influence on voting can be interpreted—post hoc, of course— in agenda-setting terms. But the concept of an agenda-setting role for the news media was put to direct empirical test in the 1968 presidential election when McCombs and Shaw (1972) simultaneously collected data on the agenda of the news media and the agenda of the public. Reasoning that any impact of the news media was most likely to be measurable among undecided voters, their study surveyed undecided voters in Chapel Hill, North Carolina, and content analyzed the local and national news media, both print and broadcasting, regularly used by these voters. The high degree of correspondence between these two agendas of political and social issues established a major link in what has become a substantial chain of evidence for an agenda-setting role of the press.

This early study also firmly established the viability of the concept of agenda setting, a limited model of media effects, vis-à-vis the concept of selective perception, a key explanatory element in the then prevailing model of limited effects. Although still undecided about their presidential ballot, some of these Chapel Hill voters were leaning toward the Republican or Democratic candidate. Using this preference, comparisons were made between these voters' agendas and two different press' agendas (viz., the total agenda of issues reported in the news *or* only the agenda of issues attributed to the preferred party and its candidates). If the correlation between voters' agenda and the total news agenda is the highest, this is evidence of agenda setting. If the correlation with the preferred party's agenda is higher, there is evidence of selective perception. Out of 24 comparisons, 18 favored an agenda-setting interpretation.

Correlations alone do not establish the causal assertion that the news media influence the public agenda. These correlations might even be spurious, an artifact resulting from a common source for both the press and public agendas. However, the rebuttal to this argument as well as new evidence buttressing the concept of an agenda-setting role for the news media was reported by Funkhouser (1973) from an intensive study of public opinion trends in the 1960s. His creative secondary analysis brought together three key elements: (a) public opinion, assessed by the Gallup Poll's question about the most important problem facing the nation; (b) press coverage, determined by a content analysis of *Time, Newsweek,* and *U.S. News and World Report*; (c) statistical indicators of "reality" for these key concerns of the 1960s. Replicating the findings from the Chapel Hill voter study, Funkhouser found substantial correspondence between public opinion and press coverage. But most important, he found little correspondence between either of these and his statistical indicators of reality. For example, press coverage and public concern about Vietnam, campus unrest, and urban riots during the 1960s peaked considerably before the actual trends measured by such indicators as the number of troops committed to Vietnam, number of campus demonstrations, and number of civil disturbances.

These initial studies probing the impact of news coverage on public opinion yielded exceptionally clean and dramatic findings. Like all good exploratory scientific expeditions, they stimulated the curiosity and insight of others, so much so that the original McCombs and Shaw (1972) report is now one of the most frequently cited articles in mass communication research. But although an initial study may be parsimonious in its statement of a new perspective, it is inevitable that a fruitful concept leads to a vast array of new and previously unasked questions.

CHARTING MEDIA INFLUENCE

The task now at hand is to chart our way through the maze of subsequent research in pursuit of some understanding about how the news media influence their audiences. Among the key ideas to be examined are:

> The nature of the news agenda and how individuals draw from this agenda in formulating their own personal agendas, with special attention to its time frame;
>
> The variety of settings in which agenda setting and the public opinion process must be considered (e.g., election campaigns vs. more quiescent times; issues and other objects of public attention and concern, e.g., political candidates);
>
> The level of analysis for this impact (individuals or the society at large).

Beyond these concerns with the agenda-setting impact of the news media on their audiences, there also is renewed interest in gatekeeping within the news media themselves. Scholars are asking about the setting of agendas within the press. Finally, to put the entire matter in a broader context, the place of agenda setting in the broader social process of agenda building must be examined as well.

Rhetoric encompasses a vast historical span of perspectives on the effects of communication. From Aristotle to Kenneth Burke, the style and substance of messages have been critically analyzed. With the advent of behavioral science analysis of mass communication, Hovland and his colleagues began to enunciate a scientific rhetoric of communication (Hovland, Janis, & Kelley, 1953). Working from a stimulus–response perspective, they quickly discovered that the messages of the mass media are not simply a stimulus eliciting a response from members of the audience. Rather a message is best considered as a set or array of stimuli impinging on the audience whose subsequent behavior is a response to a selected few of these stimuli. Among the message stimuli mapped by Hovland and his colleagues were the structure of arguments, the credibility of the communicator, and the involvement of the audience with the topic.

To understand the impact of the daily news more clearly, we also need to articulate a scientific rhetoric of agenda setting, a theory or model identifying which elements in the news and its presentation influence audience perceptions of what are the important topics of the day. Because the explicit traditional rhetoric of journalism does not include deliberate efforts to communicate an agenda of issues, it is best to think of the scientific rhetoric of agenda setting as a set of implicit *cues* provided by news media about the salience of issues, actors, and situations in the news. They are best regarded as cues because these designations of what is important emerge only after numerous repetitions across time.

Nearly all studies of agenda setting have assumed that the major cue of what is important is how frequently it is repeated. An issue reported many times is considered to be more important than one mentioned only occasionally. This is, of course, an assumption picked up by agenda-setting researchers from quantitative content analysis whose fundamental operating assumption is that the key to understanding a message, or set of messages, is to count the frequency with which some element or elements appear. This is the approach typically taken to ascertain the agenda of the news media, and because these measures typically correlate quite highly with independent measures of the public agenda, the assumption seems well founded.

Both an agenda-setting process and the frequency of appearance as the major element in its cuing process are assumed by a number of commercial services that content analyze major news media in order to alert their clients, mostly major institutions and large corporations, about impending shifts in public opinion and attention.

Although the majority of evidence in hand documents frequency of repetition as an important cue in the news messages, other elements of a scientific rhetoric of agenda setting have been tentatively identified. A few studies, including the original 1968 Chapel Hill agenda-setting study, have considered the prominence with which items are displayed in the news. Common sense suggests that audiences take note of how an item is displayed in the news, whether it appears on the front page or deep inside the newspaper, whether it warrants 2-min of film treatment on the air or is relegated to a 10-sec bulletin. The evidence to date supports our common-sense expectations, but there are only a few studies. Furthermore, these studies, as well as many others which have considered the impact of the news' visual characteristics, have only begun to faintly sketch a systematic catalog or model of visual rhetoric either for print or audio-visual media.

Another element in the scientific rhetoric of agenda setting is the degree of conflict present in the news report. Again, common sense suggests the plausibility of this cue. If people are in conflict over some issue, so the reasoning might go, it must be more important than if everyone agrees or if only a few people are voicing opinions. But then, common sense is not always affirmed by careful scientific observation, and this cue has only been observed in a single study by Taik Sup Auh (1977) at Indiana University.

But its implications are intriguing because here a value of journalism, a news value, becomes a major cue for the audience. If the role of conflict as a cue about what is important is borne out by subsequent research, it raises important ethical and value questions about the practice of journalism and its social consequences. It also suggests questions about the role of other news values as cues to importance, values which sharpen certain attributes of news stories and may affect their subsequent use by and impact on the news audience.

News values determine both which stories are told by journalists and, equally important, how these stories are told. The rhetoric of journalism is not the rhetoric of ordinary discourse, and its focus of attention is a highly attenuated portion of reality. Efforts to understand the agenda-setting impact of the news illuminate the behavioral consequences for the audience of the techniques of news writing and display.

Some simple, but highly suggestive, evidence already exists about the impact of how journalism tells its story. For example, total media attention to crime in Charlotte, North Carolina, during the 1972 presidential campaign showed little correspondence to voters' concern with crime as a major election issue (Shaw & McCombs, 1977). But media attention to crime falls into two categories: reports of specific criminal acts largely obtained from police reports and reports of crime as a social problem, such as a speech by the chief of police or a candidate for President. Audience reaction to these news stories depends on which setting is used to report criminal activity. Charlotte voters did not appear to tally the individual crime reports and conclude that crime was a problem. But when the media agenda was calculated only in terms of the news stories about crime as a social issue, there was considerable agreement between media and voters.

How a story is framed, that is, in what context and on what occasion the news media pay attention to a social issue, is crucial (Williams, Shapiro, & Cutbirth, 1983). Framing is yet another element in the rhetoric of journalism and the rhetoric of agenda setting. At this point, we perceive only dimly which rhetorical elements serve as cues to the audience about what is important and worthy of attention and thought.

EFFECTS OVER TIME

One of the most critical aspects in the concept of an agenda-setting role of mass communication is the time frame for this phenomenon. In analyzing this concept, we must examine what determines the time frame. Among the facets to be considered are: (a) the overall time frame, which is the total period of time under consideration; (b) the time lag, which is the elapsed time between the appearance of an item on the media agenda (the independent variable) and its appearance on the public agenda (the dependent variable); (c) the duration of the media agenda; (d) the duration of the public agenda measure; and (e) the optimal effect span, which is the peak association between media emphasis and public emphasis of an issue.

Each of these facets presents major questions that need close consideration and examination. But these are difficult questions to answer. For the most part, researchers have relied on guesswork and intuition in designing and implementing their investigations. Two keystone studies illustrate the uncertainties inherent in studying long-term cumulative media effects.

Stone and McCombs (1981) studied the agendas of *Time* and *Newsweek*, analyzing 6 months prior and 3 months following the fieldwork of two different public opinion surveys. Using Pearson's *r* to index the strength of the relationship between each month's media agenda and the public agenda, they sought to identify the *optimal effect span* for an agenda of six major issues. The results led to the conclusion that 4 months was the optimal span.

Winter and Eyal (1981) compared Gallup Poll data on the importance of civil rights issues with front page stories in *The New York Times* over a 22-year period. The media agenda consisted of 6-months coverage prior to each of 27 Gallup Polls. Interestingly, these findings for a single long-term issue showed a completely different picture than did Stone and McCombs' findings. Moving backward by months from the interview period, there was a monotonic decline in the relationship between the media and the public agendas. Winter and Eyal's results indicated that for civil rights issues, the optimal effect span is somewhere between 0 and 8 weeks prior to interviewing.

There are several possible explanations for the differences found in these two studies' assessment of the optimal effect span for agenda-setting effects. Stone and McCombs' analysis of the media agenda was based on the weekly cycle of news magazines, whereas Winter and Eyal used the daily cycle and larger newshole of *The New York Times*. They also focused specifically on civil rights. It is entirely plausible that different issues, and different kinds of issues, have varying optimal effect spans. If this is so, then Stone and McCombs' results reflect the averaging of time spans for a variety of issues.

Other evidence suggests that the agenda-setting potential over time is different in newspapers than in television. In the 1972 presidential campaign, Shaw and McCombs (1977) found that newspapers performed a more effective agenda-setting role than television in moving public opinion. Yet, as the election day grew closer, the roles reversed and television became the prime mover of public opinion. McCombs concluded that technological and stylistic differences between the media accounted for the different functions during distinct phases over time. For example, television news is more like the front page of a newspaper, so that readers have a longer period of experience with an issue than do viewers. But once an issue is on television, the treatment tends to be more intensive and its salience is more apparent. Although the parsimony of the agenda-setting concept declines with the necessary inclusion of such factors as media differences and issue differences, the scope is broadened to include critical journalism and public opinion variables.

ISSUES, IMAGES, AND INTEREST

For the most part, the behavioral science evidence to date is primarily about the impact of news coverage on public perception of issues, problems, and concerns. This was the starting point for agenda-setting research in McCombs and Shaw's study of undecided voters during the 1968 presidential campaign and has remained the primary focus ever since. But there is some evidence about the impact of news coverage on other kinds of agenda items.

Tracing out some of the richness of this metaphorical concept of news impact, McCombs and his colleagues, David Weaver, Doris Graber, and Chaim Eyal, followed use of the news media by panels of about 50 voters each in Lebanon, New Hampshire, Indianapolis, Indiana, and Evanston, Illinois from December 1975 until after election day in 1976. Their study showed that the news media play a major role both in setting the agenda of viable candidates and in influencing the images of these candidates. "In fact," conclude Weaver, Graber, McCombs, and Eyal (1981), "this image agenda-setting function of the media probably has more pervasive influence on the voters' early perceptions of the campaign and the final choices available at election time than does issue agenda-setting" (p. 200).

The most critical dimension of a candidate's image is name recognition, that is, voter awareness of the person as a contender for office. But news coverage does far more than teach voters who the candidates are. By focusing coverage on a few frontrunners to the sometimes almost total exclusion of their rivals, the news media play a major, albeit implicit, role in the selection of party nominees for national office. Considerable anecdotal evidence about this political impact of the news has now been buttressed by careful quantitative analysis of press coverage and voter response.

Beyond the agenda of candidates vying for office, how much influence do the news magazines, newspapers, and television have on the agenda of attributes that each candidate is perceived to possess? Again, evidence from in-depth analyses of voters during the 1976 campaign suggests that media agenda setting, particularly newspaper coverage, extends to specific image dimensions as well as to agendas of candidates and issues. Weaver et al. (1981) note: "These findings also signify that media emphasis or de-emphasis of certain image dimensions can contribute to overall voter evaluations of candidates as well as to their images of such candidates" (p. 201).

It also appears that it is easier for voters to learn about candidates and their images than it is to learn about the issues, enhancing the chances for image agenda setting. According to Weaver et al. (1981):

> Although the media presented ample information of all kinds during the 1976 campaign, they emphasized personal qualities of the candidates and campaigning activities. The voters learned accordingly. Image dimensions pertaining to personality traits and styles of the candidates were better remembered than those pertaining to job qualifications and ideology. (p. 201)

This discussion of voter behavior, like so much of the research on agenda setting, centers on the public's political agenda. But for most Americans, politics— public issues, candidates, parties, and all the minutiae of politics—are only one minor item on their larger agenda of concerns. For most people, the pictures in their heads are only fleeting images of politics. Here may lie the most important agenda-setting role of all for the news media of a stable democracy, in which politics is not a highly salient topic, raising the level of political interest among the general public above the threshold sufficient to assure reasonable learning about the issues and candidates and to assure reasonable levels of participation in the primaries and general election.

Again, in-depth analysis of the 1976 election (Weaver et al., 1981) discovered that the news media, especially television, had major influence on voters' levels of political interest during the early stages. Frequent use of television to follow politics during the primaries played a significant role in stimulating subsequent voter interest in the presidential campaign. Reminiscent of our previous discussion of the rhetoric of journalism, these findings from a lengthy and detailed analysis of voter behavior underscore the importance of carefully examining the contents of the news. The news of the day is an influential civics textbook.

VARIETIES OF EXPERIENCE

The news media, of course, are not the only textbook of life. Firsthand experience also is important. Thus, agenda-setting analyses began to dissect the national agenda and to examine issue by issue people's experiences with very different kinds of public issues. For issues such as inflation, where the news media are far from the dominant or most important source of information, extensive examinations by Winter (1980) of nearly 25 years of news coverage and public opinion trends found little evidence of any agenda-setting influence. But for issues such as foreign affairs, on which the news media have a near monopoly, there is considerable evidence of impact on public perceptions of their importance.

The explanation for this outcome lies in the distinction between obtrusive and unobtrusive issues. Obtrusive issues are those with which individuals have close personal contact. Media cues about such issues' importance are, at best, secondary sources of orientation. In contrast, unobtrusive issues are, by definition, remote from one's personal experience. Here the news media exercise a near monopoly as sources of information and orientation.

Although there is little variance in the ratings assigned issues like inflation (highly obtrusive) and foreign affairs (highly unobtrusive), issues such as unemployment fall at many different locations along the obtrusive/unobtrusive continuum. For Ohio steelworkers, unemployment is a highly obtrusive issue. For Wall Street brokers in a bull market or for tenured members of a college faculty, unemployment is unobtrusive.

The nature of people's experiences with issues—their degree of reliance on the news media as a source of information—is an important contingent condition for agenda-setting effects. Once attention is drawn explicitly to the behavior of individuals, the stage is set for laboratory experiments and their superior evidence of direct causation. Communities and entire societies can neither be trundled into the laboratory nor manipulated in order to test hypotheses about the impact of news. But individuals can—and have been!

Under the guise of a study about the contents of the daily network television news, Iyengar, Peters, and Kinder (1982) recruited subjects from the general population for two experiments in which the amount of information in a series of news broadcasts was systematically manipulated. In the first experiment, increases in the coverage of U.S. defense preparedness resulted in the increased salience of this topic. In the second experiment, increases in the coverage of defense preparedness, pollution, and inflation resulted in increased salience for the first two topics, but not for inflation. Again, the explanation for this outcome lies in the distinction between obtrusive and unobtrusive issues.

FOUR TYPES OF AGENDA SETTING

Some analyses aim at a comprehensive portrait of public opinion, examining the full array of issues before the public or an individual at some point in time. Other analyses limit themselves to a single issue or to a few issues taken one at a time. Along another dimension, some analyses of public opinion are exactly that, an analysis of *public* opinion, a portrait of how an entire community or society views issues of the day. Other analyses, more in the tradition of media effects analysis, concentrate on the thought and behavior of individuals. In short, two entirely different levels of analysis are possible: societal and individual.

Combining these two dimensions—the scope of the portrait and the level of analysis—yields a typology of four different agenda-setting impacts of the news, as can be seen in Table 1.1. With the continuing proliferation of agenda-setting studies, this typology is useful for sorting out and cataloging the findings. Typical of Type I, analysis of how the community arrays the major issues of the day, are the original Chapel Hill study (McCombs & Shaw, 1972) as well as Funk-houser's (1973) sweeping analysis of the issues of the 1960s.

Type II continues this emphasis on the major issues of the day, but shifts the

TABLE 1.1
Level of Analysis

	Society	Individual
Scope		
All issues	I	II
Single issues	III	IV

focus to how each individual arrays these concerns on his or her own agenda. Not surprisingly, as Weaver (1983) points out, this is a null category. Evidence of agenda setting here would require not only that the media influence the salience of an issue for an individual but, in fact, dictate the exact ordering of those concerns.

Recent studies have emphasized Types III and IV, the analysis of individual issues. Typical of Type III is Winter and Eyal's (1981) tracking of public opinion and press coverage on the civil rights issue across a 22-year span. Typical of Type IV, with its emphasis on individual behavior, are the experiments manipulating television newscast content conducted by Iyengar et al. (1982) and Blood's (1981) analysis of the economic issue in terms of each individual's personal and media-mediated experience. The recent trend toward Types III and IV research increases our understanding of the dynamics involved in the agenda-setting process. But eventually, we must return to Type I research for a comprehensive view of the world in which we live.

AGENDA BUILDING

The news is not cut from whole cloth. The ingredients for the day's news are largely supplied by individuals and events quite independent of the press. And the subsequent impact of news reports rests for the most part in the hands of the political system, which must take the initiative if public concern, collective or individual, is to have major consequences. Agenda setting, the creation of awareness and the arousal of public concern, is but one aspect of the larger process of agenda building, a collective process in which media, government, and the public reciprocally influence each other.

The annual State of the Union address by the President affords one window for examining these reciprocal relationships between the nation's number one newsmaker and the national press. Here is an instance where the President lays out an entire agenda of issues for action by the Congress. But this is far more than a constitutionally mandated report. Since the early days of the 20th century, Presidents have used this annual report as an occasion to address the nation directly as well as the Congress. With the arrival of television, the State of the Union address has become a major prime-time media event. To what extent does this political event set the agenda for subsequent press coverage?

Surprisingly, analysis of Jimmy Carter's 1978 State of the Union address found little evidence of presidential agenda setting (Gilbert, Eyal, McCombs, & Nicholas, 1980). Instead, it appeared that the press, through its coverage of issues prior to the State of the Union address, actually influenced the President's agenda. But this may have been due to Carter's managerial style of governing.

Replication of this analysis, using Richard Nixon's 1970 State of the Union address, did find evidence of presidential influence on subsequent press coverage (McCombs, Gilbert, & Eyal, 1982).

Continuing analysis of this interplay between the presidential agenda and national press coverage focuses on the ebb and flow of attention to specific national issues in the press, especially on the ever-changing nature and definition of national problems. At the broadest level, there are national concerns. It has been suggested that no more than three or four concerns, in turn, have dominated American public opinion since World War II. Foremost among these concerns have been economics and foreign policy.

At a more specific level are the topics that define a broad concern, such as economics. In recent years, concern with economics variously has meant concern over inflation, unemployment, tax cuts, and federal budget deficits. In reporting these topics, the news media move from issue to issue, the specific points of contention between political, business, and social groups about how to deal with these economic topics. Although the broad outlines of the news media's ability to influence the salience of economic concerns are well established, little is yet known about the dynamics of the agenda-building process that explains the ebb and flow of the specific issues which define these topics and determine their ultimate historical fate.

Part of the explanation rests with the interplay between press and public, between press and government officials, or between press and special interest groups. Part of the explanation also rests with agenda setting within the press itself. The metaphor of agenda setting has revived interest in the analysis of gatekeeping behavior within news organizations.

Crouse (1973) succinctly captured the movement of George McGovern onto the national agenda through his portrait of the news media puzzling out the meaning of the Iowa caucuses in early 1972. Finally, he noted, the typewriter of *The New York Times* reporter Johnny Apple tapped out a story about "a surprisingly strong showing for George McGovern." Arrayed behind Apple, both literally there in that Iowa room as well as in the next day's news reports, were the AP and UPI, the national television networks, and a host of other correspondents on the campaign trail. In a few strikes of the typewriter keys, McGovern moved decisively toward the top of the Democratic candidate agenda.

Reanalysis of the older gatekeeping studies also demonstrates agenda setting within the press. For example, reexamination of the classic Mr. Gates' studies demonstrated striking correlations between what was offered by the wire and what was selected by Mr. Gates (McCombs & Shaw, 1976).

For the student of public opinion, the concept of agenda setting, applied at key points in the agenda-building process, summarizes important steps in the process. For the student of journalism, the concept of agenda setting highlights critical aspects of the news gathering and writing process and helps spell out the social implications of journalistic practice and tradition.

REFERENCES

Auh, T. S. (1977). *Issue conflict and mass media agenda-setting during Bayh-Lugar senatorial campaign of 1974.* Paper presented at the meeting of the Theory and Methodology Division, Association for Education in Journalism, Madison, WI.

Blood, R. W. (1981). *Unobtrusive issues in the agenda-setting role of the press.* Unpublished doctoral dissertation, Syracuse University, Syracuse, NY.

Cohen, B. C. (1963). *The press and foreign policy.* Princeton, NJ: Princeton University Press.

Crouse, T. (1973). *The boys on the bus.* New York: Ballantine Books.

Funkhouser, G. R. (1973). The issues of the sixties: An exploratory study in the dynamics of public opinion. *Public Opinion Quarterly, 37,* 62–75.

Gilbert, S., Eyal, C. H., McCombs, M. E., & Nicholas, D. (1980). The state of the union address and the press agenda. *Journalism Quarterly, 57,* 584–588.

Hovland, C. I., Janis, I. L., & Kelley, N. H. (1953). *Communication and persuasion: Psychological studies of opinion change.* New Haven, CT: Yale University Press.

Hyman, H. H., & Sheatsley, P. B. (1947). Some reasons why information campaigns fail. *Public Opinion Quarterly, 11,* 412–423.

Iyengar, S., Peters, M. D., & Kinder, D. R. (1982). Experimental demonstrations of the "not-so-minimal" consequences of television news programs. *American Political Science Review, 76*(4), 848–858.

Kuhn, T. S. (1970). *The structure of scientific revolutions* (2nd ed.). Chicago, IL: University of Chicago Press.

Lang, K., & Lang, G. E. (1959). *The mass media and voting.* New York: Free Press.

Lazarsfeld, P. F., Berelson, B., & Gaudet, H. (1944). *The people's choice: How the voter makes up his mind in a presidential campaign.* New York: Columbia University Press.

Lippmann, W. (1922). *Public opinion.* New York: Macmillan.

McCombs, M. E. (1981). The agenda-setting approach. In D. D. Nimmo & K. R. Sanders (Eds.), *Handbook of political communication* (pp. 121–140). Beverly Hills, CA: Sage.

McCombs, M. E., Gilbert, S., & Eyal, C. H. (1982, May). *The state of the union address and the press agenda: A replication.* Paper presented at the annual meeting of the International Communication Association, Boston.

McCombs, M. E., & Shaw, D. L. (1972). The agenda-setting function of mass media. *Public Opinion Quarterly, 36,* 176–187.

McCombs, M. E., & Shaw, D. L. (1976). Structuring the 'unseen environment.' *Journal of Communication, 26*(2), 18–22.

Schudson, M. (1982). The politics of narrative form: The emergence of news conventions in print and television. *Daedalus, 111,* 97–112.

Shaw, D. L., & McCombs, M. E. (1977). *The emergence of American political issues: The agenda-setting function of the press.* St. Paul, MN: West.

Stone, G. C., & McCombs, M. E. (1981). Tracing the time lag in agenda-setting. *Journalism Quarterly, 58,* 51–55.

Weaver, D. H. (1983, September). *Media agenda-setting and public opinion.* Paper presented at the Public Opinion and Communication Seminar, Tokyo, Japan.

Weaver, D. H., Graber, D. A., McCombs, M. E., & Eyal, C. H. (1981). *Media agenda-setting in a presidential election: Issues, images, and interests.* New York: Praeger.

Williams, W., Jr., Shapiro, M., & Cutbirth, C. (1983). The impact of campaign agendas on perceptions of issues in 1980 campaign. *Journalism Quarterly, 60,* 226–231.

Winter, J. P. (1980). *Differential media-public agenda-setting effects for selected issues, 1948–1976.* Unpublished doctoral dissertation, Syracuse University, Syracuse, NY.

Winter, J. P., & Eyal, C. H. (1981). Agenda-setting for the civil rights issue. *Public Opinion Quarterly, 46,* 376–383.

2 Living with Television: The Dynamics of the Cultivation Process

George Gerbner
Larry Gross
The Annenberg School of Communications
University of Pennsylvania

Michael Morgan
University of Massachusetts

Nancy Signorielli
The Annenberg School of Communications
University of Pennsylvania

The longer we live with television, the more invisible it becomes. As the number of people who have never lived without television continues to grow, the medium is increasingly taken for granted as an appliance, a piece of furniture, a storyteller, a member of the family. Ever fewer parents and even grandparents can explain to children what it was like to grow up before television.

Television is the source of the most broadly shared images and messages in history. Although new technologies transform business and professional communications, the public and much of the research community continue to be concerned with over-the-air television, and for good reasons. Saturation and viewing time, incredibly high for decades, continue to increase. The mass ritual that is television shows no signs of weakening its hold over the common symbolic environment into which our children are born and in which we all live out our lives. For most viewers, new types of delivery systems (e.g., cable, satellite, and cassette) signal even further penetration and integration of established viewing patterns into everyday life.

And yet, far too little is known and even less is agreed upon about the dynamic role of television in our lives. The reasons for this lack of consensus include institutional resistance (high economic stakes and political interests might be affected), the relative youth of the field, the inherent clumsiness of research methods and measures, and the "hit-and-run" proclivities and sporadic funding of those who seek to understand television's overall impact. In contrast, we have been fortunate to obtain research grant support from a variety of public sources over a long period of time. We have thus been able, since 1968, to follow a fairly consistent line of theory and research on the implications of television. Our research project, called *cultural indicators*, has accumulated large amounts of data with which to develop and refine our theoretical approach[1] and the research strategy we call *cultivation analysis* (see Gerbner, Gross, Morgan, & Signorielli, 1980). In this chapter, we summarize and illustrate our theory of the dynamics of the cultivation process.

TELEVISION IN SOCIETY

Television is a centralized system of storytelling. It is part and parcel of our daily lives. Its drama, commercials, news, and other programs bring a relatively coherent world of common images and messages into every home.

Television cultivates from infancy the very predispositions and preferences that used to be acquired from other primary sources. Transcending historic barriers of literacy and mobility, television has become the primary common source of socialization and everyday information (mostly in the form of entertainment) of an otherwise heterogeneous population. The repetitive pattern of television's mass-produced messages and images forms the mainstream of a common symbolic environment.

Many of those who now live with television have never before been part of a shared national culture. Television provides, perhaps for the first time since preindustrial religion, a daily ritual of highly compelling and informative content that forms a strong cultural link between elites and the rest of the population. The heart of the analogy of television and religion, and the similarity of their social functions, lies in the continual repetition of patterns (myths, ideologies, "facts," relationships, etc.), which serve to define the world and legitimize the social order.

The stories of the dramatic world need not present credible accounts of what things are in order to perform the more critical function of demonstrating how things work. The illumination of the invisible relationships of life and society has always been the principal function of storytelling. Television today serves that function, telling most of the stories to most of the people most of the time.

---

[1]Cultural indicators began in 1967–1968 with a study for the National Commission on the Causes and Prevention of Violence. It continued under the sponsorships of the U.S. Surgeon General's Scientific Advisory Committee on Television and Social Behavior, the National Institute of Mental Health, the White House Office of Telecommunications Policy, the American Medical Association, the U.S. Administration on Aging, and the National Science Foundation.

This superimposition of a relatively homogeneous process upon a relatively diversified print and film context is a central cultural feature of our age. Television differs from other media in its centralized mass production and ritualistic use of a coherent set of images and messages produced for total populations. Therefore, exposure to the total pattern rather than only to specific genres or programs is what accounts for the historically new and distinct consequences of living with television, namely, the cultivation of shared conceptions of reality among otherwise diverse publics.

We do not deny or minimize the importance of specific programs, selective attention and perception, specifically targeted communications, individual and group differences, and research on effects defined in terms of short-run individual attitude and behavior change. But exclusive concentration on those aspects and terms of traditional effects research risks losing sight of what is basically new and significant about television as the common storyteller of our age.

Compared to other media, television provides a relatively restricted set of choices for a virtually unrestricted variety of interests and publics. Most of its programs are by commercial necessity designed to be watched by nearly everyone in a relatively nonselective fashion. Surveys show that amount of viewing follows the style of life of the viewer and is relatively insensitive to programming. The audience is always the group available at a certain time of the day, the week, and the season, regardless of the programs. Most viewers watch by the clock and either do not know what they will watch when they turn on the set or follow established routines rather than choose each program as they would choose a book, a movie, or an article. The number and variety of choices available when most viewers are available to watch are also limited by the fact that many programs designed for the same broad audience tend to be similar in their basic makeup and appeal.

According to the 1984 Nielsen Report, the television set in the typical home is in use for about 7 hrs a day, and actual viewing by persons older than 2 years averages over 4 hrs a day. With that much viewing, there can be little selectivity. And the more people watch, the less selective they can and tend to be. Most regular and heavy viewers watch more of everything. Researchers who attribute findings to news viewing or preference for action programs and the like overlook the fact that most of those who watch more news or action programs watch more of all types of programs and that, in any case, many different types of programs manifest the same basic features.

Therefore, from the point of view of the cultivation of relatively stable and common images, the pattern that counts is that of the total pattern of programming to which total communities are regularly exposed over long periods of time. That is the pattern of settings, casting, social typing, actions, and related outcomes that cuts across most program types and defines the world of television, a world in which many viewers live so much of their lives that they cannot avoid absorbing or dealing with its recurrent patterns, probably many times each day.

Thus the patterns central to cultivation analysis are those central to the world of television. They pervade most if not all programs. What matters most for the study of television is not so much what this or that viewer may prefer as what virtually no regular viewer can escape. Therefore, the focus of cultivation analysis is not on what this or that campaign may achieve but on what all campaigns are up against: a widening circle of standardized conceptions superimposed upon a more selectively used print culture and appearing to be increasingly resistant to change.

THE SHIFT FROM EFFECTS
TO CULTIVATION RESEARCH

The vast bulk of scientific inquiry about television's social impact can be seen as directly descended from the theoretical models and the methodological procedures of marketing and attitude change research. Large amounts of time, energy, and money have been spent in attempts to determine how to change people's attitudes or behaviors. By and large, however, this conceptualization of effect as immediate change among individuals has not produced research that helps us understand the distinctive features of television: massive, long-term, and common exposure of large and heterogeneous publics to centrally produced, mass-distributed, and repetitive systems of stories.

Traditional effects research perspectives are based on evaluating specific informational, educational, political, or marketing efforts in terms of selective exposure and immediately measurable differences between those exposed and others. Scholars steeped in those traditions find it difficult to accept the emphasis of cultivation analysis upon total immersion rather than selective viewing and upon the spread of stable similarities of outlook rather than of remaining sources of cultural differentiation and change. Similarly, we are all imbued with the perspectives of print culture and its ideals of freedom, diversity, and an active electorate producing as well as selecting information and entertainment from the point of view of a healthy variety of competing and conflicting interests. Therefore, many also question the emphasis of cultivation analysis upon the passive viewer being programmed from birth and the dissolution of authentic publics that this emphasis implies. These scholars and analysts argue that other circumstances do intervene and can affect or even neutralize the cultivation process, that many, even if not most, viewers do watch selectively, and that those program selections do make a difference.

We do not dispute these contentions. As we describe subsequently, we account for them in our analytic strategies. But we believe, again, that concentrating on individual differences and immediate change misses the main point of television: the absorption of divergent currents into a stable and common mainstream.

Others have, of course, suggested that mass media may involve functions and processes other than overt change. Lazarsfeld and Merton (1948) argued that the primary impact of exposure to mass communication is likely to be not change but maintenance of the status quo. Similar notions have been expressed by Glynn (1956) and Bogart (1956). Our own studies in institutional process analysis show that media content and functions reflect institutional organization, interest, and control (Gerbner 1969b, 1972). Television's goal of greatest audience appeal at least cost demands that most of its messages follow conventional social morality (cf. Weigel & Jessor, 1973).

Communications researchers have often bent over backwards to avoid simplistic, unidirectional ideas about effects, but rarely have concrete alternatives been proposed. As McQuail (1976) noted, television "is said to 'stimulate,' 'involve,' 'trigger off,' 'generate,' 'induce,' 'suggest,' 'structure,' 'teach,' 'persaude,' 'gratify,' 'arouse,' 'reinforce,' 'activate' " (p. 347); but this variety of terms masks a vagueness in many attempts to characterize media impact. Indeed, the wide variety of terms may stem from the tendency of media research to isolate and dissect pieces from the whole.

Culture cultivates the social relationships of a society. The mainstream defines its dominant current. We focus on the implications of accumulated exposure to the most general system of messages, images, and values that underly and cut across the widest variety of programs. These are the continuities that most effects studies overlook.

If, as we argue, the messages are so stable, the medium is so ubiquitous, and accumulated total exposure is what counts, then almost everyone should be affected. Even light viewers live in the same cultural environment as most others, and what they do not get through the tube can be acquired indirectly from others who do watch television. It is clear, then, that the cards are stacked against finding evidence of effects. Therefore, the discovery of a systematic pattern of even small but pervasive differences between light and heavy viewers may indicate far-reaching consequences.

A slight but pervasive (e.g., generational) shift in the cultivation of common perspectives may alter the cultural climate and upset the balance of social and political decision making without necessarily changing observable behavior. A single percentage point difference in ratings is worth millions of dollars in advertising revenue, as the networks know only too well. It takes but a few degrees shift in the average temperature to have an ice age. A range of 3% to 15% margins (typical of our cultivation differentials) in a large and otherwise stable field often signals a landslide, a market takeover, or an epidemic, and it certainly tips the scale of any closely balanced choice or decision. Cultivation theory is based on the persistent and pervasive pull of the television mainstream on a great variety of currents and countercurrents.

If that theory is correct, it is the current system of television, and not our methodology, that challenges theories of self-government predicated on print-based assumptions of ideologically diverse, distinct, and selective publics conscious of their own divergent interests. Thus, the decision to focus on what most viewers share is more than a shift of research emphasis. It is an attempt to develop a methodology appropriate to the distinct and central cultural dynamics of the age of television. This requires a set of theoretical and methodological assumptions and techniques different from those of traditional media effects research. Through the cultural indicators project, we have begun to develop such an alternative approach.

CULTURAL INDICATORS

The cultural indicators project is historically grounded, theoretically guided, and empirically supported. Like so many projects in the history of communications research, it was launched as an independently funded enterprise in an applied context, though it was based on earlier theoretical considerations (Gerbner, 1969c).

Although these early efforts (and many published reports) focused primarily on the nature and functions of television violence, the cultural indicators project was broadly conceived from the outset. Even violence was studied as a demonstration of the distribution of power in the world of television, with serious implications for the confirmation and perpetuation of minority status (Gerbner, Gross, Signorielli, & Morgan, 1979; Morgan, 1983), and the project continued to take into account a wide range of topics, issues, and concerns (Gerbner & Gross, 1976). We have investigated the extent to which television viewing contributes to audience conceptions and actions in such realms as sex and age-role stereotypes, health, science, the family, educational achievement and aspirations, politics, and religion.

The cultural indicators approach involves a three-pronged research strategy (for a more detailed description, see Gerbner, 1973). The first prong, called *institutional process analysis,* is designed to investigate the formation of policies directing the massive flow of media messages. Because of its direct policy orientation, this research is the most difficult to fund and, therefore, the least developed (for some examples, see Gerbner, 1969b, 1972). More directly relevant to our present focus are the other two prongs called *message system analysis* and *cultivation analysis.* Both relate to and help develop a conception of the dynamics of the cultivation process.

In the second prong, we record week-long samples of network television drama each year and subject these systems of messages to rigorous and detailed content analysis in order to reliably delineate selected features of the television world. We consider these the potential lessons television cultivates and use them as a source of questions for the cultivation analysis.

In the third prong, we examine the responses given to these questions (phrased to refer to the real world) among those with varying amounts of exposure to the world of television. (Nonviewers are too few and demographically too scattered for serious research purposes.) We want to determine whether those who spend more of their time with television are more likely to answer these questions in ways that reflect the potential lessons of the television world (give the "television answer") than are those who watch less television but are otherwise comparable (in terms of important demographic characteristics) to the heavy viewers. We have used the concept of cultivation to describe the contributions television viewing makes to viewer conceptions of social reality. Cultivation differential is the margin of difference in conceptions of reality between light and heavy viewers in the same demographic subgroups.

CULTIVATION: A MULTIDIRECTIONAL PROCESS

Our use of the term *cultivation* for television's contribution to conceptions of social reality is not simply a fancier word for effects. Nor does it necessarily imply a one-way, monolithic process. The effects of a pervasive medium upon the composition and structure of the symbolic environment are subtle, complex, and intermingled with other influences. This perspective, therefore, assumes an interaction between the medium and its publics.

The elements of cultivation do not originate with television or appear out of a void. Layers of demographic, social, personal, and cultural contexts also determine the shape, scope, and degree of the contribution television is likely to make. Yet, the meanings of those contexts and factors are in themselves aspects of the cultivation process. That is, although a viewer's sex, age, or class may make a difference, television helps define what it means, for example, to be an adolescent female member of a given social class. The interaction is a continuous process (as is cultivation) taking place at every stage, from cradle to grave.

Thus, television neither simply creates nor reflects images, opinions, and beliefs. Rather, it is an integral aspect of a dynamic process. Institutional needs and objectives influence the creation and distribution of mass-produced messages which create, fit into, exploit, and sustain the needs, values, and ideologies of mass publics. These publics, in turn, acquire distinct identities as publics partly through exposure to the ongoing flow of messages.

The question of which came first is misleading and irrelevant. People are born into a symbolic environment with television as its mainstream. Children begin viewing several years before they begin reading, and well before they can even talk. Television viewing is both a shaper and a stable part of certain life styles and outlooks. It links the individual to a larger if synthetic world, a world of television's own making. Most of those with certain social and psychological characteristics, dispositions, and world views—and fewer alternatives as attractive and compelling as television—use it as their major vehicle of cultural participation. The content shapes and promotes their continued attention. To the extent that television dominates their sources of information, continued exposure to its messages is likely to reiterate, confirm, and nourish (i.e., cultivate) their values and perspectives.

Cultivation should not be confused with mere reinforcement (although, to be sure, reaffirmation and stability in the face of pressures for change are not trivial feats). Nor should it suggest that television viewing is simply symptomatic of other dispositions and outlook systems. Finally, it should not be taken as implying that we do not think any change is involved. We have certainly found change with the first "television generation" (Gerbner & Gross, 1976) and with television spreading to various areas of a country (Morgan, 1984) and of life (Morgan & Rothschild, 1983). When we talk about the "independent contribution" of television viewing, we mean quite specifically that the generation (in some) and maintenance (in others) of some set of outlooks or beliefs can be traced to steady, cumulative exposure to the world of television. Our longitudinal studies of adolescents (Gerbner, Gross, Morgan, & Signorielli, 1980; Morgan, 1982) also show that television viewing does exert an independent influence on attitudes over time, but that belief structures can also influence subsequent viewing.

The point is that cultivation is not conceived as a unidirectional process but rather more like a gravitational process. The angle and direction of the "pull" depends on where groups of viewers and their styles of life are in reference to the center of gravity, the "mainstream" of the world of television. Each group may strain in a different direction, but all groups are affected by the same central current. Cultivation is thus part of a continual, dynamic, ongoing process of interaction among messages and contexts. This holds even though (and in a sense, especially because) the hallmark of the process is either relative stability or slow change.

As successive generations grow up with television's version of the world, the former and traditional distinctions become blurred. Cultivation thus implies the steady entrenchment of mainstream orientations in most cases and the systematic but almost imperceptible modification of previous orientations in others; in other words, affirmation for the believers *and* indoctrination for deviants. That is the process we call *mainstreaming*.

The observable manifestations of the process vary as a function of the environmental context and other attributes of the viewer. In order to explain these variations, however, it is necessary to describe the central components of the symbolic environment composed by television. We return to the concept of mainstreaming after a brief consideration of the values, ideology, demography, and action structure of the television mainstream itself.

THE WORLD OF TELEVISION

Message system analysis is a tool for making systematic, reliable, and cumulative observations about television content. We use message system analysis not to determine what any individual viewer (or group of viewers) might see, but to

assess the most representative, stable, and recurrent aggregate patterns of messages to which total communities are exposed over long periods of time. The
analysis is based on the premise that although findings about media content
cannot be taken at face value as evidence of impact, representative and reliable
observations of content (rather than selective and idiosyncratic impressions) are
critical prerequisites to a valid consideration of media influence. In other words,
a relatively few unambiguous, dominant, and common content patterns provide
the basis for interaction and shared assumptions, meanings, and definitions (though
not necessarily agreement) among large and heterogeneous mass publics. Message system analysis records those patterns and establishes the bases for cultivation analysis. We have been conducting annual analyses of prime time and
weekend daytime network television drama since 1969.[2]

The world of prime time is animated by vivid and intimate portrayals of over
300 major dramatic characters a week, mostly stock types, and their weekly
rounds of dramatic activities. Conventional and normal though that world may
appear, it is in fact far from the reality of anything but consumer values and the
ideology of social power.

Men outnumber women by at least 3:1 and are younger (but age faster) than
the men they meet. Young people (under 18) comprise one-third and older people
(over 65) one-fifth of their true proportion in the population. Figure 2.1 shows
the difference between the age distribution in the television world and reality.
Similarly, blacks on television represent three-fourths, and Hispanics one-third
of their share of the U.S. population, and a disproportionate number are minor
rather than major characters.

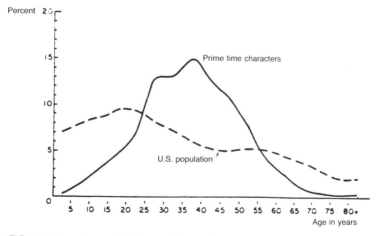

FIG. 2.1 Percentages of U.S. population and all prime time TV characters by
chronological age.

---

[2]By 1984, 2,105 programs (1,204 prime time and 901 weekend daytime), 6,055 major characters,
and 19,116 minor characters had been analyzed.

The point is not that culture should duplicate real-life statistics. It is rather that the direction and thrust of cultural amplification or neglect provide a clue to the treatment of social types, groups, and values, and yield suggestions for cultivation analysis. For example, the prominent and stable overrepresentation of well-to-do white men in the prime of life dominates prime time and indicates a relatively restrictive view of women's and minorities' opportunities and rights. As Figure 2.1 suggests, the general demography of the television world bears greater resemblance to the facts of consumer income than to the U.S. census.

The myth of the middle class as the all-American norm pervades the world of television. Nearly 7 out of 10 television characters appear in the "middle-middle" of a five-way classification system. Most of them are professionals and managers. Blue collar and service work occupies 67% of all Americans but only 25% of television characters.

In the world of prime time, the state acts mostly to fend off threats to law and order in a mean and dangerous world. Enforcing the law of that world takes nearly three times as many characters as the number of all blue-collar and service workers. The typical viewer of an average week's prime time programs encounters seemingly realistic and intimate (but usually false) representations of the life and work of 30 police officers, 7 lawyers, and 3 judges, but only 1 engineer or scientist and very few blue-collar workers. Again, nearly everybody appears to be comfortably managing on an average income of the mythical norm of middle class.

But threats abound. Crime in prime time is at least 10 times as rampant as in the real world. An average of 5 to 6 acts of overt physical violence per hour menace over half of all major characters. However, pain, suffering, and medical help rarely follow this mayhem. Symbolic violence demonstrates power, not therapy; it shows who can get away with what against whom. The dominant white men in the prime of life are more likely to be victimizers than victims. Conversely, old, young, and minority women, and young boys, are more likely to be victims rather than victimizers in violent conflicts. The analysis of content data as a message system rather than as isolated incidents of violence or sex, for example, makes it possible to view these acts in context as representing social relationships and the distribution (as well as symbolic enforcement) of the structure of power according to television.

The stability and consistency of basic patterns over the years is one of their most striking (but not surprising) features. A central cultural arm of society could hardly avoid reflecting (and cultivating) some of its basic structural characteristics, as well as more specific institutional positions and interests. Television has obviously changed on many levels (e.g., there have been ebbs and flows in the popularity and distribution of various genres, new production values, visible but token minority representation, and many short-lived trends and fads), but these changes are superficial. The underlying values, demography, ideology, and power relationships have manifested only minor fluctuations with virtually no significant deviations over time, despite the actual social changes which have occurred. The remarkable pattern of uniformity, durability, and resilience of the aggregate messages of prime time network drama explains its cultivation of both stable concepts and the resistance to change.

MODES OF CULTIVATION ANALYSIS

Our tracking and documentation of the shape and contours of the television world have led to several analytical strategies concerning the cultivation potential of television. These include analyses of the extent to which television teaches various facts about the world, of extrapolations from those facts to more general images and orientations, and of the incorporation of the lessons into viewers' personal assumptions and expectations.

Each of these involves somewhat different processes and relies on the specific findings of message system analysis to varying degrees. The content findings form the conceptual basis for the questions we ask respondents. The margins of difference ("cultivation differentials") between demographically matched light and heavy viewers' response patterns define the extent of cultivation. Where possible or appropriate, we use large surveys that were conducted for other purposes, with the accompanying advantages and limitations of secondary analysis. In any case, the questions do not mention television, and the respondents' awareness or perceptions of the source of their information are irrelevant for our purposes. Any resulting relationship between amount of viewing and the tendency to respond to these questions according to television's portrayals (with other things held constant) illuminates television's contribution to viewers' conceptions of social reality.[3]

The cases of clear-cut divergence between symbolic reality and objective reality provide convenient tests of the extent to which television's versions of the facts are incorporated or absorbed into what heavy viewers take for granted about the world. For example, television drama tends to sharply underrepresent older people. While those over 65 constitute the fastest growing segment of the real-world population, heavy viewers are more likely to feel that the elderly are a "vanishing breed"—that compared to 20 years ago, they are fewer in number, they are in worse health, and they don't live as long—all contrary to fact (Gerbner, Gross, Signorielli, & Morgan, 1980).

---

[3]In all analyses we use a number of demographic variables as controls. These are applied both separately and simultaneously. Included are sex (men, women), age (typically 18–29, 30–54, and over 55), race (white, nonwhite), education (no college, some college), income (under $10,000, $10,000–$24,999, and over $25,000), and political self-designation (liberal, moderate, conservative). Where applicable, other controls such as urban–rural areas, newspaper reading, and party affiliation are also used.

As another example, consider how likely television characters are to encounter violence compared to the rest of us. Well over half of all major characters on television are involved each week in some kind of violent action. Although FBI statistics have clear limitations, they indicate that in any 1 year less than 1% of people in the U.S. are victims of criminal violence. Accordingly, we have found considerable support for the proposition that heavy exposure to the world of television cultivates exaggerated perceptions of the number of people involved in violence in any given week (Gerbner et al., 1979; Gerbner, Gross, Morgan, & Signorielli, 1980), as well as numerous other inaccurate beliefs about crime and law enforcement. In these cases, we build upon the patterns revealed through message system analysis (e.g., concerning age and sex-roles, occupations, prevalence of certain actions, etc.) and ask viewers questions that tap what they assume to be the facts of real life with regard to these patterns.

Our investigation of the cultivation process is not limited to the lessons of television facts compared to real-world statistics. Some of the most interesting and important topics and issues for cultivation analysis involve the symbolic transformation of message system data into hypotheses about more general issues and assumptions.

The facts (which are evidently learned quite well) are likely to become the basis for a broader world view, thus making television a significant source of general values, ideologies, and perspectives as well as specific assumptions, beliefs, and images. This extrapolation beyond the specific facts derived from message system analysis can be seen as second-order cultivation analysis. Hawkins and Pingree (1982) call this the cultivation of "value systems."

One example is what we have called the "mean world" syndrome. Our message data say little directly about either the selfishness or altruism of people, and there are certainly no real-world statistics about the extent to which people can be trusted. Yet, we have found that one lesson viewers derive from heavy exposure to the violence-saturated world of television is that in such a mean and dangerous world, most people "cannot be trusted" and that most people are "just looking out for themselves" (Gerbner, Gross, Morgan, & Signorielli, 1980). We have also found that the differential ratios of symbolic victimization among women and minorities on television cultivate different levels of insecurity among their real-life counterparts, a "hierarchy of fears" that confirms and tends to perpetuate their dependent status (Morgan, 1983).

Another example of extrapolated assumptions relates to the image of women. The dominant majority status of men on television does not mean that heavy viewers ignore daily experience and underestimate the number of women in society. But it does mean that most heavy viewers absorb the implicit assumptions that women have more limited abilities and interests than men. Most groups of heavy viewers, with other characteristics held constant, score higher on our sexism scale.

Other second-order extrapolations from content patterns have also led to fruitful discoveries of more explicit political importance. For example, we have argued that as television seeks large and heterogeneous audiences, its messages are designed to disturb as few as possible. Therefore, they tend to balance opposing perspectives and to steer a middle course along the supposedly nonideological mainstream. We have found that heavy viewers are significantly and substantially more likely to label themselves as being "moderate" rather than either "liberal" or "conservative" (see Gerbner, Gross, Morgan, & Signorielli, 1982; 1984).

Finally, we have observed a complex relationship between the cultivation of general orientations or assumptions about facts of life and more specific personal expectations. For example, television may cultivate exaggerated notions of the prevalence of violence and risk out in the world, but the cultivation of expectations of personal victimization depends on the neighborhood of the viewer (see Gerbner, Gross, Morgan, & Signorielli, 1981a). Different groups may hold the same assumptions about the facts but relate to them in different ways, depending on their own situations.

Thus, the cultivation of a general conception of social reality (e.g., about women's place or violence in the world) may lead to a certain position on public issues or to some marketing decision, but it need not result in other behavior consonant with that conception. The latter (e.g., career expectation, likelihood of victimization) may be deflected by demographic or personal situations or other currents in the television mainstream. Our focus has generally been on those basic perspectives and conceptions that bear the strongest relationships to common expectations and the formation of public policy.

THE NATURE OF CULTIVATION

Since the early 1970s, the range of topics we have subjected to cultivation analysis has greatly expanded. On issue after issue we found that the assumptions, beliefs, and values of heavy viewers differ systematically from those of comparable groups of light viewers. The differences tend to reflect both the dominant patterns of life in the television world and the characteristics of different groups of light and heavy viewers.

Sometimes we found that these differences hold across-the-board, meaning that those who watch more television are more likely—in all or most subgroups— to give what we call "television answers" to our questions. But in most cases, the patterns were more complex. As we looked into the cultivation process in more and more aspects of life and society, from health-related beliefs to political orientations and occupational images (and much more), we found that television viewing usually relates in different but consistent ways to different groups' life situations and world views.

We have found that personal interaction makes a difference. Adolescents whose parents are more involved in their viewing show sharply smaller relationships between amount of viewing and perceiving the world in terms of television's portrayals (Gross & Morgan, 1985). Children who are more integrated into cohesive peer groups are less receptive to cultivation (Rothschild, 1984). In contrast, adolescents who watch cable programming show significantly stronger cultivation patterns (Morgan & Rothschild, 1983). The implication is that cultivation is both dependent on and a manifestation of the extent to which mediated imagery dominates the viewers' sources of information. Personal interaction and affiliation reduce cultivation; cable television (presumably by providing even more of the same) increases it.

Personal, day-to-day, direct experience also plays a role. We have found that the relationship between amount of viewing and fear of crime is strongest among those who have good reason to be afraid. When one's everyday environment is congruent with and reinforces television's messages, the result is a phenomenon we call *resonance*. For example, the cultivation of insecurity is most pronounced among those who live in high crime urban areas (Doob & Macdonald, 1979; Gerbner, Gross, Morgan, & Signorielli, 1980). In these cases, everyday reality and television provide a double dose of messages that resonate and amplify cultivation.

Demographic correspondence between viewers and television characters also predicts the extent and nature of cultivation. Our message system analyses have revealed consistent differences in the relative likelihood of different demographic groups to be portrayed as victims or as perpetrators of violence (known as *risk ratios*). Relationships of amount of viewing and the tendency to hold exaggerated perceptions of violence are much more pronounced within the real-world demographic subgroups whose fictional counterparts are most victimized (Morgan, 1983). The symbolic power hierarchy of relative victimization is thus reflected in differential cultivation patterns.

MAINSTREAMING

We have seen that a wide variety of factors produce systematic and theoretically meaningful variations in cultivation. We have named the most general and important of these patterns *mainstreaming*.

The mainstream can be thought of as a relative commonality of outlooks and values that exposure to features and dynamics of the television world tends to cultivate. By mainstreaming we mean the expression of that commonality by heavy viewers in those demographic groups whose light viewers hold divergent

views. In other words, differences found in the responses of different groups of
viewers, differences that can be associated with other cultural, social, and political characteristics of these groups, may be diminished or even absent from the
responses of heavy viewers in the same groups.

Mainstreaming represents the theoretical elaboration and empirical verification
of our assertion that television cultivates common perspectives. Mainstreaming
means that television viewing may absorb or override differences in perspectives
and behavior that stem from other social, cultural, and demographic influences.
It represents a homogenization of divergent views and a convergence of disparate
viewers. Mainstreaming makes television the true 20th-century melting pot of
the American people.

The mainstreaming potential of television stems from the way the institution
is organized, the competition to attract audiences from all regions and classes,
and the consistency of its messages (see, e.g., Hirsch, 1979; Seldes, 1957). In
every area we have examined, mainstreaming is the strongest and most consistent
explanation for differences in the strength and direction of television's contributions to viewer conceptions.

For example, data from the 1975, 1978, 1980, and 1983 National Opinion
Research Center (NORC) General Social Surveys combined to form the Mean
World Index provide evidence for mainstreaming. These analyses have revealed
that the overall amount of television viewing is significantly associated with the
tendency to report that most people are just looking out for themselves, that you
can't be too careful in dealing with them, and that they would take advantage
of you if they had a chance. The relationship is strongest for respondents who

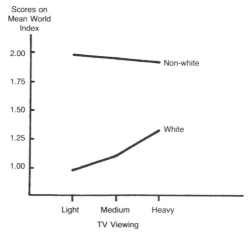

FIG. 2.2 Scores on the Mean World Index of Apprehension and mistrust for white
and nonwhite light, medium, and heavy viewers.

TABLE 2.1
Relationship Between Amount of Television Viewing and Political Self-Designation

| | Percentage Who Say They Are | | | | | | | | |
| | Liberal | | | Moderate | | | Conservative | | |
	%L	CD	Gamma	%L	CD	Gamma	%L	CD	Gamma
Overall	29	−2	−.031	34	+11	.136***	37	−9	−.120***
Controlling for:									
Sex									
Male	30	0	.001	31	+9	.119***	39	−9	−.121***
Female	29	−4	−.050	37	+11	.132***	35	−8	−.107***
Age									
Under 30	39	−3	−.045	32	+32	.150***	28	−8	−.136***
30–54	29	−4	−.074*	32	+12	.160***	39	−8	−.103***
Over 55	19	+3	.065	40	+6	.080*	41	−9	−.126***
Education									
No College	23	+2	.040	41	+6	.068**	36	−8	−.117***
Some College	36	−2	−.034	26	+8	.110**	38	−6	−.067*
Income									
Low	34	−5	−.056	36	+7	.094**	30	−2	−.051
Medium	29	−4	−.062	32	+13	.162***	36	−9	−.127***
High	28	−1	−.043	32	+12	.154***	40	−10	−.120***
Race									
White	29	−5	−.064**	34	+12	.148***	37	−7	−.105***
Nonwhite	37	+4	.076	32	+6	.087	32	−11	−.194**

	%L	CD		%L	CD		%L	CD	
Region									
Urban	35	−3	−.028	32	+9	.115***	33	−6	−.095**
Nonurban	25	−1	−.025	35	+12	.147***	40	−11	−.140***
Party									
Democrat	36	−5	−.063*	36	+8	.095**	28	−3	−.048
Independent	33	−6	−.093**	36	+11	.146***	32	−6	−.078*
Republican	14	+6	.126*	29	+12	.163***	57	−18	−.216***

Note: %L (percent light viewers) refers to the percentage of light viewers giving the "television answer." CD (cultivation differential) refers to the percentage of heavy viewers minus the percentage of light viewers giving the "television answer."

*p < .05.
**p < .01.
***p < .001.

Source: NORC General Social Surveys (1975, 1977, 1978, 1980, 1982, 1983)

have had some college education—those who are otherwise (as light viewers) the least likely to express interpersonal mistrust. (The correlation between education and the Mean World Index is $-.25, p < .001$.) Interesting specifications emerge for whites and nonwhites. As can be seen on Figure 2.2, nonwhites as a group score higher than whites on the Mean World Index, $r = .21, p < .001$. Yet there is a slightly negative association among nonwhites between viewing television and this index, suggesting that television may play an ameliorating role in their anxieties. The relationship for whites, however, is the opposite. For the majority of (white) viewers, therefore, television plays an exacerbating role. Moreover, an analysis of variance of scores on the Mean World Index by television viewing and race reveals significant main effects and a significant interaction. Thus, the heavier viewers of those groups who otherwise are least likely to hold television-related views of suspicion and mistrust are most likely to be influenced toward the relatively suspicious and mistrustful mainstream television view. In general, those who are most likely to hold a view already in the mainstream show no difference, whereas those who hold views more extreme than the television view may be brought back to the mainstream position.

Reflecting its tendency to balance divergent views and present a broadly acceptable political orientation, television also blurs traditional political differences. It can be seen in Table 2.1 and Figure 2.3 that significantly more heavy than light viewers of all political affiliations call themselves moderate. Heavy viewers are less likely to say they are conservative or liberal except among Republicans where, in a typical mainstreaming pattern, there is an extremely low number of liberals among light viewers, whereas among heavy viewers the level approaches that of the mainstream.

On the surface, mainstreaming appears to be a centering of political and other tendencies. However, a look at the actual positions taken in response to questions about a number of political issues shows that the mainstream does not always mean middle of the road. When we analyzed responses to questions in the NORC General Social Surveys about attitudes and opinions on such topics as racial segregation, homosexuality, abortion, minority rights, and other issues that have traditionally divided liberals and conservatives, we found such a division mainly among those who watch little television. Overall, self-styled moderates are closer to conservatives than they are to liberals. Among heavy viewers, liberals and conservatives are closer to each other than among light viewers. Figure 2.4 illustrates these findings.

In regard to opposition to busing, we can see that heavy-viewing conservatives are more liberal and heavy-viewing liberals more conservative than their respective light-viewing counterparts. In the second example, opposition to open housing laws, viewing is not associated with any differences in the attitudes expressed by conservatives, but among liberals we see that heavy viewing goes with a greater likelihood of such opposition. The third example shows that in response to a question about laws against marriages between blacks and whites, heavy

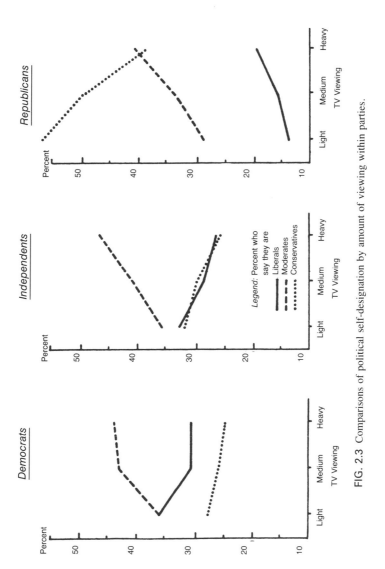

FIG. 2.3 Comparisons of political self-designation by amount of viewing within parties.

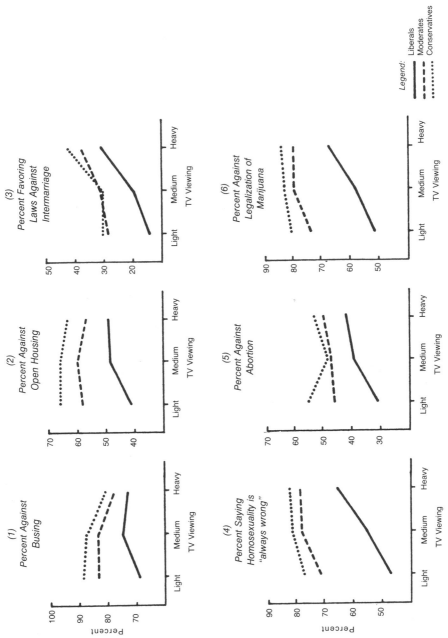

FIG. 2.4 Television viewing and positions on racial and personal rights issues by political orientation.

viewers in all groups are more likely to favor these laws than are light viewers in the same categories, but this is much more pronounced for liberals. Finally, in the cases of attitudes on homosexuality, abortion, and marijuana (examples 4, 5, and 6), there is a considerable spread between light-viewing liberals and light-viewing conservatives, but once again, the attitudes of heavy-viewing liberals and conservatives are closer together. This is due primarily to the virtual collapse of the typical liberal opinion among heavy-viewing liberals. We have also noted (Gerbner, Gross, Morgan, & Signorielli, 1982; Gerbner et al., 1984) that although the mainstream runs toward the right on political issues, it leans toward a populist stance on economic issues, setting up potentially volatile conflicts of demands and expectations.

Mainstreaming has been found to explain differences in within-group patterns in terms of the cultivation of images of violence (Gerbner, Gross, Morgan, & Signorielli, 1980), conceptions of science and scientists (Gerbner, Gross, Morgan, & Signorielli, 1981c), health-related beliefs and practices (Gerbner, Gross, Morgan, & Signorielli, 1981b; Gerbner, Morgan, & Signorielli, 1982), sex-role stereotypes (Morgan, 1982; Signorielli, 1979), adolescent career choices (Morgan & Gerbner, 1982), views of racial and sexual minorities (Gross, 1984), as well as the ways in which television relates to academic achievement (Morgan & Gross, 1982) and other issues. Mainstreaming also explains variations in the intersection of patterns reflecting different modes of cultivation, such as in the distinction between general assumptions about the prevalence of violence and perceived personal risks (Gerbner et al., 1981a).

An increasing number of studies conducted by independent investigators in the United States and abroad contributes to the development and refinement of cultivation theory (e.g., Bonfadelli, 1983; Bryant, Carveth, & Brown, 1981; Hawkins & Pingree, 1982; Pingree & Hawkins, 1981; Singer & Singer, 1983; Tan, 1979, 1982; Volgy & Schwarz, 1980; Weimann, 1984; Williams, Zabrack, & Joy, 1983). We have moved from our early focus upon across-the-board consequences of television viewing (which still holds some of the most compelling evidence of television's contributions to conceptions of social reality) to a further examination of the systematic processes of mainstreaming and resonance.

Our research has revealed a number of mainstreaming patterns. The emerging models have two characteristics in common. First, heavy viewers in one or more subgroups are more likely to reflect in their responses what they have seen on television than are light viewers in the same subgroups. Second, the difference between light and heavy viewer conceptions is greatest in those groups in which the light viewers' conceptions are the farthest away from what might be seen as the television mainstream. As we can see in the illustration of different models of the cultivation process (Fig. 2.5, graphs a through e), the light–heavy viewer differences need not point in the same direction or involve all subgroups. But except for graph f, they all reflect the cultivation process and relate to its center of gravity, the television mainstream.

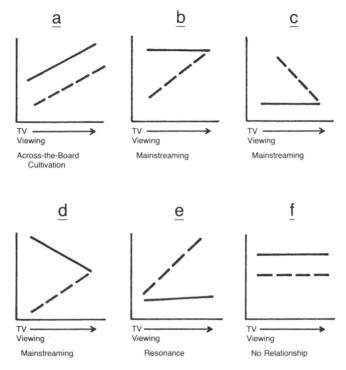

FIG. 2.5 Models of cultivation.

In summary, our theory of the cultivation process is an attempt to understand and explain the dynamics of television as a distinctive feature of our age. It is not a substitute for, but a complement to, traditional approaches to media effects research concerned with processes more applicable to other media. Designed primarily for television and focusing on its pervasive and recurrent patterns of representation and viewing, cultivation analysis concentrates on the enduring and common consequences of growing up and living with television: the cultivation of stable, resistant, and widely shared assumptions, images, and conceptions reflecting the institutional characteristics and interests of the medium itself. Our explorations of this process in many ways and contexts have been enriched and confirmed by studies of a growing number of independent investigators in the United States and abroad and have led to the development of some theoretical models for further testing and elaboration.

We believe that television has become the common symbolic environment that interacts with most of the things we think and do. Therefore, understanding its dynamics can help develop and maintain a sense of alternatives and independence essential for self-direction and self-government in the television age.

REFERENCES

Bogart, L. (1956). *The age of television.* New York: Ungar.

Bonfadelli, H. (1983). Der Einfluss des Fernsehens auf die Konstruktion der Sozialien Realitat: Refunde aus der Schweiz zur Kultivierungshypothese. *Rundfunk und Fernsehen, 31,* 415–430.

Bryant, J., Carveth, R. A., & Brown, D. (1981). Television viewing and anxiety: An experimental examination. *Journal of Communication, 31*(1), 106–119.

Doob, A. N., & Macdonald, G. E. (1979). Television viewing and fear of victimization: Is the Relationship Causal? *Journal of Personality and Social Psychology, 37*(2), 170–179.

Gerbner, G. (1969a). Dimensions of violence in television drama. In R. K. Baker & S. J. Ball (Eds.), *Violence in the media* (Staff Report to the National Commission on the Causes and Prevention of Violence, pp. 311–340). Washington, DC: U.S. Government Printing Office.

Gerbner, G. (1969b). Institutional pressures upon mass communicators. In P. Halmos (Ed.), *The sociology of mass communicators* (Sociological Review Monographs No. 13, pp. 205–248). England: University of Keele.

Gerbner, G. (1969c). Toward "cultural indicators": The analysis of mass mediated message systems. *AV Communication Review, 17*(2), 137–148.

Gerbner, G. (1972). The structure and process of television program content regulation in the U.S. In G. A. Comstock & E. A. Rubinstein (Eds.), *Television and social behavior,* Vol. 1: *Content and control* (pp. 386–414). Washington, DC: Government Printing Office.

Gerbner, G. (1973). Cultural indicators: The third voice. In G. Gerbner, L. Gross, & W. H. Melody (Eds.), *Communications technology and social policy* (pp. 555–573). New York: Wiley.

Gerbner, G., & Gross, L. (1976). Living with television: The violence profile. *Journal of Communication, 26*(2), 172–199.

Gerbner, G., Gross, L., Signorielli, N., Morgan, M., & Jackson-Beeck, M. (1979). The demonstration of power: Violence profile no. 10. *Journal of Communication, 29*(3), 177–196.

Gerbner, G., Gross, L., Signorielli, N., & Morgan, M. (1980). Aging with television: Images on television drama and conceptions of social reality. *Journal of Communication, 30*(1), 37–47.

Gerbner, G., Gross, L., Morgan, M., & Signorielli, N. (1980). The "mainstreaming" of America: Violence profile no. 11. *Journal of Communication, 30*(3), 10–29.

Gerbner, G., Gross, L., Morgan, M., & Signorielli, N. (1981a). Final reply to Hirsch. *Communication Research, 8*(3), 259–280.

Gerbner, G., Gross, L., Morgan, M., & Signorielli, N. (1981b). Health and medicine on television. *The New England Journal of Medicine, 305*(15), 901–904.

Gerbner, G., Gross, L., Morgan, M., & Signorielli, N. (1981c). Scientists on the TV screen. *Society, 18*(4), 41–44.

Gerbner, G., Gross, L., Morgan, M., & Signorielli, N. (1982). Charting the mainstream: Television's contributions to political orientations. *Journal of Communication, 32*(2), 100–127.

Gerbner, G., Gross, L., Morgan, M., & Signorielli, N. (1984). Political correlates of televison viewing. *Public Opinion Quarterly, 48,* 283–300.

Gerbner, G., Morgan, M., & Signorielli, N. (1982). Programming health portrayals: What viewers see, say, and do. In D. Pearl, L. Bouthilet, & J. Lazar (Eds.), *Television and behavior: Ten years of scientific progress and implications for the 80's* (Vol. II, pp. 291–307). Washington, DC: U.S. Government Printing Office.

Glynn, E. D. (1956). Television and the American character: A psychiatrist looks at television. In W. Y. Elliot (Ed.), *Television's impact on American culture* (pp. 175–182). Lansing: Michigan State University Press.

Gross, L. (1984). The cultivation of intolerance: Television, blacks and gays. In G. Melischek, K. E. Rosengren, & J. Stappers (Eds.), *Cultural indicators: An international symposium* (pp. 345–364). Vienna: Austrian Academy of Sciences.

Gross, L., & Morgan, M. (1985). Television and enculturation. In J. Dominick & J. Fletcher (Eds.), *Broadcasting research methods* (pp. 221–234). Boston: Allyn & Bacon.

Hawkins, R. P., & Pingree, S. (1982). Television's influence on social reality. In D. Pearl, L. Bouthilet, & J. Lazar (Eds.), *Television and behavior: Ten years of scientific progress and implications for the 80's* (Vol. II, pp. 224–247). Washington, DC: U.S. Government Printing Office.

Hirsch, P. (1979). The role of television and popular culture in contemporary society. In H. Newcomb (Ed.), *Television: The critical view* (2nd ed., pp. 249–279). New York: Oxford University Press.

Lazarsfeld, P. F., & Merton, R. K. (1948). Mass communication, popular taste, and organized social action. In L. Bryson (Ed.), *The communication of ideas* (pp. 95–118). New York: Harper.

McQuail, D. (1976). Alternative models of television influence. In R. Brown (Ed.), *Children and television* (pp. 343–360). Beverly Hills, CA: Sage.

Morgan, M. (1982). Television and adolescents' sex-role stereotypes: A longitudinal study. *Journal of Personality and Social Psychology, 43*(5), 947–955.

Morgan, M. (1983). Symbolic victimization and real-world fear. *Human Communication Research, 9*(2), 146–157.

Morgan, M. (1984). *Television and the erosion of regional diversity.* Paper presented at the meeting of the International Association for Mass Communications Research, Prague, 1984.

Morgan, M., & Gerbner, G. (1982). TV professions and adolescent career choices. In M. Schwarz (Ed.), *TV and teens: Experts look at the issues* (pp. 121–126). Reading, MA: Addison-Wesley.

Morgan, M., & Gross, L. (1982). Television and educational achievement and aspirations. In D. Pearl, L. Bouthilet, & J. Lazar (Eds.), *Television and behavior: Ten years of scientific progress and implications for the 80's* (Vol. II, pp. 78–90). Washington, DC: U.S. Government Printing Office.

Morgan, M., & Rothschild, N. (1983). Impact of the new television technology: Cable TV, peers, and sex-role cultivation in the electronic environment. *Youth and Society, 15*(1), 33–50.

Pingree, S., & Hawkins, R. (1980). U.S. programs on Australian television: The cultivation effect. *Journal of Communication, 31*(1), 97–105.

Rothschild, N. (1984). Small group affiliation as a mediating factor in the cultivation process. In G. Melischek, E. R. Rosengren, & J. Stappers et al. (Eds.), *Cultural indicators: An international symposium* (pp. 377–388). Vienna: Osterreichischen Akademie der Wissenschaften.

Seldes, G. (1957). *The new mass media: Challenge to a free society.* Washington, DC: American Association of University Women.

Signorielli, N. (1979, April). *Television's contribution to sex-role socialization.* Paper presented at the seventh annual Telecommunications Policy Research Conference, Skytop, PA.

Singer, J. L., & Singer, D. G. (1983, July). Psychologists look at television: Cognitive, developmental, personality and social policy implications. *American Psychologist,* pp. 826–834.

Tan, A. S. (1979). TV beauty ads and role expectations of adolescent female viewers. *Journalism Quarterly, 56*(2), 283–288.

Tan, A. S. (1982). Television use and social stereotypes. *Journalism Quarterly, 59*(1), 119–122.

Volgy, T., & Schwarz, J. E. (1980). Television entertainment programming and sociopolitical attitudes. *Journalism Quarterly, 57*(1), 150–155.

Weigel, R. H., & Jessor, R. (1973). Television and adolescent conventionality: An exploratory study. *Public Opinion Quarterly, 37,* 76–90.

Weimann, G. (1984). Images of life in America: The impact of American T.V. in Israel. *International Journal of Intercultural Relations, 8,* 185–197.

Williams, T. M., Zabrack, M. L., & Joy, L. A. (1983). The portrayal of aggression on North American television. *Journal of Applied Social Psychology, 12*(5), 360–380.

3 Social Learning of Aggression from Television

Alexis S. Tan
Texas Tech University

It is evident from recent reviews of television research that scholarly, public, and television industry concerns have moved beyond the early preoccupation with television violence and subsequent aggressive behavior in viewers. A recent report of the National Institute of Health on television and behavior, for example, devotes about 16% of its total pages to television violence and aggression, and relatively new research topics such as the structure of television programs and family influences on viewing are emphasized (Pearl, Bouthilet, & Lazar, 1982). The range of television effects studied by researchers has expanded. We are now interested not only in aggression in viewers, but also in television's influence on prosocial behaviors and attitudes, perceptions of social reality, role socialization, cognitive and social development, health behaviors, the development of imagination, and school performance (e.g., Pearl et al., 1982; Singer & Singer, 1983).

Nevertheless, the interest in television violence and aggression lingers, and with it the accompanying controversy. The reasons for this continued interest include: (a) television programming, for the most part, continues to be violent; (b) violence in our communities is an everyday reality; (c) after 2 decades of intensive research, there is still considerable disagreement within the research community on whether television violence causes aggression in the real world.

There is general consensus that exposure to television violence can cause short-term arousal and modeling effects. The problem arises when laboratory results are extrapolated to the real world. Most social and behavioral scientists who have studied television accept the relationship between televised violence

41

and subsequent aggressive behavior in viewers as positive and causal. Rubinstein (1982), for example, points out that: "Most television researchers look at the totality of evidence and conclude, as did the Surgeon General's advisory committee, that the convergence of most of the findings about televised violence and later aggressive behavior supports the positive conclusion of a causal relationship" (p. 104).

A few recent studies, using longitudinal field designs and causal statistical models, offer evidence contrary to this conclusion. Milavsky, Kessler, Stipp, and Rubens (1982), after a 3-year study of the development of aggressive patterns in elementary and high school children, found no signficant association between exposure to violence in television and subsequent change in aggression. Milavsky et al. conclude that short-term, modeling effects probably do exist, as shown by the experimental laboratory studies; however, they stress that "these short-term effects found experimentally do not lead to stable patterns of aggression" (p. 155). On the other hand, other longitudinal studies have found evidence of a significant, positive relationship. Time-lag surveys of preschool children over a period of 1 year (Singer & Singer, 1983) indicate that heavy viewing of aggressive-action adventure and cartoon shows was linked to later aggression. Furthermore, neither existing family aggression patterns nor aggression levels in children prior to viewing television violence could explain away these results. Adding to the debate is an interpretation of the Milavsky et al. study by Cook, Kendzierski, and Thomas (1983) who point out some weaknesses of the basic regression model used and conclude that the effects of viewing televised violence on later aggression are consistently positive, small, and causal.

The emerging picture, then, is far from complete. We can expect more data to be collected using field designs and time-lag models as the causal hypothesis continues to be tested in the real world. This is a positive development, as even more televised violence becomes available to children via video recorders and cable television. The analysis of data, however, can be meaningful only if interpreted within the framework of theory that can explain why particular relationships exist and their underlying processes.

The objective of this chapter is to present a theoretical model that can explain some of these hypotheses and findings. This model, social learning theory (Bandura, 1977), is not the only theory that can explain the relationship between televised violence and subsequent aggression in viewers. Other theories and models can also do this, among them the various information-processing models of learning (Huesmann, 1982), television viewing and arousal models (Zillmann, 1982), and aggression-cue models (Berkowitz & LePage, 1967; Turner & Layton, 1976). Social learning theory, however, is probably the most comprehensive. It can explain not only why televised violence is likely to be modeled and how it is learned, but also why the relationship in the real world between exposure to televised violence and subsequent aggression, although positive and causal, is in most cases small.

SOCIAL LEARNING THEORY

Bandura (1977) formulated his social learning theory as a general explanation of human behavior. It is an eclectic theory in that it does not subscribe to "one-sided determinism" explanations of human behavior in which either environmental forces (as in classical learning theories) or internal dispositions (as in drive theories) are considered the primary determinants of action. Instead, social learning theory considers both external and internal determinants to be important in the acquisition of response tendencies. Although Bandura (1983) has more recently been interested in the application of social learning theory to explain self-directed change in the individual, the theory was originally used to explain how new response tendencies (e.g., aggressive acts) could be learned by observation and modeling (Bandura, 1977).

In its most basic form, social learning theory explains how matching performances can result from modeling an observed behavior (see Fig. 3.1). An external event—the behavior to be modeled—is the starting point in the social learning process. Events that are distinctive, evaluated positively, simple, prevalent, and useful will be attended to. Attention, the first step in social learning, is also determined by attributes of the actor—his or her perceptual capabilities (e.g., attention span), arousal level (some degree of emotional arousal facilitates attention to related stimuli), perceptual set, and acquired preferences.

Once an event has been attended to, the next step in social learning is retention. Retention is accomplished by symbolic coding (using symbols to represent the event mentally), cognitive organization (sorting out the event into steps and components), symbolic rehearsal (e.g., mentally going over the event), and enactive rehearsal (acting out the event). Cognitive attributes of actors such as their ability to learn and their existing cognitive structures determine the extent to which the event is remembered. Whether the remembered event becomes part of the actor's regular behavioral repertoire depends on certain production processes. These include internal conception or how accurately the event has been remembered, observation of the enactments by self or others, and accuracy of feedback from others or by self. The actor's physical capabilities and the availability of component subskills (e.g., physical strength) also determine the extent to which the act will be regularly performed.

Finally, motivational processes within the individual affect performance of the learned act. External, vicarious, and self-initiated rewards determine the frequency of matching performances.

A SOCIAL LEARNING ANALYSIS OF AGGRESSION

Aggression is a complex behavior with many complex origins, and again, we turn to social learning theory to understand the mechanisms of human aggression in the real world.

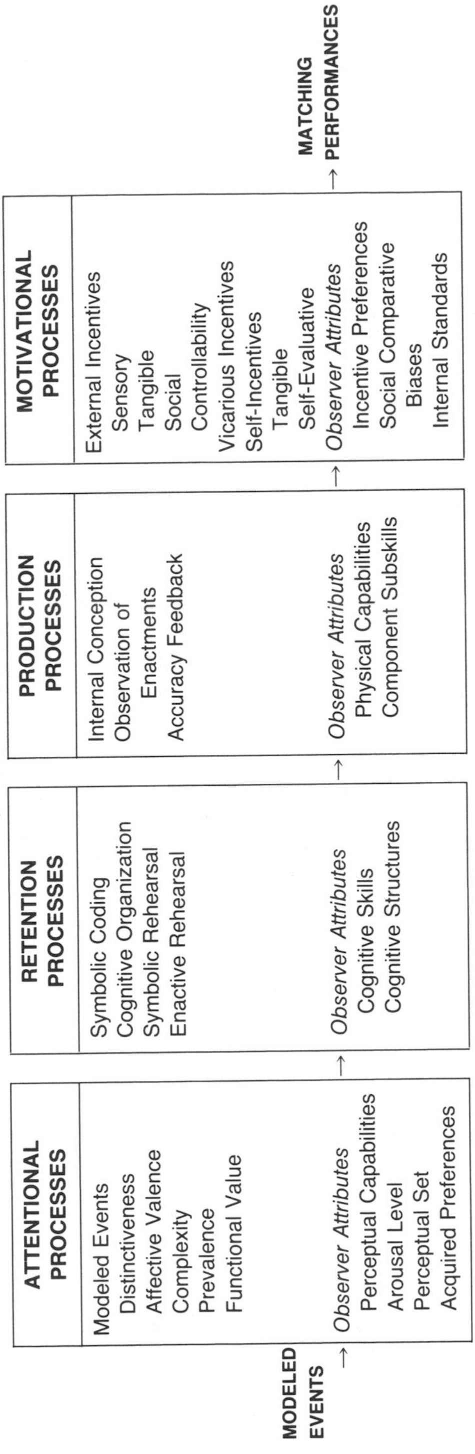

FIG. 3.1 The social learning model (from Bandura, 1977)

In the social learning view, aggression is "behavior that results in personal injury and physical destruction" (Bandura, 1979, p. 316). Although this definition considers physical harm and psychological impairment to be "personal injury," most studies of aggression have focused on direct assaultive behavior with explicit intent to injure or destroy. Thus, the component of aggression that has received the most attention has been physical injury. Not all behavior leading to physical injury, however, is perceived as aggression. Judgmental factors often determine how people label these behaviors. For example, behaviors will more likely be judged as aggressive when observers attribute personal injury and injurious intent to the actor (Bandura, 1973; Rule & Nesdale, 1976). Aggression, then, is a complex behavior that includes not only physically and psychologically injurious behavior but also judgmental factors that lead observers to label some forms of harmful conduct as aggression and others as benevolence (Bandura, 1979).

In a social learning analysis of aggression, the origins of aggression are first identified. These include observational learning, reinforced performance, and biological determinants. Aggressive instincts remain dormant unless they are instigated by modeling influences, aversive treatment, incentive inducements, instructional control, or bizarre symbolic control. Finally, aggressive acts are regulated by reinforcements, which can take the form of external reinforcements, punishment, vicarious reinforcement, or self-reinforcement (see Fig. 3.2). Our concern in this chapter is to show that aggression in the real world is instigated and regulated by many conditions.

Figure 3.2 shows that observational learning is only one of the many possible origins of aggression and that modeling influences (the most likely effect of exposure to televised violence) is only one of the many instigators of aggression. Also, aggression is regulated by several conditions. The performance in the real world of a learned aggressive act depends primarily on reinforcement. Quite simply, aggressive behaviors that are rewarded will be performed, whereas those that are punished will remain dormant. Any analysis of the effects of televised violence on subsequent aggressive behavior should consider not only the modeling influences on the actor but also the environmental conditions in which the learned act is or can be performed. For example, one should not expect a strong, positive causal relationship between exposure to televised violence and subsequent aggression in a social environment (e.g., school) where aggression is consistently punished or where reinforcements are not available.

SOCIAL LEARNING
AND TELEVISION VIOLENCE RESEARCH

In this section, some hypotheses and results of recent research on television violence and aggressive behavior are discussed from a social learning perspective (see Pearl et al., 1982, for a comprehensive review). The objective is to provide

FIG. 3.2 A social learning analysis of aggression
(from Bandura, 1979).

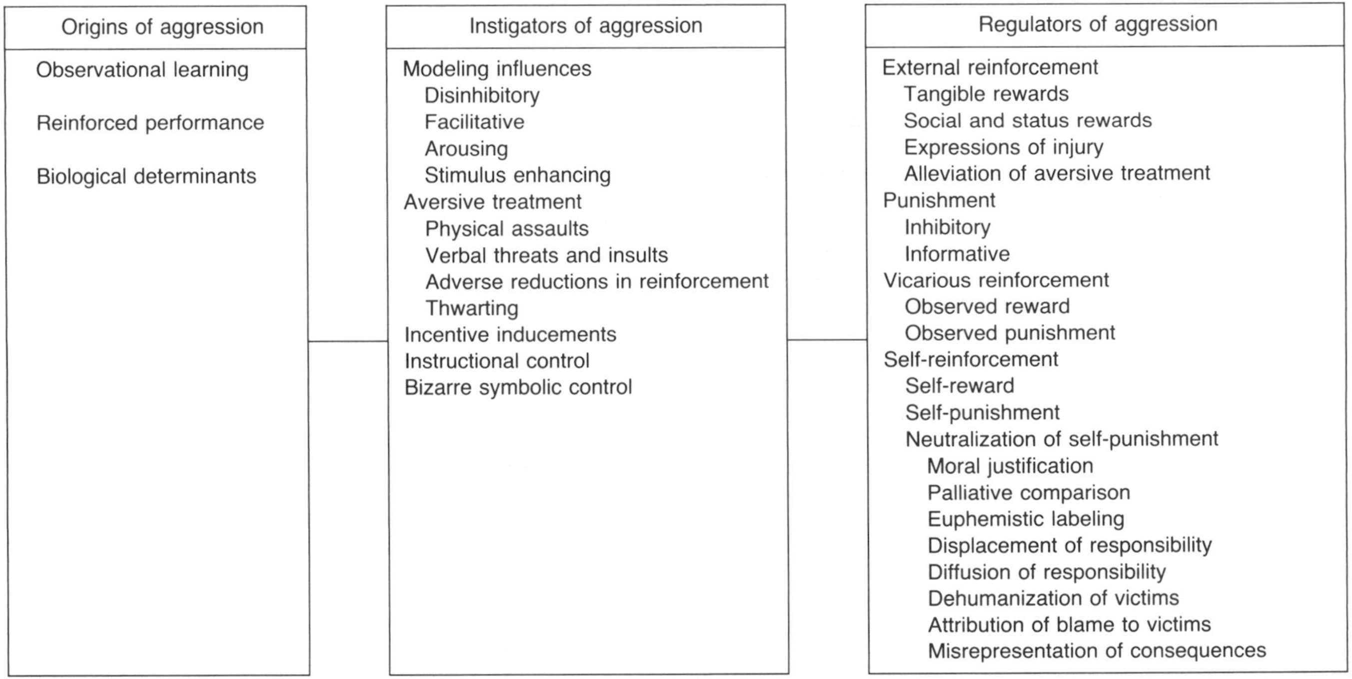

Origins of aggression	Instigators of aggression	Regulators of aggression
Observational learning	Modeling influences	External reinforcement
Reinforced performance	Disinhibitory	Tangible rewards
Biological determinants	Facilitative	Social and status rewards
	Arousing	Expressions of injury
	Stimulus enhancing	Alleviation of aversive treatment
	Aversive treatment	Punishment
	Physical assaults	Inhibitory
	Verbal threats and insults	Informative
	Adverse reductions in reinforcement	Vicarious reinforcement
	Thwarting	Observed reward
	Incentive inducements	Observed punishment
	Instructional control	Self-reinforcement
	Bizarre symbolic control	Self-reward
		Self-punishment
		Neutralization of self-punishment
		Moral justification
		Palliative comparison
		Euphemistic labeling
		Displacement of responsibility
		Diffusion of responsibility
		Dehumanization of victims
		Attribution of blame to victims
		Misrepresentation of consequences

a theoretical framework for the interpretation and understanding of results of recent studies.

Attention to Televised Violence

Social learning of a behavior begins when an event that can be modeled is made available to the actor. The first concern, then, is the availability of televised violence as events that can be learned.

Television violence has been defined by researchers in many ways, and these many definitions are the cause of some controversy. Perhaps the best known definition is given by Gerbner, Gross, Morgan, and Signorielli (1980), who define television violence as: "the overt expression of physical force (with or without a weapon, against self or others) or other compelling action against one's will on pain of being hurt or killed, or actually hurting or killing" (p. 11). This definition considers only the physical pain component of violence, whether it occurs in a realistic, fantasy, or humorous context. It does not include violence to property and behaviors leading to emotional or psychological injury (Signorielli, Gross, & Morgan, 1982).

The CBS Office of Social Research (1976–1977), in its monitoring project of violence in network television programming, similarly confines the definition of televised violence to physical harm. Violence in television is defined as: "the use of physical force against persons or animals, or the articulated, explicit threat of physical force to compel particular behavior on the part of a person" (p. 4).

The Gerbner and CBS definitions of television violence are similar in that both emphasize the physical harm component. A major difference is that the CBS definition does not include injurious acts presented in a humorous context; the Gerbner definition considers all physically injurious acts to be violence, regardless of context.

Content analyses over the past decade by Gerbner and his colleagues show that the frequency of violence in television has remained consistently at a high level. Signorielli et al. (1982), using Gerbner's definition, report that 80.9% of all television programs and 91.9% of weekend daytime programs contained some violence in 1979, compared to 81.3% and 93.8%, respectively, in 1967. The mean number of violent acts for all programs in 1979 was 4.98 (also 4.98 in 1967); the mean for weekend daytime programs was 4.58 in 1979 (4.72 in 1967). We can conclude from these data that violent acts on television, particularly those that depict physically injurious behaviors, are readily available to the audience, thus presenting many opportunities for modeling influences.

Availability of the event to be modeled is not a sufficient condition for learning. One must also be able to show that the potential learner pays attention to the event. Out of the thousands of messages a person is exposed to each day, to what extent do violent television contents stand out and attract his or her attention?

According to social learning theory (Fig. 3.1), we attend to events that are distinctive, evaluated positively, prevalent, and functional. Most violent acts shown in television fulfill at least one of these conditions. Violent acts are distinctive because of fast paced action which sets them apart from the rest of the program (e.g., dialogue); they are often shown to be preferred solutions to interpersonal conflicts and are evaluated positively by observers when committed by good guys or when shown to be effective in the pursuit of valued consequences. Most televised violence is simple in that the violent act is often shown in a few sequences lasting a few minutes or less; violence is prevalent, occurring with regularity in prime time and weekend programming; it can be functional, especially for children, because the presentation of violent acts in television as effective strategies for solving problems can provide guidance for the resolution of problems in real life. Given this assessment of television violence, we can expect viewers to be more attentive to violent acts in television than to other depicted behaviors.

This hypothesis has not been tested directly; however, it has indirect support in studies of cognitive processing of general television contents. Levin and Anderson (1976) report, for example, that children's attention to segments in children's programs was predicted by, among other conditions, high levels of physical activity, movement, and auditory changes in the programs. Although both violent and nonviolent acts in television could fulfill one or more of these conditions, it is reasonable to expect that television violence, because it is generally depicted with a high level of physical movement and auditory stimuli (e.g., a gun being fired), will attract and hold the attention of viewers, especially children.

Comprehension of Televised Violence

Social learning theory requires not only that the violent act in television be attended to, but also that the sequences in the act be understood and remembered by the viewer. Understanding the physical moves in televised violent behavior should facilitate retention of that event. Unfortunately, there is little empirical analysis of the cognitive processes involved in remembering specific violent acts from television. We know that even single exposures to televised violence can be remembered by children for up to 6 months (Bandura, 1973; Hicks, 1968). We also know that aggressive acts observed on television are more likely to be modeled when these acts are rehearsed through daydreaming, imaginative play, or other aggressive fantasies (Rosenfield et al., 1978). However, we know little of how televised violent acts are remembered, what is remembered, and the conditions facilitating retention.

A few studies have investigated the extent to which children understand the meaning of a televised violent act within the context of the accompanying narrative. Most of these studies indicate that young viewers (up to 8 years) are often unable to infer implications and linkages between scenes in television programs. Collins (1982, 1983) concludes from this evidence that young children typically do not understand the context (e.g., motives and consequences) in which violent acts are presented on television. According to social learning theory, violent acts leading to negative consequences or instigated by antisocial motives should elicit little modeling behaviors from viewers. However, when these motives and consequences are not understood by the viewer, then such acts will be modeled. Conversely, children will be less likely to imitate televised aggression when they are made to understand, as through adult intervention, the antisocial motives and negative consequences of the observed violence (Collins, 1973).

The discussion so far presents some theoretical justification for the expectation that specific violent acts on television will be attended to and learned. Social learning theory is concerned not only with direct modeling (the learning of specific acts) but also with symbolic modeling, in which the actor generalizes from a specific televised behavior he or she has learned to other similar behaviors and situations. For example, if a television viewer observes and learns that a specific aggressive act is a preferred and effective means of resolving interpersonal conflict, he or she may accept the principle that aggressive behavior in general (as a class of behaviors) is an acceptable and effective means of solving problems. Most studies of television violence assume symbolic modeling to be the process by which aggressive behavior is learned from television. In field studies particularly, aggression measured in real life does not necessarily correspond to behaviors coded as violent in television. Symbolic modeling, then, is taken to be the most common effect of exposure to televised violence.

Enactment of Learned Aggressive Behaviors

Obviously, people do not enact all the aggressive behaviors they have learned from observation. According to social learning theory, matching performances will result only when the actor is motivated to enact the learned behaviors. Motivational processes are activated by reinforcements for the aggressive act, which disinhibit its performance in the real world.

Normally, people are inhibited from acting aggressively because of external regulators such as social norms, fear of punishment, fear of reprisal (e.g., the target of aggression may retaliate), guilt feelings, and the anxiety normally associated with violence (Bandura, 1979). The probability that learned aggressive acts will be performed is increased when these sources of inhibition are neutralized. One way that disinhibition can occur is by the reinforcement of aggression either before the actor observes the model, vicariously by observing the model being rewarded, or after a matching performance of the learned aggressive act.

Preobservation Reinforcement.   The extent to which aggression is rewarded in the actor's everyday social environment is an important determinant of whether learned aggressive acts will be performed. Early studies of television violence indicated that the children most likely to behave aggressively after viewing televised violence are those who are already predisposed to aggression (Surgeon General's Scientific Advisory Committee, 1972). Two variables that determine this predisposition are sex and family attitudes. A number of early studies showed that boys performed more aggressive acts after exposure to television violence than did girls (Bandura, 1965). Chaffee and McLeod (1972) reported that the positive relationship between exposure to televised violence and subsequent aggressive behavior was weaker among children whose parents punished or disapproved of aggression.

Vicarious Reinforcement.   A number of laboratory and field studies has shown that television violence which is rewarded, not punished or justified as vengeance or self-defense, is more likely to elicit subsequent viewer aggression than televised violence which is not rewarded, punished, or perceived by the viewer to be unjustified (Bandura, 1979; Pearl et al., 1982; Tan, 1981). Also, the perceived effectiveness of the televised violent act in achieving desired goals can have reinforcing qualities. In a survey of adolescents, Hartnagel, Teevan, and McIntyre (1975) found that respondents who perceived television violence as often effective in achieving goals of the aggressors were more likely to engage in subsequent aggressive behavior than respondents who did not see these behaviors as effective.

Postobservation Reinforcement.   Several laboratory studies indicate that children will perform aggressive acts when they are promised rewards or when they are actually rewarded for doing so (Bandura, 1965; Hicks, 1975). Promised or delivered rewards facilitate matching performances of aggressive acts learned from television; they are also a sufficient condition for the performance of aggression even when no prior observational learning has occurred (Bandura, 1979).

Self-Generated Reinforcements.   These "self-reinforcements" play an important role in controlling aggressive behavior. As Bandura (1975) sees it: "After people acquire standards of conduct through modeling and selective reinforcement, they partly regulate their own actions by self-created consequences. They do things that give them self-satisfaction and a sense of self worth but refrain from conduct that produces self-devaluative consequences" (p. 254).

To many people, the deliberate infliction of physical harm to another often leads to self-devaluative consequences (e.g., feelings of guilt). Through cognitive restructuring, however, many are able to justify the performance of what would normally be a censurable act. Cognitive restructuring, in the social learning model, can take many forms. One is euphemistic labeling which is construing a reprehensible act (e.g., violence) in terms of high moral principle, thus conferring it some respectable status. Another is palliative comparisons, that is, contrasting a self-deplored act with other more deplorable acts committed by other people. A third strategy for cognitive restructuring is displacing and diffusing responsibility. Milgram (1974) has shown, for example, that people are willing to injure others physically to a severe degree when a legitimate authority (e.g., the experimenter) approves of their conduct and accepts responsibility. A fourth strategy is attributing blame to the victim. For example, capital punishment is sometimes justified by convincing oneself that the victim deserved it.

Two other cognitive restructuring strategies that have been studied are dehumanizing the victim and reducing personal responsibility. In a series of laboratory experiments, Bandura (1975) showed that dehumanizing the victims by labeling them as an "animalistic, rotten bunch" was a potent disinhibitor of aggression, as was reducing personal responsibility of the subjects for the aggessive act.

TELEVISION VIOLENCE RESEARCH
FROM A SOCIAL LEARNING PERSPECTIVE

Most current research on television violence and aggression uses longitudinal field designs in which exposure to television violence, viewer aggression, and control variables are measured over a period of time ranging from 1 year (Singer & Singer, 1980, 1981) to 10 years (e.g., Lefkowitz, Eron, Walder, & Huesmann, 1977). Control variables often measured are aggression level at Time 1 (e.g., Milavsky et al., 1982) and family characteristics such as self-described values, attitudes toward discipline and child rearing, and belief systems (e.g., Singer & Singer, 1983).

With some notable exceptions (e.g., Milavsky et al., 1982), these field studies have found significant positive correlations between viewing televised violence and subsequent aggressive behavior. The relationships are usually interpreted as causal (e.g., Huesmann, 1982); however, they are also typically small, with correlations ranging from 0.15 to 0.30 (Chaffee, 1972; Huesmann, 1982). Thus, in the typical field study, exposure to televised violence explains only from 2.25% to 9% of subsequent aggression in viewers. Both critics and proponents of the hypothesis that television violence leads to aggressive behavior have pointed to these results as supportive of their respective viewpoints. Critics say that the relationship is too small to be meaningful; proponents say that although small, the correlations are consistently positive and supportive of a causal intepretation.

From a social learning perspective, these correlations are exactly what should be expected. This discussion of television violence and subsequent modeling behaviors leads one to expect a causal, positive relationship. However, these correlations cannot be expected to be substantial, considering that television

FIG. 3.3. Social learning of aggression from television.

TV Violence → ATTENTIONAL PROCESSES → RETENTION PROCESSES → REPRODUCTION PROCESSES → Matching Performance

Matching Performance
1. Imitation of specific violent act
2. Generalized aggression
3. Approval of aggression

ATTENTIONAL PROCESSES

I. *Attributes of TV Violence*
1. Rewards: tangible, social
2. Punishment
3. Justification: revenge or self-defense
4. Effectiveness in achieving goals
5. Perpetrator's motivation—intent to injure
6. Real or fantasy
7. Similarity of perpetrator to viewer
8. Prevalence
9. Simplicity

II. *Observer Attributes*
1. Arousal level: anger, frustration, annoyance, aversive treatment
2. Perceptual capabilities: age, intelligence
3. Acquired preferences and social norms: sex, family, and peer values
4. Biological factors
5. Physical capabilities

RETENTION PROCESSES

I. *Symbolic Processes and Cognitive Organization*
1. Representation of the violence act in symbolic codes: words, images
2. Understanding motivations for the violent act
3. Attribution of responsibility to the perpetrator
4. Approval for the violent act
5. Generalization of approval to other aggressive acts

II. *Symbolic Rehearsal*
1. Mental rehearsal of the specific violent act
2. Violence fantasies

III. *Enactive Rehearsal*
1. Opportunity for motor rehearsal
2. Feedback

III. *Observer Attributes*
1. Perceptual capabilities
2. Physical capabilities

REPRODUCTION PROCESSES

I. *Retrieval of Symbolic Representations*

II. *Observation of Results of Enactments*
1. Sensory incentives: affective valence
2. Tangible incentives
3. Social incentives: peer approval, status

III. *Regulators of the Enactment (of Aggression)*
1. External rewards: tangible, social, alleviation of aversive treatment
2. Punishment
3. Self-reinforcements: self-rewards, self-punishment
4. Neutralization of self-punishment: cognitive reorganization

IV. *Observer Attributes*
1. Arousal level
2. Acquired preferences
3. Biological factors
4. Physical capabilities
5. Incentive preference

violence is just one of the many possible instigators of aggression in the real world. Further, the enactment of learned aggressive acts in the real world is regulated by many inhibitors (see Fig. 3.2).

No one equation can account for all possible causes and regulators of aggression. Social learning theory identifies some of the important variables relevant to our discussion. In Figure 3.3, I have broken down the modeling of aggressive behavior from television into the social learning processes of attention, retention, and reproduction. Within each process, I have identified the variables that should be accounted for. Their inclusion in the analysis of television violence and subsequent viewer aggression is imperative from a social learning perspective.

In conclusion, the viewing of television violence is only one of the many factors that could lead to aggression in the real world. The relationship between exposure to television violence and subsequent aggressive behavior in viewers is probably causal; however, this relationship cannot be expected to be substantial or a major explanation of aggression in the real world. From the viewpoint of social learning theory, to do so would be bad theoretical reasoning and simply an exercise in futility.

ACKNOWLEDGMENTS

I would like to thank Albert Bandura for making available some of his recent publications. I take sole responsibility, however, for the interpretation of social learning theory presented in this chapter.

REFERENCES

Bandura, A. (1965). Influence of models' reinforcement contingencies on the acquisition of imitative responses. *Journal of Personality and Social Psychology, 1*, 589–595.

Bandura, A. (1973). *Aggression: A social learning analysis.* Englewood Cliffs, NJ: Prentice-Hall.

Bandura, A. (1975). Disinhibition of aggression through diffusion of responsibility and dehumanization of victims. *Journal of Research in Personality, 9*, 253–269.

Bandura, A. (1977). *Social learning theory.* Englewood Cliffs, NJ: Prentice-Hall.

Bandura, A. (1979). Psychological mechanisms of aggression. In M. von Cranach, K. Foppa, W. Lepenies, & D. Ploog (Eds.), *Human ethology: Claims and limits of a new discipline* (pp. 316–379). Cambridge: Cambridge University Press.

Bandura, A. (1983). Model of causality in social learning theory. In S. Sukemune (Ed.), *Advances in social learning theory.* Tokyo: Kaneko-shoho.

Berkowitz, L., & LePage, A. (1967). Weapons as aggression-eliciting stimuli. *Journal of Personality and Social Psychology, 7*, 202–207.

CBS, Inc., Office of Social Research. (1976–1977). *Network prime-time violence tabulations for the 1976–77 season and instructions to coders* (Research Rep.). New York: Author.

Chaffee, S. H. (1972). Television and adolescent aggressiveness (overview). In G. A. Comstock & E. A. Rubinstein (Eds.), *Television and social behavior: Vol. 3:Television and adolescent aggressiveness.* Washington, DC: U.S. Government Printing Office.

Chaffee, S. H., & McLeod, J. M. (1972). Adolescent television use in the family context. In G. A. Comstock & E. A. Rubinstein (Eds.), *Television and social behavior: Vol. 3: Television and adolescent aggressiveness* (pp. 239–313). Washington, DC: U.S. Government Printing Office.

Collins, W. A. (1973). The effect of temporal separation between motivation, aggression, and consequences: A developmental study. *Developmental Psychology, 8,* 215–221.

Collins, W. A. (1982). Cognitive processing in television viewing. In D. Pearl, L. Bouthilet, & J. Lazar (Eds.), *Television and behavior: Ten years of scientific progress and implications for the eighties* (Vol. 2, pp. 9–23). Washington, DC: U.S. Government Printing Office.

Collins, W. A. (1983). Interpretation and inference in children's television viewing. In J. Bryant & D. A. Anderson (Eds.), *Children's understanding of television: Research on attention and comprehension* (pp. 125–150). New York: Academic Press.

Cook, T., Kendzierski, D., & Thomas, S. (1983).The implicit assumptions of television research: An analysis of the 1982 NIMH report on *Television and Behavior. Public Opinion Quarterly, 47,* 161–201.

Gerbner, G., Gross, L., Morgan, M., & Signorielli, N. (1980). The "mainstreaming" of America: Violence profile no. 11. *Journal of Communication, 30,* 10–29.

Hartnagel, T. F., Teevan, J. J., Jr., & McIntyre, J. J. (1975). Television violence and violent behavior. *Social Forces, 54,* 341–351.

Hicks, D. J. (1968). Short- and long-term retention of affectively varied modeled behavior. *Psychonomic Science, 11,* 369–370.

Hicks, D. J. (1975). Imitation and retention of film-mediated aggressive peer and adult models. *Journal of Personality and Social Psychology, 2,* 97–100.

Huesmann, L. R. (1982). Television violence and aggressive behavior. In D. Pearl, L. Bouthilet, & J. Lazar (Eds.), *Television and behavior: Ten years of scientific progress and implications for the eighties* (Vol. 2, pp. 126–137). Washington, DC: U.S. Government Printing Office.

Lefkowitz, M., Eron, L., Walder, L., & Huesmann, L. (1977). *Growing up to be violent: A longitudinal study of the development of aggression.* New York: Pergamon Press.

Levin, S. R., & Anderson, D. R. (1976). The development of attention. *Journal of Communication, 26*(2), 126–135.

Milavsky, J. R., Kessler, R., Stipp, H., & Rubens, W. (1982). Television and aggression: Results of a panel study. In D. Pearl, L. Bouthilet, & J. Lazar (Eds.), *Television and behavior: Ten years of scientific progress and implications for the eighties* (Vol. 2, pp. 138–157). Washington, DC: U.S. Government Printing Office.

Milgram, S. (1974). *Obedience to authority: An experimental view.* New York: Harper & Row.

Pearl, D., Bouthilet, L., & Lazar, J. (Eds.). (1982). *Television and behavior: Ten years of scientific progress and implications for the eighties* (Vol. 2). Washington, DC: U.S. Government Printing Office.

Rosenfield, E., Maloney, S., Huesmann, L. R., Eron, L. D., Fischer, P. F., Musonis, V., & Washington, A. (1978). *The effect of fantasy behaviors and fantasy-reality discrimination upon the observational learning of aggression.* Paper presented at the meeting of the International Society for Research on Aggression, Washington, DC.

Rubinstein, E. (1982). Introductory comments (violence and aggression). In D. Pearl, L. Bouthilet, & J. Lazar (Eds.), *Television and behavior: Ten years of scientific progress and implications for the eighties* (Vol. 2, pp. 104–107). Washington, DC: U.S. Government Printing Office.

Rule, B. G., & Nesdale, A. R. (1976). Emotional arousal and aggressive behavior. *Psychological Bulletin, 83,* 851–863.

Signorielli, N., Gross, L., & Morgan, M. (1982). Violence in television programs: Ten years later. In D. Pearl, L. Bouthilet, & J. Lazar (Eds.), *Television and behavior: Ten years of scientific progress and implications for the eighties* (Vol. 2, pp. 158–174). Washington, DC: U.S. Government Printing Office.

Singer, D. G., & Singer, J. L. (1980). Television viewing and aggressive behavior in preschool children: A field study. *Annals of the New York Academy of Science, 347,* 289–303.

Singer, D. G., & Singer, J. L. (1981). Television and the developing imagination of the child. *Journal of Broadcasting, 41,* 373–387.

Singer, J. L., & Singer, D. G. (1983). Psychologists look at television: Cognitive, developmental, personality, and social policy implications. *American Psychologist, 38*(7), 826–834.

Surgeon General's Scientific Advisory Committee on Television and Social Behavior. (1972). *Television and growing up: The impact of televised violence* (Report to the Surgeon General, United States Public Health Service). Washington, DC: U.S. Government Printing Office.

Tan, A. S. (1981). *Mass communication theories and research.* Columbus, OH: Grid Publishing.

Turner, C. W., & Layton, J. F. (1976). Verbal imagery and connotation as memory-induced mediators of aggressive behavior. *Journal of Personality and Social Psychology, 33,* 755–763.

Zillmann, D. (1982). Television viewing and arousal. In D. Pearl, L. Bouthilet, & J. Lazar (Eds.), *Television and behavior: Ten years of scientific progress and implications for the eighties* (Vol. 2, pp. 53–67). Washington, DC: U.S. Government Printing Office.

4 A Priming Effect Analysis of Media Influences

Leonard Berkowitz
Karen Heimer Rogers
University of Wisconsin

On studying the aftereffects of such crimes as the Jack the Ripper murders, Gabriel Tarde (1912) noted that the national attention given to these brutal acts seemed to trigger similar attacks elsewhere. He labeled the crimes following the well-publicized acts of violence "suggesto-imitative assaults" and concluded that "epidemics of crime follow the line of the telegraph."

Although Tarde identified this phenomenon over 80 years ago, scientific support for his thesis has only recently begun to accumulate. For example, Berkowitz and Macaulay (1971) found that there was a significant increase in the rate of violent, but not property, crimes following several sensational murders in the 1960s (including President Kennedy's assassination). Phillips has published much more impressive evidence in a series of studies of the consequences of widely publicized suicides. In 1974 he reported that when a famous person's suicide received considerable attention from the mass media, there was a rise in the number of people who also took their own lives. Furthermore, the greater the publicity given to the suicide story, the greater seemed to be the impact. In another study (Phillips, 1979), the rate of automobile accidents was also found to rise in the days following media attention to a suicide. Interestingly, single vehicle mishaps accounted for much of the increase in this latter study, and the drivers in these cases tended to be more similar to the suicide victim than were any other pasengers in the car. Later research adds to the generalizability of these findings. Phillips (1980) demonstrated that highly publicized suicide-murders were also followed by an increase in noncommercial airplane crashes.

All of this research suggests that media depictions of violence can prompt people in the audience to act aggressively toward others or themselves, even when the portrayals of violence are fictional. We argue here that violent scenes on television and movie screens can have effects essentially similar to the reactions producing the suggesto-imitative assaults described by Tarde and "the contagion of violence" just discussed. However, in addition to these negative outcomes, prosocial behavior may also be promoted by the mass media (Liebert, Sprafkin, & Davidson, 1982; Rushton, 1979). Any comprehensive account of media effects must deal with both these negative and positive influences, and we make such an attempt here.

A number of psychological processes can contribute to these anti- and prosocial effects. Concentrating on just a few of these processes, this paper is mainly concerned with the role of the audience's thoughts. We propose that when people witness, read, or hear of an event via the mass media, ideas are activated which, for a short period of time, tend to evoke other semantically related thoughts. These thoughts can, under some circumstances, justify conduct similar to that portrayed by the communication, lead the viewers to anticipate the benefits they themselves might derive for this kind of behavior, and even activate semantically related behavioral inclinations.

PRIMING EFFECTS, ASSOCIATIVE NETWORKS, AND SPREADING ACTIVATION

In the past, Berkowitz (1973, 1974) employed principles of conditioning to account for many of the media effects to be discussed here. We now suggest, however, that the concepts of cognitive-neoassociationism (Anderson & Bower, 1973; Landman & Manis, 1983) provide a better framework for the analysis of these phenomena. People's reactions to the messages they read, see, or hear in the media depend considerably on the way the message is interpreted and the thoughts and memories that are consequently activated. The cognitive-neoassociationist formulation gives explicit attention to these matters.

We need not be concerned here with the intricacies of this conceptual scheme or with the controversies regarding a number of details (cf. Klatzky, 1980; Landman & Manis, 1983; Wyer & Hartwick, 1980; Wyer & Srull, 1981, for a more comprehensive discussion). Summarizing this formulation, elements of thought, feeling, and prior memories are seen as nodes in a network interconnected by associative pathways. The strength of these associative pathways is a function of a variety of factors, including contiguity, similarity, and semantic relatedness.

The present formulation adds the concept of spreading activation advanced by Collins and Loftus (1975) and others to these structural notions. According to this conception, when a thought element is activated, or brought into focal awareness, the activation radiates out from this particular node along the asso ciative pathways to other nodes. As a consequence, for some time after a concept is activated, there is an increased probability that it and associated thought elements will come to mind again, creating what has been termed a *priming effect*. It is as if some residual excitation has remained at the activated node for a while, making it easier for this and other related thoughts and feelings to be reactivated. Extrapolating from this analysis, we maintain that the aggressive ideas suggested by viewing violence in the mass media can prime other semant- ically related thoughts, heightening the chances that other aggressive ideas will come to mind during this period. It should be noted that all of this can occur automatically and without much conscious thought. Cognitive theorists now differentiate between automatic and controlled processing (e.g., Shiffrin & Schneider, 1977). Where controlled processing presumably requires conscious attention, the memory effects just mentioned take place passively and involuntarily.

In recent years, social psychologists have demonstrated that priming effects can have a considerable impact upon the personality impressions that are formed soon afterward. In one such study (see Wyer & Hartwick, 1980; Wyer & Srull, 1981), subjects engaged in a sentence construction task in which they were required to use three of the four words presented on each trial. Some of the sentences had aggressive connotations, and others suggested only neutral ideas. The proportion of sentences associated with aggression was also varied. After 1 hour, 1 day, or 1 week, participants were required to read an ambiguous paragraph about a target person and rate the person. As the researchers predicted, the greater the proportion of aggression-related sentences the subject had been exposed to previously, the more unfavorable was the evaluation of the target person. This effect decreased with the passage of time, yet was still noticeable even after 24 hours. The use of the aggression-related words in the sentence construction task had apparently activated other aggression-related thoughts, which colored the participants' judgment of the target for a time afterward.

Bargh and Pietromonaco (1982) have shown that a priming effect can operate automatically and even without awareness. Subjects in their experiment were unknowingly exposed to single words, some of which were semantically asso- ciated with hostility. The participants were then asked to rate a target person on the basis of a brief description. When a greater proportion of hostility-related words were presented, subjects' evaluations of the target person were more negative, even though they had not been consciously aware of the priming words.

Links with Emotion Components

The present formulation makes use of some recent developments in cognitive psychology maintaining that externally presented ideas can activate specific action tendencies as well as certain kinds of thoughts and recollections. This formulation builds upon the network analyses of emotion advanced by such writers as Bower

(1981), Clark and Isen (1982), Lang (1979), and Leventhal (1980), which postulate associative connections between thoughts, memories, and feelings. Lang (1979), for example, has suggested that thought, memory, and feeling nodes are associatively (and especially, semantically) related to other concepts in memory and to the expressive behaviors and autonomic responses. As in the other theories of emotion just cited, the activation of any of the components in the network presumably evokes the other units to which it is linked. Such a connection was demonstrated by Isen and her associates when they found that a positive mood facilitates recall of information in memory having a positive meaning (cf. Clark & Isen, 1982). Or consider the Velten (1968) mood induction procedure. As the subjects read a series of affectively toned positive or negative statements, they presumably recall conceptually similar incidents in their past history having the same affective tone and thus tend to have expressive-motor reactions and feelings somewhat similar to those they had experienced in those situations. The activated components summate and reverberate as the subjects go from one statement to the next, and they then consciously experience (to some extent) the feelings associated with the statements they read.

We suggest that due to the associative connections among units of feelings and expressive-motor reactions, situationally evoked ideas can trigger involuntary actions and even some more controlled behaviors that are semantically associated with the ideas. Lang's (1979) theory of emotional imagery is consistent with this suggestion in that is postulates semantic connections between "the cognitive structure of the image" and "specific patterns of physiological and behavioral responding" (p. 506). Greenwald's (1970) discussion of the ideomotor mechanism in performance control is also supportive of the present formulation. On reviewing the available evidence, he concluded, along with William James, that the perceptual image or idea of an action can initiate the performance of this behavior. Also in keeping with the present analysis, Anderson (1983) has provided evidence that when a self-referent category is activated in memory, people report intentions regarding their own future behaviors that are congruent with the category. The thought of themselves carrying out the action evidently activates a readiness to perform the behavior. Later in this paper, we consider a number of conditions that might influence the degree to which media-induced thoughts are translated into open action.

APPLICATIONS TO RESEARCH FINDINGS

Prosocial Influences and Priming Effects

Several experiments employing children and young adults have reported that people seeing a display or helpfulness or generosity are often inclined to be helpful or generous themselves (Hearold, 1979; Liebert et al., 1982; Rushton,

1979). The communication's influence, of course, probably does not occur in these instances through the reduction of the audience's restraints. Furthermore, the effects produced are often relatively short-lived (Liebert et al., 1982; Rushton, 1979) and do not result in lasting learning. Rather, the viewers appear to have been spurred temporarily into action. The first step in such a process might involve a priming effect in which there is an activation of thoughts semantically related to the depicted occurrence.

Such a priming effect has been demonstrated by Hornstein and his colleagues (Blackman & Hornstein, 1977; Holloway, Tucker, & Hornstein, 1977; Hornstein, LaKind, Frankel, & Manne, 1975) in a series of experiments concerned with the impact of good news. The subjects in these studies listened to a news program on the radio that happened to be playing while they were ostensibly waiting for the experiment to begin, and then engaged in bargaining with a peer. Those who listened to a news story of prosocial behavior were relatively cooperative in their bargaining, particularly if the report was of someone who had intentionally given help (Holloway et al., 1977).

Ratings made following the bargaining session indicate that the radio story not only told the listeners that they ought to be generous when dealing with others; it also affected the participants' view of human nature and the social world around them. After hearing the prosocial news, the subjects had a stronger expectation that their bargaining partner would cooperate with them; moreover, they also thought that there were more people who led "clean, decent lives" and who were "basically honest." Integrating their results with comparable observations published by other investigators, Blackman and Hornstein (1977) concluded that "people function as social actuaries, relying upon the information they receive from the mass media and other sources . . . to make generalized inferences about human nature" (p. 303).

Our cognitive perspective affords an easy interpretation of these findings. First we note the tendency for generalization to occur. In the Hornstein research, as in other experiments (e.g., Aderman & Berkowitz, 1970; Collins & Getz, 1976; Sprafkin, Liebert, & Poulos, 1975), even though the portrayed prosocial behavior was quite different from the acts the subjects would carry out, the communication influenced their subsequent actions. The subjects apparently were responding to semantically related concepts (e.g., helpfulness, cooperation) that had been activated in their minds when they heard the news story and were not simply and narrowly imitating the reported conduct. Furthermore, in at least some studies the activation spread some distance along the associated pathways to other prosocial concepts such as honesty (Blackman & Hornstein, 1977) or good work and rule obedience (Friedrich & Stein, 1973). The present formulation maintains that the influence of mass communication is due in large part to the activation of concepts and propositions semantically related to the event depicted. If the viewer or listener has no ideas that are semantically related to the reported event, the person will not be affected in the same manner. The finding that

Sesame Street's prosocial scenes had little effect on the behavior of every young children (Silverman & Sprafkin, 1980) might be explained in this way. Alternative explanations are always possible, yet it may be that the youngsters lacked the concepts and propositions in memory that could be related to the prosocial behavior that they viewed.

As has been discussed, the thoughts activated by the communication often do not persist, and its impact typically declines with the passage of time. Priming effects usually subside as the initiating stimulus recedes into the past. In addition to bringing related ideas to mind, Hornstein has noted that the portrayed event evidently also affects the observers' estimates of the prevalence of prosocial behavior in their social world. Such a finding can be explained by the availability heuristic. Readily recalling the dramatic (i.e., vivid) instance of altruism reported in the mass media, the participants automatically assume this conduct to be relatively frequent and likely.

Studies of the Priming Effects
Due to Television and Movie Violence

Our formulation is based on the results of studies of the effects of viewing aggression. Several fine reviews of this research now exist (e.g., Andison, 1977; Comstock, 1975; Comstock, Chaffee, Katzman, McCombs, & Roberts, 1978; Geen, 1976; Liebert et al., 1982; Murray & Kippax, 1979; Palmer & Door, 1980). On the basis of these studies most researchers agree that the depiction of violence in the media increases the chances that people in the audience will act aggressively themselves. Meta-analyses of the published studies support such a conclusion (Andison, 1977; Hearold, 1979). There is some controversy, however, regarding the magnitude of this effect (see, e.g., Comstock, 1975; Cook, Kendzierski, & Thomas, 1983), and no claim is made here as to how important media depictions are relative to the other sources of antisocial conduct. Additionally, as most arguments in this research area center on the long-range effects of frequent exposure to violent scenes (see Eron, Huesmann, Lefkowitz, & Walder, 1972; Milavsky, Kessler, Stipp, & Rubens, 1982), we focus mainly on experiments in which the participants see only one or a few aggressive movies. The consequences of repeated viewing of violence receive much less emphasis here, with findings from investigations of this issue discussed only when they are pertinent to a particular theoretical point.

Are There Shortcomings in the Traditional Interpretation? Some of the problems that arise in the traditional analyses of media aggression can be overcome by our priming effect analysis. Many of the theories advanced to account for the effects of observed violence hold that observers learn what is appropriate conduct, and also become aware of the likelihood of obtaining rewards for a given act, when that type of action is portrayed in the media (e.g., Bandura,

1965, 1971, 1973). It is not our intention to deny or minimize the importance of this learning. However, if observational learning refers to the lasting acquisition of novel behavior or new knowledge, all media influences cannot be attributed to such learning. Some media effects are fairly transient (e.g., Buvinic & Berkowitz, 1976; Doob & Climie, 1972; Mann, Berkowitz, Sidman, Starr, & West, 1974), as if the observed event had activated reactions or thoughts only for a relatively brief period of time. The studies of the impact of widely publicized suicide stories conducted by Phillips also obtained evidence of a "time decay." Bollen and Phillips (1983), for example, have reported that suicide rates were unaffected when more than 10 days had lapsed from the time media attention was given to the story of someone taking his or her life. It is suggested here that at least part of this time decay is due to the usual attenuation of the priming effect that occurs with the passage of time (cf. Wyer & Srull, 1981).

The often demonstrated generality of the media influence also seems troublesome for those observational learning interpretations that are couched in terms of imitation. Although the imitation construct implies that the viewer's behavior physically resembles the depicted action, most of the experiments in this area employ aggression measures that are physically very different from the portrayed conduct. Illustrating such a generalization, Phillips (1983) reported that between 1973 and 1978, there was a significant tendency for well-publicized heavyweight championship prizefights to be followed by an increase in homicides throughout the United States. Because these homicides are not simply a reproduction of the behavior portrayed by the media, rather than account for these findings in terms of imitation or modeling it may be more accurate to say that the observers responded to the meaning of the media event and exhibited behavior having the same general meaning. The depicted event may lead to a priming effect by activating semantically related ideas and behavioral tendencies.

Many researchers support the knowledge transmission interpretation of media influences, which holds that these influences arise in large part through a permission-giving (or disinhibitory) process. People in the audience are supposedly disposed to engage in some antisocial behavior but are reluctant to do so until the media tells them, directly or indirectly, that the behavior is permissible or even profitable. An example of such an analysis can be found in Wheeler's (1966) discussion of behavioral contagion. Also along these lines, Comstock and his associates (Comstock, 1980; Comstock et al., 1978) emphasized the disinhibitory effects of viewing violence, maintaining that the media depiction of aggression reduces the audience's reluctance to engage in such antisocial behavior.

We do not contest the idea that media events can lessen observer inhibitions by suggesting that the actions they are tempted to carry out may profit them in some way (Bandura, 1965) or might be appropriate in the given situation. Indeed, a good number of Wisconsin experiments have demonstrated a permission-giving phenomenon (e.g., Berkowitz & Geen, 1967; Berkowitz & Rawlings, 1963).

Rather, we maintain that relatively temporary aggression-enhancing influences are due not only to a disinhibitory process.

Priming of Aggression-Related Ideas.   There is both direct and indirect evidence that the observation of aggression evokes aggression-related thoughts and ideas in viewers. For example, the research by Wyer and Srull (1981) and Bargh and Pietromonaco (1982) has already been cited as a demonstration of how the priming effect can influence one's reaction to others. In these studies, presenting the participants with words having hostile connotations led them to make hostile evaluations of an ambiguous target person. Carver, Ganellan, Froming, and Chambers (1983) extended this research by showing that people who watched a brief film depicting hostile interaction between a businessman and his secretary subsequently perceived more hostility in an ambiguous stimulus person. An investigation of the consequences of aggressive humor (Berkowitz, 1970) is conceptually similar to these studies. In this experiment, young women were asked to listen to a tape recording of either a hostile (Don Rickles) or nonaggressive (George Carlin) comic routine. They then rated a job applicant. The results showed that exposure to the hostile comedy led to harsher evaluations of the applicant, even when the subjects had not been provoked by the person they were judging.

Berkowitz, Parker, and West (cited in Berkowitz, 1973, pp. 125–126) offered indirect support for the contention that observed aggression evokes other aggression-related thoughts. They asked school children to read either a war comic book (*Adventures of the Green Berets*) or a neutral comic book (*Gidget*) and then to complete sentences by choosing one of two words presented. Children who read the war comic were more likely to choose words with aggressive connotations than were youngsters who read *Gidget*. Exposure to the violent scenes in the former condition apparently brought aggression-related ideas to mind so that the words with aggressive meanings seemed more appropriate in constructing the sentences.

In the foregoing instances, the initial communication evidently primed aggression-related ideas, which then affected the subjects' interpretation of an ambiguous target person or the choice of stimulus words. These activated ideas might also change the viewers' impressions of the desirability of aggression, at least temporarily. And so, other studies have shown that people seeing violent encounters are at times inclined to favor the use of violence in interpersonal conflict. Such an effect has been reported by Leifer and Roberts (1972) and Drabman and Thomas (1974) in experiments with school children. In addition, Malamuth and Check (1981) found that after males viewed movies depicting sexual violence, they were more apt to indicate that violence against women was occasionally acceptable. Even the mere presence of weapons might also produce a heightened acceptance of violence at times. The participants in an experiment by Leyens and Parke (1975) who were shown slides of weapons were more willing to severely punish an available target than were their counterparts who had seen only neutral slides.

Conceptions of Others: The Cultivation Thesis. The notion that viewing violence may lead to greater acceptance of aggression has been taken a step further by Gerbner and his associates (e.g., Gerbner, Gross, Morgan, & Signorielli, 1980; Gerbner, Gross, Signorielli, Morgan, & Jackson-Beeck, 1979). These researchers argued that television violence not only produces a relatively temporary change in observers' attitudes concerning aggression, but may also cultivate a lasting conception of the social environment as wicked and dangerous. As television programs often portray a world full of violence, danger, and evil, it is suggested that those who watch TV frequently develop a perception of social reality that is consistent with this usual depiction of life and society.

The Gerbner argument has received some empirical support. Perhaps the best evidence can be found in research in which subjects are exposed to only one violent communication. For instance, Thomas and Drabman (1977) found that youngsters who were shown a television detective scene were later apt to say that other children would want to behave aggressively in their interactions. These viewers might also think that aggression was relatively frequent in their environment. The findings obtained by Hornstein and his colleagues (e.g., Blackman & Hornstein, 1977) are also congruent with Gerbner's cultivation thesis, even though these studies measured the perception of prosocial behavior. In the Hornstein experiments, participants who listened to a news story portraying helpful behavior were inclined to guess that benevolence was relatively prevalent in their social worlds.

Studies of the effects of repeated viewing of violence, however, do not consistently support Gerbner's thesis. On one hand, Gerbner et al. (1979) reported that adolescents who watched a great deal of television were especially likely to overestimate the amount of violence in society and believe that the social world was dangerous. Yet, a study based on a national sample of the British television audience (Wober, 1978) found no indications that viewers perceived the world as evil. Moreover, Doob and MacDonald (1979) showed that the relationship between television viewing and fear of crime was eliminated in a Toronto sample when the actual incidence of crime in the viewers' areas was controlled statistically. Gerbner et al. (1980) answered this challenge by publishing a statistical analysis of data from a national sample of adults which shows a relationship between heavy television viewing and later perceptions of danger. Cook et al. (1983) took a position somewhere between that of Gerbner and his critics. On examining the published data, they concluded that watching television can influence general beliefs about the world, but suggested that this cultivation effect was "extremely modest" (p. 174).

The discrepancies in this research may be explained by two different possibilities. First, recall that media reports seem to activate semantically related thoughts only for a brief period. It is during this time that the viewers, guided by the availability heuristic, might exagerrate the prevalence of antisocial behavior in the world around them. It may be, however, that other crucial influences must be present for the activated ideas to be learned so that one's conception of the world is affected for an appreciable length of time. These influences are not always present, and furthermore, viewers do not necessarily always accept television depictions as unbiased representations of social reality.

The second possibility is that one's estimate of the prevalence of violence and crime may not affect the perception of personal susceptibility to danger. Such a notion was proposed by Hawkins and Pingree (1980), who suggested that a heavy diet of television increases the perceived frequency of antisocial behavior in the social world but does not necessarily create the belief that the viewers are themselves likely to be victimized. Tyler (1980) conducted a path analysis of data gathered from east and west coast cities which lends some support to this suggestion. He demonstrated that mass media reports of crimes influenced respondents' estimates of the crime rate in their neighborhoods but did not alter their sense of personal susceptibility to crime. This latter perception was influenced by their own or another's personal experience with crime, however.

Both theory and empirical research thus suggest that vivid portrayals of antisocial behavior on television and radio create at least a short-lived belief that this kind of behavior is relatively frequent in the social environment. Yet, additional factors apparently have to operate if these activated judgments are to be turned into a persistent perception of the world and/or are to affect the sense of being personally in danger.

Evoking an Action Tendency.   The research reviewed to this point indicates that media communications can activate particular thoughts and ideas. Now we must deal with the question of whether specific action tendencies are also incited. In the earlier discussion of network analyses of emotion, it was proposed that the activation of particular ideas in memory may radiate outward to activate associated feelings, expressive movements, and even action tendencies. Do we have any evidence that media-activated thoughts can generate such behavioral inclinations?

The aggressive humor experiment mentioned earlier (Berkowitz, 1970) points to such a possibility. Listening to the hostile comic routine resulted in harsh treatment of another person. Better evidence is provided by Carver et al. (1983), who showed that male undergraduates primed to have aggressive thoughts (by means of a sentence construction task) subsequently delivered the most intense electric shocks to a fellow student whenever that person made a mistake. Apparently, thinking about aggressive ideas led to aggressive acts.

Experiments on the effects of aggression-associated cues in the surrounding environment also provide support for our contention. Only one such study need be mentioned here, as this body of research is discussed in a later section.

Josephson (1981) conducted an experiment in which deliberately frustrated boys viewed an excerpt from a popular television program that was either violent or nonviolent in nature. The boys then played a game of floor hockey in which they could exhibit naturalistic aggression against their opponents. Because the villains in the violent program used walkie-talkies in the course of their misdeeds, Josephson hypothesized that the presence of a walkie-talkie would serve as a retrieval cue reminding the subjects exposed to the violent movie of the aggression they had seen. They presumably would thus reexperience the thoughts and feelings that had earlier been evoked by this film. In some cases, therefore, the adult referees supervising the game carried walkie-talkies. The boys were found to be most aggressive if they had previously watched the violent program and if the referees carried the aggression-associated walkie-talkies. This retrieval cue evidently enhanced or reawakened the activation of aggressive ideas evoked by the violent film.

Worchel (1972) provided indirect evidence suggesting that violent scenes can incite aggressive inclinations. In this experiment, male and female campers were first shown either a brief prizefight scene, an interesting movie about boats, or no film. The subjects were then told that they could either participate in an aggressive activity (a pie fight) or in a boating activity (riding on a raft). The activity that the youngsters first chose was generally congruent with the movie they had seen, as if the film had evoked an "appetite" for that type of behavior. Worchel then had a second experimenter pressure the boys and girls to select either the activity that was consistent or the one that was inconsistent with the movie they had watched. When the campers were again asked to state their preferences, they overwhelmingly reacted against the pressure if it had been inconsistent with the film (in keeping with expectations suggested by reactance theory). Both films had evidently generated a desire for a particular type of activity, and the subjects countered the opposing pressure with an even stronger insistence on this activity.

Disinhibition and Indifference. The notion that viewing violence activates aggression-related thoughts can also explain other consequences of media depictions of violence. So far it has been suggested that these activated ideas can: (a) affect the audience's evaluations of an ambiguous stimulus person, (b) lead viewers to increase their estimates of the frequency of aggressive and other antisocial acts in the social world, (c) incite inclinations to aggressive behavior, and (d) strengthen the belief that aggression is desirable or acceptable at times. All of these possible reactions, especially the increased acceptance of aggression, can result in a reduction in restraints against aggression and might even abate the observers' anxiety about aggression.

This process has been discussed by some authors as the "trivialization of aggression." As viewers are repeatedly exposed to violence, they tend to regard this behavior as more acceptable, or at least as relatively unimportant, so that they are more indifferent to aggression generally. One indication of this has been mentioned in the discussion of Malamuth and Check's (1981) experiment, but much more direct evidence has been provided by Zillmann and Bryant (1982). Supporting Gerbner's cultivation thesis, the men and women in this experiment who were exposed to a massive amount of filmed sex scenes gave the highest estimate of the prevalence of unusual sexual practices in the general population, and they were also least likely to object to the open display of pornography. Furthermore, those subjects who had been exposed to the heavy diet of sex scenes favored the shortest terms of imprisonment for a convicted rapist. Rape had evidently become a more trivial matter for them. Perhaps the activation of sexual-aggression ideas in these people, which led to greater acceptance of such behavior, also diminished sexual-aggressive concerns.

We would expect that such a reduction in aggression anxiety would be accompanied by a decrease in physiological arousal. Such a possibility is suggested in a study by Thomas, Horton, Lippincott, and Drabman (1977). These researchers asked children and college students to watch either a fictional portrayal of violence or a nonaggressive movie and then to view a film clip depicting realistic aggression. Both the youngsters and the college students exhibited less emotionality (in terms of changes in skin resistance) in reaction to the realistic aggression if they had previously viewed the fictional aggressive incident. A similar finding has been reported by Geen (1981), who suggested that the earlier observation of aggression was likely to lessen the viewers' sensitivity to cues that normally restrain their aggression.

The important point in this argument, it must be clear, is that the lower arousal presumably indicates a reduced concern about aggression and not a decreased inclination to aggression. Supporting this contention, Thomas (1982) published evidence that when men had been previously angered, exposure to an aggressive television program resulted in lower heart rates than did viewing a neutral movie. Nevertheless, in spite of their lower arousal level, those who observed the televised depiction of aggression also tended to give the person who had angered them more electric shocks soon afterwards. It seems that these men, evidently having calmed down somewhat, were less anxious about aggression (because of the aggression-approving ideas activated by the violent program) but still punished their tormentor more severely.

CONDITIONS FACILITATING THE DISPLAY
OF OVERT AGGRESSION

Of course, there is a substantial gap between the media-activated ideas, feelings, and action tendencies on one hand and the open display of behavior on the other. Various intervening variables may influence the chances that people viewing violence will be overtly assaultive themselves.

The Communication's Meaning

One factor that may affect the relationship between observed events in the media and viewers' subsequent behavior is the communication's meaning for the audience. Aggression is, so to speak, in the mind of the beholder; unless the scenes depicted are considered aggressive by viewers, aggression-related thoughts will not be activated.

In their study of the effects on behavior of viewing contact sports, Berkowitz and Alioto (1973) assumed that most people think of aggression as the deliberate injury of another. They hypothesized that contact sports are most likely to stimulate aggressive inclinations in the onlookers when they believe the players are trying to hurt each other. The university men participating in the experiment were angered and then exposed to a film either of a prizefight or a football game. Additionally, the subjects were led to interpret the observed contest either as aggressive in nature (the opponents were trying to injure each other) or as nonaggressive (the contestants were professionals unemotionally engaged in their business). At the end of the movie, when given a chance to shock the person who had angered them earlier, the men who had seen the supposedly aggressive encounter were more punitive. It was apparently necessary for the subjects to define the action they had witnessed as aggressive if the event was to activate strong aggression-related ideas and responses. Also consistent with this proposal, Donnerstein and Berkowitz (1983) have reported that the intensity of their male subjects' punishment of a woman who had provoked them earlier was significantly correlated with the rated aggressiveness of the movie they had seen before they could deliver the shocks. Once again, it seems that the observers' definition of the scene as aggressive activated aggression-related thoughts and other aggression-facilitating reactions in them, which strengthened the punishment they gave to the provocateur.

Other Aggressive Ideas. Besides imparting an aggressive meaning to the witnessed event, the observers might also have other aggressive thoughts at the time they watch this occurrence which can intensify the activated aggressive inclinations. Evidence for this contention is found in an experiment by Turner and Berkowitz (1972). Male college students were first provoked and then watched a movie of a prizefight. Most of the men were asked to think of themselves either as the winner of the fight or the referee. The others simply watched the movie without any specific instructions. Additionally, half of the subjects in each condition were asked to think "hit" each time the victor landed a blow and were thus induced to have aggressive ideas. Later, all participants were given the opportunity to shock the person who had previously tormented them.

In general, the men attacked their tormentor most severely if they had imagined themselves as the winner and had thought "hit" with each punch they saw on the screen. The "imagine-self" finding in this experiment is reminiscent of the results reported more recently by Anderson (1983). The college students in Anderson's study who had previously imagined themselves carrying out a certain kind of behavior expressed the strongest intentions of later engaging in that action. The "hit" ideas could have served as aggression retrieval cues, especially for those who had thought of themselves as the fight victor. When subjects said the word "hit" and at the same time imagined themselves punching their opponents, memories of past experiences with fighting may have come to mind. Thoughts, feelings, and expressive movements related to the aggression they had exhibited at these times might have been activated by the word "hit" so that their present aggression was intensified.

Turner was the first to recognize how the words we employ in our thoughts can function as aggression retrieval cues to affect our subsequent behavior. Based upon investigations of memory processes, he predicted that words having aggressive meanings would be powerful activators of aggressive inclinations to the degree that they could easily evoke images. It was hypothesized that these high imagery-aggressive words would serve as better retrieval cues for prior aggressive episodes stored in memory. Thus, they should strongly activate other aggression-related thoughts and inclinations. Turner and Layton (1976) attempted to test this prediction by asking their subjects to learn lists of words that were either high or low in imagery value and representative of either aggressive or neutral ideas. They then gave the participants an opportunity to shock a partner. All of the subjects were physiologically aroused as they administered the shocks by exposing them to white noise at the time. Turner's hypothesis was supported by the finding that subjects were most punitive if they had previously encountered the high imagery-aggressive words.

Identification with Characters.   Several authors (e.g., Dorr, 1981; Tannenbaum & Gaer, 1965) have suggested that the observer's identification with the media characters influences the extent to which they are affected by the witnessed occurrence. In line with the present formulation, we suggest that viewers who identify with the actors they see are vividly imagining themselves as these characters and are thinking of themselves as carrying out the depicted actions. Such an identification with the aggressor in a movie should active high imagery-aggressive thoughts, and the subsequent priming of this kind of idea might influence subsequent behavior. The previously cited experiment by Turner and Berkowitz (1972) supports this analysis, as does a later study by Leyens and Picus (1973). In the latter investigation, the angry subjects who had been asked to imagine themselves as the victor of the filmed fight were most aggressive later toward the person who had insulted them, presumably because of their high level of aggression-related thoughts as they watched the film.

Taken together, these findings suggest that a highly aggressive imagination might keep the influence of the media exposure alive. In accord with this position,

Bandura (1971) maintained that the observers' imaginal and verbal representations of a witnessed incident can perpetuate the effects of that event. It is also possible that children's aggressive make-believe play can increase the probability that overt aggression will be displayed following the viewing of media violence. In all of these cases, we believe, continuing to think about the filmed violence and one's own aggression in the depicted situation prolongs the media-generated activation of aggressively related ideas and expressive-motor reactions. Singer and Singer (1981) have published results consistent with this contention. They found that children whose play was guided by a prosocial theme displayed little aggression afterward. Their prosocial thoughts could have activated ideas and feelings that were incompatible with aggression, thereby lessening their aggressive tendencies.

The Audience's Interpretation of the Observed Aggression.   Besides defining an action as aggressive or nonaggressive, viewers may give other meanings to the witnessed behavior. For example, they might regard the depicted action as justified or unjustified, as deserved retribution for an earlier insult, as a profitable act for the aggressor, or as risky behavior which could have negative consequences. Perhaps because of a spreading activation to related concepts, these meanings often generalize, providing a context within which observers interpret their own aggressive actions. Many studies have now demonstrated that the audience's willingness to attack someone is influenced greatly by the observed aggressor's outcomes (Bandura, 1965, 1971). The viewers appear to draw a lesson from what they see: What happens on the screen (or is reported in the media) might also happen to them if they exhibit the same behavior (Bandura, 1971; Comstock, 1980; Comstock et al., 1978; Huesmann, 1982). Our cognitive conception can be readily applied to this phenomenon: When observers witness the consequence of the aggressor's action, other occasions in which there was the same type of outcome are recalled. With this kind of outcome now vividly in mind, as the availability heuristic suggests, the viewers might overestimate the frequency and probability of the same type of consequence. Thus, observing desirable consequences for a given behavior may increase viewers' willingness to perform that kind of behavior themselves, whereas seeing an actor punished for engaging in a certain act may make viewers reluctant to follow suit.

Furthermore, as Goranson (1969) has shown, an audience can be affected by the outcome of the aggression they watch even if the movie aggressor is not directly affected by his violence. This study reported that angry subjects attacked their tormentor only weakly after learning that the victim in the violent film they watched died of the injuries he received. Under these circumstances, the possibility that violence might have unfortunate consequences apparently dominated the observers' thoughts, and these ideas evidently led them to restrain their aggression. However, we must recognize that the subjects in this experiment neither held ill feelings toward the victim in the movie nor associated that character with someone whom they might have wanted to hurt. On the other hand, if the filmed victim had only suffered somewhat, rather than died, the angry observers might have regarded the victim's pain as gratifying for them. The observed aggression could then have been seen as successfully leading to a desired consequence (i.e., revenge), and the end result might have been a disinhibition (Berkowitz, 1974; Donnerstein & Berkowitz, 1981).

We should not neglect the observed outcome of the aggression if we hope to gain a comprehensive understanding of the effects of movie violence. Indeed, the "good old westerns" may have affected their viewers adversely because they never showed aggression having any tragic consequences; although characters were shot and fell down, no real suffering was seen. Interestingly, films on Japanese television, which portray about the same amount of violence as U.S. television movies, are much more likely to show victims suffering and to depict the hero, or protagonist, in the movie as the victim (Iwao, Pool, & Hagiwara, 1981). This emphasis on good characters' pain could lessen the audience's willingess to act aggressively themselves.

Viewers' inhibitions against violent acts may also be affected by their attitudes toward the observed aggressor and/or the aggression victim. Numerous investigations, initiated by Berkowitz and Rawlings (1963) and then replicated by Berkowitz and his co-workers (Berkowitz, 1965; Berkowitz, Corwin, & Heironimus, 1963; Berkowitz & Geen, 1967; Berkowitz, Parke, Leyens, & West, 1974; Berkowitz & Powers, 1979) and others (e.g., Geen & Stonner, 1973; Hoyt, 1970; Meyer, 1972), provide support for this contention. In these studies, angered men were led to regard the victim in the violent movie they were about to see as either bad and unpleasant or as a good person. At the conclusion of the film, all of the men were given a chance to punish another student who had insulted them earlier. The experiments uniformly found that the angered subjects attacked the tormentor more severely after they had seen the immoral "bad guy" being beaten up than when they had observed the "good guy" being hurt.

Berkowitz interpreted these results as being due to differences in the perceived justification of the witnessed aggression. That is, the subjects presumably thought of the aggression against the immoral character as somewhat justified, whereas the more favorable victim's beating was seen as morally unwarranted. The observers then interpreted their own possible attacks on their tormentor in the same way. That is, the good, justified aggression shown on the screen activated other ideas of morally proper aggression. However, other researchers have extended the original findings in a way that suggests a slightly different interpretation. Hoyt (1970) and other investigators (Geen & Stonner, 1973, 1974; Meyer, 1972) demonstrated that provoked observers were most punitive toward their insulter if they had been led to think of the witnessed violence as vengeance for an earlier injustice. This suggests that the angered subjects saw themselves as having been mistreated, and therefore, they extrapolated from the movie-activated thoughts of revenge to their own situation. As a result, their inhibitions against aggression were reduced. Subjects who had not been angered, however, might have regarded these ideas as inappropriate or even wrong, which would be expected to create increased restraints (Geen & Stonner, 1973). Geen (1976) concluded from all this that the subjects deduced whether aggression was appropriate in their situation by comparing their own motivational state with that of the actors. They also made use of cues from the filmed violence in deciding upon the appropriate course of action. In any case, whatever the exact meaning of the observed aggression, the context in which it occurs clearly can affect the viewers' inhibitions against aggression.

Nature of the Available Target.   The probability that overt aggression will follow media depictions of violence also depends on the nature of the potential target. Of course, viewers are unlikely to aggress against someone who is capable of punishing them. But more interesting is the discovery that angry observers who view violence later tend to direct their strongest aggression toward those people in their environment whom they associated with the victim (Berkowitz & Geen, 1967; Donnerstein & Berkowitz, 1981; Geen & Berkowitz, 1966, 1967). In most of these studies, provoked participants were shown a film fight and then were given an opportunity to punish the person who had angered them. On the whole, the participants punished their tormentor more severely when he had the same name as the loser of the observed fight than when his name was the same as the winner or was not used at all in the movie.

A more recent unpublished experiment by Donnerstein and Berkowitz (1983) extends the generality of this phenomenon. Male subjects were first provoked by a woman (the experimenter's accomplice) and then some were exposed to a film clip in which a woman was assaulted by two men. As in earlier experiments, when these subjects were given an opportunity to punish the insulting female accomplice, their aggression was more intense if she had the same name as the movie victim than if she had a different name. It is possible that as the angry viewers watched the filmed assault after having been provoked by a woman, thoughts about the pleasure of attacking a woman were activated. These thoughts could have been strengthened when the subjects then faced the female accomplice having the same name as the film victim, perhaps because her name functioned as a retrieval cue. The result was strong aggression toward her. In general, then, potential targets will be aggressed against if they remind viewers of the victim of the observed violence, especially if that violence was gratifying to the viewers.

The Reality of the Media Depiction.   All of the factors just mentioned, such as the meaning of the witnessed event, obviously will affect the observers only to the extent that they attend to this occurrence. Moreover, the likelihood of viewers being influenced increases when they are highly involved in the observed scene, thinking of themselves as carrying out the portrayed behaviors. The reality of the media depiction can determine how involved they will be in the scene that they observe.

A number of experiments suggest that viewers are more likely to be aggressively incited by a violent occurrence if this event is realistic rather than make-believe. Feshbach (1972) exposed the children in his study to a film of a campus riot. He told the youngsters either that the film was a fictitious Hollywood movie or that it was a newsreel of an actual riot. Later, all children were given the opportunity to punish a peer. Feshbach found that those youngsters who had seen the supposedly real violence were most aggressive. Berkowitz and Alioto (1973) extended this finding to young adults. The angry college men in their experiment were more punitive toward their provocateur after watching a war scene that was described as realistic rather than staged. Other research, although not a controlled laboratory study, has suggested that the constructiveness of children's play is more negatively influenced by realistic rather than stylistic portrayals of aggression (Noble, 1973).

Geen and his co-workers have conducted research that adds to our understanding of this phenomenon. An experiment by Geen and Rakosky (1973) suggests that when viewers define the witnessed aggression as fictitious, they tend to distance themselves psychologically from the event so that it has less impact on them. When the subjects in this study were reminded that the fight they were about to see was fictional, they subsequently were less physiologically aroused by it than were their counterparts not given this reminder. Consistent with this finding, Geen (1975) later reported that angry men who observed the film of a real rather than a staged fight were more likely to maintain high levels of physiological arousal during the movie and to give their tormentor strong punishment soon afterwards. It appears that people who believe a violent incident to be make-believe will be less likely to have aggression-activating thoughts.

A similar effect has been noted when observers focus on the artistic nature of the scene. Leyens, Cisneros, and Hossay (1976) exposed their subjects to aggression-related pictures and asked some of them to attend to the pictures' aesthetic qualities. The results showed that these "decentration" instructions led the subjects to be less hostile toward a person who had insulted them earlier than were their counterparts who were not asked to attend to the aesthetic qualities. (The subjects seeing the aggressive pictures without the aesthetic focus were more aggressive than controls seeing nonaggressive pictures.) The researchers noted that the attention to the aesthetic qualities had not changed the pictures' aggressive meaning, so this attention might have only led to a weaker activation of aggression-facilitating ideas.

On the basis of their findings, Leyens et al. suggested that it may be possible to attenuate the aggression-inciting capacity of violent communications without imposing censorship by teaching viewers to attend to the aesthetic or physical aspects of the movies they watch. Such a possibility is interesting. More evidence comes from research led by Huesmann and Eron (Huesmann, Eron, Klein, Brice, & Fischer, 1983). These investigators emphasized the reality versus fictional dimension, asking the youngsters in their experimental condition to write essays about why violence on television was both unreal and bad. Based on social psychological studies of role playing, this technique was intended to inculcate an unfavorable attitude toward violent programs as well as strengthen the children's awareness of the fictional nature of these shows. The researchers found that the training procedure led the experimental subjects to be rated by peers as less aggressive than their controls. However, the relationship between viewing violence and aggression, which existed in the control condition, disappeared when the children were exposed to the training procedure. The experimental condition children might have learned to think about televised violence in a way that dampened the aggression-activating capacity of these aggressive movies.

CONCLUSION

The concern expressed by the American public about the high levels of violence in our media generally stems from both the fear that young children will learn to regard aggression as a viable alternative in problem solving and the fear that many persons will become indifferent to the suffering caused by violence. Attention to these matters is certainly warranted. However, in addition to these concerns, the present paper emphasizes another type of danger: People can get ideas from the communications reporting violent incidents, and for a short time afterwards at least, these thoughts can help foster antisocial behavior.

We must recognize that the media can promote prosocial as well as antisocial behavior. As has been suggested, the media are capable of activating thoughts and memories that can facilitate helpfulness, kindness, and the like. The outcome depends on the type of action (and its consequences) that is communicated.

Newspapers, radio, and television create news as well as report it. Socially desirable behavior can be promoted if instances of such conduct are well publicized. On the other hand, the likelihood of aggression can be enhanced by the depiction of violent incidents either in realistic or fictional form. (However, it may be that realistic portrayals of violence are much more apt to have these adverse consequences, assuming that they are vivid enough to capture the audience's full attention.)

The current analysis has dealt only with research exploring the effects of exposure to one or a few media communications. Frequent viewing could lead to an even smaller effect as the audiences become desensitized to the scenes or stories reported by the media. We address this possibility in our earlier discussion of the "trivialization of aggression" or "desensitization to aggression." Such a process could be described as follows: When viewers are exposed to repeated violence, they might become habituated to events of this type so that there is a decreasing priming effect and a decline in the activation of aggression-related ideas and inclinations. The desensitization, then, reflects this reduced activation.

This paper has implicitly rejected this habituation interpretation of desensitization. Rather, it has been suggested that the effects that researchers have attributed to a desensitization to aggression might be due to an increased acceptance of aggressive behavior. Theoretically, aggressive ideas have a greater probability of being activated with repeated exposure to violence, and as a result, the observers are more apt to think (at least for a short time) that aggression is proper or worthwhile. Because of this increased acceptance of aggression, their concerns and anxiety about aggression are attenuated. From this perspective, the reduction in physiological arousal resulting from several viewings of aggressive movies might reflect a decreased level of internal conflict or lowered aggression anxiety, but not a decline in the observer's inclination to aggression. The study by Thomas (1982) supports this thesis.

Yet, even if we accept that desensitization to aggression involves habituation, we need not necessarily conclude that repeated exposure to aggressive scenes will lead to a lower likelihood of overt aggression. Although the habituation could weaken both the ideas and inclinations facilitative of aggression, the ideas and other responses that tend to inhibit overt aggression may also be weakened. Available evidence suggests, although only tentatively, that any habituation might result in a faster decrease in the inhibitory as compared to the facilitative tendencies. Once again, overt aggression would be more likely.

This does not mean that antisocial and prosocial actions are inevitable when antisocial or prosocial incidents are reported in the media. The mass communications only influence the likelihood that such behavior will occur. Many other intervening variables can affect the probability that the media-activated thoughts will be translated into actual behavior. Several of these factors have been discussed in this paper. When all of these influences are taken into account, there may be only a relatively small chance that any given viewer will actually engage in the witnessed behavior. Yet, considering the size of the audiences reached by mass communications, even a small probability becomes significant in practicality. Even if the odds are only in 1 in 100,000 that viewing aggression will result in open violence, in an audience of 10,000,000 there would be 100 acts of aggression! These figures are hypothetical—the probabilities may have been vastly underestimated, indeed. Regardless of statistical predictions, however, we must decide as a society whether the practical significance of such figures indicates a price that we are willing to pay.

REFERENCES

Aderman, D., & Berkowitz, L. (1970). Observational set, empathy, and helping. *Journal of Personality and Social Psychology, 14,* 141–148.

Anderson, C. A. (1983). Imagination and expectation: The effect of imagining behavioral scripts on personal intentions. *Journal of Personality and Social Psychology, 45,* 293–305.

Anderson, J., & Bower, G. (1973). *Human associative memory*. Washington, DC: Winston.

Andison, F. (1977). TV violence and viewer aggression: A cumulation of study results 1956–1976. *Public Opinion Quarterly, 41*, 314–331.

Bandura, A. (1965). Vicarious processes: A case of no-trial learning. In L. Berkowitz (Ed.), *Advances in experimental social psychology* (Vol. 2). New York: Academic Press.

Bandura, A. (1971). *Social learning theory*. New York: General Learning Press.

Bandura, A. (1973). *Aggression: A social learning analysis*. Englewood Cliffs, NJ: Prentice-Hall.

Bargh, J., & Pietromonaco, P. (1982). Automatic information processing and social perception: The influence of trait information presented outside of conscious awareness on impression formation. *Journal of Personality and Social Psychology, 43*, 437–449.

Berkowitz, L. (1970). Aggressive humor as a stimulus to aggressive responses. *Journal of Personality and Social Psychology, 16*, 710–717.

Berkowitz, L. (1973). Words and symbols as stimuli to aggressive responses. In J. Knutson (Eds.), *Control of aggression: Implications from basic research*. Chicago: Aldine-Atherton.

Berkowitz, L. (1974). Some determinants of impulsive aggression: Role of mediated associations with reinforcements for aggression. *Psychological Review, 81*, 165–176.

Berkowitz, L., & Alioto, J. (1973). The meaning of an observed event as a determinant of its aggressive consequences. *Journal of Personality and Social Psychology, 28*, 206–217.

Berkowitz, L., Corwin, R., & Heironimus, M. (1963). Film violence and subsequent aggressive tendencies. *Public Opinion Quarterly, 27*, 217–229.

Berkowitz, L., & Geen, R. (1967). Stimulus qualities of the target of aggression: A further study. *Journal of Personality and Social Psychology, 5*, 364–368.

Berkowitz, L., & Macaulay, J. (1971). The contagion of criminal violence. *Sociometry, 34*, 238–260.

Berkowitz, L., Parke, R., Leyens, J-P., & West, S. (1974). The effects of justified and unjustified movie violence on aggression in juvenile delinquents. *Journal of Research in Crime and Delinquency, 11*, 16–24.

Berkowitz, L., & Powers, P. (1979). Effects of timing and justification of witnessed aggression on the observers' punitiveness. *Journal of Research in Personality, 13*, 71–80.

Berkowitz, L., & Rawlings, E. (1963). Effects of film violence on inhibitions against subsequent aggression. *Journal of Abnormal and Social Psychology, 66*, 405–412.

Blackman J., & Hornstein, H. (1977). Newscasts and the social actuary. *Public Opinion Quarterly, 41*, 295–313.

Bollen, K., & Phillips, D. (1983). Imitative suicides: A national study of the effects of television news stories. *American Sociological Review, 47*, 802–809.

Bower, G. (1981). Mood and memory. *American Psychologist, 36*, 129–148.

Buvinic, M., & Berkowitz, L. (1976). Delayed effects of practiced versus unpracticed responses after observation of movie violence. *Journal of Experimental Social Psychology, 12*, 283–293.

Carver, C., Ganellen, R., Froming, W., & Chambers, W. (1983). Modeling: An analysis in terms of category accessibility. *Journal of Experimental Social Psychology, 19*, 403–421.

Clark, M., & Isen, A. (1982). Toward understanding the relationship between feeling states and social behavior. In A. Hastorf & A. Isen (Eds.), *Cognitive social psychology*. New York: Elsevier/North Holland.

Collins, A., & Loftus, E. (1975). A spreading-activation theory of semantic memory. *Psychological Review, 82*, 407–428.

Collins, W., & Getz, S. (1976). Children's social responses following modeled reactions to provocation: Prosocial effects of a TV drama. *Journal of Personality, 44*, 488–500.

Comstock, G. (1975). *Television and human behavior: The key studies*. Santa Monica, CA: Rand.

Comstock, G. (1980). New emphasis in research on the effects of television and film violence. In E. Palmer & A. Dorr (Eds.), *Children and the faces of television*. New York: Academic.

Comstock, G., Chaffee, S., Katzman, N., McCombs, M., & Roberts, D. (1978). *Television and human behavior.* New York: Columbia University Press.

Cook, T. D., Kendzierski, D. A., & Thomas, S. V. (1983). The implicit assumptions of television research: An analysis of the 1982 NIMH report on *Televison and Behavior. Public Opinion Quarterly, 47,* 161–201.

Donnerstein, E., & Berkowitz, L. (1981). Victim reactions in aggressive erotic films as a factor in violence against women. *Journal of Personality and Social Psychology, 41,* 710–724.

Donnerstein, E., & Berkowitz, L. (1983). *Effects of film content and victim association on aggression behavior and attitudes.* Unpublished study, University of Wisconsin–Madison.

Doob, A., & Climie, R. (1972). Delay of measurement and the effects of film violence. *Journal of Experimental Social Psychology, 8,* 136–142.

Doob, A., & MacDonald, G. (1979). Televison viewing and fear of victimization: Is the relationship causal? *Journal of Personality and Social Psychology, 37,* 170–179.

Dorr, A. (1981). Television and affective development and functioning: Maybe this decade. *Journal of Broadcasting, 25,* 335–345.

Drabman, R., & Thomas, M. (1974). Does media violence increase children's toleration of real-life aggression? *Developmental Psychology, 10,* 419–421.

Eron, L., Huesmann, L., Lefkowitz, M., & Walder, L. (1972). Does television violence cause aggression? *American Psychologist, 27,* 253–263.

Feshbach, S. (1972). Reality and fantasy in filmed violence. In J. Murray, E. Rubinstein, & G. Comstock (Eds.), *Television and social behavior* (Vol. II, pp. 318–345). Washington, DC: Department of Health, Education, and Welfare.

Friedrich, L., & Stein, A. (1973). Aggressive and prosocial television programs and the natural behavior of preschool children. *Monographs of the society for research in child development, 38,*(4, Serial No. 151).

Geen, R. (1975). The meaning of observed violence: Real vs. fictional violence and effects of aggression and emotional arousal. *Journal of Research in Personality, 9,* 270–281.

Geen, R. (1976). Observing violence in the mass media: Implications of basic research. In R. Geen & E. O'Neal (Eds.), *Perspectives on aggression.* New York: Academic.

Geen, R. (1981). Behavioral and physiological reactions to observed violence: Effects of prior exposure to aggressive stimuli. *Journal of Personality and Social Psychology, 40,* 868–875.

Geen, R., & Berkowitz, L. (1966). Name-mediated aggressive cue properties. *Journal of Personality, 34,* 456–465.

Geen, R., & Berkowitz, L. (1967). Some conditions facilitating the occurrence of aggression after the observation of violence. *Journal of Personality, 35,* 666–676.

Geen, R., & Rakosky, J. (1973). Interpretations of observed violence and their effects of GSR. *Journal of Experimental Research in Personality, 6,* 289–292.

Geen, R., & Stonner, D. (1973). Context effects in observed violence. *Journal of Personality and Social Psychology, 25,* 145–150.

Geen, R., & Stonner, D. (1974). The meaning of observed violence: Effects on arousal and aggressive behavior. *Journal of Research in Personality, 8,* 55–63.

Gerbner, G., Gross, L., Morgan, M., & Signorielli, N. (1980). The "mainstreaming" of America: Violence profile no. 11. *Journal of Communication, 30,* 10–29.

Gerbner, G., Gross, L., Signorielli, N., Morgan, M., & Jackson-Beek, M. (1979). The demonstration of power: Violence profile no. 10. *Journal of Communication, 29,* 177–195.

Goranson, R. (1969). *Observed violence and aggressive behavior: The effects of negative outcomes to the observed violence.* Unpublished doctoral dissertation, University of Wisconsin.

Greenwald, A. G. (1970). Sensory feedback mechanisms in performance control: With special reference to the ideo-motor mechanism. *Psychological Review, 77,* 73–99.

Hawkins, R., & Pingree, S. (1980). Some processes in the cultivation effect. *Communication Research, 7,* 193–226.

Hearold, S. (1979). *Meta-analysis of the effects of television on social behavior*. Unpublished doctoral dissertation, University of Colorado, Boulder.

Holloway, S., Tucker, L., & Hornstein, H. (1977). The effects of social and nonsocial information on interpersonal behavior of males: The news makes news. *Journal of Personality and Social Psychology, 35*, 514–522.

Hornstein, H. A., LaKind, E., Frankel, G., & Manne, S. (1975). The effects of knowledge about remote social events on prosocial behavior, social conception, and mood. *Journal of Personality and Social Psychology, 32*, 1038–1046.

Hoyt, J. (1970). Effect of media violence "justification" on aggression. *Journal of Broadcasting, 16*, 455–464.

Huesmann, L. (1982). Violence and aggression. In National Institute of Mental Health, *Televison and behavior: Ten years of scientific progress* (Vol. 1). Washington, DC: U.S. Government Printing Office.

Huesmann, L., Eron, L., Klein, L., Brice, P., & Fischer, P. (1983). Mitigating the imitation of aggressive behaviors by changing children's attitudes about media violence. *Journal of Personality and Social Psychology, 44*, 899–910.

Iwao, S., de Pool, I. S., & Hagiwara, S. (1981). Japanese and U.S. media: Some cross-cultural insights in TV violence. *Journal of Communication, 31*, 28–36.

Josephson, W. (1981). *Television violence and children's aggression: Disinhibition, elicitation or catharsis?* Paper presented at the meetings of the Canadian Psychological Association.

Klatzky, R. (1980). *Human memory* (2nd ed.). San Francisco: Freeman.

Landman J., & Manis, M. (1983). Social cognition: Some historical and theoretical perspectives. In L. Berkowitz (Ed.), *Advances in experimental social psychology* (Vol. 16). San Francisco: Academic.

Lang, P. J. (1979). A bio-informational theory of emotional imagery. *Psychophysiology, 16*, 495–512.

Leifer, A., & Roberts, D. (1972). Children's response to television violence. In J. Murray, E. Rubinstein, & G. Comstock (Eds.), *Television and social behavior* (Vol. 2.). Washington, DC: U.S. Government Printing Office.

Leventhal, H. (1980). Toward a comprehensive theory of emotion. In L. Berkowitz (Ed.), *Advances in experimental social psychology* (Vol. 13). New York: Academic.

Leyens, J-P., Cisneros, T., Hossay J.-F. (1976). Decentration as a means for reducing aggression after exposure to violent stimuli. *European Journal of Social Psychology, 6*, 459–473.

Leyens, J-P., Parke, R. (1975). Aggressive slides can induce a weapons effect. *European Journal of Social Psychology, 5*, 229–236.

Leyens, J-P., & Picus, S. (1973). Identification with the winner of a fight and name mediation: Their differential effects upon subsequent aggressive behavior. *British Journal of Social and Clinical Psychology, 12*, 374–377.

Liebert, R., Sprafkin, J., & Davidson, E. (1982). *The early window: Effects of television on children and youth* (2nd ed.). New York: Pergamon.

Malamuth, N., & Check, J. (1981). The effects of mass media exposure on acceptance of violence against women: A field experiment. *Journal of Research Personality, 15*, 436–446.

Mann, J., Berkowitz, L., Sidman, J., Starr, S., & West, S. (1974). Satiation of the transient stimulating effects of erotic films. *Journal of Personality and Social Psychology, 30*, 729–735.

Meyer, T. (1972). Effects of viewing justified and unjustified real film violence on aggressive behavior. *Journal of Personality and Social Psychology, 23*, 21–29.

Milavsky, J., Kessler, R., Stipp, H., & Rubens, W. (1982). *Television and aggression: The results of a panel study*. New York: Academic Press.

Murray, J. (1980). *Television and youth: 25 years of research and controversy*. Boys Town, NE: Boys Town Center for Study of Youth Development.

Murray, J., & Kippax, S. (1979). From the early window to the late night show: International trends in the study of television's impact on children and adults. In L. Berkowitz (Ed.), *Advances in experimental social psychology* (Vol. 12). New York: Academic.

Noble, G. (1973). Effects of different forms of filmed aggression on children's constructive and destructive play. *Journal of Personality and Social Psychology, 26,* 54–59.

Palmer E., & Dorr, A. (Eds.). (1980). *Children and the faces of television: Teaching, violence, selling.* New York: Academic.

Phillips, D. (1974). The influence of suggestion on suicide: Substantive and theoretical implications of the Werther effect. *American Sociological Review, 39,* 340–354.

Phillips, D. (1979). Suicide, motor vehicle fatalities, and the mass media: Evidence toward a theory of suggestion. *American Journal of Sociology, 84,* 1150–1174.

Phillips, D. (1980). Airplane accidents, murder, and the mass media: Towards a theory of imitation and suggestion. *Social Forces, 58,* 1001–1024.

Phillips, D. (1983). The impact of mass media violence on U.S. homicides. *American Sociological Review, 48,* 560–568.

Rushton, J. (1979). Effects of prosocial television and film material on the behavior of viewers. In L. Berkowitz (Ed.), *Advances in experimental social psychology* (Vol. 12). New York: Academic.

Shiffrin, R., & Schneider, W. (1977). Controlled and automatic human information processing: II. Perceptual learning, automatic attending, and a general theory. *Psychological Review, 84,* 127–190.

Silverman, L., & Sprafkin, J. (1980). The effects of *Sesame Street's* prosocial spots on cooperative play between young children. *Journal of Broadcasting, 24,* 135–147.

Singer, J., & Singer D. (1981). *Television imagination, and aggression.* Hillsdale, NJ: Lawrence Erlbaum Associates.

Sprafkin, J., Liebert, R., & Poulos, R. (1975). Effects of a prosocial televised example on children's helping. *Journal of Experimental Child Psychology, 20,* 119–126.

Tannenbaum, P., & Gaer, E. P. (1965). Mood changes as a function of stress of protagonist and degree of identification in film-viewing situation. *Journal of Personality and Social Psychology, 2,* 612–616.

Tarde, G. (1912). *Penal philosophy.* Boston: Little, Brown.

Thomas, M. (1982). Physiological arousal, exposure to a relatively lengthy aggressive film, and aggressive behavior. *Journal of Research in Personality, 16,* 72–81.

Thomas, M., & Drabman, R. (1977). *Effects of television violence on expectations of others' aggression.* Paper presented at the meetings of the American Psychological Association, San Francisco.

Thomas, M., Horton, R., Lippincott, E., & Drabman, R. (1977). Desensitization to portrayals of real-life aggression as a function of exposure to television violence. *Journal of Personality and Social Psychology, 35,* 450–458.

Turner, C., & Berkowitz, L. (1972). Identification with film aggressor (covert role taking) and reactions to film violence. *Journal of Personality and Social Psychology, 21,* 256–264.

Turner, C., & Layton, J. (1976). Verbal imagery and connotation as memory induced mediators of aggressive behavior. *Journal of Personality and Social Psychology, 33,* 755–763.

Tyler, T. R. (1980). Impact of directly and indirectly experienced events: The origin of crime-related judgments and behaviors. *Journal of Personality and Social Psychology, 39,* 13–28.

Velten, E. (1968). A laboratory task for the induction of mood states. *Behavior Research and Therapy, 6,* 473–482.

Wheeler, L. (1966). Toward a theory of behavioral contagion. *Psychological Review, 73,* 179–182.

Wober, J. (1978). Televised violence and paranoid perception: The view from Great Britain. *Public Opinion Quarterly, 42,* 315–321.

Worchel, S. (1972). The effect of films on the importance of behavioral freedom. *Journal of Personality, 40,* 417–435.

Wyer, R., Jr., & Hartwick, J. (1980). The role of information retrieval and conditional inference processes in belief formation and change. In L. Berkowitz (Ed.), *Advances in experimental social psychology* (Vol. 13.). New York: Academic.

Wyer, R., Jr., & Srull, T. (1981). Category accessibility: Some theoretical and empirical issues concerning the processing of information. In E. Higgins, C. Herman, & M. Zanna (Eds.), *Social cognition* (Vol. 1.). Hillsdale, NJ: Lawrence Erlbaum Associates.

Zillmann, D., & Bryant, J. (1982). Pornography, sexual callousness, and the trivialization of rape. *Journal of Communication, 32,* 10–21.

Zillmann, D., Bryant, J., Comisky, P., & Medoff, N. (1981). Excitation and hedonic valence in the effect of erotica on motivated intermale aggression. *European Journal of Social Psychology, 11,* 233–252.

5

The Functions and Effects of Pornography: Sexual Communications versus the Feminist Models in Light of Research Findings

Neil M. Malamuth, Victoria Billings
University of California, Los Angeles

A very large mass media industry exists throughout the world that produces sexually explicit stimuli including books, magazines, video cassettes, and movies. Generally referred to as the pornography or erotica[1] industry, it is estimated that its yearly profits exceed those of the general movie and record industries combined (Steinem, 1983). Reliable data on the actual consumption of such stimuli are available, however, only in the area of magazines (Shepher & Reisman, in press). The Target Group Index (1974, 1978) provides data on the readership of the 13 most popular magazines, and when figures for the total adult readership are examined, it is found that 5 are erotica publications. Statistics for adult male readership show that the combined readership of *Playboy* and *Penthouse* exceeds the combined readership of *Time* and *Newsweek*.

It is therefore surprising that relatively little systematic attention has been paid to this topic by media researchers, particularly social scientists. Little experimental research was available until the creation of the presidential Commission on Obscenity and Pornography (1970) (referred to hereafter as "the commission"). Since the commission's research, there has been a paucity of published scientific research on this topic until very recently.

In this chapter, we first discuss problems of definition in addressing the subject of pornography. Next, we present two theoretical models that have been proposed

---

[1]As noted later, the terms *pornography* and *erotica* are used interchangeably herein to refer to sexually explicit stimuli without any pejorative meaning necessarily intended.

83

to describe the functions and effects of pornography. Third, we consider empirical research findings relevant to the theoretical models.

DEFINITION OF PORNOGRAPHY

There have been numerous attempts to define pornography and to distinguish between what some consider acceptable erotica as opposed to unacceptable pornography. Etymologically, pornography refers to "writings about prostitutes" (*porne*, prostitute *graphein*, to write). Attempts at definition have included those emphasizing (a) the intent of the producer to elicit erotic responses from the consumer (e.g., Gould, 1977), (b) the effects on the consumer, such as sexual arousal (e.g., Falwell, 1980), and (c) the portrayal of the characters within the stimuli, such as degrading or demeaning of women (Longino, 1980). Attempts to distinguish pornography from erotica have included those suggesting that the former portrays unequal power in sexual relations whereas the latter depicts males and females to be of equal power and in mutually consenting relations (Steinem, 1980). However, as various writers have noted (e.g., Goldstein, Kant, & Hartmann, 1973), definitions and distinctions of this nature are frought with subjective elements that render scientifically operational definitions difficult to construct. For the purposes of the present chapter, therefore, we adopt the approach suggested by Smith (1976b) to use the terms *pornography* and *erotica* interchangeably without any pejorative meaning to refer to sexually explicit stimuli. We feel that a definition in terms of sexual explicitness more readily lends itself to operationalization because it may be based on the presence or absence of references to certain anatomical areas of the body (e.g., breasts, penis, etc.).

THEORETICAL MODELS

Historically, varied theoretical positions have been advanced regarding the functions and effects of pornography. Elsewhere (Malamuth & Billings, 1984) we discuss six such models. In this chapter, we focus on two differing perspectives that have guided a large segment of systematic research in this area. These are the sexual communications model and the feminist model.

The following discussion presents the central ideas of these two models, and we consider three central questions: (a) Is pornography's basic function sexual or political/ideological communication, and what are the effects of pornography? (b) What type of information is cited by the proponents of each model to support their position? (c) How is women's portrayal in pornography conceptualized by each model? In a later section, we examine recent research data in light of these two theoretical models.

The Sexual Communications Model

Functions and Effects of Pornography

Numerous writers have contended that pornography is essentially communication relating to sexuality that has no discernible negative effects and may have varied beneficial effects in the realms of fantasy, sex education, and artistic expression (e.g., Gagnon, 1977; Gordon, 1980). For the purposes of explication, we distinguish between the sexual interest and the artistic variations of the sexual communications model, although they espouse the same basic viewpoint. The former variant focuses on the needs of the consumer of pornography, whereas the latter focuses on the needs of the artistic creator. These viewpoints generally treat current pornographic forms (e.g., magazines and movies) as modern versions of sexual expression manifested throughout history in paintings, sculpture, drawings, and graphics of various types. They consider pornography a natural result of the fact that humans are sexual beings. They perceive historical, and by extension current, attempts to curtail the content and/or distribution of pornography as reflecting an antisexual attitude that fears that greater availability of sexual communications would lessen restrictions on the free expression of sexuality.

The Sexual Interest Version.   The sexual interest variant contends that consumers are attracted to pornography in a desire to fulfill their sexual curiosities and needs. The functions and effects of pornography, according to this theoretical approach, are either restricted to the realm of fantasy (e.g., Gagnon, 1977) or to providing desirable communications that are often lacking in many people's sex education (e.g., Wilson, 1978). For example, in emphasizing the view that pornography is limited to the fantasy world, Gagnon (1977) writes:

> Pornography is fantasy sex, consumed by people who know it is fantasy . . . In the fantasy world of the book or theater they are released from responsibility from the realness of life. Unlike real life they do not have to perform or succeed, they are having a momentary and pleasant escape from daily constraints, from sexual victory or defeat. (p. 357)

The Artistic Version.   The artistic variant emphasizes the artistic need to express sexuality. Pornography is viewed as a harmless or even socially beneficial form of artistic self-expression which creates a fantasy world built about sexual interest (Charney, 1981; Michelson, 1971). For example, Michelson (1971) writes:

> In whatever art form, pornography documents man's archetypal concern with sexuality . . . pornography is the private confrontation of individual psyche with

its sexual needs. The larger cultural engagement with pornography is the public confrontation with archetypal—and usually subliminal—sexual impulses. Pornography then, for better or for worse, is the imaginative record of man's sexual will. (p. 5)

Supporting Information

Exponents of the sexual communications model often turn to examples from primitive and Eastern culture to demonstrate not only the universality of sexual communication but its positive social function and erotic or instructive value. For instance, Abramson and Hayashi (1984) say that in premodern Japan, sexually explicit stimuli fulfilled one of three purposes: (a) to symbolize fertility, (b) to illustrate a "sex manual", or (c) to create sensual feelings. Under the influence of Western morality, the Japanese imposed restrictions on pornography at certain periods in their history. Even today, visual materials still must not show genital and pubic hair. With this one exception, pornography now appears throughout Japanese society. Themes such as rape are common and yet rape rates in Japan are relatively low (this issue is discussed further later in this chapter).

Proponents of this model also emphasize the assertion of sexual interest in all cultures, despite religious restrictions and irrespective of political beliefs. Smith (1983) argues that the emergence of more openly erotic Western art work in the 19th century by conservative artists such as David and Degas, as well as radicals like Rodin and Toulouse-Lautrec, shows that "erotic art has never been determined by either the politics of the artist nor his social status . . . the interest of the artist in the visual aspects of sex is apparently universal" (p. vii).

Certain periods and works are considered to represent breakthroughs in the West in sexual expression, such as the publication in the 17th century of Arentino's *Pleasures*, an erotic work with accompanying illustrations of intercourse. This work remained popular for 2 centuries and produced a genre of copulation prints (Foxon, 1965) paralleling Japanese and Chinese erotic prints. The increase in pornography production in that century is cited by several observers as a sign of both sexual curiosity and need (Foxon, 1964; Gordon, 1980). Gordon argues that pornography appeared in the West as soon as it was technically possible to provide mass communication and communicators were freer of church regulation.

Portrayal of Women

In contrast to the feminist perspective, the portrayal of women in pornography is not seen as a critical feature by proponents of the sexual communications view. Therefore, exponents of the communications model often touch on this subject lightly, if at all, in considering historical and cross-cultural material. However, when women's portrayal is considered, it usually is viewed as a reflection of the particular culture or of the female's biological sexual role. Sexual communication in a sexually tolerant society is expected simply to reflect the greater freedom of sexual expression women are presumed to have under these conditions.

An example of the emphasis on sexual communication as presenting more positive images of women in more sexually tolerant societies is Kronhausen and Kronhausen's (1961, 1978) stress on women's portrayal in Chinese and Indian erotica. Eastern erotica picture women as more sexually active than in the Western tradition, which emphasizes passivity and the male superior position for intercourse. The Kronhausens (1961) point out that an ancient Chinese treatise on sex stressed: "Man should give the woman complete satisfaction every time he engages in sexual intercourse with her, but he should allow himself to ejaculate only on certain specified occasions" (p. 241). They also emphasize the gentle persuasion and sweetness of Chinese erotica. Japanese erotica display more aggression, the Kronhausens acknowledge, but the emphasis on female sexual organs is almost equal to that of the males.

In addition to the rape theme in Japanese erotica, a feature of women's portrayal that has attracted the attention of exponents of the sexual communications model is the eroticization of Chinese foot binding. In his discussion of erotic symbolism, Ellis (1936) noted this practice of compressing females' feet. He considered its appeal an exaggeration of the general sexual drive. Ellis believed the foot was selected because of ancient customs glamorizing the foot and because of the beauty standard which valued the petite. In contrast to the feminist perspective, he explicitly rejected the oppression of women or their political status as being related to foot binding. Ellis cites the small waist and use of the corset to diminish the waist to enhance sexual attractiveness as a Western example of erotic symbolism.

The Feminist Model

Functions and Effects of Pornography

The subject of pornography has received considerable attention from feminist writers (e.g., Brownmiller, 1975; Gager & Schurr, 1976; Russell, 1980; Steinem, 1980) who view it as an important reflector and creator of male subjugation of women. In contrast to the sexual communications model, feminists do not see the subject of pornography in terms of sexual permissiveness versus repression, but in terms of sexist propaganda conveying a political ideology of male domination/female subordination (Morgan, 1980).

Feminists contend that the functions and effects of pornography need to be understood within the larger context of male–female relations. They do not object to the depiction of sexual content per se, but feminists voice strong objections to what they perceive as the expression of an antifemale ideology in pornography that portrays women in roles contrary to the goals of women's liberation. According to this view, women are typically depicted as objects to be used to serve the pleasure of men; they are degraded, dehumanized, and frequently shown as both willing and unwilling victims of abusive and violent acts:

> Pornography, like rape, is a male invention, designed to dehumanize women, to reduce the female to an object of sexual access, not to free sensuality from moralistic or parental inhibition. The staple of porn will always be the naked female body, breasts and genitals exposed, because as man devised it, her naked body is the female's "shame," her private parts the private property of man, while his are the ancient, holy, universal, patriarchal instrument of his power, his rule by force over her. Pornography is the undiluted essence of antifemale propoganda. (Brownmiller, 1975, p. 443)

> Pornography's *most fundamental message* about women which, whether inspired by wishful thinking, or a deep fear and ignorance of female sexuality—is essentially that "all women are whores." (Blackstone, 1984, p. 9)

Why should an ideology of male domination and abuse of women be expressed in the context of sexual themes? This ideology is particularly evident here, according to feminists, because historically in partriarchal societies, where men hold the reins of power, the woman's worth was strongly linked to her sexuality. Feminists contend that pornography has effects beyond the fantasy realm. It supports similar attitudes and behavior toward women in reality and consequently contributes to a cultural climate where acts of discrimination and violence against women are more likely to occur and be accepted.

Supporting Information

As evidence of the propagandistic nature of pornography, LaBelle (1980) argues that it uses the eight techniques listed by Brown (1963) as universally employed in propaganda campaigns. Similarly, Casalis (1975) analyzed *Penthouse* magazine from the perspective of an ideology, showing phrases which objectified women (e.g., bust-waist-hip measurements) as a salient personal characteristic. Other features were the magazine's engagement against the women's liberation movement and incorporation of this movement's ideas into a context that is ideologically compatible with the magazine. For instance, the sexually liberated woman is presented, but her achievements are trivialized in profiles of women who are featured as "pets."

Others have stressed the close association between pornography and political groups or movements. Griffin (1981) presents the Nazi movement in Germany as an example of the use of imagery similar to the domination and humiliation motifs of pornography to assert authoritarian domination, particularly over Jews. By stressing the high emphasis on control and authoritarian themes, Griffin seeks to demonstrate that the main impulse behind this genre of sexual motif is not actually sex, but political oppression.

Portrayal of Women

The portrayal of women is seen as the most salient feature of pornography by feminists due to women's status as an oppressed and exploited group. Women are also considered to be the group most apt to be controlled through sexual imagery, although other groups such as children and blacks can be portrayed in similar ways.

Historically, a number of observers have pointed to the misogynistic strain in art and literature which deals either directly or indirectly with sex and relations between men and women. The characters of the witch (Masters & Lea, 1964) and Eve (Phillips 1984) represent examples of sexual women as evil. Thompson (1979), in his survey of 17th century pornographic works published in England, writes: "A common characteristic of virtually every book and every type that we shall be examining is its underlying contempt for women. Women are created for the satisfaction of men and satisfaction means physical domination. Women are paradoxically depicted as either tempresses or victims, Messalinas or Lucreces, ravenous or ravished" (p. 12). He argues that even the female rogue was portrayed unsympathetically as "rampart lesbian and unfaithful wife" (p. 33). He found that women often were depicted as seductresses far out of proportion to what the female embracement of this sexual role actually could have been. Where women were pictured as sexual, they usually were cast into the role of the whore. Even in such ancient Western sexual works as Ovid's *Metamorphosis,* which remained a popular work of sexual fiction through the Middle Ages (Stone, 1977), rape was a frequent motif and women were pictured on the one hand as being chased and coerced or tricked into having sex, usually with a god, and on the other hand as being held responsible for the act.

Rush (1980) notes the growth of sexual imagery involving children, citing statistics from a 1977 *Los Angeles Times* article which estimates that 40% of the $2.5 billion porn industry comes from child pornography. Rush argues that the use of children in sexual imagery is not a matter of simple sexual interest but an appeal to sexually exploit the weak, the same motivation for women's portrayal in pornography.

Although much feminist concern about pornography's effects has focused on violence, feminists also have been concerned about the effects of more muted messages in sexual imagery, including domination and bondage (Lederer, 1980). This is seen not as a harmless fantasy outlet but a means for symbolically or actually constraining women. In contrast to the views presented by the sexual communications' model, Brownmiller (1984) and Dworkin (1981) argue that sexual fetishism, especially Chinese foot binding, is related to and reinforces political bondage of women. Levy's (1966) study of Chinese foot binding and related art and literature documents how bondage was linked both to sex and politics and how this connection was reinforced by cultural media. The crippling practice of foot binding began as foot wrapping by court dancers. But the practice was widened and the wrappings tightened to become bindings because both political and religious leaders wanted to restrict the movement of women and cut back on such rights as freer association with unrelated men. The practice became glamorized and subjected to beauty standards as time went on. Because it originated in the upper class where women did not do physical labor, the practice operated like a fashion, affecting those most interested in imitating the rich. What would be considered pornography entered the process as an increasingly commercial and secular culture produced sex books with novelized narratives. A specific genre of these, the Lotus Literature, dealt directly with the erotic properties of the bound foot. This literature not only explained how to become sexually aroused by the bound foot but provided defenses of the practice and a distorted historical account which ignored its intent to constrain women. Levy notes that fallacious ideas about the bound foot appearing in the Lotus Literature were believed by some males past the middle of the 20th century.

A similar historical instance is the tight lacing of women's waists, popular in Europe from the Renaissance to the 19th century. Lewisohn (1956) notes that the corset appears both in Greek myth and in historical practice as a chastity belt for potentially adulterous wives. Kunzle (1972) notes that an erotic fashion magazine helped to make what was initially a chastity item into a sexual fetish. The magazine ran drawings which gave the corseted woman and the corset fitting an erotic connotation. As opposition to tight lacing mounted, especially among physicians, the corset magazine continued to defend the practice, with the support of male and female readers.

RESEARCH FINDINGS

In light of the foregoing discussion of the sexual communications and feminist models, there appear to be four central questions that merit empirical testing: (a) Does the content of pornography reflect an ideology regarding male–female relations in addition to its portrayal of nudity and sexual explicitness? (b) Does pornography change sexual responses such as sexual arousal and activities? (c) Does pornography affect social relations between males and females that relate to political/ideological roles? (d) Does pornography affect crimes such as rape?

Content of Pornography

There have been relatively few systematic content analyses of pornography in differing media; the generalizability of the findings is therefore quite limited. Perhaps the most thorough analysis was that of Smith (1976a, 1976b), who analyzed the content of 428 "adults only" paperbacks published between 1968 and 1974 and sampled from five states. The nature of the social relations described in these books, according to Smith (1976b), was of a "machismo world" in which the most common theme was:

> The young, probably rich, sleek, cool, restrained and poised beauty, the depths of her sexual desires unstirred as yet (particularly, if married, by her husband), until Superstud arrives, who, despite her initial resistance and piteous pleas for mercy, rather quickly and relentlessly unlocks her sexual passion to take her to totally unimagined heights leaving her begging for his continued ministrations. (p. 23)

Smith (1976a, 1976b) found that 20% of the sexual episodes in these books depicted a rape, with less than 3% of the attackers meeting any negative consequences. The vast majority of such violence was by males against females. Moreover, the victim was rarely portrayed as having regrets about having been raped. The number of rapes portrayed doubled from 1968 to 1974.

Malamuth and Spinner (1980) conducted a content analysis that focused on the frequency of sexual aggression in the cartoons and pictorials of *Playboy* and *Penthouse* magazines between 1973 to 1977, inclusive. They found that on the average about 10% of the cartoons were sexually violent throughout this 5-year period. For pictorials, there was an increase in sexual violence from about 1% in 1973 to 5% in 1977. Such aggression was almost exclusively directed by males against females.

Dietz and Evans (1982) classified 1,760 heterosexual pornographic magazines according to the imagery depicted on the cover, comparing the imagery depicted in 1970 to 1981. Whereas in 1970, when the pornography commission had completed its research, magazine covers depicting a woman posed alone had predominated, such imagery constituted a much smaller percentage by 1981. In contrast, bondage and domination imagery increased very markedly since 1970 and in 1981 constituted 17.2% of the magazine covers, second in frequency only to the depiction of couples in sexual activity.

Conclusions.   In terms of overt violence and domination, it appears that an increasing percentage of sexually explicit media portray such themes. Further, although there have not been systematic studies specifically addressing the issue of an "ideology" of male dominance/female submission in pornography, the content analytic studies to provide some support for the assertion that such an ideology is frequently communicated. It is important that future research closely analyze additional dimensions of erotic stimuli to assess the extent to which a sexist ideology is portrayed in contrast to an imagery of positive relations involving mutual respect, affection, and the like.

Sexual Responses

Sexual Arousal

There are a great deal of data to support the obvious conclusion that erotic stimuli often stimulate sexual arousal. In the present analysis, however, we examine data bearing on a more complex question: Does exposure to erotica produce changes in the degree to which people are sexually aroused in subsequent exposures to sexually explicit materials? Writings on this issue have suggested every possible outcome. Some writers (e.g., Longford Committee, 1972) have contended that repeated exposure to pornography results in enhanced sexual arousal and interest in such materials (i.e., an enhancement effect). Others (e.g., Sonenschein, 1969; Steiner, 1970) have argued that repeated exposure to pornography results in reduced arousal and lack of interest (i.e., habituation or satiation effect). An additional possibility is that while exposure to pornography may produce short-term changes in sexual arousal, no long-term changes occur (i.e., null effect).

It should be noted at this point that the research has been conducted almost exclusively with adult populations due to the ethical barriers to exposing minors to pornographic stimuli within a research context. Consequently, the ability to assess the potential influence of erotica on patterns of sexual arousal (and other responses) is limited given that the first experiences with pornography for most people takes place during adolescence (Commission on Obscenity and Pornography, 1970). Further, it may be that patterns of sexual arousal are established prior to reaching adulthood and that exposures that have profound effects in childhood may not have comparable effects later in life.

Enhancement Effect.   There is little evidence that exposure to pornography produces changes in arousal patterns so as to result in greater sexual arousal to pornographic depictions. One study did suggest an intriguing possibility concerning the conditions under which an enhancement effect may occur. Unfortunately, this study is frought with methodological problems. Schaefer and Colgan (1977) exposed six control and two experimental male subjects to pornographic literature in sex sessions over a 2-week period. In each of these sessions, subjects read the same six-page erotic materials, followed by a novel one-page erotic passage. Immediately following each session, the experimental subjects ejaculated (reinforcement condition), whereas the control subjects did not (nonreinforcement condition). Subjects' sexual arousal to the various stimuli was assessed by means of direct genital measures (i.e., penile tumescence).

The results showed that for the control subjects there was a decrease in penile tumescence across trials to the same six-page pornographic stimulus, whereas no differences across trials were found for the novel erotic stimuli. For experimental subjects, there was an increase in arousal responses across trials for both same and novel pornographic passages. These data were interpreted by the authors as suggesting that reinforcement may play a crucial role in mediating the effects of exposure to pornography. Habituation occurs when exposure is not followed by orgasm, and an enhancement effect may occur when exposure is immediately followed by reinforcement (i.e., ejaculation).

There are serious limitations in Schaefer and Colgan's study (1977) that render any generalizations from their data highly suspect. For example, the authors do not indicate whether subjects were randomly assigned to the experimental and control conditions. In addition, the very small and unequal sizes of the samples cast serious doubts on the validity of the statistical tests used.

Habituation Effect.   Varied studies conclude that repeated exposure to erotica will, under many circumstances, result in less sexual arousal to and reduced interest in such materials. These studies include both experimental and survey research.

The first clear experimental study demonstrating habituation was conducted as part of the research of the commission (Howard, Reifler, & Liptzin, 1971). This study found that repeated exposure of male college students to erotica for 90 min a day, 5 days a week for 5 weeks, resulted in a reduction in sexual arousal to erotic stimuli as well as reduced interest in such pornography. Following 2 months of nonexposure, however, there was a recovery in sexual arousal to levels that were not significantly different from those prior to the repeated exposure procedure (recovery of interest levels was not specifically assessed).

Criticism of this research has been made by Cline (1975). He argues that exposure to any stimulus or experience (e.g., sexual intercourse, food, etc.) for 5 days a week for 3 consecutive weeks is likely to lead to habituation. Furthermore, he points out that these data do not address the question of whether more realistic levels of exposure to pornography in a "natural environment" lead to lasting habituation effects.

Two recent experiments used dosage levels of pornography that were somewhat more realistic than those used by Howard et al. (1971). Zillmann and Bryant (1984) randomly assigned male and female college students to one of three exposure conditions or to a no-exposure condition. In each of the three exposure conditions, subjects viewed six 8-min films per session. A session was held each week for 6 consecutive weeks. In the massive pornography exposure condition, subjects viewed six pornographic films per session. In the moderate pornography exposure condition, subjects viewed three pornographic films and three nonsexual films each session. In the no pornography exposure condition, only nonsexual films were viewed. All of the pornographic films were sexually explicit (i.e., hardcore) unedited portrayals that did not depict violent activities. The nonsexual films were chosen to be educational and entertaining. In the seventh week of the research, all subjects were exposed to three films: (a) a softcore nonviolent heterosexual film, (b) a hardcore film portraying nonviolent heterosexual activities, and (c) a hardcore film depicting sadomasochism and bestiality. Sexual arousal to all of these three films was assessed by means of heart rate and blood pressure.

On the whole, the study's results clearly demonstrated that repeated exposure to pornography may result in habituation to similar stimuli. Further, this research highlights the importance of the degree of exposure (e.g., massive vs. moderate) and the similarity between stimuli (e.g., hardcore, softcore, or sadomasochistic/ bestiality). It appears that the higher the levels of exposure and the greater the similarity between the exposure and test stimuli, the greater the degree of habituation. (Other important aspects of this experiment are discussed later in this chapter.)

Another experiment that provided some evidence of a habituation effect (Ceniti & Malamuth, 1984) highlighted the importance of individual differences as a mediator of exposure effects. Subjects were first classified on the basis of their penile tumescence to rape and to mutually consenting depictions into one of three groups: force-oriented, nonforce-oriented, or unclassifiable. Those classified as force-oriented had evidenced relatively high levels of sexual arousal to rape depictions as compared to mutually consenting portrayals. Those classified as nonforce-oriented had shown relatively little arousal to rape depictions but had become relatively aroused to mutually consenting portrayals. Subjects labeled as unclassifiable had shown little arousal to either type of depiction. Following this classification, subjects were randomly assigned to one of three exposure groups: sexually violent, sexually nonviolent, or control exposure conditions. Those assigned to the sexually violent condition were exposed to 10 sexually violent stimuli over a period of 4 weeks. These included feature-length films and written and pictorial depictions. Subjects in the sexually nonviolent condition were exposed to 10 similar media presentations depicting sexually nonviolent activities only. Subjects in the control condition were not exposed to any stimuli during this 4-week period. Soon after completion of the exposure phase, subjects returned for a postexposure laboratory session in which they were presented with four depictions that were similar in theme to those in the preexposure session. Penile tumescence scores and self-reports of sexual arousal were obtained.

Results revealed that force-oriented subjects exposed to either sexually violent or nonviolent stimuli were less aroused by the rape depictions in the postexposure session than those in the control condition. A similar pattern occurred with the nonrape depictions for these subjects, though it was considerably less pronounced. No evidence of a similar habituation pattern was obtained for either nonforce-oriented or unclassifiable subjects, with these subjects not showing any significant differences among the three exposure conditions. As noted earlier, these data highlight the importance of individual differences in satiation effects and suggest that such effects may be quite limited when relatively realistic levels of exposure are involved.

Sexual Activities.   Several studies have assessed the impact of exposure to erotic stimuli on heterosexual and autoerotic activities. The methodology consisted of exposing subjects to sexual stimuli and then requesting that they complete a questionnaire about their sexual activities within a given time period. Subjects' reports were then compared with those of a control group that was not exposed to pornography. Some of these studies included a pretest report of sexual activities prior to the exposure phase. Amount of exposure in these studies has varied from one session (e.g., Byrne & Lambert, 1971; Fisher & Byrne, 1978) to several sessions extending over several weeks (e.g., Howard et al., 1971; Mann, Berkowitz, Sidman, Starr, & West, 1974; Mann, Sidman, & Starr, 1970). The effects of exposure have been assessed within 24 hours (e.g., Amorso, Brown, Preusse, Ware, & Pilkey, 1971; Fisher & Byrne, 1978), 1 week later (e.g., Byrne & Lambert, 1971; Mann et al., 1971, 1974), and as long as 2 months after exposure (Howard et al., 1970).

In general, the results of these studies revealed no long-term changes in subjects' established sexual activities (e.g., Ceniti & Malamuth, 1984; Commission on Obscenity and Pornography, 1970; Kutchinsky, 1978). Although a number of studies found that for some subjects there were increases in various sexual activities such as discussions about sex, sexual daydreams, sexual fantasies, masturbation, and intercourse (e.g., Davis & Braucht, 1971; Mann et al., 1971, 1974), these changes generally did not last beyond a 24-hour period. Furthermore, such changes were not found for the majority of subjects. When changes occurred, they were generally in the domain of established sexual behaviors (e.g., when an increase in masturbation or intercourse occurred, it was in subjects who were already engaging in these activities prior to participation in the research). It should be noted, however, that the sexual stimuli used generally portrayed conventional sexual activities such as intercourse and masturbation. Very few studies used nonconventional, deviant, or criminal sexual depictions (e.g., pedophilia, incest, rape, etc.), although these are quite frequently portrayed in the pornography currently available on the market.

An experiment by Fisher and Byrne (1978) indicates that some subjects' sexual activities may be affected by exposure to erotica beyond a very brief period. In this study, male and female undergraduates were first asked to complete a questionnaire inquiring about their sexual behaviors during the preceding 2 days. Then, all subjects were exposed to a pornographic film. They were asked to rate their reactions to this film in terms of sexual, evaluative, and affective responses. On the basis of these reactions, subjects were later classified for the purposes of analysis as erotophobes (those who rated the film as relatively pornographic) or erotophiles (those who rated the film as relatively nonpornographic). At the end of the session, subjects were given a sealed envelope containing the same questionnaire as that completed prior to exposure to the erotic film. They were instructed to open the envelope 2 days later, complete the questionnaire at that time, and mail it back to the experimenters.

The findings indicated that erotophobes showed a significant increase in established sexual activities from pre- to postexposure, whereas erotophiles did not show significant changes. However, a possible methodological problem with this study should be noted. The preexposure reports of sexual activities were gathered in the laboratory, whereas the postexposure data were mailed in. It might be that erotophobes (who in addition to rating the film as pornographic also were found to have relatively negative attitudes toward sex) were more reluctant to report sexual activites when questioned in the lab but were more comfortable in reporting such activities when the questionnaire was completed in the privacy of their homes. Thus, the difference in the settings used for completing the questionnaire may have caused the difference in the sexual activities in the pre-versus postexposure comparison rather than the intervening film. This competing explanation notwithstanding, the importance of individual differences as a crucial dimension for research on the effects of pornography is evident in this study.

Although these research data do not generally reveal lasting changes in sexual responses as a function of exposure to pornography, there have been some clinical reports and research studies on the use of pornography in therapeutic settings that have suggested otherwise. For example, Wishnoff (1978) exposed women with high levels of anxiety about sex to explicit sexual movies. Compared with control groups, such exposure was found to lower sexual anxiety and increase self-reported willingness to engage in sexual behavior under appropriate circumstances. Gillan (1978) and Yaffe (1982) reviewed similar data, as well as findings from studies on the use of pornography to treat male impotence. They concluded that such stimulation therapy may result in considerable improvement for some patients but that other therapeutic interventions are clearly required as well.

In addition to helping in the treatment of individuals who already have sexual problems, it has been suggested that pornography plays an important social role in helping prevent the development of sexual problems. Wilson (1978), former director of research for the commission, points out that there are substantial survey and clinical data to show that close to 50% of North American married couples have significant sexual problems, with about 20% of survey respondents rating their present sex life as unsatisfactory. Moreover, Wilson points out, the principal sources of such dissatisfaction appear to be lack of information, general anxiety about sex, and inability to communicate freely with one's partner about sex. He indicates that some men and women report that exposure to pornography provided them with sex information, reduced their sexual inhibitions, increased their willingness to discuss sex with others, caused them to try "new things," and generally improved their sexual relationship. Therefore, Wilson concludes that pornography may indeed help prevent the development of clinical sexual problems.

Conclusions.   Experiments that have exposed subjects to pornographic materials and examined changes in arousal patterns or sexual activities have not revealed lasting changes. In contrast, there are reports from studies focusing on the use of pornography to prevent and alleviate sexual problems suggesting that exposure to pornography has had long-term effects. Additional research is clearly needed to examine this apparent contradiction and to establish the mediating conditons that may determine the nature and duration of any changes in sexual responses occurring as a function of exposure to erotica.

Social Relations

In this section, we examine the research findings on the effects of pornography on responses associated with social relations. More specifically, we consider the extent to which exposure to erotica may affect perceptions, beliefs, attitudes, and behavior relevant to male–female relations.

Sexually Aggressive Stimuli.   A series of studies examined the impact of exposure to stimuli that fuse sexual and aggressive elements (e.g., Donnerstein, 1980, 1983, 1984; Donnerstein & Berkowitz, 1981; Malamuth & Check, 1980, 1981, 1983, in press; Malamuth, Haber, & Feshbach, 1980). As these studies have been reviewed in detail elsewhere (Donnerstein, 1984; Malamuth, 1984; Malamuth & Donnerstein, 1982), we describe only their general conclusions here. The data across these laboratory and field experiments support the proposition that exposure to stimuli that combine violent and sexual content may increase males' acceptance of violence against women, beliefs in rape myths (e.g., that rape victims derive pleasure from being assaulted), and aggressive behavior as measured by the willingness to deliver unpleasant stimuli (e.g., electric shock) against a woman. Similarly, Linz, Donnerstein, and Penrod (1984) found that exposure to several feature-length, sexually aggressive films resulted not only in desensitization to media portrayals of sexual violence but also to reduced sensitivity to the plight of a rape victim. Taken as a whole, these data clearly show that under certain circumstances exposure to pornographic stimuli that fuse sexual and aggressive elements affects perceptions and behavior in socially undesirable directions. In addition, the data suggest that the message about male–female relations and/or aggression is the critical dimension that determines whether negative effects occur rather than sexual explicitness per se. However, these findings also indicate that there may be particularly potent effects of the combination of sexual and aggressive elements that exceed those found when aggressive stimuli appear in a nonsexual context (e.g., Donnerstein & Berkowitz, 1981).

Nonaggressive Sexual Stimuli.   As Steinem (1980) suggests, sexually explicit stimuli that do not depict blatant aggression may nonetheless vary a great deal in their content vis-à-vis the messages portrayed regarding males and females and the relations between the two genders. It is this variability in content that may partially explain the contrasting findings obtained with nonaggressive sexual stimuli. Other factors such as the hedonic valence and arousal levels stimulated may also need to be considered (see Zillmann, 1984, for a thorough discussion of the importance of these dimensions). On the one hand, data suggest that various types of sexually explicit stimuli, such as those depicting males and females in relations that involve equal power, mutual respect, and/or loving relations, do not increase antisocial responses (e.g., Commission on Obscenity and Pornography, 1970) and may even reduce them (e.g., Baron & Bell, 1977; Malamuth, 1978). On the other hand, a very different effect is evident in the research of Zillmann and Bryant (1984).

As described earlier, this research included four exposure conditions: massive pornography exposure, moderate pornography exposure, no pornography exposure (but exposure to neutral stimuli), or no prior exposure at all. Three weeks following the conclusion of the exposure phase of the research, subjects returned to the laboratory for a final session. At that time, they estimated the frequency of various sexual practices among adults, reported their beliefs about the necessity for regulating pornography, reported the degree of their support for the women's liberation movement, and recommended punishment in a mock-jury rape case. Males were also administered a scale assessing sexual callousness toward women. Results showed that exposure to massive and moderate amounts of pornography significantly increased males' and females' perceptions of the popularity of various sexual practices in society, including unusual sexual behavior such as sado-masochism and bestiality. In addition, exposure to pornography increased approval and support for such practices by both genders. Exposure also significantly affected reactions to rape. For example, massively exposed subjects prescribed far less severe punishment for this crime than control subjects. Further, exposure to pornography was found to reduce support for the women's liberation movement. Finally, males exposed to massive amounts of pornography exhibited greater callousness toward women than males in the control group.

How can these findings be explained? Zillmann and Bryant (1984) point out that the pornography used in their research depicts women as socially nondiscriminating, as hysterically euphoric in response to just about any sexual or pseudosexual stimulation, and eager to accommodate seemingly any and every sexual request. Such portrayals, they suggest, may convince even females of the hyperpromiscuous, accepting nature of women. This view may affect the credibility of the rape victim. In general, the authors suggest that "massive exposure to pornography appears to contribute to beliefs about sexual desire and sexual conduct that are not conducive to respect for the opposite (or the same) sex" (pp. 134–135).

Zillmann and Bryant's data are important in at least two respects. First, they suggest that some of the antisocial effects documented with sexually aggressive media stimuli (e.g., Malamuth & Check, 1980, 1981) may also occur with stimuli that do not directly focus on sexual coercion or violence. Second, the importance of cumulative effects that may not be detected with single media exposures is clearly highlighted by the longitudinal nature of this study.

Conclusions. The findings show that pornographic media stimuli may affect varied responses relevant to social relations. These data by no means indicate that such effects are limited to sexually explicit materials; similar effects may occur with stimuli that are not sexually explicit. However, considerable data clearly reveal that exposure to sexually violent media affects perceptions, attitudes, and beliefs in a manner that may contribute to a cultural climate that is more accepting of actual violence against women. Moreover, the data suggest that exposure to violent pornography may increase males' aggression in the laboratory. Considerable caution must be exercised, however, in generalizing directly from such aggression to violence in nonlaboratory settings.

Recent data suggest that some of the negative effects of exposure to certain types of pornography (e.g., trivialization of rape) may not be limited to stimuli that are clearly violent but may also occur with nonviolent erotic portrayals such as those portraying women as insatiable, nondiscriminating sexual creatures. It is also apparent that exposure to various forms of sexually explicit stimuli, such as those portraying men and women in roles that involve equal power, mutual respect, and loving relationships, does not increase antisocial responses and may indeed reduce them.

Criminal Behavior

In a national survey of American adults, Abelson, Cohen, Heaton, and Sluder (1970) found that close to half of the respondents believed that pornography is one of the causes of rape. To examine this possibility with empirical research, we consider two types of approaches: (a) correlational studies assessing a possible relationship between the availability and/or consumption of pornography in differing areas and the rates of sex crimes[2] in these places and (b) retrospective studies comparing rapists' and control groups' exposure to pornography. For a discussion of the limitations of such methods, the reader is referred to Nelson (1982) and Court (1984).

Before evaluating the research, we would like to point out that in examining the possible relationship between pornography consumption and crime, the focus is on deviant behavior, that is, behavior that is not socially sanctioned. To the extent that pornography may be a manifestation of beliefs and "scripts" portraying a widely accepted cultural ideology, effects may be more likely in culturally sanctioned behaviors than in deviant responses (e.g., if pornography portrays an

---

[2]The use of the term *sex crimes* to refer to violent acts such as rape may be inappropriate due to the implication that such crimes are primarily motivated by sexual needs. However, due to the extensive use of this phrase in the relevant literature, it is also employed herein.

ideology of male dominance over women, effects may occur in culturally accepted expressions of such an ideology rather than in criminal behavior).

Sex Crimes.   Studies examining a possible relationship between the consumption of pornography and sex crimes have generally used one of two approaches. One has been to assess whether changes in the availability of pornography were associated with corresponding changes in the rate of sex crimes. The second approach has been to compare different countries and/or states to determine whether there is a correlation between the amount of pornography consumed and the rate of sex crimes. Some studies used a combination of these two approaches (e.g., Court, 1984).

As part of the research of the commission, a number of studies analyzed the relation between changes in laws regulating the availability of pornography and the frequency of sex crimes. Some of these studies focused on Denmark. In the 1960s, the Danish government gradually relaxed restrictions on the sale of pornography and eliminated all restrictions on sales of pornographic books in 1967 and on all other erotic media in 1969. Using Copenhagen police statistics, investigators (e.g., Ben-Veniste, 1970; Kutchinsky, 1973) reported a reduction in the number of sex offenses occurring at the time restrictions on pornography were lifted. Closer examination of the data suggested that these reductions reflected real decreases in some sex crimes such as voyeurism, but in other crimes, the changes appear to be best explained by society's increasing tolerance for sexual activities such as homosexuality (Kutchinsky, 1973; Court, 1984). It is clear, however, that there was no reduction in the occurrence of rape. Conflicting data have been reported, with some studies suggesting no change in rape rates following the liberalization of pornography laws, whereas other studies indicate some minor increases in this violent crime (Bachy, 1976; Court, 1984; Kutchinsky, 1978).

In an analysis of sex crimes in the United States, Kupperstein and Wilson (1970) examined the FBI Uniform Crime Statistics from 1960 and 1969 and found an increase in that time period both in the availability of pornography and sex crimes. Although these data appear to show a correlational link, the investigators found that the rise in sex offenses did not exceed the proportional rise in other crimes. Kupperstein and Wilson (1970) concluded that "for the moment, the question of the relationship between availability of erotic materials and sex crimes must remain open to further question" (p. 32).

In an analysis of the availability of pornography throughout the world, Court (1984) concludes that there is evidence to suggest that certain types of pornography, particularly violent pornography, contribute to the occurrence of sex crimes. A note of caution must be raised regarding this research, however, because the selection of varied countries and/or states was not random and may reflect selection of individual examples that may or may not be representative. Further, although the data do appear to offer some correlation between the availability of pornography and sex crimes, there does not seem to be a sufficient basis to conclude with confidence that a causal connection exists.

A study that examined all states in the United States was reported by Baron and Straus (1984), who analyzed whether there was a relationship between rates of rape and the extent to which sex magazines are part of the popular culture of each state (i.e., magazine sales). They found that there was a strong correlation between the popularity of pornography magazines and the incidence of rape. In contrast, a much weaker correlation was obtained between sex magazine consumption and general rates of nonsexual violent crime. The correlation between pornographic magazine consumption and rape rates remained statistically significant even following the partialing out of the potential contribution of various control variables. These investigators appropriately caution that such a correlation is suggestive but not a sufficient basis for establishing a causal connection.

Although various sources of data suggest that there may be some correlation between the consumption of pornography and the incidence of violent sexual crimes, there are also examples of countries where the rate of consumption of pornography in general, as well as violent pornography in particular, is high but the incidence of rape is relatively low. Earlier in this chapter we referred to the work of Abramson and Hayashi (1984) who note the high rate of sexual violence in the Japanese media. These writers also point out that Japan has a relatively low incidence of reported rape. They suggest that a combination of factors, including the existence of strong internal constraints (e.g., an emphasis from early childhood on not committing shameful acts), results in the low frequency of rape.

The research of Abramson and Hayashi as well as examples from countries such as Denmark should alert us to the fact that any causal connection between the availability of pornography and antisocial behavior, if one indeed exists, is bound to be a complex relationship mediated by many other factors. Considerable variability may exist in susceptibility to the influences of media stimuli such as violent pornography both among cultures and among individuals within a culture (Malamuth & Check, in press). Moreover, if certain media messages within pornography have an antisocial impact, the expression of such influences may be strongly affected by cultural norms. For example, there may be a low rate of violence within Japan, but it is a culture that appears to have a high degree of inequality between the genders and a history of considerable violence against other societies. Although pornography is not likely to have been a major cause of such patterns, it may be conjectured that the violent nature of Japanese pornography may reflect and perpetuate sexism and other behaviors despite effective constraints against actually committing violent acts prohibited by culture.

Conclusions.   Both within the United States and in comparing a number of other countries, a positive correlation has been found between greater availability and/or consumption of pornography and higher rates of rape. These data are clearly insufficient to infer any direct causal connection between these variables. In addition, there are examples of certain countries that have relatively high levels of available pornograpy and relatively low rape rates. It is also clear that in certain countries (e.g., Denmark) the liberalization of pornography laws did not result in a massive increase in the occurrence of rape, although it is also apparent that contrary to widely publicized views there was no decrease in such crimes. Nonetheless, the positive correlation points to the need for further research addressing the hypothesis that there may be some complex causal relationship between the availability of pornography and the committing of antisocial acts by some people, within some cultural environments.

Rapists and Pornography Exposure.   A number of retrospective studies using survey-interview methods have sought to determine whether exposure to pornography may be related to deviant behavior. The general approach has been to examine whether there are differences in the amount of exposure to pornography by rapists and various groups of sex deviants in comparison to control samples. Methodological criticisms of these studies are discussed in Cline (1975) and Lederer (1980). Here we also consider the possibility that focusing on amount of exposure may be oversimplistic.

The findings of these studies (e.g., Cook & Fosen, 1970; Davis & Braucht, 1973; Goldstein et al., 1973; Propper, 1970; Walker, 1970) have been inconsistent. Some suggest that pornography exposure may indeed have contributed to the development of antisocial and deviant behaviors, whereas others find no support for this conclusion. Indeed, some of the latter studies suggest that rapists were exposed to less pornography than control comparison groups. Rather than discussing the many differences among these varied studies, we focus in greater detail on one, the research of Goldstein et al. (1973). Methodologically, this study appears to be one of the best in this area; it is frequently cited as providing no support for the hypothesis that pornography exposure may contribute to antisocial behavior.

The findings of Goldstein et al. (1973) indicate that in general rapists reported less exposure to pornography in adolescence than the control comparison groups. However, various aspects of these data appear to indicate that the type of pornography rapists were exposed to and the degree to which they were affected by it may have differed. For example, rapists reported an earlier age of peak experience with pornography. In addition, they were far more likely to have encountered pornographic photos displaying explicit sexual acts (rather than nudes) at an early age and to have had greater desire to imitate the activity portrayed in pornography (although they were less likely to have actually done it). Rapists were more likely to relate daily masturbation to thoughts of erotica, to have developed a stronger interest in pornography early in life, to have become repeatedly aroused by a particular theme, and to have more feelings of frustration and guilt related to their pornography exposure than control subjects.

Although Goldstein et al. (1973) did not specifically inquire about pornography involving coercive sex themes, it is clear from their interviews that media depictions involving sexual violence (e.g., motorcycle films depicting "gang bangs") frequently became part of rapists' daydreams and fantasies. In addition, they report that 55% of the rapists (as compared to 9% of the controls) used scenes from pornography in their fantasies and daydreams. In light of the content analyses reported earlier, which reveal an increasing degree of sexual violence within erotic stimuli, it seems likely that such depictions would affect rapists' sexual fantasies and daydreams. It may be relevant to note at this point that programs for treating rapists (e.g., Abel, Blanchard, & Becker, 1976, 1978; Brownell, Hayes, & Barlow, 1977) place considerable emphasis on changing their sexually violent fantasies in modifying their antisocial behavior. This suggests that if media depictions including violent pornography stimulate violent fantasies (Malamuth, 1981), then for some individuals such fantasies may affect behavior. Further, the data of Schaefer and Colgan (1977) may be relevant here. This research pointed to the possible importance of masturbation as increasing the likelihood of long-term effects of pornography (see also McGuire, Carlisle, & Young, 1965, on masturbatory conditioning). These data may be relevant to rapists' more frequent use of pornography during masturbation.

How can we account for the data suggesting that rapists had less exposure to pornography in childhood but were affected by it more? This and other studies suggest that rapists were more likely to come from home environments where education about sexuality was highly restricted and sex was generally treated as a taboo subject. (The relatively minimal exposure to erotica may have been a byproduct of this taboo attitude.) With such a background, it might be expected that exposure to pornography would exert a relatively more powerful influence on rapists' responses because it would be a primary source of information and stimulation. Consistent with this view are the data of Fisher and Byrne (1978) suggesting that individuals with a history of restrictive sexual socialization reacted more negatively to pornography but at the same time were more behaviorally affected by it.

Conclusions. The data in this area are limited and vulnerable to varied methodological criticisms, but some findings indicate that rapists had less exposure to pornography than controls, although their early exposure may have involved more hardcore material than that of control subjects. Further, the data suggest that rapists were more likely to have been strongly affected by their exposure to pornography than were controls. We speculate that rapists' relatively restrictive sexual socialization and education may have made them more likely to be affected by pornography. To the extent that pornography does present a certain ideology about male–female relations, it might be theorized that rapists' ideas about sexuality and heterosexual relations may indeed have been significantly affected by exposure to pornography. Had they had other sources of education about sexuality and male–female relations in their childhood, they might have been less likely to have been as strongly affected by pornography exposure.

CONCLUDING COMMENTS

Our review of the research literature suggests that the sexual communications model of pornography may be overly limited in its scope. The data indeed are consistent with the view that erotic materials play diverse roles relevant to sexuality, such as expressions of sexual needs and ideas, enhancement of sexual arousal, and even therapeutic aid. However, content analytic data, findings from experimental studies focusing on social relations, and correlational research assessing the relation between pornography consumption and violence against women provide some support for the feminist model in its call for greater attention to the ideological/political messages communicated by sexually explicit materials. Particularly relevant messages for future research to investigate systematically are those regarding the nature of women and men, their roles, and relations.

We began this chapter by noting the surprising paucity of social scientific research on pornography, despite the tremendous size of this mass media industry. Our review of the existing research literature points to some progress but clearly highlights the compelling need for much more systematic, programmatic research. In an area where strong personal opinions abound, researchers using the tools of social science have a potentially important role to play in proceeding beyond the level of opinions to the realm of data that are open to challenge and/or replication by other investigators' research.

REFERENCES

Abel, G. G., Blanchard, E. B., & Becker, J. V. (1976). Psychological treatment of rapists. In M. Walker & S. Brodsky (Eds.), *Sexual assault: The victim and the rapist* (pp. 99–115). Lexington, MA: Lexington Books.

Abel, G. G., Blanchard, E. B., & Becker, J. V. (1978). An integrated treatment program for rapists. In R. Rada (Ed.), *Clinical aspects of the rapist* (pp. 161–214). New York: Grune & Stratton.

Abelson, H., Cohen, R., Heaton, E., & Suder, C. (1970). *Public attitudes toward and experience with erotic materials* (Technical Reports of the Commission on Obscenity and Pornography, Vol. 6, pp. 1–137). Washington, DC: U.S. Government Printing Office.

Abramson, P. & Hayashi, H. (1984). Pornography in Japan: Cross-cultural and theoretical considerations. In N. M. Malamuth & E. Donnerstein (Eds.), *Pornography and sexual aggression* (pp. 173–183). New York: Academic Press.

Amorso, D. M., Brown, M., Preusse, M., Ware, E. E., & Pilkey, D. W. (1971). *An investigation of behavioral, psychological and physiological reactions to pornographic stimuli* (Technical Reports of the Commission on Obscenity and Pornography, Vol. 8, pp. 1–40). Washington, DC: U.S. Government Printing Office.

Bachy, V. (1976). Danish "permissiveness" revisited. *Journal of Communication, 26,* 40–43.

Baron, L., & Straus, M. A. (1984). Sexual stratification, pornography and rape. In N. M. Malamuth & E. Donnerstein (Eds.), *Pornography and sexual aggression* (pp. 185–209). New York: Academic Press.

Baron, R. A., & Bell, P. A. (1977). Sexual arousal and aggression by males: Effects of type of erotic stimuli and prior provocation. *Journal of Personality and Social Psychology, 35,* 79–87.

Ben-Veniste, R. (1971). *Pornography and sex crime—The Danish experience* (Technical Reports of the Commission on Obscenity and Pornography, Vol. 7, pp. 245–261). Washington, DC: U.S. Government Printing Office.

Blackstone, P. (1984). *Pornography and prostitution.* Unpublished manuscript, Victoria, British Columbia, Canada.

Brown, J. A. (1963). *Techniques of persuasion.* New York: Penguin Books.

Brownell, K. D., Hayes, S. C., & Barlow, D. H. (1977). Patterns of appropriate and deviant sexual arousal: The behavioral treatment of multiple sexual deviations. *Journal of Consulting and Clinical Psychology, 45,* 1144–1155.

Brownmiller, S. (1975). *Against our will: Men, women and rape.* New York: Simon & Schuster.

Brownmiller, S. (1984). *Femininity.* New York: Simon & Schuster.

Byrne D., & Lambert J. (1971). *The effects of erotic stimuli on sexual arousal, evaluative responses, and subsequent behavior* (Technical Reports of the Commission on Obscenity and Pornography, Vol. 8, pp. 41–67). Washington, DC: U.S. Government Printing Office.

Casalis, M. (1975). The discourse of *Penthouse*: Rhetoric and ideology. *Semiotica, 15,* 355–391.

Ceniti, J., & Malamuth, N. M. (1984). Effects of repeated exposure to sexually violent and nonviolent stimuli on sexual arousal to rape and nonrape depictions. *Behaviour Research and Therapy, 22,* 535–548.

Charney, M. (1981). *Sexual fiction.* New York: Methuen.

Cline, W. B. (1975). *Where do you draw the line? An exploration into media violence, pornography, and censorship.* Provo, UT: Brigham Young University Press.

Commission on Obscenity and Pornography. (1970). *Report of the Commission on Obscenity and Pornography.* New York: Random House.

Cook, R. F., & Fosen, F. H. (1971). *Pornography and the sex offender: Patterns of exposure and immediate arousal effects of pornographic stimuli* (Technical Reports of the Commission on Obscenity and Pornography, Vol. 7, pp. 149–162). Washington, DC: U.S. Government Printing Office.

Court, J. (1984). Sex and violence: A ripple effect. In N. M. Malamuth & E. Donnerstein (Eds.), *Pornography and sexual aggression* (pp. 143–172). New York: Academic.

Davis, K. E., & Braucht, G. N. (1971). *Exposure to pornography, character and sexual deviance: A retrospective survey* (Technical Reports of the Commission on Obscenity and Pornography, Vol. 7, pp. 173–243). Washington, DC: U.S. Government Printing Office.

Dietz, P. E., & Evans, B. (1982). Pornographic imagery and prevalence of paraphilia. *American Journal of Psychiatry, 139,* 1493–1495.

Donnerstein, E. (1980). Aggressive-erotica and violence against women. *Journal of Personality and Social Psychology, 39,* 269–277.

Donnerstein, E. (1983). Erotica and human aggression. In R. Geen & E. Donnerstein (Eds.), *Aggression: Theoretical and empirical reviews* (Vol. 2, pp. 127–154). New York: Academic.

Donnerstein, E. (1984). Pornography: Its effects on violence against women. In N. M. Malamuth & E. Donnerstein (Eds.), *Pornography and sexual aggression* (pp. 53–81). New York: Academic.

Donnerstein, E., & Berkowitz, L. (1981). Victim reactions in aggressive-erotic films as a factor in violence against women. *Journal of Personality and Social Psychology, 41,* 710–724.

Dworkin, A. (1981). *Pornography: Men possessing women.* New York: Putnam.

Ellis, H. (1936). *Studies in the psychology of sex* (Vol. II). New York: Random House.

Falwell, J. (1980). *Listen America.* Garden City, NY: Doubleday.

Fisher, W. A., & Byrne, D. (1978). Individual differences in affective, evaluative, and behavioral responses to an erotic film. *Journal of Applied Social Psychology, 8*, 355–365.

Foxon, D. (1965). *Libertine literature in England 1600–1745*. New Hyde Park, NY: University Books.

Gager, N., & Schurr, C. (1976). *Sexual assault: Confronting rape in America*. New York: Grosset & Dunlap.

Gagnon, J. H. (1977). *Human sexualities*. Glenview, IL: Scott, Foresman.

Gillan, P. (1978). Therapeutic uses of obscenity. In R. Dhavan & D. Davies (Eds.), *Censorship and obscenity* (pp. 127–147). Totowa, NJ: Rowman & Littlefield.

Goldstein, M. J., Kant, H. S., & Hartmann, J. J. (1973). *Pornography and sexual deviance*. Los Angeles: University of California Press.

Goldstein, M. J., Kant, H. S., Judd, L. L., Rice, C. J., & Green, R. (1970). *Exposure to pornography and sexual behavior in deviant and normal groups* (Technical Reports of the Commission on Obscenity and Pornography, Vol. 7, pp. 1–89). Washington, DC: U.S. Government Printing Office.

Gordon, G. (1980). *Erotic communications: Studies in sex, sin and censorship*. New York: Hastings House.

Gould, L. (1977). Pornography for women. In J. H. Gagmen (Ed.), *Human sexuality in today's world*. Boston: Little Brown.

Griffin, S. (1981). *Pornography and silence: Culture's revenge against nature*. New York: Harper & Row.

Howard, J. L., Reifler, C. B., & Liptzin, M. B. (1971). *Effects of exposure to pornography* (Technical Reports of the Commission on Obscenity and Pornography, Vol. 8, pp. 97–132). Washington, DC: U.S. Government Printing Office.

Johnson, W. T., Kupperstein, L., & Peters, J. (1971). *Sex offenders' experience with erotica* (Technical Reports of the Commission on Obscenity and Pornography, Vol. 7, pp. 163–171). Washington, DC: U.S. Government Printing Office.

Kronhausen, E., & Kronhausen, P. (1961). The psychology of pornography. In A. Ellis & A. Arbarbanel (Eds.), *The encyclopedia of sexual behavior* (pp. 848–859). New York: Hawthorn.

Kronhausen, P., & Kronhausen, E. (1978). *The complete book of erotic art* (Vol. 2). New York: Bell.

Kunzle, D. (1972). The corset as erotic alchemy: From Rocco Galanterie to Montaut's Physiologies. In T. B. Hess & L. Nochlin (Eds.), *Women as sex object: Studies in erotic art, 1730–1970* (pp. 91–165). New York: Newsweek.

Kupperstein, L., & Wilson, W. C. (1971). *Erotica and anti-social behavior: An analysis of selected social indicator statistics* (Technical Reports of the Commission on Obscenity and Pornography, Vol. 7, pp. 311–323). Washington, DC: U.S. Government Printing Office.

Kutchinsky, B. (1971). *Towards an explanation of the decrease in sex crimes and pornography in Copenhagen: A survey of attitudes* (Technical Reports of the Commission on Obscenity and Pornography, Vol. 7, pp. 263–310). Washington, DC: U.S. Government Printing Office.

Kutchinsky, B. (1973). Eroticism without censorship: Sociological investigations on the production and consumption of pornographic literature in Denmark. *International Journal of Criminology and Penology, 1*, 217–225.

Kutchinsky, B. (1978). Pornography in Denmark—A general survey. In R. Dhavan & C. Davies (Eds.), *Censorship and obscenity* (pp. 111–126). London: Martin Robertson.

LaBelle, B. (1980). The propaganda of misogyny. In L. Lederer (Ed.), *Take back the night: Women on pornography* (pp. 174–178). New York: William Morrow.

Lederer, L. (Ed.). (1980). *Take back the night: Women on pornography*. New York: William Morrow.

Levy, H. S. (1966). *Chinese footbinding: The history of a curious erotic custom*. New York: Walton Rawls.

Lewisohn, R. (1956). *A history of sexual customers*. New York: Bell.

Linz, D., Donnerstein, E., & Penrod, S. (1984). The effects of long term exposure to filmed violence against women. *Journal of Communication, 34,* 130–147.

Longford Committee. (1972). *Pornography: The Longford Report.* London: Coronet Books.

Longino, H. E. (1980) Pornography, oppression and freedom: A closer look. In L. Lederer (Ed.), *Take back the night: Women on pornography* (pp. 40–54). New York: William Morrow.

Malamuth, N. M. (1978). *Erotica, aggression, and perceived appropriateness.* Paper presented at the annual convention of the American Psychological Association, Toronto.

Malamuth, N. M. (1981). Rape fantasies as a function of exposure to violent-sexual stimuli. *Archives of Sexual Behavior, 10,* 33–47.

Malamuth, N. M. (1984). Aggression against women: Cultural and individual causes. In N. M. Malamuth & E. Donnerstein (Eds.), *Pornography and sexual aggression* (pp. 19–52). New York: Academic Press.

Malamuth, N. M., & Billings, V. (1984). Why pornography? Models of functions and effects. *Journal of Communication, 34,* 117–129.

Malamuth, N. M., & Check, J. V. P. (1980). Penile tumescence and perceptual responses to rape as a function of victim's perceived reactions. *Journal of Applied Social Psychology, 10,* 528–547.

Malamuth, N. M., & Check, J. V. P. (1981). The effects of mass media exposure on acceptance of violence against women: A field experiment. *Journal of Research in Personality, 15,* 436–446.

Malamuth, N. M., & Check, J. V. P. (1983). Sexual arousal to rape depictions: Individual differences. *Journal of Abnormal Psychology, 92,* 55–67.

Malamuth, N. M., & Check, J. V. P. (in press). Effects of aggressive-pornography on beliefs in rape myths: Individual differences. *Journal of Research in Personality.*

Malamuth, N. M., & Donnerstein, E. (1982). Effects of aggressive-pornographic mass media stimuli. In L. Berkowitz (Ed.), *Advances in experimental social psychology* (Vol. 15, pp. 103–136). New York: Academic.

Malamuth, N. M., Haber, S. & Feshbach, S. (1980). Testing hypotheses regarding rape: Exposure to sexual violence, sex differences, and the "normality" of rapists. *Journal of Research in Personality, 14,* 127–137.

Malamuth, N. M., & Spinner, B. (1980). A longitudinal content analysis of sexual violence in the best-selling erotic magazines. *The Journal of Sex Research, 16,* 226–237.

Mann, J., Berkowitz, L., Sidman, J., Starr, S., & West, S. (1974). Satiation of the transient stimulating effects of erotic films. *Journal of Personality and Social Psychology, 30,* 729–735.

Mann, J., Sidman, J., & Starr, S. (1971). *Effects of erotic films on sexual behaviors of married couples* (Technical Reports of the Commission on Obscenity and Pornography, Vol. 8, pp. 170–254). Washington, DC: U.S. Government Printing Office.

Masters, R. E. L., & Lea, E. (1964). *The anti-sex: The belief in the natural inferiority of women; studies in male frustration and sexual conflict.* New York: Julian Press.

McGuire, R. J., Carlisle, J. M., & Young, B. G. (1965). Sexual deviations as conditioned behavior: A hypothesis. *Behaviour Research and Therapy, 2,* 185–190.

Michelson, P. (1971). *The aesthetics of pornography.* New York: Herder & Herder.

Morgan, R. (1980). Theory and practice: Pornography and rape. In L. Lederer (Ed.), *Take back the night: Women on pornography* (pp. 134–140). New York: William Morrow.

Nelson, E. C. (1982). Pornography and sexual aggression. In M. Yaffe & E. C. Nelson (Eds.), *The influence of pornography on behaviour* (pp. 170–248). London: Academic.

Phillips, J. (1984). *The history of an idea: Eve.* San Francisco: Harper & Row.

Propper, M. M. (1971). *Exposure to sexually oriented materials among young male prison offenders* (Technical Reports of the Commission on Obscenity and Pornography, Vol. 9, pp. 313–404). Washington, DC: U.S. Government Printing Office.

Rush, R. (1980). Child pornography. In L. Lederer (Ed.), *Take back the night: Women on pornography* (pp. 71–81). New York: William Morrow.

Russell, D. E. H. (1980). Pornography and violence: What does the new research say? In L. Lederer (Ed.), *Take back the night: Women on pornography* (pp. 218–238). New York: William Morrow.

Schaefer, H. H., & Colgan, A. H. (1977). The effect of pornography on penile tumescence as a function of reinforcement and novelty. *Behavior Therapy, 8,* 938–946.

Shepher, J., & Reisman, J. (in press). Pornography: A sociobiological attempt at understanding. *Ethology and Sociobiology.*

Smith, B. (1983). *Erotic art of the masters: The 18th, 19th and 20th centuries.* New York: Galley.

Smith, D. D. (1976a). *Sexual aggression in American pornography: The stereotype of rape.* Paper presented at the annual meeting of the American Sociological Association, New York.

Smith, D. D. (1976b). The social content of pornography. *Journal of Communication, 26,* 16–33.

Sonenschein, D. (1969). Pornography: A false issue. *Psychiatric Opinion, 6,* 11–18.

Steiner, G. (1970). Night words. In D. A. Hughes (Ed.), *Perspectives on pornography* (pp. 240–250). New York: St. Martin's Press.

Steinem, G. (1980). Erotica and pornography: A clear and present difference. In L. Lederer (Ed.), *Take back the night: Women on pornography* (pp. 35–39). New York: William Morrow.

Stone, L. (1977). *The family, sex and marriage in England 1500–1800.* London: Weidenfeld & Nicolson.

Target Group Index. (1974). New York: Axiom Market Research Bureau.

Target Group Index. (1978). New York: Axiom Market Research Bureau.

Thompson, R. (1979). *Unfit for modest ears: A study of pornographic, obscene and bawdy works written or published in England in the second half of the seventeenth century.* London: Macmillan.

Walker, E. C. (1971). *Erotic stimuli and the aggressive sexual offender* (Technical Reports of the Commission on Obscenity and Pornography, Vol. 7, pp. 91–147). Washington, DC: U.S. Government Printing Office.

Wilson, W. C. (1978). Can pornography contribute to the prevention of sexual problems? In C. B. Qualls, J. P. Wincze, & D. H. Barlow (Eds.), *The prevention of sexual disorders: Issues and approaches.* New York: Plenum.

Wishnoff, R. (1978). Modeling effects of explicit and nonexplicit sexual stimuli on the sexual anxiety and behavior of women. *Archives of Sexual Behavior, 7,* 455–461.

Yaffe, M. (1982). Therapeutic uses of sexually explicit material. In M. Yaffe & E. C. Nelson (Eds.), *The influence of pornography on behaviour* (pp. 119–150). London: Academic.

Zillmann D. (1984). *Connections between sex and aggression.* Hillsdale, NJ: Lawrence Erlbaum Associates.

Zillmann, D., & Bryant, J. (1984). Effects of massive exposure to pornography. In N. M. Malamuth & E. Donnerstein (Eds.), *Pornography and sexual aggression* (pp. 115–138). New York: Academic.

6 Television Addiction

Robin Smith
University of Minnesota

TELEVISION ADDICTION
IN THE SCIENTIFIC LITERATURE

Until recently, most research on television has been concerned with the effects of particular content on behavior. The effects of viewing television per se have rarely been addressed. Yet concerns about such effects constitute a widespread and growing portion of the popular literature on television.

A look at the scientific literature reveals many interesting hypotheses about the nature and causes of television addiction, but few hard facts. The review that follows is organized around several persistent themes in the scientific literature on television addiction: (a) TV addiction is a form of escape to a fantasy world that is pathological in nature; (b) TV addicts use television to reduce stress; (c) the personal relationships of TV addicts are disturbed; (d) middle-class viewers are more susceptible to TV addiction; and (e) TV addicts become addicted because of television's sensory arousal potential.

These themes cut across two historical phases of television research. In the 1950s, when television use became widespread, there was much concern about the effects of the viewing experience, including its potentially addictive power. Several classic studies (e.g., Himmelweit, Oppenheim, & Vince, 1958; Schramm, Lyle, & Parker, 1961) addressed these issues, particularly the question of "displacement" of other activities, such as reading and family interaction, by television. Although some observations by these investigators led them to posit the existence of a television addiction syndrome, there were no systematic attempts to define and study it. In the 1960s, attention turned to the content of television programs, especially violence, and the issue of addiction to the medium dropped out of the literature. The 1970s saw a revival of interest in the issue of the effects of the medium per se and an increase in discussions of television addiction. However, although our conceptual and methodological research tools are much more sophisticated than those of the early days of television research, the level of discussion remains speculative, and uninformed opinion abounds. At the same time, parents and educators are increasingly turning to behavioral scientists for answers to their questions about the potentially addictive effects of television. What follows is a review of what scientists have to offer at the present time.

Escape Theories.   Many mental health professionals have assumed that television addiction is an avoidance pattern that interferes with mechanisms for problem-solving (Barragan, 1976). For example, Meerlo (1954) reported a case of television addiction and reactive apathy. In this report, the girl is said to have become addicted to television and become unable, until treated, to distinguish between the world of television fantasy and the real world.

Another psychiatrist (Glynn, 1956) described the following case:

> A 24-year-old musician, daughter of an adoring, constantly present, constantly acting mother, quarrels with her parents and gives up her own quite busy professional life. She turns to the television set, and soon is spending 10 or 12 hours a day watching it, constantly sitting before it, transfixed, drinking beer or eating ice cream, lost and desperate if the set is turned off. Making a joke one day, she said, "Boy, I don't know what I would do for a mother if that tube ever burned out." This girl, of real intellectual attainment, was completely indifferent as to what the programs actually were. (p. 178)

Children are represented in the following statement:

> It is undoubtedly true that television addicts exist, and among children who are psychologically disturbed in a serious way . . . The child who becomes addicted to the excitement of televison is usually one who is not well-grounded in reality and not able to make a clear distinction between the real and fantasy world . . . The child who becomes addicted to the dream world of television is usually schizoid or suffering from very unsatisfactory personal relations, at home or with the peer group or both. (Schramm et al., 1961, p. 167–168)

Stress-Reduction Theories.   Several investigators have suggested that television addiction may be the result of overuse of television viewing as a stress-reduction technique. Singer (1980) proposed that "if TV has a potential addictive power, it arises from the fact that it reduces negative affect by substituting somebody else's thoughts for your own thus minimizing painful private rehearsals of one's own problems" (p. 49). Zillmann, Hezel, and Medoff (1983) provide evidence consistent with the notion that people select programs that hold the greatest promise of relief from negative affective states.

Television viewing is frequently mentioned as a coping mechanism for dealing with stress in everyday life (Greenberg, 1974; Murray & Kippax, 1979; Schramm et al., 1961). The statements of self-designated addicts also tend to emphasize the "escapist" function of television. Yet only Pearlin (1959) has attempted to examine the relationship between "escapist viewing" and stress, and he found a significant relationship between them in a questionnaire study. However, his measures of both these variables reflect the lack of methodological sophistication in the research on television in the 1950s. For example, stress was determined by answers to four questions indexing "aspiration frustration," "blind faith in people," and "feelings of despair." Today more comprehensive and standardized scales are available which measure stress as a function of life events found to predict the onset of a wide range of disorders, from depression (Rahe, 1979) to drug dependence (Duncan, 1976). With an adequate definition of television addiction, it should be possible to directly investigate the role of stress in compulsive television viewing.

Social Maladjustment Theories.   Investigators have also speculated that the television addict suffers from unsatisfactory personal relationships (Freedman, 1961; Schramm et al., 1961). Some evidence for this is found in reports that heavy viewing by children is related to conflict with parents (Schramm et al., 1961) and to difficulty in making friends (Himmelweit et al., 1958; Schramm & Roberts, 1971). Murray (1972) found that, among 5- and 6-year-old males in inner-city homes, very heavy viewers were most likely to have problems of social adjustment, to be interpersonally passive, less persistent, and shyer.

It seems important at this point to clarify a distinction between amount of viewing and addiction to television. For some investigators, heavy viewing is synonymous with addiction to television. For example, Himmelweit et al., (1958) designated as "addicts" the one third of each age group in their study that spent the longest time viewing. No estimates of the actual number of hours of viewing per week were reported for this group, although it was stated that on weekdays heavy viewers watched television for half the time available between the end of school and going to bed.

Given the complexity of the descriptions of television addiction, this definition seems too simplistic. In addition, people may be addicted but actually watch a relatively normal amount of television due to constraints on their time. In fact, Himmelweit et al. intensively interviewed a small sample of subjects and found one or two who were heavy viewers because they had just moved into a new neighborhood and had not yet made friends. One or two others felt they did not have enough outlets for their energy. Heavy viewing per se may be a consequence of lack of behavioral options in the environment and not necessarily a good indicator of television addiction.

Social Class Theories.   The social class hypothesis is based on evidence for the operation of a middle-class taboo against television viewing. For example, Edgar (1977) surveyed 298 Australian families who never owned a television set or who had gotten rid of one. He found that this group was characterized by a higher socioeconomic status and educational level than the general population. The chief reasons cited for not owning a television were that "it is addictive" and that television constituted a threat to family life.

Geiger and Sokol (1959) speculated that because behavior involving gratification but subject to cultural taboos is likely to lead to addiction, television addicts would be found predominantly among middle-class persons who were constant viewers. Other investigators have suggested that the appeal of "forbidden fruit" may contribute to television addiction (Schramm et al., 1961). For example, Shapiro (1965) describes one patient who maintained that "he must avoid watching any television since he might enjoy it, want to watch more, become addicted to it, and want to do nothing else and then, what would become of the book he was writing?" (p. 44).

Arousal Theories.   Another notion frequently encountered in the scientific literature might be called the arousal hypothesis. Zuckerman (1979) speculated that although television provides little in the way of novel sensation, the television addict might be called a stimulation seeker. Maccoby (1951) reasoned that television addiction might result when a person "becomes accustomed to a heightened level of excitement and organizes much of his learned excitement at that particular level" so that "his behavior will be disrupted if the level of excitement declines, and he will be restless, bored, ill-at-ease" (p. 441–442) until he resumes the activity. In other words, the sensory arousal potential of television leads the viewer to seek more and more stimulation until a dependence, and addiction, results.

In summary, there are many untested assumptions about television addiction in the psychological literature. Given the extent of popular concern, psychologists have a responsibility to base their conclusions about television addiction on sound scientific evidence, little of which exists.

DEFINING TELEVISION ADDICTION

Logically, the first step in a scientific investigation of this phenomenon would be to derive a definition of what to look for—to define television addiction. Scientists concerned with addiction processes in general have pointed out the necessity that addiction be "first of all specifically and carefully defined so that we know what we are talking about and what is excluded from the definition" (Lindesmith, 1966, p. 92). An adequate definition of television addiction would enable scientists to develop criteria that would separate addicts from heavy viewers or any other group.

For example, in an extensive questionnaire study of the members of Alcoholics Anonymous, Jellinek (1952) found that a perceived "loss of control" discriminated between two categories of drinkers: (a) habitual symptomatic excessive drinkers and (b) alcohol addicts. Also, Zinberg and Jacobson (1974) distinguished controlled drug users from addicts in a group of physicians and suggested that the extent and diversity of the person's social relationships are crucial in determining whether the person becomes a controlled or compulsive user. Such discriminational criteria might also be developed for television addiction.

At this point, a definition of television addiction that can be translated into research on the issue does not exist in the scientific literature. Therefore, a generally accepted theoretical notion of addiction processes that could be applied to the case of television in particular would be useful.

Addiction Theory

The notions that addiction is not a purely physiological phenomenon and that narcotics are not the sole source of addiction now seem to be widely accepted. In fact, most theoretical efforts now focus on the dominance of the psychological processes in drug dependence. Addiction is often seen as a primarily psychological phenomenon, "a constellation of behaviors that constitute a way of life" (Cummings, 1979, p. 1121–1122). The nature of the primary reward provided by the drug is most often conceived of as a mental state.

In sum, researchers have been unable to link addiction with any one drug or class of drugs. Rather, the literature supports a dynamic psychological view of a "complex individual system interacting with personal history and environmental factors to yield an addiction" (Nathan & Lansky, 1978, p. 714). However, there do not seem to be characteristic personality patterns that differentiate drug abusers from nonabusers. Earlier studies claimed to find personality characteristics that were particular to addicts, but these studies were plagued with methodological problems (reviewed by Gendreau & Gendreau, 1970; Nathan & Lansky, 1978) and/or circular reasoning. A particularly common methodological problem is in appropriate comparison groups or the lack of control groups. The circular reasoning employed by the theoreticians in this field is described by Zinberg (1975):

The idea that certain personality types seek out drug experience because of a specific, early, unresolved developmental conflict, and that such people predominate in the addict group or in the much larger group of controlled users, is based on retrospective falsification. That is, looking at drug users and especially addicts, after they have become preoccupied with their drug experience, authorities assume that these attitudes and this personality state are similar to those the user had before

the drug experience, and thus led to it. Then "evidence" from the users developmental history and previous object relationships is marshalled to show that the
addicted state was the end point of a long-term personality process. (p. 568)

Results reported by Vaillant and Milofsky (1982) from a prospective study
of the etiological factors in alcoholism support this viewpoint. Although most
theorists are suspicious of the notion of the "addiction-prone" personality, it is
recognized that psychological factors are involved in the decision to use drugs,
the effects of those drugs, the course of the dependence, and the efficacy of
different treatment methods. Briefly reviewed here are three recent theories of
addiction processes that might be regarded as new directions in the thinking in
this field. They represent psychoanalytic, physiological, and behaviorist
perspectives.

Zinberg (1975) described ways in which the social conditions of the addict
have an impact on ego function. His treatment-oriented theory is grounded in
the post-Freudian, ego-adaptive school of psychoanalysis. He claims that the
relative autonomy of the addict's ego from both id (instinctual drives) and forces
in the external environment is impaired. This results when addicts lose varied
sources of stimulus nutriment. That is, they are alienated from family and friends
and declared deviant by society.

Some fascinating new theoretical developments have emerged from research
on the endogenous opioids. Recently, opiate receptors have been discovered
along the principal routes of pain stimuli in the brain and spinal cord. In addition,
opiate receptors have been found in areas associated with emotional responses
and hormone control as well as the amygdala and hippocampus areas thought
to be involved in reward systems and memory. This is of special interest in light
of the evidence that cocaine, amphetamines, nicotine, barbiturates, ethyl alcohol,
and the opiates all serve as reinforcers for operant behavior in monkeys (Meyer,
1974).

Although the endorphins have not yet been implicated in addiction processes,
it has been suggested that a defect in the endorphin system may play a role in
explaining why some individuals are more vulnerable to drug addiction than
others (Goldstein, 1981). A second possibility is that addiction may result from
suppression or impairment of the endogenous system due to the habitual use of
exogenous opiates.

Yet a third and possibly more likely role has been suggested. Goldstein (1981)
cites evidence linking insensitivity to pain with overproduction of endorphins.
It is possible that such differences in psychophysiological responsiveness may
help to account for vulnerability to addiction. Consistent with this is evidence
reported by Martin and Inglis (1965) that pain thresholds for addicts were lower
than those for nonaddicts.

Finally, a very promising theory of addiction processes has been offered within
the context of a general theory of motivation. Solomon and Corbit (1974) use

addiction as an empirical model for all acquired motivation. Their opponent-process theory of motivation implies that addiction is "the inevitable consequence of a normally functioning system that opposes affective or hedonic states" (p. 144). In addition, addiction is seen as a possible consequence of any repeated pleasure. Because this theory (Solomon & Corbit, 1974) seems to be potentially the most useful one for understanding television addiction, a more extensive description of it follows. More recent empirical tests are discussed in Solomon (1980).

The theory assumes the existence of central nervous system mechanisms that operate to reduce the intensity of many affective states. The intensity reduction is accomplished by *opponent processes*, which are automatically recruited when either a pleasurable or aversive stimulus results in an affective reaction. These opponent processes are strengthened by use and weakened by disuse. Furthermore, it is assumed that the establishment of some types of acquired motivation (through the exercise of these processes) does not depend on conditioning and is not associative in nature.

In sum, the current theoretical consensus is that addiction is primarily a psychological phenomenon, with a possible physiological substrate in the endorphin system. There are no clearly specified physiological or biochemical mechanisms that mediate addiction processes, and there seems to be no limit to the number of potentially addictive substances and experiences. The nature of the reward in addiction is thought to be the achievement of a pleasurable (or nonaversive) affective state. Finally, variations in environmental and sociocultural factors are thought to play a major role in determining vulnerability to addiction, choice of substance of experience, and mode of expression in behavior.

RELEVANCE OF ADDICTION THEORY
TO TELEVISION VIEWING

It is clear that the theoretical consensus allows for the possibility of the television viewing experience to develop into an addiction. Solomon, in particular, explicitly attempts to generalize his model of addiction to a variety of pleasurable experiences, from love and attachment to thrill-seeking behavior. In his theory, there are no limitations on the types of experience that could lead to addiction; he regards this as an empirical question. In terms of guidelines for a theory of addiction to television, the aforementioned theories point to the affective domain as an area of behavior in which to expect differences between addicts and nonaddicts, particularly with regard to: (a) affective state during and after viewing, (b) feelings of control over viewing behavior, and (c) feelings about one's social relationships and role in society.

Zinberg's theory leads to only very general predictions about the affective state of the addict—namely, that addicts will feel alienated from family, friends, and society and will feel unable to control their viewing behavior due to a deterioration in ego function. Solomon's theory would predict that, if televison viewing is a potentially addictive experience, an A state attained while viewing should be followed by an opposite B state after viewing in those who are vulnerable to addiction. With repeated exposure, the A state will lessen in intensity and the B state will strengthen. If the B′ state is unpleasant, which is a reasonable assumption given that viewing television is probably not an initially aversive experience, it will drive operant behavior, such as turning on the television, to reduce it. Finally, if the A′ and B′ states become conditioned, addicts should feel hemmed in and unable to control their viewing behavior.

There is some evidence that the previously described affective states are characteristic of television addicts. An analysis of the popular literature on television addiction lends support to the notion that addiction processes may determine the television viewing behavior of some people.

The Popular Literature on Television Addiction

In order to discover the particular manifestations in viewing behavior that an addiction to television would cause, a content analysis of the popular literature was undertaken and is reported here. The use of popular literature on behavior for psychological research is often overlooked as a rich source of hypotheses about behavior. The popular literature on television addiction contains descriptions of addictive behavior by self-designated addicts and by their families.

A literature search was undertaken to gather references to television addiction in the popular literature. The 1975–1979 issues of the *Reader's Guide to Periodical Literature* were consulted for articles on television addiction and closely related topics. In addition, several recent popular books (e.g., *The Plug-In Drug, Four Arguments for the Elimination of Television*) yielded many more descriptions. Finally, current newspaper and magazine articles contributed to the analysis.

Inspection of these statements suggested 12 categories of statements about television addiction:

1. Television functions as a sedative. "Another symptom of TV dependency is using it to obliterate pain, tension, or anxiety" (Brown, 1980, p. 52).

2. Addiction does not bring satisfaction. "I remember turning on television when I was a child and having that vapid feeling after watching hours of TV . . . it just didn't give back a real feeling of pleasure. It was like no orgasm, no catharsis, very frustrating" (quoted in Winn, 1978, p. 26).

3. There is an absence of selectivity. "True TV junkies are spiked on whatever flits across the herz line and they don't even read *TV Guide*" (Brown, 1980, p. 48).

4. Addicts feel a loss of control over their viewing. "I can't turn it off. I feel sapped, will-less, enervated" (quoted in Winn, 1978, p. 25).

5. Addicts lose a sense of time passing. "The next thing I know it's eleven o'clock and I'm watching the Johnny Carson show, and I'll realize I've spent the whole evening watching TV! What's more, I can't stand Johnny Carson! But I'll sit there watching him. I'm addicted to TV" (quoted in Winn, 1978, p. 28).

6. Television provides meaning and purpose in their lives. For soap opera addicts, "soap operas seem to comprise the reality which dominates their lives" (Winsey, 1979, p. 32).

7. Their time is structured around the television set. "You're also in trouble, say former TV freaks, when TV competes with more important involvements—compulsive soap-opera watching keeps you off your job, a rigid nighttime viewing schedule takes the place of sex, hobbies, or social life" (Brown, 1980, p. 52).

8. They feel they watch too much television. "The self-confessed televison addict often feels he 'ought' to do other things" (Winn, 1978, p. 25).

9. They feel angry with themselves for giving in to its effects. "All the while we were watching I'd feel terribly angry at myself for wasting all that time watching junk" (quoted in Winn, 1978, p. 26).

10. They can't wait to get back to television when they've been away. "Television promised so much richness I could hardly wait for it" (quoted in Winn, 1978, p. 26).

11. They try to quit and fail. "And I'm embarrassed to admit that after only two weeks of 'cold turkey,' I found myself standing on Fifth Avenue with my nose pressed against the Sony showroom window. I needed to shoot up" (English, 1977, p. 184).

12. They experience withdrawal symptoms when they try to quit. "I was very restless. I discovered that television had acted as a tranquilizer. Without it, I had to work to overcome my nervousness" (Tannehill, 1979, p. 59).

A look at the popular literature provides more specific information on the quality of the affective dynamics that might be found in television addiction. For example, addicts say they feel sedated and lose awareness of time passing or feel angry while watching television. After viewing, there is a vapid feeling or feelings of guilt and restlessness. In addition, they clearly report feeling unable to control their viewing behavior. Finally, there are also indications of specific overt behavior that is characteristic of television addiction (e.g., turning it on as soon as one gets home, trying to quit but failing, etc.). These statements are clearly consistent with the predictions derived from addiction theory and go beyond such predictions by providing information about the specific overt behavior and quality of feelings in television addiction.

It seems likely that, if television addiction is a real process, these behaviors should be related so as to constitute a syndrome. An operational definition of television addiction for the purposes of research would consist of the covariation of items measuring each of the behaviors that have been listed. If these items are tapping into the same construct—television addiction—it should be possible to find a new variable or factor that would account for most of the variance in the item correlation matrix.

A test of this model would constitute one approach to the question. That is, television addiction could be conceived of as a general process, such that individual scores reflect both error variance and a true score on that variable. By contrast, another approach looks for individual consistencies in the operation of psychological processes. It is assumed that a particular process may not be a general one, but would be operating in a subset of the population. The second research strategy to the question of television addiction would be to determine whether such a variable might describe the viewing behavior and affect of a subset of a population. The research reported here represents an attempt to combine both approaches to determine whether television addiction exists as it has been described.

The most direct method would be to ask people to rate their own behavior on the addiction dimensions previously described and to examine these responses to determine whether an addiction factor is characteristic of all subjects' responses or whether it describes the behavior of only a small though significant number.

THE SURVEY

A questionnaire was written to test some of the hypotheses about television addiction described in previous sections. It was administered by mail to a sample of 984 adults living in Springfield, Massachusetts, in the spring of 1982. In this section, the questionnaire design, survey administration, and response rate are described. Also, the specific hypotheses about television addiction are set forth, and a discussion of the demographic characteristics of the respondents is included.

Questionnaire Design

The questionnaire consisted of seven parts. Sections A, B, and C contained items about television viewing, including those written to assess TV addiction. The remaining sections contained items assessing demographic characteristics (e.g., age, sex, income, etc.) of the respondents, stress due to life events, activity level, and values. In some cases, there were clear expectations based on the literature about the direction of the relationships between television addiction and the other variables (e.g., stress); in other cases (e.g., values), there were no clear expectations.

The television addiction scale (Section B) consisted of 27 items. Of these, 18 were derived from statements on TV addiction in the popular literature (the "addict items"). The remaining 9 items consisted of those that might be considered normal kinds of behavior (I forget to watch a TV show that I want to see) or deviance of another sort (I have fears of losing control or going crazy). Examples of the addict items and their associated content analysis categories are as follows:

1. When I come home from work, school, or shopping, I turn on the TV within 5 minutes. (10)
2. When I'm watching TV at night, I go to bed later than I plan to. (7)
3. I'll watch anything that's on TV. (3)

Respondents were asked to rate their own behavior on these items on a 5-point scale from 0 (never) to 4 (always). It was hypothesized that, if television addiction exists as a general syndrome, responses to these items would covary such that a factor analysis would reveal the existence of a general factor composed of these items. Alternatively, if television addiction is not a general phenomenon, but specific to a subset of the population, a small but significantly greater than chance number of respondents will score 3 (often) or 4 (always) on 12 of 18 items. The probability of any one subject showing this pattern of responses on these items is .02. Therefore, at least 11 of the total 491 respondents (the obtained sample size) would show this pattern if television addiction underlies their responses. This test is referred to as the binomial analysis because the binomial distribution pairs each total score with its probability (assuming sampling from a stationary Bernoulli process).

Section A included items assessing amount of television viewing, number of favorite shows, number of televisions available to watch, proportion of free time spent viewing, and amount of time spent viewing with others. It was hypothesized that although television addicts may not watch more television in terms of number of hours due to constraints on the free time available, they may report spending all or most of their free time watching TV. In addition, they would be more likely to describe themselves as addicted to television on the items in which that response was an alternative. There were no clear expectations about relationships between television addiction and the other items in this section, but it was deemed important and interesting to discover if such relationships exist.

Section C contained an attitude scale in which half of the items assessed positive attitudes and half assessed negative attitudes. Respondents were asked to rate their agreement with these statements about television on a scale from 1 (strongly disagree) to 5 (strongly agree). A total attitude index was obtained for each respondent by subtracting the mean negative item score from the mean positive item score, so that sign as well as magnitude of the index was informative. Space for comments was also provided. The second negative item (TV is addictive) was of particular interest. It was hypothesized that addicts would be more likely to agree or strongly agree with that statement, as well as have more generally negative attitudes toward television.

Basic demographic information was obtained from items in Section D. These variables included age, sex, race, marital status, education, income, employment status, occupation, and household composition. There were no clear expectations here about the characteristics of television addicts because the popular literature did not single out any particular group as being more susceptible and the self-descriptions of television addicts seem to include males and females, single and married people, housewives and professionals, and so on. There is the notion in the scientific literature that middle-class persons may be more susceptible due to the operation of a middle-class taboo against television viewing (Geiger & Sokol, 1959). Items in this section enabled this notion to be tested.

The role of stress in television addiction was assessed by the scale items in Section E. These items and their weights were derived from a life events inventory developed by Cochrane and Robertson (1973). A total amount of life stress is calculating by adding the weights of the events checked as occurring in the past year for each respondent. It was hypothesized that television addicts' mean score on life stress would be higher than that of the rest of the population if television addiction is a coping mechanism as claimed. Section E also included items assessing happiness in the last 3 months, self-description of "sociability," and physical handicaps.

Section F included a scale assessing frequency of various activities such as studying, reading, attending parties, and going to concerts. In addition, one of the items assessed frequency of playing video games, as the previous video game question assessed only home use. It was hypothesized that television addicts would be less active, in terms of engaging in fewer activities (except watching TV) less often, than the rest of the population. An activity index was calculated for all respondents by adding the scores, ranging from 0 (never) to 4 (every day), for each item on this scale.

Finally, Section G included a values scale. Respondents were asked to rate the extent to which several kinds of goals were important to them personally, ranging from 1 (not important) to 5 (very important). There were no clear expectations about the relationship between values and television addiction.

The back cover of the questionnaire included a request for further comments. Finally, a Spanish translation of the questionnaire was made available to the 80 respondents with Hispanic surnames.

Results

In order to determine whether television addiction existed either as a "state" or a "trait" in this sample, two types of statistical tests were performed on the survey data. First, a confirmatory factor analysis examined the amount of variance accounted for by the hypothesized 18-item addiction factor in the responses to the 27-item addiction scale. This 18-item addiction factor hypothesis was derived from the content analysis of the literature on television addiction. The confirmatory factor analysis was essentially a test of a trait model. The second type of analysis, the binomial test previously referred to, examined the plausibility of a state model. The results of both sets of analyses are reported here, along with the descriptive statistics on the addiction scale and relations of addiction scale scores with other variables.

Confirmatory Factor Analysis.   In answer to the question "Does TV addiction exist?" this analysis determined how well the hypothesized addiction factor accounted for the variance in the responses to the addiction scale. The results indicated that a one-factor solution explained the variance fairly well, but not as well as a two-factor solution. In order to assess the adequacy of the hypothesized one-factor solution, a total of nine factor analyses were conducted to explore the consequences of different methods of factor extraction, rotation, and criteria for the number of factors to be extracted. The results of all these analyses converged on the conclusion that a two-factor model was the best explanation for the pattern of item covariances in the addiction scale. The details of these analyses are to be presented elsewhere (Smith, in preparation). Here I focus on describing those two factors. Because essentially the same factor structures emerged repeatedly over all analyses, I describe the factor structure from just one of those analyses, which used the principal factors method with iterated communality estimates, quartimax rotation, and number of factors limited to two.

Table 6.1 presents the results of this analysis. Factor 1 included seven variables, all addict items. It accounted for 70.9% of the two-factor variance. Factor 2 also contained all addict items, three loading above criterion, and it accounted for the remaining 29.1% of the variances. The first factor included items that assessed feelings of depression and nervousness when respondents could *not* watch TV and behavior that indicated feelings of loss of control ("can't walk away," "can't stop," "watch anything"). An independent dimension is represented by the three items in Factor 2. These assessed feelings of guilt, anger, and depression about, during, and after viewing.

Using the two factors obtained from this analysis, factor scores were computed for the respondents. Scores on Factor 1 were positively correlated with both number of hours of viewing per week, $r = .28$, $p<.001$, and proportion of free time spent viewing TV, $r = .40$, $p < .001$, as well as several other variables. It should be noted that the second correlation is higher than the first, suggesting that proportion of free time spent viewing televison may be a better indicator of excessive viewing than number of hours. These two measures are related but not totally redundant because the correlation between proportion of free time spent viewing and number of hours is only .45, $p<.001$.

Binomial Analysis.   This analysis tested for the existence of a small but significant number of respondents who scored above the criterion on the addict

TABLE 6.1
Items Loading Above Criterion for Solution Employing Principal
Factors with Quartimax Rotation and Number of Factors
Limited to Two

Factor Number	Eigenvalue after Rotation	Item Number	Item Content	Factor Loading
1	4.64	16	I feel depressed when I can't watch TV.	.68
		25	When I'm watching TV, I feel like I can't stop.	.64
		24	I feel nervous when I can't watch TV.	.61
		27	I can't walk away from the TV once it is on.	.57
		17	I can't think of anything to do on the weekends and holidays.	.51
		3	I'll watch anything that's on TV.	.51
		14	I lose track of the time while I'm watching TV.	.50
	Criterion --			
		1	When I come home from work, school, or shopping, I turn on the TV within 5 minutes.	.49
		10	I cancel other plans in order to watch TV.	.48
		2	When I'm watching TV at night, I go to bed later than I plan to.	.47
		5	I feel guilty about how much TV I watch.	.44
		18	I sneak peeks at the TV when no one is around.	.43
2	1.91	9	I feel depressed after watching TV.	.64
		11	While I'm watching TV, I feel angry at myself for watching TV.	.56
		5	I feel guilty about how much TV I watch.	.51
	Criterion --			
		15	I feel guilty when someone else sees me watching TV.	.47
		13	I have decided to give up TV for periods of time.	.45
		4	I feel nervous after watching TV.	.45
		8	I forget to watch a TV show that I want to see.	.41

items and thus might be called television addicts. The probability was less than .02 that 10 or more respondents would obtain a score of 3 or 4 on 12 or more of the 18 addict items if measurement error was the major source of item variance. The null hypothesis could not be rejected on the basis of the results. That is, none of the respondents scored at or above the criterion.

In sum, the binomial analysis did not support the notion that there is a small but significant number of televison addicts (as defined by the popular literature) in the population.

Descriptive Statistics.   Finally, descriptive statistics revealed that "never" was the most frequent response for 17 of the 18 addict items. This indicated that most respondents found television addiction to be completely atypical of them. On a scale of 0 (never) to 4 (always), the mean score for each respondent's average on the addiction items was 0.61, with a standard deviation of 0.4. An index of each respondent's total score on the addiction items was also computed. Of a possible range of 0 to 72, the mean was 10.77, with a standard deviation of 7.15.

This does not reflect a response set because all but two of the eight distributions of responses to the other items were either negatively skewed or approximately normal in distribution. Only items 20 (I avoid watching TV . . .) and 22 (I have fears of losing control or going crazy) were found to be atypical of most respondents.

In sum, the behavior and feelings hypothesized to be characteristic of television addicts were found to be rated as highly uncharacteristic of themselves by the large majority of respondents. It is very unlikely that this reflects a response set because seven of the nine items which were not deemed to be addict items were rated very differently by the respondents.

Other types of items provided information on television addiction. One asked respondents to choose between the following alternatives as a self-description: (1) I avoid watching TV, (2) I watch TV very rarely, (3) I watch TV now and then, (4) I watch TV every day, and (5) I'm addicted to TV. Of the 11 respondents who chose (5), only 1 scored above 36 on the total addiction item index. These 11 subjects viewed an average of 55.63 hours of television a week (the average amount for the entire sample of 491 respondents was 26.74), with a range of 34 to 90 hours. The average age of the self-described addicts was 46, with a range of 26 to 82 years. Their average score on the total addiction item index was 26.18, with a range of 18 to 43 (compared to a mean of 10.77 for the entire sample). The standard deviation was 7.32, which is comparable to that of the entire sample. For the entire sample, the Pearson product moment correlation between the total index and the subject's response to this self-description item was .26 ($p<.001$). However, the correlation between reponse to this item and number of hours in television viewing was .49 ($p<.001$). Number of hours spent viewing television correlated only .25 ($p<.001$) with the total index.

In sum, there was a moderate but significant relationship between the amount of television viewing and score on the 18 addict items, but a strong relationship between amount of viewing and tendency to call oneself a television addict. The relationship between score on the addict items and tendency to call oneself an addict is also moderate.

Finally, three items on the attitude scale assessed attitudes about television which are relevant to addiction. Of all respondents, 64% either agreed or strongly agreed that television is addictive. In addition, 53% either agreed or strongly agreed that television allows people to escape their problems. However, only 28% agreed or strongly agreed that television makes people more passive. The most frequent response category for this attitude was neither agree nor disagree.

Thus, although most respondents agree that television is addictive, only 11 called themselves addicts, and these individuals watched almost twice as much television as the average viewer. Most respondents found the behavior and feelings in the addict items to be very atypical of themselves, although self-described addicts scored higher on this scale.

CONCLUSION

The results of both the binomial analysis and the factor analyses of the survey data failed to support the hypothesis that television addiction exists in the form hypothesized. That is, neither approach to the question of the existence of the syndrome—either as a general trait in the population or as a pattern characteristic of a small but significant group—yielded support for the hypothesis. In the binomial analysis, none of the 491 respondents scored at or above the criterion on the addict items. In order to be statistically significant, at least 10 respondents should have shown this pattern. The factor analyses revealed that a two-factor model was better able to account for the item covariance than the hypothesized addiction factor. These two factors were composed of items deemed characteristic of addicts, but they represent independent dimensions. The first factor, which accounted for most of the variance, represented feelings of loss of control over viewing behavior, absence of program selectivity, loss of a sense of time passing while viewing, withdrawal symptoms when unable to watch, and using television as a source of meaning and purpose. A second factor represented feelings of guilt about amount of viewing, anger for giving in to watching television, and depression after viewing. This suggests that negative affect may be independent of actual viewing behavior.

There are four possibilities as to how extremes on these independent dimensions may be expressed in the behavior of a single individual. One might score high on both dimensions, a pattern which would be characteristic of television addicts according to the definition used in this study. If this pattern was significant, however, it would have become evident in the binomial analysis because both dimensions are composed of addict items. A second pattern would be that of low scores on both dimensions. This is probably the norm, given the shape of the response distributions to the addict items. A third pattern, high scores on Factor 1 and low scores on Factor 2, would indicate that there may be a subgroup that views a lot of television and derives a sense of structure and purpose from it, but does not feel guilty, angry, or depressed about their viewing habits. Whether or not these people might be television addicts is an empirical question. It would be important to examine their scores on the other variables thought to be related to addiction, such as feelings of alienation from society and friends, amount of life stress, and so forth. A final pattern is low scores on Factor 1 and high scores on Factor 2. For lack of a better term, this might be called a neurotic pattern because it would indicate feelings of anger, guilt, and depression in the absence of excessive television viewing. This is the pattern about which least is known, except that perhaps it reflects a middle-class bias against television viewing such as that reported by Geiger and Sokol (1959).

Finally, the descriptive data on the responses to the addict items indicated that the majority found this behavior completely atypical of themselves. And yet, 65% believed that television is addictive, and 11 respondents called themselves addicts. It was observed that, for these 11 respondents, the mean number of hours per week spent viewing was more than double the mean for the entire sample. However, all but 1 of the 11 scored below criterion on the addict item scale. Television addiction exists as a popular concept and as a self-label for heavy viewers, but it was not possible to document its existence in this sample as a behavioral syndrome such as that described in the popular literature.

How does one then account for the anecdotal evidence? One possibility is that television addiction exists, and this study failed to find it. In purely statistical terms, by perhaps falsely failing to reject the null hypothesis, a Type II error has been committed. The power of the test was in fact limited by the low variance in the responses to the addict items. It would be possible to increase the power of future tests by raising the alpha level, but that would increase the probability of a Type I error. It would be preferable to increase the sample size. This leads to the question of how important such a phenomenon is if, despite its robust and regular appearance in anecdotes and magazine articles, a systematic attempt to find addicts requires a very large sample. Contrast this with the results of the classic midtown Manhattan study, in which 1,660 residents were interviewed for symptoms of emotional impairment. The study revealed a startlingly high frequency (23.4%) of marked to severe symptom formation or incapacity among the residents (Srole et al., 1962). The present study found that although a small number of people called themselves addicts, by behavioral self-rating they did not show the classic symptoms described in the literature. Television addiction does not appear to be a robust phenomenon.

However, the popularity of the notion of television as "plug-in drug" is enduring. One possible source of this image lies in the nature of the viewing experience. The only study to date that examines the nature of the viewing experience in adults (Csikszentmihalyi & Kubey, 1981) found that television watching, of all life activities measured in the course of 1 week, was the least challenging, involved the least amount of skill, and was most relaxing. The investigators found that among 104 adults who filled out self-reports when signaled by a beeper, the typical viewing experience is characterized by low feelings of potency, moderate cheerfulness, and high relaxation. Affective states reported while reading were nearly identical, but television viewing was experienced as having fewer cognitive requirements and involving lower feelings of potency. One source of the image of television as drug may lie in such perceived effects on mood and cognitive activity. The present study found that the majority of respondents agree that television helps people escape their problems. In this sense, television is perceived as having a sedative effect, although few people were willing to believe that television actually makes people more passive.

The popular image of television as a drug may also derive from a pervasive fear, or at least ambivalence, about technology and its effects. Despite the powerful impact of video technology on popular culture, its symbolic significance is often ignored.

An explicit link between the power of religious symbols and the power of television technology has been made by the contemporary theologian Harvey Cox (1973), who writes of television as the "electronic icon":

> Technological artifacts become symbols when they are "iconized," when they release emotions incommensurate with their mere utility, when they arouse hopes and fears only indirectly related to their use, when they begin to provide foci for the mapping of cognitive experience. (p. 282)

The point is that such value judgments about the power of the medium and fears about its effects on consciousness may be contributing to the popular image of television as a drug. If this is so, it is useful to consider the notion of television addiction as a second-order conviction (Benjamin, 1961). First-order convictions are those based on scientifically sound evidence that have yet to be tested directly. Second-order convictions are not based on unsound evidence, but primarily on wishes, needs, or fears and often represent compliance with a subcultural value system. Benjamin suggests that when second-order convictions persist, there exists a need in society for accepting them. Evaluation of this argument is beyond the scope of this chapter, but the notion is useful for thinking about television addiction, considering the lack of evidence for its existence.

ACKNOWLEDGMENTS

The research reported here was part of a doctoral dissertation submitted to the graduate school of the University of Massachusetts in Amherst in partial fulfillment of the requirements for the PhD degree in psychology. This research was supported by a doctoral dissertation grant (No. BNS-8116876) from the National Science Foundation and by a

Grant-in-Aid-of-Research from Sigma Xi, the scientific research honor society. This chapter was written while the author held a National Research Service Award from the National Institute of Mental Health. I would like to thank my dissertation committee members, Daniel R. Anderson, Arnold Well, Edward Tronick, and Peter Rossi for their generosity in sharing time and help toward this project. I also want to thank Jennings Bryant for his encouragement of my work and the opportunity to contribute to this volume. Finally, I want to thank Patricia Collins and Eric Pierce for their valuable assistance in data coding and analysis.

REFERENCES

Arlen, M. J. (1976, December 6). What we do in the dark. *The New Yorker*, pp. 192, 194, 197.

Barragan, M. (1976). The child-centered family. In P. J. Guerin (Ed.), *Family therapy: Theory and practice*. New York: Gardner.

Benjamin, J. (1961). Knowledge, conviction, and ignorance. *Journal of Medical Education, 36*, 117–132.

Brown, J. (1980, October). Turned on, tuned in, strung out. *High Times*, pp. 46–52.

Cochrane, R., & Robertson, A. (1973). The life events inventory: A measure of the relative severity of psycho-social stressors. *Journal of Psychosomatic Research, 17*, 135–139.

Cox, H. (1973). *The seduction of the spirit: The use and misuse of people's religion*. New York: Simon & Schuster.

Csikszentmihalyi, M., & Kubey, R. (1981). Television and the rest of life: A systematic comparison of subjective experience. *Public Opinion Quarterly, 45*, 317–328.

Cummings, N. A. (1979). Turning bread into stones: Our modern antimiracle. *American Psychologist, 34*, 1119–1129.

Duncan, D. F. (1976). Stress and adolescent drug dependence: A brief report. *IRCS Medical Science, 4*, 381.

Edgar, P. (1977). Families without television. *Journal of Communication, 27*, 73–77.

English, D. (1977, February). Are you a secret TV addict? *Vogue*, pp. 184–185.

Florman, S. C. (1981). *Blaming technology: The irrational search for scapegoats*. New York: St. Martin's.

Freedman, L. Z. (1961). Daydream in a vacuum tube. In W. Schramm, J. Lyle, & E. B. Parker (Eds.), *Television in the lives of our children* (pp. 189–194). Stanford, CA: Stanford University Press.

Geiger, K., & Sokol. R. (1959). Social norms in television watching. *American Journal of Sociology, 65*, 174–181.

Gendreau, P., & Gendreau, L. P. (1970). The "addiction-prone" personality: A study of Canadian heroin addicts. *Canadian Journal of Behavioral Science, 2*, 18–25.

Glynn, E. D. (1956). Television and the American character: A psychiatrist looks at television. In W. Y. Elliot (Ed.), *Television's impact on American culture*. East Lansing: Michigan State University Press.

Goldstein, A. (1981). Endorphins and addiction. In H. Schaffer & M. E. Burglass (Eds.), *Classic contributions in addictions* (pp. 421–432). New York: Brunner/Mazel.

Greenberg, B. S. (1974). Gratifications of television viewing and their correlates for British children. In J. Blumler & E. Katz (Eds.), *The uses of mass communications: Current perspectives on gratifications research*. Beverly Hills, CA: Sage.

Himmelweit, H. T., Oppenheim, A. N., & Vince, P. (1958). *Television and the child*. London: Oxford University Press.

Jellinek, E. M. (1952). Phases of alcohol addiction. *Quarterly Journal of Studies on Alcohol, 13*, 673–684.

Lindesmith, A. R. (1966). Basic problems in the social psychology of addiction and a theory. In J. A. O'Donnell & J. C. Ball (Eds.), *Narcotic addiction* (pp. 91–109). New York: Harper & Row.

Maccoby, E. E. (1951). Television: Its impact on school children. *Public Opinion Quarterly, 15,* 421–444.

Mander, J. (1978). *Four arguments for the elimination of television.* New York: William Morrow.

Martin, J., & Inglis, J. (1965). Pain tolerance and narcotic addiction. *British Journal of Social and Clinical Psychology, 4,* 224–229.

Meerlo, J. A. M. (1954). Television addiction and reactive apathy. *Journal of Nervous and Mental Disease, 120,* 29–91.

Meyer, R. E. (1974). On the nature of opiate reinforcement. In P. G. Bourne (Ed.), *Addiction* (pp. 21–45). New York: Academic.

Murray, J. P. (1972). Television in inner-city homes: Viewing behavior of young boys. In E. A. Rubinstein, G. A. Comstock, & J. P. Murray (Eds.), *Television and social behavior* (Vol. 4, pp. 345–368). Washington, DC: U.S. Government Printing Office.

Murray, J. P., & Kippax, S. (1979). From the early window to the late night show: International trends in the study of television's impact on children and adults. In L. Berkowitz (Ed.), *Advances in experimental social psychology* (Vol. 12, pp. 253–320). New York: Academic.

Nathan, P. E., & Lansky, D. (1978). Common methodological problems in research on the addictions. *Journal of Consulting and Clinical Psychology, 46,* 713–726.

Pearlin, L. I. (1959). Social and personal stress and escape television viewing. *Public Opinion Quarterly, 23,* 255–259.

Peele, S. (1979). Redefining addiction: II. The meaning of addiction in our lives. *Journal of Psychedelic Drugs, 11,* 289–297.

Rahe, R. H. (1979). Life change events and mental illness: An overview. *Journal of Human Stress, 5,* 2–10.

Schramm, W., Lyle, J., & Parker, E. B. (1961). *Television in the lives of our children.* Stanford, CA: Stanford University Press.

Schramm, W., & Roberts, D. F. (1971). Children's learning from the mass media. In D. F. Roberts & W. Schramm (Eds.), *The process and effects of mass communication* (rev. ed.). Urbana: University of Illinois Press.

Shapiro, D. (1965). *Neurotic styles.* New York: Basic Books.

Singer, J. (1980). The powers and limitations of television: A cognitive-affective analysis. In P. H. Tannenbaum (Ed.), *The entertainment functions of television* (pp. 31–65). Hillsdale, NJ: Lawrence Erlbaum Associates.

Smith, R. (in prep.). Television addiction.

Solomon, R. L., & Corbit, J. D. (1974). An opponent-process theory of motivation: I. Temporal dynamics of affect. *Psychological Review, 81,* 119–145.

Srole, L., Langner, T. S., Michael, S. T., Kirkpatrick, P., Opler, M. K., & Rennie, T. A. C. (1962). *Mental health in the metropolis.* New York: McGraw-Hill.

Tannehill, C. S. (1979, January). Turned on but tuned out. *Redbook,* pp. 58–59.

Vaillant, G. E., & Milofsky, E. S. (1982). The etiology of alcoholism: A prospective viewpoint. *American Psychologist, 37,* 494–503.

Windell, J. (1981, July 19). Experts disagree: Does TV enslave viewers? *Oakland Press,* p. E-1.

Winn, M. (1977). *The plug-in drug.* New York: Bantam.

Winsey, V. (1979, April). How soaps help you cope. *Family Health, 11,* pp. 30–32.

Zillmann, D., Hezel, R. T., & Medoff, N. J. (1983). The effect of affective states on selective exposure to televised entertainment fare. *Journal of Applied Social Psychology, 10,* 323–339.

Zinberg, N. E. (1975). Addiction and ego function. *The Psychoanalytic Study of the Child, 30,* 567–588.

Zinberg, N. E., & Jacobson, R. (1974). *The social controls of non-medical drug use.* Washington, DC: Drug Abuse Council.

Zuckerman, M. (1979). *Sensation seeking: Beyond the optimal level of arousal.* Hillsdale, NJ: Lawrence Erlbaum Associates.

7 Television and Its Educational Impact: A Reconsideration

Samuel Ball, Patricia Palmer, Emelia Millward
University of Sydney, Australia

The question of television's educational impact is a perennial and predictable one. Those of us associated with this research area know that as early as 1951 there were many studies of how the new medium was affecting students (Belsen, 1956; Dale & Williams, 1960; Witty, 1951). The myriad of studies later referred to by Comstock and Fisher (1975) is testimony to the persistent nature of the topic. Of course, each major communications medium seems to carry with it a debate about its educational impact. One can make reference, for example, to the 1930s debate on the impact of radio on education (radio was said to be a negative influence on home study habits) and the still earlier debate on the impact of the print medium when the so-called penny-dreadfuls (mass-produced pre-comic magazines) whetted the interests of our ever decadent youth.

Before televison is in turn superseded by some new medium (some form of computerized cathode ray tube, perhaps), it might be useful to look at how the focus of the research on television and education has been fine tuned since about 1970. As we look at the increased sophistication of our questions, our research techniques, and our findings, we can learn something not only about television's impact but about the conduct of research on educational issues more generally.

The earlier years of research on television's effects on education and on the student tended to take the form of attempts to answer questions that assumed a direct and generalized association or impact. An example of this may be found in the research that considered television's relationship to student IQ, student achievement, and reading. Since about 1970, a different line of research has looked at the social learning that comes from television viewing. Partly because of the newer social-outcome focus, the television research field has also become interested in contextual factors that influence the type of television viewing, the quality of the viewing process, and the resulting impacts on education.

It is our contention that education in both the narrow sense of subject-specific learning outcomes, and in the broader sense of the comprehensive development of new citizens is affected both directly and indirectly by television. How well children learn at school is not only influenced by what they know upon entering but also by the values and attitudes they hold and by the social interactions and roles they see as appropriate. Television's influence in all these areas has not been uniformly well researched, but a pattern of results is beginning to emerge.

First, we briefly consider the direct influence of television on IQ, achievement, and reading. We then turn to the indirect factors of social learning, context, and viewing processes.

TELEVISION VIEWING AND IQ

One of the first, simple questions looked at by researchers was: What is the association between viewing television and intellectual capacity? Early evidence suggested that a relationship existed between intelligence of the viewer and the time spent watching. A comparison of viewers and nonviewers showed significantly lower intelligence among viewers (Scott, 1956), and this has been supported by some later studies (Himmelweit, Oppenheim, & Vince, 1958; Morgan & Gross, 1980; Sharman, 1979; Starkey & Swinford, 1974). These correlational results led televison critics to interpret a causal relationship. The charge was that viewing television lowers IQ. However, more sophisticated critics, even in the early days of TV, noted what appeared to be a more complex relationship between amount of viewing and IQ. For example, Schramm, Lyle, and Parker (1961) carried out extensive research in 10 communities in the United States and Canada and found that high intelligence (IQ over 115) was positively related to heavy viewing up to the age of 11, but this relationship was reversed in the following years. Lyle and Hoffman (1972), using Lorge-Thorndike scores, found results similar to those reported by Schramm et al. In the sixth grade, bright students tended to be among the heaviest viewers, whereas in the tenth grade, they were more likely to be among the lighter viewers.

This finding has not yet been accounted for satisfactorily. There is clearly not a pattern of gradual or sudden deterioration of the IQs of heavy viewers. If that were so, the test-retest reliability of IQ tests would also be deteriorating seriously. One tenable hypothesis worth investigating is that most television programs are matched to the interests and abilities of bright younger children, who outgrow this level over time. Meanwhile, the less bright children grow into this level. In any case, chronological age seems to be a complicating factor in analyzing the question of the relationship between amount of viewing and intelligence.

TELEVISION AND SCHOOL ACHIEVEMENT

The earliest studies of television's effect on school achievement compared viewers with nonviewers, but results were not conclusive. Durham (1952), comparing 1,000 sixth and seventh graders, and Greenstein (1954), comparing 67 sixth graders, found no significant differences between the learning of viewers and nonviewers. Witty (1951) and Scott (1956), however, found reason to suggest that excessive viewing is associated with slightly lower grades in school.

Later studies have compared relative amounts of viewing with achievement scores, but many have failed to show a clear relationship. Ridder (1963) and Quisenberry and Klasek (1976) both failed to find any relationship between hours of viewing and general school achievement. Childers and Ross (1973) assessed quantity and quality of viewing and related these to grade point average and results on the Iowa Basic Skills Tests. Multiple and partial regression analyses showed a slightly negative, but not significant, relationship between grade point average and television viewing. They concluded that neither quantity nor quality of viewing is a predictor of school achievement.

Anderson and MacGuire (1978) assessed 300 third and fourth graders on several measures: verbal IQ, nonverbal IQ, achievement on a locally standardized math test, word meaning, and paragraph comprehension. Two-way ANOVAs (three levels of viewing by three levels of IQ) disclosed no significant differences. More recently, Anderson (1982) gave 275 fifth- and sixth-grade subjects a math test and measures of word meaning and reading achievement from the Stanford Achievement Test. No evidence of a negative relationship between television viewing and these measures was found.

However, other studies seem to indicate that some negative relationship does exist between overall school achievement and amount of television viewing. Clemens (1983) gathered data through the 1981 Pennsylvania Educational Quality Assessment for Grades 5, 8, and 11. Negative correlations were found for all groups, though television viewing accounted for only a small percentage of variance in achievement. Goodwin (1983) carried out an ex post facto study using a major national data set gathered in 1980 by the National Opinion Research Centre and known as "High School and Beyond." Standardized reading scores and teachers' assessments of achievement were correlated with viewing time for 43,000 students in 10th and 11th grades. He concluded that increased viewing time was a statistically significant indicator of lower achievement. Correlational studies, of large samples, such as the last two cited, have the problem of small correlations becoming statistically significant. In neither case did the television viewing measure account for more than a few percentage points of the variance in school achievement.

Sharman's (1979) study of 271 sixth-grade children in Melbourne, Australia, went beyond simple correlations, using path analysis to explore the relationships among many variables, including school performance and television viewing.

Overall school achievement, as rated by teachers, and amount of television viewing were not found to be significantly related. However, amount of television viewing had a positive effect on social studies comprehension.

Gadberry (1977) considered not only amount of television viewing but also the type of program, and correlated these measures with both achievement and grades for effort. A positive relationship was established for first graders between school achievement and cartoons, educational programs, and news. There was a negative relationship with adventure shows for the same group. By contrast, effort grades were negatively related to total amount of viewing.

A firm conclusion cannot be drawn about the relationship between school achievement and television viewing. Studies cannot be readily compared because of the different ways of measuring school achievement and because of the methodological problems that occur in much of the published research. In addition, measures of achievement and those of television viewing seem too global to produce meaningful results. Results suggest that the relationship between achievement and viewing may be quite complex and that research focusing on specific school subjects may show different effects for different knowledge areas at different grade levels. It would be surprising if any of the statistically significant results could be interpreted as accounting for much of the actual variability in children's achievement scores.

TELEVISION AND READING

Reading is an interesting area in itself because it is closely related to intelligence and because it is a prerequisite for satisfactory learning in school. A negative impact of television on reading has seemed intuitively obvious to many parents and teachers. However, reviews of studies investigating the relationship between time spent viewing and reading performance (e.g., Lehr, 1981; Neuman, 1980; Wagner, 1980) have noted that research is limited. Generally, no clear relationship between the two factors has been found. Angle (1981) did find a negative relationship between attitudes toward reading and amount of television viewing, for fifth-grade students. Once again, more specific measures show effects in some areas. Smeyser (1980) measured type as well as amount of viewing for first graders, relating them to results on a reading subtest of the SRA Achievement Series. After controlling for IQ, partial correlation coefficients showed a negative relationship between early reading achievement and amount of entertainment viewing time for boys. In this research, there were no significant relationships between viewing habits and early reading achievement for girls.

Considering the lack of clear findings in all these areas (IQ, achievement, and reading), Singer and Singer have suggested a possible complex interactive relationship. It may be that heavy television viewers from low IQ groups are stimulated by viewing and their reading may improve, whereas brighter children who watch a great deal of television may read less and move to lower levels of school achievement than would be expected from their initial capacities (Singer & Singer, 1983). The suggestion remains empirically unverified.

TELEVISION AND THE DEVELOPMENT
OF SPECIFIC COGNITIVE SKILLS

Since about 1970, the question of television's educational impact has been recast in more sophisticated terms of specific educational outcomes related to specially produced children's programs. In this, the *Sesame Street* evaluative research was a pioneer. *Sesame Street* used techniques and qualities of commercial television as an entertainment medium to teach a range of skills and attitudes to young children. These were in the areas of early language and number skills, problem solving, and reasoning skills, as well as social and emotional development (Polsky, 1974). Early summative evaluations of the extent to which children learned from *Sesame Street* indicated that overall there were gains in the skills taught directly in the series. Younger children appeared to gain more than older children. Disadvantaged children who viewed frequently gained as much as advantaged frequent viewers and gained more than advantaged infrequent viewers. But advantaged infrequent viewers gained more than disadvantaged infrequent viewers, perhaps because they had other sources for learning the knowledge and skills taught (Ball & Bogatz, 1970).

The data from the early evaluations were reanalyzed in 1975. It was argued that the experimental conditions introduced extra material and involved mothers; hence, effects could not be attributed solely to viewing the series. However, when comparisons were confined to frequent and infrequent viewers in the control group, significant differences were still found, though they were not as general as for the experimental group (Cook & Conner, 1977; Watkins, Huston-Stein, & Wright, 1981).

Another program, the *Infinity Factory*, was produced by the Education Development Centre and was designed to facilitate the understanding of basic math skills used in everyday life (decimal numbers, measurement, scaling). A magazine format was used, with each program featuring one main theme involving two or three basic skills or concepts. A test of the effects of viewing eight programs was conducted on 1,000 students, and all groups (whites, blacks, and Latinos) showed significant gains on the posttest (Bryant, Alexander, & Brown, 1983). These studies show that programs designed to teach as well as entertain can develop young children's skills in particular subject areas. Frequent exposure to these programs can produce significant learning in such subjects.

Research by Cohen and Salomon (1977b/1979) also suggests that certain forms and formats of television may teach certain cognitive skills and styles. In their view, filmic codes serve as representations of mental skills. For example, a zoom-in represents the mental operation of analyzing a stimulus into parts. Showing an object from several different angles may be parallel to the mental skill of perspective taking.

A longitudinal study of children in Israel who were exposed to *Sesame Street* provided further support for this idea. When the series was introduced, the children had experienced little television. Preschoolers who saw the series gained skills in content areas such as letter matching and classification. Second and third graders, however, acquired additional skills such as perspective taking, which according to Salomon (1977b) were conveyed in the film's codes. This suggests that children learn from television in different ways. They learn the skills presented as content, including program formats which facilitate the understanding of content, and they learn general television forms that provide symbolic codes of the medium. Some of these forms have the possibility of teaching cognitive skills directly.

TELEVISION AND EDUCATION
IN SOCIAL RELATIONSHIPS

As we have noted, evaluations of specially produced television programs for children demonstrate that TV can 'teach' successfully in some of the traditional academic skills areas. It may even be more effective in forming certain cognitive skills. However, education is usually understood to have a broader meaning, including an understanding of one's society and the development of a perspective toward one's place in the world. Schools have traditionally embraced this aspect of education in their curriculum statements, with perhaps mixed success in actual performance. Recent research indicates that the major educational impact of television viewing may well be in teaching children about society and about themselves. We should note that this social learning, in turn, contributes to the effectiveness of more academic learning in school.

Noble (1983) conducted a series of studies about children's learning from, and use of, entertainment-oriented programs shown on commercial television. He quotes the finding of Greenberg (1974) that children themselves give as their main reasons for watching television to learn about things and to learn about themselves. This is supported by results of studies of children's learning from two very different programs, a nature series, *Australia Naturally*, and an American series, *Happy Days*. Regarding the former program and based on the answers of 240 children aged 7 to 11, Noble (1983) reports that "children acquired the moral messages . . . with more force than they acquired factual information." These were messages such as "being careful not to upset the delicate balance of nature" (p. 105). From *Happy Days*, adolescents reported they learned how to be "spunky" (i.e., sexy) and "how to be themselves" (Noble, 1983, pp. 110–111).

Early adolescence may be a time when children make special use of television to learn about social relationships. In her exploratory study of 14-year-old girls, Palmer (1982) found a particular use of programs such as serial dramas by some girls in which they studied social interaction and its outcomes over a period of time, discussed it with friends, and related it to their own lives. On the basis of intensive interviews with 40 girls, she developed the concept of a *primer*, that is, a television program watched regularly with keen interest, to which priority is given over alternative programs or other home activities. Even those girls who usually put homework before viewing television would reverse their priorities for such a program. The term primer conveys a sense of the influence of such programs in initiating girls into appropriate social behaviors.

Palmer found that a primer was not chosen on the basis of individual taste alone, but was usually one of a small number of favorites discussed in a group of close girlfriends. Together they decided which programs were most true-to-life, speculated on future plot developments, and exchanged views on how they would behave in a similar situation. Sometimes they acted out the exciting parts, reproducing them as accurately as possible.

Little is known about the process whereby children make use of television content to understand themselves and their social environment. Palmer's description of 14-year-old girls raises the possibility that children actively engage in teaching each other about social relationships by using televison content as a kind of "demonstration model." Younger children are known to play games based on television characters and events (Palmer, 1983). The process of reviewing television content in this way seems akin to the more deliberate behavior of adolescents.

The study of television's contribution to children's understanding of social life is not straightforward. The social context in which children are placed has an important bearing on what they take from the many examples of social relationships portrayed on television. Not surprisingly, the concepts and methods of research studies that examine television's educational role within its social context represent a departure from more narrowly defined psychological research designs. Yet they are built on them. Early evaluations of *Sesame Street*, for example, showed that the social context of viewing was relevant to learning outcomes; children whose mothers were encouraged to have their children watch showed greater gains in skills taught by the program (Ball & Bogatz, 1970). Promotion of mother's coviewing was later established by Salomon (1977a) as related to greater improvement in skills, especially for children from working-class homes.

Walling (1976) was also concerned with the effect of parental interaction on learning from television, but adopted a broader definition of learning. He was interested in what he called *informal learning* from commercial television programs because of an assumed link between this kind of learning and the child's overall socialization. Using a combination of interview and experimental methods with 24 first-grade students and their mothers, Walling established that informal learning was greatly enhanced when parents interacted with their children during and about television viewing. His conceptualization of commercial television programs as providing material that entered into a child's socialization also led him to call for methods that took account of the social context of television viewing, specifically, more experimental research in naturalistic settings over longer periods of time (Walling, 1976).

There has indeed been a recent development of observational and ethnographic techniques in the study of television within families. Studies by Lull (1982a, 1982b), Bryce (1980), and Anderson and his colleagues (Anderson et al., 1979; Meyer, Traudt, & Anderson, 1980) are concerned with describing patterns of television behavior within families and relating them to social processes beyond the immediate viewing environment. However, these studies do not specifically address the question of the impact of television in relation to children. We now turn to studies that do focus on television and children within a family context. Being a developing area, a range of different theoretical approaches is being applied, with the emphasis as much on process and context as upon outcomes.

THE FAMILY CONTEXT

Messaris (1982) states a concern about "the various ways in which parent and television together may contribute to a child's developing stock of knowledge about the real world and, in particular, the child's sense of the nature of society and social relationships" (p. 581). Much recent work has begun to look at the family context of television viewing to explain television's effects more comprehensively.

Bronfenbrenner (1975) speculates that the proliferation of television sets in American homes and the separation of adult and child viewing areas are contributing to increased alienation of children from the older generation. His ideas receive some support from Gross and Walsh (1980) who found that parents' coviewing and control over children's viewing decreased with the increase in the number of television sets in the family. It also helps to explain the finding that, in the United States at least, positive relationships between amount of viewing and socioeconomic level or intelligence are not now consistently found. Family socialization patterns and other contextual factors (e.g., where the TV set is situated) are now more likely to relate to heavy viewing than IQ and socioeconomic measures (Wartella, Alexander, & Lemish, 1979).

Brown and Linné (1976) define the family as a mediator of television's effects in a conventional S-IV-R model, where television is the stimulus and the family an intervening variable. They argue that "the family acts as a filter to the child's experience of television" and this process "actively affects the type of influence television has on the child" (Brown & Linné, 1976, p. 84).

Singer and Singer (1981) have conducted research on parents as "mediators" of television effects in which they set up four different treatment groups using the parents of 141 preschool children. The three experimental groups were trained to stimulate imagination with television or toys, to stimulate language and cognition similarly, or to limit the amount of their child's viewing. Parents kept viewing records of their children at intervals during 1 year, and observers rated their free play on eight occasions in the same period. Parents in the imaginative play and those in the cognitive skills groups were successful in promoting these features in their child's play. Children in these two groups also reduced their viewing time. No effects were present for the other two groups. It seems that merely limiting the amount of television viewing, without actively participating while children are watching, is ineffective in aiding development of imagination or language. Singer and Singer are now following the same 5- and 6-year-olds through the third and fourth grade and relating their abilities at school and play to their television viewing and their parents' style of mediation or filtering of television.

Another approach to conceptualizing the child-family-television relationship is that of Chaffee, McLeod, and Atkin (1971) who established two different dimensions of child-parent communication with regard to television: concept orientation and socio-orientation. Concept orientation refers to a focus on the free expression of ideas; socio-orientation places emphasis on harmonious relationships and obedience to authority. Using this dichotomy, Chaffee, McLeod, and Atkin (1971) characterized four family types: laissez-faire (low on both orientations), protective (high on socio-orientation), pluralistic (high on concept orientation), and consensual (high on both—the child is exposed to controversial ideas but constrained to maintain harmonious relationships). They found that those children from pluralistic homes gave considerable attention to media news reports and spent little time with television, whereas those from protective homes were heavy users and showed little interest in news. Those from laissez-faire and consensual homes differed little from the norm. These dimensions of family communication were also linked to student achievement, with children from pluralistic homes making better grades in school. By contrast, adolescents from consensual homes received the lowest grades in social studies.

Messaris and Kerr (1983) have used this conceptual framework as a basis for investigating the range and type of comments made by mothers to their children about television. This study was based on interview data from 336 mothers of elementary school children. Mothers were asked to indicate (on a 4-point scale) how often they had made various kinds of critical comments about the relationship between television and reality and how often they had supplemented information on television in the previous 6 months. After controlling for amount of television viewing, coviewing, and the child's age, concept orientation was found to be positively related to nondirective critical comments about the behavior of television characters and to "broadening" information giving. It seems that children within families that encourage free inquiry have their understanding further enhanced by the commentary their mother provides while viewing television. Interestingly, mothers from both types of families affirmed the negative aspects of society as portrayed on television in their comments to children.

A second study by Messaris (1983), based on the observation of 113 families, is concerned with actual family conversations about television. He describes two different kinds of conversations: those involving behavioral prescriptions and those that are information-oriented. The latter are germane to this chapter. Information-oriented conversations are those in which "information about some aspect of the real world is sought and/or given following a televised portrayal of our reference to that aspect of the world" (Messaris, 1983, p. 294). According to Messaris, children often make requests for further information, some of which deal with the subjects of formal education (e.g., history or geography). What may be more important than the specific learning inspired by television requests, however, is what parents convey about "the value of trying to go beyond what one is given in this or any other medium" (Messaris, 1983, p. 297). Messaris found great variation in how parents treated their children's requests, with some being completely unresponsive, or even annoyed, and others answering questions at great length. A few parents took the initiative to quiz their children about television content and rewarded correct answers. These two studies give strong indications that the patterns of use of televison content in discussions with parents may provide one of the explanatory links between television viewing and performance at school.

A RECONSIDERATION OF TELEVISION AND EDUCATION

The totality of a child's experience away from school forms the basis for his or her schooling. For example, families that encourage children to be active and curious about their television viewing at home are developing attitudes toward knowledge and experience which are congruent with the kind of learning usually promoted at school as appropriate for successful achievement. It is important that teachers also acknowledge the integrity of the experiences children bring to their schooling. For many children, a large part of this will consist in "the unplanned curricular messages of television" (Berry, 1980, p. 80).

Tripp (1983) has conducted research in classrooms to explore what aspects of the two realms of the child's experience overlap, when and in what ways. Ten teachers from primary and secondary schools were employed to conduct a 10-week study in three phases. In the first, teachers documented any reference to television viewing that occurred during their classes. The second phase was spent exploring those instances when television intruded into schoolwork. In the third phase, the teacher encouraged students to make use of television in lessons.

The study found evidence of widespread understanding on the part of children that television was not a legitimate part of schooling, which is reinforced by examples of teachers disallowing children's use of knowledge from television shows in class discussions. As a result, children sometimes deliberately disguised the source of their information. When encouraged to talk about television in class, some children became disruptive, possibly because they considered such talk frivolous.

Children also seem able to discriminate between different kinds of television programs according to their acceptability to teachers. In a survey of teachers in South Australia (Australian Council for Children's Film and Television, 1981) 30% of the teachers reported that children initiated talk with them about news and documentary programs, but only 19.2% reported the same for soap operas and serial dramas. By contrast, 9% reported children talking to each other about documentaries; 33% reported that children discussed soap operas and serials. Unlike the children, teachers seem unwilling to relate to the real television interests of their pupils. Tripp (1983) argues that such a delegitimation of television viewing puts at a disadvantage the pupil whose chief environmental enrichment has been the television.

CONCLUSIONS

We have argued that television has some direct impact on children's learning at school but that this impact varies depending on a variety of factors. Thus, it is not tenable to maintain the validity of general statements that television is good or bad for school achievement, reading, and academic aptitude. However, we have also argued that television teaches children about their society and about appropriate ways of behaving in society. It is through such learning that educational processes are filtered; thus, indirectly, television again can be seen to affect children's learning. A child who has become alienated from family and learned that physical aggression is the proper first response to frustration will make a different kind of student than one who has viewed television with active parental participation and learned that thoughtful reflection is the proper first response to frustration.

Television affects children's educational achievements both directly and indirectly. In an earlier paper, Ball (1976) argued that a precise evaluation of the direct impact of television is methodologically impossible. It remains so. However, from the evidence at our disposal based on a variety of research methodologies, it is clear that television is a tool whose educational impact can vary widely in quality and in degree. Viewing of appropriate television programs adequately filtered by a sensitive family can have positive impact, both directly and indirectly, on the education of children. Teachers must recognize that television is a major part of our children's experiences, and consequently, teachers should be willing to share the pedagogical dais with television. Likewise, as a community, we must look for ways to encourage the sensible use of the new teaching tool called television.

REFERENCES

Anderson, C. (1982). Some correlations of TV viewing. *Alberta Journal of Educational Research, 28*,(1), 58–68.

Anderson, C., & MacGuire, T. (1978). The effect of TV viewing on the educational performance of elementary school children. *Alberta Journal of Educational Research, 24*(3), 156–163.

Anderson, J. A., Traudt, P. J., Acker, S. R., Meyer, T. P., Donohue, T. R. (1979). *An ethnological approach to a study of televiewing in family settings.* Paper presented at the annual meeting of the Western Speech Communication Association, Los Angeles. (ERIC Document Reproduction Service No. ED 172 282)

Angle, B. (1981). The relationship between children's televiewing and the variables of reading attitude, reading achievement, book reading and IQ in a sample of fifth grade children. *Dissertation Abstracts International, 41* 3501A.

Australian Council for Children's Film and Television. (1981). *Survey of Teachers' Perceptions of the Impact of Television on the Children They Teach.* Adelaide, Australia.

Ball, S. (1976). Methodological problems in assessing the impact of television. *Journal of Social Issues, 32*, 8–17.

Ball, S., & Bogatz, G. (1970). *A summary of major findings in "The First Year of Sesame Street": An evaluation.* New York: Educational Testing Service.

Belsen, W. A. (1956). Learning and attitude changes resulting from viewing a television series, "Bon Voyage." *British Journal of Educational Psychology, 26*, 31–38.

Berry, G. L. (1980). Children, television and social class roles: The medium as an unplanned educational curriculum. In E. L. Palmer & A. Dorr (Eds.), *Children and the faces of television* (pp. 71–81). New York: Academic.

Bronfenbrenner, U. (1975). The origins of alienation. In U. Bronfenbrenner & M. A. Mahoney (Eds.), *Influences on human development* (2nd ed., pp. 658–677). Hinsdale, IL: Dryden.

Brown, J. R., & Linné, O. (1976). The family as a mediator of television's effects. In R. Brown (Ed.), *Children and television* (pp. 184–198). London: Collier-Macmillan.

Bryant, J., Alexander, A., & Brown, D. (1983). Learning from educational programs. In M. Howe (Ed.), *Learning from educational television: Psychological and educational research* (pp. 1–30). New York: Academic.

Bryce, J. W. (1980). *Families and television: An ethnographic approach.* Unpublished doctoral dissertation, Columbia University, New York.

Chaffee, S., McLeod, J., & Atkin, C. (1971). Parental influences on adolescent media use. *American Behavioral Scientist, 14*(3), 323–240.

Childers, P., & Ross, J. (1973). The relationship between viewing television and student achievement. *Journal of Educational Research, 66*(7), 317–319.

Clemens, M. (1983). The relationship between television viewing, selected student characteristics and academic achievement. *Dissertation Abstracts International, 43* 2216A.

Cohen, A. A., & Salomon, G. (1979). Children's literate television viewing: Surprises and possible explanations. *Journal of Communication, 3*, 156–163.

Comstock, G., & Fisher, M. (1975). *Television and human behavior: A guide to the pertinent scientific literature.* Santa Monica, CA: The Rand Corp.

Cook, T., & Conner, R. (1977). Sesame Street around the world: The educational impact. *Studies of Communication, 26*(2), 155–169.

Dale, E., & Williams, H. A. (1960). Mass media. In C. W. Harris (Ed.), *Encyclopedia of educational research* (pp. 791–2). New York: Macmillan.

Durham, F. (1952). The effects of television on school achievement of children. *School Life, 34,* 88–89.

Gadberry, S. (1977). *Television viewing and school grades: A cross-lagged longitudinal study.* Paper presented at the biennial meeting of the Society for Research in Child Development, New Orleans.

Goodwin, E. (1983). The relationship of school achievement to time spent watching television among 10th and 12th grade pupils in United States high schools: An analysis of high school and beyond. *Dissertation Abstracts International, 43,* 2835A.

Greenberg, B. S. (1974). Gratifications of television viewing and their correlates for British children. In J. G. Blumler & E. Katz (Eds.), *The uses of mass communications: Current perspectives on gratifications* (pp. 71–91). Beverly Hills, CA: Sage.

Greenstein, J. (1954). The effects of television on elementary school grades. *Journal of Educational Research, 48,* 161–176.

Gross, L. S., & Walsh, R. P. (1980). Factors affecting parental control over children's television viewing: A pilot study. *Journal of Broadcasting, 24,* 411–419.

Himmelweit, H., Oppenheim, A., & Vince, P. (1958). *Television and the child.* New York: Oxford University Press.

Lehr, F. (1981). Television viewing and reading performance. *Reading Teacher, 35*(2), 230–233.

Lull, J. (1982a). A rules approach to the study of television and society. *Human Communication Research, 9,* 3–16.

Lull, J. (1982b). How families select television programs: A mass-observational study. *Journal of Broadcasting, 26,* 801–811.

Lyle, J., & Hoffman, H. (1972). Children's use of television and other media. In E. A. Rubinstein, G. A. Comstock, & J. P. Murray (Eds.), *Television and social behavior* (Vol. 4, pp. 129–256). Washington, DC: U.S. Government Printing Office.

Messaris, P. (1982). Parents, children and television. In G. Gumpert & R. Cathcart (Eds.), *Inter/media: Interpersonal communication in a media world* (pp. 580–598). New York: Oxford University Press.

Messaris, P. (1983). Family conversations about television. *Journal of Family Issues, 4*(2), 293–308.

Messaris, P., & Kerr, D. (1983). Mothers' comments about TV: Relation to family communication patterns. *Communication Research, 10*(2), 175–194.

Meyer, T. P., Traudt, P. J., & Anderson, J. A. (1980). Nontraditional mass communication research methods: An overview of observational case studies of media use in natural settings. In D. Nimmo (Ed.), *Communication yearbook 4* (pp. 261–275). New Brunswick, NJ: Transaction Books.

Morgan, M., & Gross, L. (1980). Television viewing, IQ, and academic achievement. *Journal of Broadcasting, 24*(2), 117–133.

Neuman, S. (1980). *The relationship between television viewing and reading behaviour.* Paper presented to the annual meeting of the International Reading Association, St. Louis.

Noble, G. (1983). Social learning from everyday television. In M. J. Howe (Ed.), *Learning from television: Psychological and educational research* (pp. 101–124). London: Academic.

Palmer P. M. (1982, August). *Symbolic interactionism and the study of television viewing: Possibilities and perversions.* Paper presented at the Sociological Association of Australia and New Zealand Conference, Sydney.

Palmer P. M. (1983). *Favourite TV programmes: What children say and the games they play* (Progress Report No. 2, TV: The Child's View). University of Sydney: Department of Government.

Polsky, R. M. (1974). *Getting to Sesame Street: Origins of the Children's Television Workshop.* New York: Praeger.

Quisenberry, N., & Klasek, C. (1976). *The relationship of children's viewing to achievement at the intermediate level.* Southern Illinois University, Carbondale, IL, ED143336.

Ridder, J. (1963). Pupils' opinions and the relationship of television viewing to academic achievement. *Journal of Educational Research, 57*(4), 204–206.

Salomon, G. (1977a). Effects of encouraging Israeli mothers to co-observe Sesame Street with their 5-year olds. *Child Development, 48,* 1146–1151.

Salomon, G. (1977b). *The language of media and the cultivation of mental skills.* Report on 3 years of research submitted to the Spencer Foundation.

Scott, L. (1956). Television and school achievement. *Phi Delta Kappan, 38,* 25–28.

Schramm, W., Lyle, J., & Parker, E. (1961). *Television in the lives of our children.* Stanford, CA: Stanford University Press.

Sharman, K. (1979). *Children's television behaviour: Its antecedents and relationships to school performance.* ACER Occasional Paper 14.

Singer, J., & Singer, D. (1981). *Television, imagination and aggression: A study of preschoolers.* Hillsdale, NJ: Lawrence Erlbaum Associates.

Singer, J., & Singer, D. (1983). Implications of childhood television viewing for cognition, imagination and emotion. In J. Bryant, & D. Anderson (Eds.), *Children's understanding of television: Research on attention and comprehension* (pp. 265–295). New York: Academic.

Smeyser, S. (1980). Study of the relationship between television viewing habits and early reading achievement. *Dissertation Abstracts International, 41,* 4972A.

Starkey, J., & Swinford, H. (1974). *Reading: Does television viewing time affect it?* Northern Illinois University, De Kalb. ED090966.

Tripp, D. H. (1983). *Television and schooling* (Working Paper 15, Active Eye Project). Perth: Murdoch University.

Wagner, L. (1980, December). The effects of TV on reading. *Journal of Reading,* pp. 201–206.

Walling, J. I. (1976). The effect of parental interaction on learning from television. *Communication Education, 25,* 16–24.

Wartella, E., Alexander, A., & Lemish D. (1979). The mass media environment of children. *American Behavioral Scientist, 23,* 33–52.

Watkins, B., Huston-Stein, A., & Wright, J. (1980). Effects of planned television programming. In E. L. Palmer, & A. Dorr (Eds.), *Children and the faces of television: Teaching, violence, selling* (pp. 49–70). New York: Academic.

Witty, P. (1951). Television and high school students. *Education, 72,* 242–251.

8 Using Television to Best Advantage: Research for Prosocial Television

Jerome Johnston
The University of Michigan

James S. Ettema
Northwestern University

Television brings a wide array of social interactions into the living room or classroom, providing many models of behavior, emotional responses, and the consequences of their expression. Usually, because shows are intended by their creators to entertain, social learning from them would be considered incidental. But occasionally, shows are purposely designed to promote or change social behavior. Whether effects are intended or not, television that models socially valued behaviors, responses, attitudes, or beliefs is prosocial television. This is television used to best advantage.

What is known about television's capacity to elicit socially valued responses? What are the varieties of prosocial television? Can highly effective television of this type be engineered? What role can social research play in its creation? These are the themes of this chapter. We do not consider shows that teach cognitive skills (e.g., *The Electric Company*), nor campaigns such as Chemical People, which use television to exhort and catalyze community action, but not to provide models of social behavior. Our focus is on one category of television: programs which model socially valued responses for viewers.

EXAMPLES OF PROSOCIAL IMPACTS OF TELEVISION

Television can elicit prosocial behavior, but there are qualifications. In the late 1960s, the positive reception accorded to shows such as *Mister Rogers' Neighborhood* and *Sesame Street* pointed to television's potential for positive benefits to an audience of children. A few researchers in the early 1970s began exploring the potential of broadcast television in this regard. The early research focused on the effects on children's altruistic behaviors (generosity, helping, cooperation) of viewing concentrated amounts of television shows that modeled such behaviors. Stein and Friedrich (1972) had children watch 12 shows from *Mister Rogers' Neighborhood*; other children watched Batman and Superman cartoons. Viewing the aggressive television content was associated with increased interpersonal aggression for those children who were above average in such aggression before viewing; the prosocial content led to increased prosocial behavior, but only for lower socioeconomic status children. The effects could not be detected two weeks later. In short, the research indicated that under the right conditions, a television diet can elicit behavior similar to what is viewed for viewers with certain characteristics, but not for all viewers.

In a later study, Friedrich and Stein (1975) found that viewing *Mister Rogers* resulted in all viewers being able to describe more prosocial behaviors, even though none of them produced these behaviors when observed. Television altered their knowledge, but it did not affect behavior. In this same study, viewers and nonviewers were subsequently trained through role-playing in ways to be helpful to their friends. Children who had viewed *Mister Rogers* were more helpful than those who had not. This finding indicates that television can be an important ingredient in educational efforts that require the unique characteristics of television, especially by providing a model or schema for new behaviors. It also provides a caution. When mere viewing appears to have no impact on behavior, viewers may have been predisposed nonetheless. Other research has estimated television's potential to influence social interaction skills (e.g., Fryear & Thelen, 1969; Gorn, Goldberg, & Kanungo, 1976) and self-control (e.g., Friedrich & Stein, 1973; Sprafkin & Rubinstein, 1983). The research establishes television's potential to shape behavior when the environment and/or TV diet is specially manipulated. As is the case with television's role in cultivating or triggering antisocial behavior, it is not known what effect prosocial programming has when it is imbedded randomly in a viewer's total diet of viewing.

In the mid- to late 1970s, many attempts were made to exploit television's prosocial potential. Many of these programs were for older children and sought outcomes other than behavioral change. A notable example is *Freestyle*, a 13-part dramatic series for 9- to 12-year-olds. It was designed to alter sex-role stereotypes regarding appropriate behavior for boys and girls. The summative evaluation showed the power of the medium to alter beliefs, attitudes, and interests under a variety of conditions. Johnston and Ettema (1982) studied 7,000 children in seven cities to examine the effects of the series when (a) viewed at home with minimal encouragement; (b) viewed at school, with viewing required but with no discussion or activities afterward; and (c) viewed at school supplemented by teacher-led discussion and support activities. The dependent measures used in their pre-post design were self-completed assessments in three domains:

1. beliefs about boys' and girls' competence in nontraditional activities—girls in sports and boys in child care, for example;
2. attitudes about boys and girls engaging in nontraditional activities ("Is it a good idea for girls to play football?");
3. interests in performing nontraditional activities for their gender.

In total, there were 20 indices of impact—eight belief measures, eight attitude measures, and four interest measures.

Those who viewed the shows in schools watched all 13 episodes, and their results represent the effects of heavy viewing. Among female viewers, there were significant changes on 50% of the belief and attitude measures, and an increased personal liking for mechanical activities. There were fewer changes in male viewers. Males changed on only 25% of the belief and attitude measures, and showed no increased interest in activities in the nontraditional domain for boys—nurturance (e.g., child care).

Those who viewed the shows at home provided a test under almost natural conditions. Changes were found for only the heaviest viewers, that is, seven or more shows for females and 10 or more for males. Heavy viewing resulted in change only in the topic of females performing mechanical tasks (e.g., young girls repairing a bike; or building a model; adult women as auto mechanics). Females and males alike changed their beliefs and attitudes about girls in these activities; females also showed increased personal interest in mechanics.

These findings indicate that: viewing a modest amount of purposefully constructed prosocial dramatic programming can alter beliefs, attitudes, and even interests of viewers; belief and attitude change can generalize beyond show-specific concepts; size of effects interact with viewer predisposition (girls vs. boys in this case); effects are more easily achieved with some topics than others (e.g., mechanics is easier than assertiveness or leadership); and effects are more easily achieved with some types of outcomes than others (e.g., attitudes and beliefs are changed more easily than personal preferences).

Those who viewed and discussed the shows in school showed very large changes on most measures. Typically, the size of the changes were double that of heavy viewing alone, although in two instances mere viewing had as large or larger changes associated with it. Specifically, class discussion probably has two effects. In attitude change, confronting the problem (girls hearing and confronting boys, and vice versa) is more powerful than simply viewing confrontation on the screen, and adult-mediated discussion can make up for deficiencies in dramatic production. In the end, given a set of affective goals, television can achieve a great deal, but there are tradeoffs. Incorporating programming into an educational setting with carefully planned mediation activities typically enhances measured impact, but mobilizing schools to use the programming is very costly. To achieve similar effect sizes at home probably requires more programming and more efforts to encourage viewing. (For more detailed reviews of TV's potential to shape prosocial behavior, see e.g., Murray, 1980; Rushton, 1982; Watkins, Huston-Stein, & Wright, 1980.)

WHAT IS IT?
DIMENSIONS OF PROSOCIAL TELEVISION

The prosocial literature in the early 1970s focused on the altruistic behavior found in purposive television shows such as *Mister Rogers' Neighborhood.* Subsequently, prosocial television has come to include a wide array of programming types. A comprehensive definition of the term is impossible, but it can be discussed along a number of useful dimensions including content domain, outcome sought, and the function of the television component in an overall strategy for change.

Content Domains

Many prosocial shows fall in the domain of mental health or personal social adjustment. Series such as *Mister Rogers' Neighborhood* or segments from *Sesame Street* are designed to help young children better understand and cope with feelings of anger, disappointment, fear, or ennui associated with fighting, new situations, or even the death of a loved one. In the *Up & Coming* series, teenagers wrestle with abortion, cheating, and racism. *ABC After School Specials* show children and teens struggling with conflicts as weighty as parental alcoholism. Commercial networks provide occasional specials on popular social adjustment themes (e.g., teen-age sexuality or drug use), and particular shows within commercial series can be found that deal with adjustment themes (e.g., *Eight Is Enough, Family, Happy Days*).

Another category might be called societal adjustment in that the shows try to alter dysfunctional stereotypes. It includes shows that portray minority groups in a favorable light such as *Big Blue Marble* and *Villa Alegre.* Considering girls as minorities, *Freestyle* tried to portray them as capable of achievement in traditionally masculine areas such as mechanics and science. In response to concern for childhood arson, *Code Red* portrayed a child arsonist being adopted, loved, and giving up his predilection for conflagration. Illustrative of the breadth of the prosocial net is the Children's Television Workshop (CTW) series *3-2-1 Contact.* Aimed at 9- to 12-year-olds, its goals are not to teach science per se, but break down stereotypes of scientists as dull white males and make the subject of science appear interesting.

Another area is health, although most shows about health try to provide information rather than models of good health behavior. One of the best known shows devoted to health was *Feeling Good*, created by CTW in the mid-1970s. This series covered a wide variety of health topics, ranging from arthritis to nutrition. Except for *Feeling Good*, most health campaigns use television as only one component in an articulated mass media campaign to alter health behaviors.

Goals

The goal of producers of most commercial shows that come to be called prosocial is to entertain and thereby attract as large an audience as possible. Some producers, however, seek to present worthwhile topics in the course of entertaining their audience. For example, Norman Lear—producer of *All in the Family*—chose to have Archie Bunker deal with such topics as heart attack and rape, and to resolve them in socially valued ways. Presumably, these segments were motivated by considerations other than entertainment. Bill Cosby teamed up with CBS to produce *Fat Albert*, a series for children that is decidedly prosocial in intent. Still, entertainment is essential to such a series.

Among noncommercial and educational producers, entertainment may also be a goal because holding an audience is the sine qua non for other socialization goals. *Freestyle* is an example of a show with the ultimate goal of changing its audience, but with the more immediate goals of entertaining, presenting comprehensible messages, and providing programming acceptable to the educational community. As we have argued elsewhere, these more immediate goals influenced its production as much as, or even more than, the ultimate goals of changing stereotypes (Johnston & Ettema, 1982).

In regard to ultimate goals, distinctions can be made regarding the aspirations for changing the audience. The three most common categories are beliefs (or perceptions of reality), attitudes, and behaviors. *Big Blue Marble* and most of the programming funded by the Emergency School Aid Act (e.g., *Villa Alegre*, *Carrascolendas*) are examples of shows that attempted to alter viewers' beliefs and attitudes toward others. Through the use of multicultural casts and stories about various nonwhite groups, the producers hoped "to reduce the racial isolation" felt by minorities in this country. *Freestyle's* central goal was to alter sex-role stereotypes. *Fat Albert* and *Mister Rogers* are examples of series with goals in the affective and behavioral domains. Some programs deal with emotional adjustment with the aim of having the audience understand and accept their own feelings of anger or loneliness. Other programs try to teach task persistence, caring, cooperation, and the like. The belief, attitude, behavior distinction is useful in understanding the varieties of goals implicit in prosocial efforts, but architects of these series are often not conversant with the terms.

Intervention Strategy

There is a large body of literature on strategies for changing beliefs, attitudes, and behaviors, but the knowledge is rarely applied systematically in prosocial projects. We consider first the strategies implicit in projects as a whole; later we examine more carefully the strategies contained in the video component by itself.

An examination of existing programs and projects highlights some differences in strategies. A basic distinction can be made between prosocial strategies designed for home and school consumption. Home-based strategies depend on incidental learning. The show (and perhaps the promotion related to the show) must carry the entire burden for developing and maintaining attention; for communicating clearly to the target audience; and for teaching and motivating individual response to the messages. The research on *Freestyle* demonstrates that the potential for change is greatly enhanced in the school setting. Even when the school setting is used only for viewing, the effects are much stronger because viewing is assured.

A few shows targeted for home consumption try to extend their influence with print material, as in the cases of *Sesame Street* and *3-2-1 Contact*, which have subscription magazines and other materials that reinforce the themes of the shows. Interestingly, PBS rules that forbid advertising also prohibit informing the audience about these magazines. For children's shows, adult mediation (parent coviewing and commentary) is also considered important in achieving program impact.

In school and other instructional settings much more can be done with non-video components. The audience is captive and led by either a teacher or trained group facilitator. This person can help viewers comprehend and apply the messages to their own situations; they can orchestrate group response to the televised materials and provide additional training and activities. Almost all shows designed for school use include a teacher guide with suggested discussion questions and ancillary activities.

CTW routinely includes community outreach with its projects. *3-2-1 Contact* is designed to be viewed in homes and schools. To extend its influence, CTW distributes a teacher guide like most shows with a school orientation. In addition, in conjunction with the Girl Scouts, they developed a merit badge program centered around science projects illustrated on the shows. They also have encouraged science museums to label with the *3-2-1 Contact* logo exhibits that relate to the themes in the shows. *Freestyle* provides a teacher guide with suggested discussion questions and activities appropriate to the classroom. A comic book extends the video lessons in a print medium. The project even created a prototype community outreach plan in which churches and other community organizations were used as vehicles to organize meetings for parents in which the shows would be viewed and discussed. This was designed to help parents surface their own feelings about changing gender-role expectations and to provide them with ideas on how to discuss the shows with their children (Kossler, 1980).

The most articulated social interventions are found in the health arena, especially the Stanford Heart Disease Prevention Program and the Minnesota Heart Health Project. They frequently lay out elaborate plans for change based on the best available theories of persuasion, interpersonal influence, and intrapersonal change. They often include mass media campaigns as well as community outreach. Most of these campaigns are informational and do not use the prosocial strategy of modeling desired behavior. An exception is the Friends Are Good Medicine campaign of the California Department of Mental Health. Solomon (1982) provides an excellent review of the evolving theories of change and of the effectiveness of the various campaigns designed around these theories.

RESEARCH FOR PROSOCIAL TELEVISION

What makes effective prosocial video? There is a large and growing body of research on this question. A variety of program characteristics have been isolated, analyzed, and related to viewer responses such as attention, comprehension, and behavior. Although this research draws upon the work of developmental and social psychologists, it can also be seen as the beginning of an applied science of prosocial television.

Formal Elements

Huston et al. (1981) isolated and analyzed formal elements such as visual tricks (i.e., special effects) and elements of audio presentation such as singing and other sorts of music, noise, and dialogue from various sources. In much the same vein, Watt and Krull (1974) developed a number of entropy variables, which essentially are measures of various changes in the audio and visual tracks of programs.

These types of formal elements have received most research attention as independent variables in analyses of children's attention to televised stimuli. Watkins et al. (1980) were able to generate a veritable catalog of elements related to attention drawing upon the formative research for CTW productions and other research. Positive correlates of attention include lively music, clear and simple language in short sentences, children's voices, changes in sound and sound effects, and animation. Corresponding negative correlates include song and dance numbers, long and complex speeches, men's voices, and live animals.

In an interesting departure from the focus on attention, Salomon (1979) has argued that certain formal elements of television are analogous to, and help develop, certain mental operations. For example, zooming-in to emphasize one part of a complex whole both represents and promotes analysis of a whole into its parts. Similarly, showing an object from different angles represents and promotes perspective taking. Salomon provides evidence that as children become more adept at decoding these formal visual elements, they are better able to learn the content of messages that employ them. Similarly, Collins (1983; Collins, Wellman, Keniston, & Westby, 1978) suggests that such formal elements can affect the complexity of inferences necessary to grasp the plot of a program. Thus, formal elements may have an impact on comprehension as well as attention.

Studies of the relationship between formal elements and children's attention has already proven useful in the development of purposive, prosocial television. The success of *Sesame Street* in achieving its cognitive and affective goals, for example, rests in part upon that program's ability to hold children's continuing interest, if not constant attention. However, this research does not yet provide a set of principles that can be used to engineer television with high attention value. One problem is that the formal elements that have been isolated and analyzed do not constitute anything like a language of television for expressing any sort of content. Huston et al. (1981) suggest that, in principle, these elements can be used to convey any content but that, in fact, the use of the elements is correlated with particular content due to production conventions and decisions. They found, for example, that the use of particular formal features did not distinguish between humorous and serious programming but did distinguish between animated and live action and between children's commercial, children's noncommercial, and prime time programming. They also found, as television and film makers could readily verify, that the dramatization of aggression, particularly nonverbal aggression, is characterized by a package of specific formal elements. Similarly, Watt and Krull (1974) found that, for prime time programming, their entropy variables could be reduced to two factors: dynamics, which measured changes in audio and visual tempo, and unfamiliarity, which measured the occurrence of new or unfamiliar scenes. For commercials, however, the variables could be reduced to two quite different factors, one essentially auditory, the other visual (Wartella & Ettema, 1974). It seems that formal elements are bound up with the content and even the purpose of television (i.e., education, entertainment, or persuasion). Thus, the intent to use or avoid particular formal elements will constrain if not determine content.

Viewer Characteristics

If the conventions of the television creator complicate the issue, so do characteristics of the television viewer. Level of cognitive development is one such complication. Most of the generalizations concerning the relationship between formal elements and attention rest upon research with younger children. Wartella and Ettema (1974) argue, however, that the hold of formal elements on attention should decline as children become more adept at processing content and thus are able to attend selectively to material of central importance to the plot or message. An implication of this argument is that attention does not translate in some direct and automatic fashion into other outcomes such as comprehension. Younger children's attention may be firmly held by certain formal features, but they still may not comprehend the plot or message. Older children probably do not need to attend to each flicker of the tube slavishly to get the point. Indeed Lorsch, Anderson, and Levin (1979) found that induced attention to an episode of *Sesame Street* did not increase learning. In fact, they suggest that comprehension of the material guided attention rather than vice versa, confirming the common-sense notion that kids who don't "get it" will probably "tune out." We are reminded, then, that attention is an active process intimately related to other abilities and processes.

Program Formats

From one point of view, the molecular formal elements of the television stimuli are the most fundamental features of the medium. From another point of view, however, the molar distinction between program formats is very basic. Most existing prosocial television programs can be sorted into one of two general formats: the short segment or "bit" format exemplified by *Sesame Street* and the narrative or story-line format exemplified by *Freestyle*. There has been little systematic analysis of the impact of format on such outcomes as attention, comprehension, or even affective response to programs. *Sesame Street* was conceived as a short segment format, and the research on attention, comprehension, and impact has all been done on these short segments, which are the hallmark of that series. The research (e.g., Paulson, 1974) does indicate that the short segment format can effectively promote prosocial outcomes (e.g., cooperation). Similarly, the summative evaluation of *Freestyle* indicates that the narrative format, can also be effective with older children and more complex messages (Johnston & Ettema, 1982).

Freestyle is of further interest because the formative research for that program compared these two format types. Early in the development of the series, three pilot programs were produced. One used short segments to present brief, often verbal, messages; another used narratives to present dramatic portrayals of the desired prosocial behaviors; a third used a hybrid of the two. The results of a multisite test indicated that the series' counter-stereotypical messages were least understood in the story-line format, but the narrative was well understood by the 9- to 12-year-old audience and was the overwhelming favorite of both children and teachers (LaRose, 1979; Williams, 1978).

The affective response to the narrative weighed heavily in the choice of a format for the series, but it was not the only factor. The educational advisors had argued throughout the project that a narrative format in which one or two topics could be treated in depth was mandated by the complex prosocial goals of the series. The executive producer, on the other hand, concluded that the narrative format offered the possibility of more entertaining television for 9- to 12-year-olds (Johnston & Ettema, 1982). Much as with the molecular formal elements, the format of a program is more a feature of form than of content, but it is another feature with important implications for how content is communicated and even for what can be communicated.

Structural Elements

A considerable body of literature has begun to develop on children's understanding of narratives in a variety of media. Several structural elements of the narrative format have been isolated and analyzed. One such element is the temporal separation of plot events (e.g., motive, action, and consequence), which has been a focus of research by Collins and his associates (see Collins, 1983, for a review). One study indicated that when a protagonist's motive and subsequent aggressive act were in very close temporal proximity, the implicit motive-act relationship was readily understood by second and fifth graders. But when the motive and the aggression were separated by 4 minutes, the relationship was less comprehensible, particularly for the second graders (Purdie, Collins, & Westby, 1979). Successful integration of motives and aggressive acts has, in turn, been related to a more negative evaluation of the aggressor (Costanzo, Coie, Grumet, & Farnill, 1973). Once again, the level of cognitive development looms large as a mediator in the relationship between features of television and viewer response. Also important is the social knowledge children bring to the viewing situation.

Another structural element that has been related to comprehension is the use of action to highlight the narrative's message. Calvert, Watkins, Huston-Stein, and Wright (1979), for example, found that children's recall of themes in an episode of *Fat Albert and the Cosby Kids* was enhanced when the thematic material was accompanied by high levels of action. Recall was reduced, however, when the material was presented through dialogue only. The *Freestyle* research drew similar conclusions. Johnston and Ettema (1982) found that viewers usually recall best the most dramatic scenes from an episode. When the intended message is imbedded in such scenes viewers are more likely to understand the show's main message. When the message is contained in a scene in which the actors simply verbalize the message, viewers also learn the message, but only if they happen to recall the scene. Because such scenes are rarely among the more dramatic, viewers seldom remember them. These findings suggest that it is not sufficient to embed a complex counter-stereotypical message in an interesting story or even to verbalize the message at some point in the story. "Rather the drama must be so intimately related to the intended lesson that they cannot be understood apart from each other. More than that the drama must *be* the lesson" (Johnston & Ettema, 1982, p. 111).

The scenes in which the *Freestyle* messages were verbalized came to be called by the series' creators "Ah-ha! scenes." Presumably upon seeing them, children would exclaim, "Ah-ha! Now I understand." Results showed, however, that this labeling strategy had limited success. Similarly, Watkins (1978) found that a verbal explanation of themes in *Fat Albert and the Cosby Kids* did not enhance comprehension. On the other hand, Susman (1976) found that labeling the act of sharing in a program with a game show format increased children's sharing behavior. Similarly, Friedrich and Stein (1975) found that verbal labeling provided in a postviewing session enhanced kindergartners' comprehension of the message and, to a lesser extent, actual helping behavior. In an attempt to explicate such apparently contradictory results, Stein and Friedrich (1975) suggest that labels are most effective when presented before and/or after the action or story rather than within or throughout it. Differing results may also reflect differing message contents and viewers' ages.

Modeling Strategies

At a level of complexity beyond structural elements, Lovelace and Huston (1983) identify three modeling strategies for conveying prosocial messages. One such strategy is to model only the prosocial behavior to be promoted. Based upon their review of many studies, which typically exposed young children to short segments of positive behaviors such as social interaction, Lovelace and Huston conclude that this strategy can facilitate learning and performance, particularly when the behaviors are presented in small, sequential steps. They acknowledge, however, that opportunities for drama are quite limited when only the prosocial behavior can be shown. Thus, the strategy may be of limited use when a program must draw and hold an audience on its own, but it may have real value in classroom and therapeutic applications.

Another strategy with limited but still useful applications is to present models who encounter difficulties when exhibiting prosocial behavior (e.g., confrontation with a parent). The television show dramatizes the conflict, but it is unresolved as the program ends. Programs such as *On the Level* and *Self Incorporated* (Agency for Instructional Television) have used this trigger strategy and are typically designed to spur discussion among children in a classroom. The formative research on several such programs indicates that children do comprehend these stories and do tend to generate prosocial rather than antisocial resolutions to the problems portrayed (Rockman, 1976, 1980). However, other research suggests quite limited potential for prosocial change (Johnston, Blumenfeld, & Isler, 1983).

The third strategy is to create and resolve the difficulties encountered by the prosocial model within the program. This approach has been employed by *Mister Rogers, Freestyle,* and most commercial programs with prosocial themes. Lovelace and Huston (1983) suggest that programs using this strategy can effectively transmit prosocial content to children, in part because these programs can be highly engaging. The authors recommend, however, that contrary to current practice, a substantial part of the story be devoted to the prosocial behavior and its positive consequences and that the program be supplemented with postviewing rehearsal or discussion to consolidate understanding and promote adoption of the desired outcomes.

Freestyle is of particular interest because it developed the strategy into a clearly articulated and consistently applied formula. Key elements of the formula included a standardized plot line in which featured characters chose to engage in nonstereotypical behaviors but encountered difficulties in doing so. Sometimes these problems were created by others, but often the difficulties were of the character's own making. Eventually, the character overcame the difficulties by fully mastering the nonstereotypical behavior and was richly rewarded for doing so.

Form-Content Relationships

The form and content of television cannot be easily disentangled. The choice of particular formal or structural elements is likely to place constraints on content, and the choice of particular content is likely to imply the use of certain elements. It is appropriate, then, to consider more explicitly the relationship between the form and content of prosocial television. In the face of great diversity in these relationships, we present two examples.

The summative evaluation of *Freestyle* indicated that the series was more effective in some content areas than others. For example, both male and female viewers increased their estimate of the proportion of girls competent in mechanical and athletic activities. However, children did not increase their estimates of the number of girls competent in assertiveness and reasonable risk taking. It may be that children's beliefs about girls' willingness to take risks are more resistant to change than their beliefs about girls' abilities as athletes. On the other hand, it may be that the behavioral skills were more difficult to convey via television (even with teacher mediation). Competence in such concrete activities as athletics can often be conveyed in a single image—a girl scores the winning touchdown, and the lesson is clear. Competence in the much more abstract behavioral skills is not so easily portrayed.

Freestyle attempted to embody these behavioral skills in a dramatic story and to make them more comprehensible with the "Ah-ha!" scenes. However, the behavioral skills were not always as central to the story as they might have been, and the verbalizations were easily ignored. Had the scripts been different, the results might also have been. But perhaps the behavioral skills were simply too complex and abstract to be conveyed via television, which sought to entertain as well as educate. Indeed, a number of the script writers (all seasoned Hollywood professionals) said that effective drama deals more with emotions than with abstract ideas and that *Freestyle's* messages, particularly those about behavioral skills, were often not amenable to dramatic presentation. Most writers spoke of a compromise between the entertainment and educational goals of the series. Only a few spoke in terms of a synthesis.

Another example of the problematic relationship between the form and content of television comes from analysis of *Sesame Street* segments dealing with emotions. From interviews with 3- to 5-year-olds, Lasker and Bernath (1974) concluded that anger was understood better than pride. Not surprisingly, they found that anger segments were better understood than pride segments. They also found, however, that the pride segments were more attentively watched and that the anger and pride segments themselves differed in almost every aspect of form discussed earlier. The pride segments were marked by such formal features as fast-paced editing and music, which probably accounted for their high attention value, whereas the anger segments were not. The anger segments were typically structured around a sequence beginning with an anger-provoking incident, followed by a labeling of the emotion and then a resolution. The pride segments did not have such a clear sequence but instead had a strong line (e.g., song or visual montage) running through the segment which celebrated rather than explained the idea of pride. One is left to speculate whether these differences in the segments are the result of production habits on the part of the *Sesame Street* creative staff or reflect something in the nature of the emotions themselves.

Principles of Program Design

The attempt to generate principles for using television to best advantage has made a good beginning with the extensive and still growing literature on children's responses to prosocial television. Indeed, the research of Huston and Wright and Collins should serve as models for programmatic research in the social sciences. It is clear, however, that we do not yet have principles that will allow us to engineer products with guaranteed attention value, comprehensibility, and effect. The principle that song and dance numbers are negatively related to attention may predict preschoolers' response to segments of *Sesame Street*, but might not predict their older brothers' and sisters' responses to music television (MTV). Form, content, and viewer interact in many highly complex and yet-to-be-charted ways.

Further, it is not clear that principles for assembling at will the forms and features of television to precisely manipulate viewers' responses can ever be generated. The notion that television is a bundle of discrete elements that can be disentangled and then rewoven as desired is simplistic at best. The meaning of television rests on a set of symbolic conventions, but these conventions are rooted not only in the history of television but also in the history of cinema and storytelling itself. These symbolic conventions can be manipulated toward a variety of ends, but this manipulation will probably always be more an act of creation than a feat of engineering. In the last section, we return to the implications of this for the production of prosocial television.

NEEDED RESEARCH

We do not wish to be too pessimistic about the value of research. The basic research of Collins and others is very important, but research that is more consciously applied is also needed. Together, such studies would comprise the applied science of prosocial television. Here are some of the topics in need of study.

Goals

What can television do best and what should be left for other means of social-ization? New social problems will continually be identified, only some of which can be ameliorated with television. Prior research has identified some of tele-vision's strengths, but bold new experimentation is needed to map TV's areas of potency. A current social problem is substance use among teens. Part of the problem may lie in inaccurate stereotypes held by adolescents regarding the consequences of using cigarettes, alcohol, or illicit substances. It is known that television is a good medium for correcting stereotypes. But another component in substance use is the motivation and skill of saying no in the face of peer pressure to try a substance. Can television help here? It may be able to model saying no, but can it enhance the viewer's will to turn down an offer?

As another example, prosocial responses to situations are often ones that are less self-centered (cooperation, helping others) or that require mastery and con-frontation rather than avoidance. Yet research indicates that adolescents are most likely to assume that the most self-centered solution to a problem is the best solution, even though adults would consider many of these solutions short-sighted (Johnston et al., 1983). Can delayed gratification and unselfish strategies be modeled for teens and adults?

To address these issues, unabashedly practical research is needed. Programs must be created and their effects studied. The programs must be real programs created for real—not laboratory—audiences.

The Process of Effects

Research is needed on a number of video strategy issues related to character identification, attention, and comprehension. It has long been assumed that iden-tification with the model in a film/television drama is important to a viewer's adopting the modeled behavior. However, as Dorr (1982) points out, this is only an assumption in need of further testing.

If identification is found to be important, what are the characteristics that lead to identification? They clearly are not the same for all viewers. For example, Reeves (1979) showed that the strength and activity dimensions of television characters are important for young male viewers, whereas physical attractiveness is more important for young females. More needs to be known about the relevant characteristics to guide in the casting and story-line development of prosocial television.

A related issue is comprehension. How attentive must a viewer be to com-prehend the messages in the show? The traditional assumption has been that devices such as dramatic music and scene shifts are needed to rivet the viewers' attention if they are to comprehend the embedded messages. But the work of Lorsch et al. (1979) suggests that some level of comprehension is a prerequisite for holding attention. Devices and tricks to hold attention may be important, but they are insufficient to lead to comprehension.

How important is comprehension to the adoption of prosocial response? In educational television with purely cognitive goals, comprehension is an end in itself. But for affective programming aimed at teaching social behavior or attitudes through modeling, it is unclear whether viewers must comprehend the social situation portrayed in order to adopt the prosocial response illustrated.

Formative Research

Even if substantial progress is made in deriving principles of video design, formative research will always be necessary in purposive prosocial projects. Attention to the methods of formative research is itself a worthwhile endeavor. The traditional purview of formative research is testing the appeal, comprehensibility, and effects of program material. Regarding appeal, La Rose (1980) points to the frequent confounding of two facets: attracting an audience and attending to the media content once attracted. On the practical side, he cites Smith (1978) who found a shortcut to expensive field testing with the target audience. In the development of *Freestyle*, teachers were asked to review scripts for segments being planned and to estimate children's interest in the story. Their ratings correlated as high as $r = .73$ with the "likability" ratings of a large sample of children who viewed the completed segments. LaRose also reviews the research on CTW's famous distractor method of assessing attention of viewers and lays out a worthwhile agenda for research on the role of attention in viewers' processing of program content. In short, the indispensable formative evaluation should itself be a subject for research with the aim of enhancing its contribution in prosocial projects.

Intervention Strategy

A number of issues relate not to the production strategies for individual shows, but to the orchestration of shows in a larger strategy for education and change. More information is needed on the amount of viewing required to achieve certain effects and the associated persistence of such effects. The *Freestyle* research documented the different levels of effect obtainable by encouraged home viewing, captive school viewing, and viewing in school supplemented by discussion. Although it is difficult to establish criteria representing sufficient change, the research helped bracket what is required to achieve different levels. For prosocial outcomes that are widely valued, more research is needed on this question.

Considering the cost of a single high quality half-hour production, the number of shows is an important consideration.

By and large, research on prosocial effects has looked only at short-term effects. Two exceptions are O'Connor's (1972) study with social isolates and the study of *Freestyle*. Both found remarkable persistence of effects that had been obtained largely with media. What effects are most resistant to change? Which dissipate in a short time?

Rarely is television alone a sufficient tool in the effort to induce prosocial responses in viewers. Yet we are only beginning to understand the interplay between video and nonvideo components. The *Freestyle* research showed that teacher-mediated viewing had a large multiplier effect, but what teacher behaviors account for this? Most teacher guides include interesting questions for discussion, but they do not represent strategically designed inquiry (for a critique, see Johnston et al., 1983). Even the basic assumption that adult mediation will enhance effects does not always apply. Sprafkin and Rubinstein (1983) found one situation in which mediation of the prosocial television diet diminished the effects. Under what conditions are postviewing discussion and role playing critical factors in the overall strategy?

We also know very little about how the video component could facilitate mediation efforts. When behavioral change is sought, the most common approach is to model the desired behaviors in the video component on the expectation that the viewer will attend, identify, and model the behavior. Any adult mediation of the message depends entirely on the skill of the adult who must know what to do and say. Attempts to be more overt and didactic on the show itself frequently "turn off" the audience. *Freestyle's* "Ah ha!" scenes were not recalled by viewers. But in a creative smoking prevention program, McAlister, Puska, Koskela, Pallonen, and Maccoby (1980) showed that a counseling group on television could provide the link to local counseling groups throughout Finland led by nonprofessional volunteer counselors. Much more experimentation is needed in this area.

It is routine for projects to produce magazines and other ancillary materials, yet almost nothing is known about their impact. Do print materials play a critical role?

Television is a mass medium, yet it clearly shows some of its strongest prosocial effects on small segments of an audience. O'Connor's film for socially isolated preschoolers was just a story to nonisolates, but to the isolates it was a plan for survival in a preschool setting which demanded social interaction (O'Connor, 1972). Sprafkin and Rubinstein (1983) took entertainment television and calmed the aggressive tendencies of institutionalized children. Much more research is needed to ferret out who can profit most from prosocial television.

All of the research that shows positive effects from viewing is based on subjects who were induced to view or who were exposed to an artificial diet of prosocial programming. How can this be replicated in the natural setting? Schools and therapeutic settings are effective milieus in which to have people view and discuss appropriate shows. But it is impractical to expect schools to incorporate extensive viewing into the curriculum, and therapeutic settings are populated by only the select few in need of help. How can various agents of socialization (schools, clubs, churches) be enlisted to encourage intensive viewing of special shows or series? In the home-viewing sites of the *Freestyle* evaluation, teachers played a minimal role. They reminded their students once a week to watch the show at home. With this small bit of encouragement, each show was viewed by 33% of the target group, a very large proportion by Nielsen standards. Schools rarely play this role of linking agent, yet it may have great potential. Children's Television Workshop has had community outreach efforts for every series it has produced. Others might learn from their experience what is entailed in collaborating with existing community organizations or in setting up a network of regional coordinators and promoters.

When a target audience is narrowly defined, network distribution may not be the best approach. With the proliferation of 128-channel cable, there are new possibilities for delivering specialized prosocial programming to segments of the population. Video disc and video tape are other possibilities, and dial-up programming may become feasible in the future. These new distribution possibilities must be paired with creative approaches to link up with target audiences.

THE ROLE OF RESEARCH IN THE CREATION
OF PROSOCIAL TELEVISION

Formative research might always be important to the success of any purposive television enterprise. But although highly useful, formative research cannot fully determine television design principles.

Much has been made of the role of formative research in the development of *Sesame Street* and other CTW productions. Land (1971) characterizes the involvement of the researchers with the television professionals as a "fusion" of talents, but a close reading of this and other reports (e.g., Lesser, 1974) indicates that the production and research groups remain in separate departments, each with clearly defined responsibilities. Further, as Land (1971) notes, the production department was the "first among equals" (p. 5). How, then, did the researchers participate in decision making? Land reports that during the development of *Sesame Street*, for example, the educational advisors drew up a list of proposed goals for the series, but the production staff selected the actual goals based on the requirements of the television medium. It seems that the researchers and other advisors proposed, but the television producers disposed.

The role of research and researchers in the development of prosocial television should not—indeed, cannot—be taken for granted. In our studies of *Freestyle* (Ettema, 1980, 1982; Johnston & Ettema, 1982), we further examined this role and found that the production staff, and the executive producer in particular, was the first among equals in this organization as well. This authority rested not so much on formal position within the organization as on informal but effective bases of power. It was, after all, the executive producer and his staff that dealt with the central task facing any prosocial television enterprise: getting a television show "in the can." The researchers and educational advisors certainly did play a role, but given the state of the art in curriculum development and television research, they usually could not provide the precise and unequivocal advice necessary to control the activities of the production staff (Ettema, 1980). As we have argued, television must be more created than engineered. The development of *Freestyle* was more an artistic than a scientific experiment.

The idea of an artistic experiment may emphasize the importance of the television creators, but it does not deny the importance of the television researchers. Research cannot determine the design of the programs, but it can focus and direct the work of the television creators toward important problems that must be solved by the design. For example, the *Freestyle* pilot testing revealed that messages about behavioral skills in the narrative pilot were poorly understood by 9- to 12-year-olds. The executive producer concluded that more screen time would have to be devoted to behavioral skills. However, the researchers argued that the behavioral skills had to be portrayed not simply more often, but more concretely. The structure of the *Freestyle* series is the result of the executive producer's attempt to solve this and other such problems defined and clarified by the researchers.

Given the potential for a highly valuable, if highly constrained, role for research and researchers in the production of purposive television, further analysis could usefully be directed toward the ways in which researchers do—and more important, could—participate in the production process. In addition to our studies of *Freestyle* and the literature on Children's Television Workshop (Connell & Palmer, 1971; Land, 1971; Lesser, 1974; Mielke & Swinehart, 1976; Palmer, 1972), the Agency for Instructional Television has attempted to monitor and learn from its own development process (Middleton, 1979; Sloan, 1980). Such organizational analysis may be more the province of media sociologists than the social psychologists who have written most extensively about prosocial television. If, however, social psychologists and other researchers are to participate in the creation of prosocial television, they must participate in the process of creation. And if they participate in the process, it is important to understand exactly where, when, and how they can and do participate. In the case of *Freestyle*, the researchers had access only to the executive producer. But access to others in the production organization (e.g., writers) is, perhaps, possible.

In the case of *Freestyle*, the researchers served primarily as formative evaluators by testing prototype materials at the behest of the executive producer, but access at other points in the process, particularly in the beginning when basic decisions about intervention strategy are being made, is possible and desirable.

Thus, in the case of *Freestyle*, there were important constraints on how the researchers participated. Those who plan and manage any future projects should carefully analyze how researchers can participate in the creation of the programs, given the constraints of time and money and given the understanding that principles of prosocial television and the results of formative research yield not so much the design of the program itself as the problems which must be solved by that design.

THE POLITICS OF PROSOCIAL TELEVISION

But all of this is academic as resources for prosocial television disappear. Most of the shows discussed in this chapter are the result of government funding. Through producer initiative or its complement (i.e., requests for proposals) various branches of the federal government have provided funding to production houses around the country to produce shows in particular topic areas, mostly for child audiences. For example, *Sesame Street* (at least in its early years) and *Up & Coming* were funded largely by the Department of Education, *Freestyle* by the National Institute of Education (NIE), and *3-2-1 Contact* by a consortium of the National Science Foundation, Department of Education, and the Corporation for Public Broadcasting. Such funding is not easily allocated by government divisions; purposive education of the public in matters other than physical health is highly unpopular in the United States. There is almost no prosocial theme that is not controversial in some way. The *Freestyle* experience is illustrative.

In the early 1970s, gender inequity was identified as a problem embedded in school practices and also in the very fabric of U.S. society. It was argued that girls and boys were being misled by societal stereotypes. The prevailing Cinderella myth led girls to make choices in their schooling that would leave them ill-prepared to take a job, a realistic expectation for most adult women. By the mid-1970s there was a sufficiently broad mandate in the Ford and Carter administrations to permit NIE to allocate $3 (and later $4) million to the creation of a television series that would help ameliorate the problem; thus, *Freestyle* was born. By 1978, when the shows premiered on PBS, they were well received throughout the country. But 2 years later, national educational priorities had shifted, and gender equity was replaced by the back-to-basics movement. Gender equity was viewed as a softheaded liberal notion. Conservatives inside and outside of the Reagan administration began an effort to dismantle NIE. In this process, NIE's support of *Freestyle* was cited as an attempt to subvert traditional American values regarding appropriate sex roles and in so doing, the series was undermining parental authority.

It is understandable that gender equity might have its opponents, but it is less obvious that science education would. Yet the highly successful *3-2-1 Contact* has had to struggle for its funding. Few in Congress or the administration are critical of attracting more youth to the study of science. But to some, television that tries to show how much fun science can be is vaguely suggestive of a national science curriculum, and a number of groups fear this.

We have argued that more effective prosocial television could result from the growth of what we have called an applied science of prosocial television. But this science will be of little use if there are no new productions to which it can be applied. In a society in which critics are always highlighting some social ill or other, and in which television is such a prominent fixture, it would be a shame not to develop to its fullest television's potential for prosocial ends.

REFERENCES

Calvert, S., Watkins, B., Huston-Stein, A., & Wright, J. C. (1979). *Immediate and delayed recall of central and incidental television content as a function of formal features.* Paper presented to the Society for Research in Child Development, San Francisco.

Collins, W. A. (1983). Interpretation and inference in children's television viewing. In J. Bryant & D. Anderson (Eds.), *Children's understanding of television* (pp. 125–150). New York: Academic.

Collins, W. A., Wellman, H., Keniston, A., & Westby, S. (1978). Age-related aspects of comprehension and inference from a televised dramatic narrative. *Child Development, 49,* 389–399.

Connell, D. D., & Palmer, E. L. (1971). Sesame Street: A case study. In J. D. Halloran & M. Gurevitch (Eds.), *Broadcaster/researcher cooperation in mass communication research.* Leeds, England: Kavanagh & Sons.

Costanzo, P. R., Coie, J. D., Grumet, J. F., & Farnill, D. (1973). A re-examination of the effects of intent and consequence on children's moral judgments. *Child Development, 44,* 154–161.

Dorr, A. (1982). Television and affective development and functioning. In D. Pearl, L. Bouthilet, & J. Lazar (Eds.), *Television and behavior: Ten years of scientific progress and implications for the eighties: Vol. II. Technical reviews.* Washington, DC: U.S. Government Printing Office.

Ettema, J. S. (1980). The role of educators and researchers in the production of educational television. *Journal of Broadcasting, 24,* 487–498.

Ettema, J. S. (1982). The organizational context of creativity: A case study from public television. In J. S. Ettema & D. C. Whitney (Eds.), *Individuals in mass media organizations: Creativity and constraint* (pp. 91–106). Beverly Hills, CA: Sage.

Friedrich, L. K., & Stein, A. H. (1973). Aggressive and prosocial television programs and the natural behavior of preschool children. *Monographs for the Society for Research in Child Development, 38*(4, Serial No. 151).

Friedrich, L. K., & Stein, A. H. (1975). Prosocial television and young children: The effects of verbal labelling and role playing on learning and behavior. *Child Development, 46,* 27–38.

Fryear, J. L., & Thelen, M. H. (1969). Effect of sex of model and sex of observer on the imitation of affectionate behavior. *Developmental Psychology, 1,* 298.

Gorn, G. J., Goldberg, M. E., & Kanungo, R. N. (1976). The role of educational television in changing the intergroup attitudes of children. *Child Development, 47,* 277–280.

Huston, A. C., Wright, J. C., Wartella, E., Rice, M. L., Watkins, B. A., Campbell, T., & Potts, R. (1981). Communicating more than content: Formal features of children's television programs. *Journal of Communication, 31,* 32–48.

Johnston, J., Blumenfield, P., & Isler, L. (1983). *Using television to promote adolescent mental health. Vol. 2: Process and effects in classroom settings.* Ann Arbor: University of Michigan, Institute for Social Research.

Johnston, J., & Ettema, J. (1982). *Positive images: Breaking stereotypes with children's television.* Beverly Hills, CA: Sage.

Kossler, J. (1980). A community outreach experiment to increase non-school viewing. In J. Johnston, J. Ettema, & T. Davidson (Eds.), *An evaluation of Freestyle: A television series to reduce sex-role stereotypes* (pp. 253–260). Ann Arbor: University of Michigan, Institute for Social Research.

Land, H. W. (1971). *The Children's Television Workshop: How and why it works.* Jericho, NY: Nassau Board of Cooperative Educational Services.

LaRose, R. (1979). *Final report on formative evaluation of Freestyle.* Unpublished manuscript, University of Southern California, Los Angeles.

LaRose, R. (1980). Formative evaluation of children's television as mass communication research. In B. Dervin & M. J. Voigt (Eds.), *Progress in communication sciences* (Vol. 2, pp. 275–297). Norwood, NJ: Ablex.

Lasker, H., & Bernath, N. (1974). *Status of comprehension study of Sesame Street affect bits.* New York: Children's Television Workshop. (ERIC Document Reproduction Service No. ED 086 203)

Lesser, G. S. (1974). *Children and television: Lessons from Sesame Street.* New York: Vintage Books.

Lorsch, E. P., Anderson, D. R., & Levin, S. R. (1979). The relationship of visual attention to comprehension of television. *Child Development, 50,* 722–727.

Lovelace, V., & Huston, H. C. (1983). Can television teach prosocial behavior? *Prevention in Human Services, 2,* 93–106. .

McAlister, A., Puska, P., Koskela, K., Pallonen, U., & Maccoby, N. (1980). Mass communication and community organization for public health education. *American Psychologist, 35*(4), 375–379.

Middleton, J. (1979). *Cooperative school television and educational change.* Bloomington, IN: Agency for Instructional Television.

Mielke, K. W., & Swinehart, J. W. (1976). *Evaluation of the "Feeling Good" television series.* New York: Children's Television Workshop.

Murray, J. P. (1980). *Television and youth: 25 years of research and controversy.* Boys Town, NE: Boys Town Center for the Study of Youth Development.

O'Connor, R. D. (1972). Relative efficacy of modeling, shaping, and the combined procedures for modification of social withdrawal. *Journal of Abnormal Psychology, 79,* 327–334.

Palmer, E. L. (1972). Formative research in educational television production: The experience of the Children's Television Workshop: In W. Schramm (Ed.), *Quality in instructional television.* Honolulu: University Press of Hawaii.

Paulson, F. (1974). Teaching cooperation on television: An evaluation of "Sesame Street" social goals program. *AV Communication Review, 22*(3), 229–246.

Purdie, S., Collins, W. A., & Westby S. (1979). *Children's processing of motive information in a televised portrayal.* Unpublished manuscript, Institute of Child Development, University of Minnesota, Minneapolis.

Reeves, B. (1979). Children's understanding of television people. In E. Wartella (Ed.), *Children communicating: Media and development of thought, speech, understanding.* Beverly Hills, CA: Sage.

Rockman S. (1976). *Formative evaluation of Self Incorporated programs.* Bloomington, IN: Agency for Instructional Television.

Rockman S. (1980). *On the Level: Final report on formative evaluation.* Bloomington, IN: Agency for Instructional Television.

Rushton, J. P. (1982). Television and prosocial behavior. In D. Pearl, L. Bouthilet, & J. Lazar (Eds.), *Television and behavior: Ten years of scientific progress and implications for the eighties: Vol. II. Technical reviews.* Washington, DC: U.S. Government Printing Office.

Salomon, G. (1979). *Interaction of media, cognition and learning.* San Francisco: Jossey-Bass.

Sloan, K. R. (1980). *Thinking through television.* Bloomington, IN: Agency for Instructional Television.

Smith K. (1978). The utilization of teacher feedback in ETV development. *Educational Technology, 18,* 49–51.

Solomon, D. S. (1982). Health campaigns on television. In D. Pearl, L. Bouthilet, & J. Lazar (Eds.), *Television and behavior: Ten years of scientific progress and implications for the eighties: Vol. II. Technical reviews.* Washington, DC: U.S. Government Printing Office.

Sprafkin, J., & Rubinstein, E. A. (1983). Using television to improve the social behavior of institutionalized children. In J. Sprafkin, C. Swift, & R. Hess (Eds.), Rx television: Enhancing the preventive impact of TV [Special issue]. *Prevention in Human Services, 2*(1/2), 107–114.

Stein, A. H., & Friedrich, L. K. (1972). Television content and young children's behavior. In J. P. Murray, E. A. Rubinstein, G. A. Comstock (Eds.), *Television and social behavior. Vol. 2: Television and social learning.* Washington, DC: U.S. Government Printing Office.

Stein, A. H., & Friedrich, L. K. (1975). The effects of television content on young children. In A. D. Pick (Ed.), *Minnesota symposia on child psychology* (Vol. 9). Minneapolis: University of Minnesota Press.

Susman E. J. (1976). *Visual imagery and verbal labeling: The relation of stylistic features and television presentation to children's learning and performance of prosocial content.* Unpublished doctoral dissertation, Pennsylvania State University, University Park.

Wartella E., & Ettema, J. S. (1974). A cognitive developmental study of children's attention to television commercials. *Communication Research, 1,* 69–88.

Watkins, B. (1978). *Children's attention to and comprehension of prosocial television: The effects of plot structure, verbal labeling and program form.* Unpublished doctoral dissertation, University of Kansas, Lawrence.

Watkins, B. A., Huston-Stein, A., & Wright, J. C. (1980). Effects of planned television programming. In E. L. Palmer & A. Dorr (Eds.), *Children and the faces of television: Teaching, violence, and selling* (pp. 49–69). New York: Academic.

Watt, J. H., Jr., & Krull, R. (1974). An information theory measure for television programming. *Communication Research, 1,* 44–68.

Williams, F. (1978). *Project Freestyle: National sites results.* Los Angeles: University of Southern California. (ERIC Document Reproduction Service No. ED 157 104)

9 Minorities and the Mass Media

Bradley S. Greenberg
Michigan State University

In 1978, Greenberg and Atkin (1978, 1982) collated the current state of social research on minorities and television, particularly as it related to television's potential for young people's acquisition of social information about minorities. The present paper assesses what has been found in the interim. Our earlier effort indicated that a good deal of content in various media forms had been systematically examined and that a fair body of research in the early 1970s had accompanied some major public television programming efforts directed at youngsters, but that little had been accomplished in terms of isolating the impact of minority characters and minority-dominated programming directed at the larger public or at youngsters. A half decade has not altered this pattern substantially.

Two reviews largely confirm this state of affairs. One (Comstock & Cobbey, 1979), prepared for the same symposium as our own 6 years ago, yielded these general propositions:

1. Ethnic minority children have a distinctive orientation toward television and other mass media (p. 105);
2. Children of ethnic minorities have different tastes and preferences in television programming (p. 107);
3. The behavioral response of children and adolescents to television portrayals is in part dependent on ethnic minority membership (p. 108);
4. Ethnic minority children have information needs that give particular prominence to television as a source of guidance (p. 110).

The second did not confine itself to such general statements nor young respondents, although they constitute the prominent set. Poindexter and Stroman (1981) proposed that:

1. Blacks have been underrepresented; there has been a trend toward increased visibility; stereotyping and negative connotations of blacks continue; and blacks typically appear in minor roles and in low-status occupational roles on television;

2. Blacks tend to rely heavily on television figures for information, including information about blacks and the black community;

3. Blacks have distinct tastes and preferences in TV programs, are among its heaviest consumers, except for news and public affairs, and prefer to watch shows which feature black characters;

4. Black children tend to believe in the reality of television, to learn behaviors from televised models, and to be influenced by television commercials.

It is again possible to report extensively on what kinds of portrayals of minorities may be found in the various media; there has been a substantial improvement in the quality and kinds of content analyses found. Now, we can look at some studies conducted at multiple points in time across a decade and more accurately discern trends, if any. There is far more interest in portrayal features that include personality characteristics, power dimensions, and more subtle role features (e.g., family roles). New studies focus on minorities contained in children's programming. Further, intriguing content analyses stem from examining cross-race portrayals and interactions within the same episodes.

Mass media content is analyzed to facilitate hypotheses about what may be learned from such programming, what may be believed, or what behavioral postures may develop. Here, a single major focus has emerged in the research literature, namely, an examination of content and character-preference differences between minority and majority viewers, especially children. Indeed, the large majority of the field and experimental studies produced since 1978 focus on youth, and I do not attempt to deal here with the handful of studies that have studied adult minorities and the media. The emerging studies on content and character preferences attempt to trace the origins and consequences of those choice patterns for both minority and majority youths. A segment of these studies uses content and character preferences as a basis for postulating social learning outcomes, and I assimilate those within that segment of this review. Thus, this chapter is organized into a rather detailed examination of the content analytic work that has emerged since our last review, followed by a look at independent studies that begin to ask questions about social effects and effectiveness. A final section outlines new research on what appear to be missed opportunities and totally new ones in a changing mass media environment.

MINORITY PORTRAYALS IN THE MEDIA

Entertainment Portrayals

The studies reported can be grouped into three major sets of findings. First are those that count the presence or absence of minorities in media content and compare these head counts with those found for other minorities and for the majority. Second are studies that typically attempt to assess whether the presence of a minority is of major or minor proportions and what their social and demographic characteristics are. Third, a relatively new and incisive approach, is the extent to which those minorities are like or unlike majority characters on the same show, and further, the manner and frequency with which the minority characters interact with the majority characters.

Head Counts.   One decade-long study has been conducted by Seggar, Hafen, and Hannonen-Gladden (1981), with content samples from 1971, 1973, 1975, and 1980, inclusive of some 18,000 character portrayals. The first two periods focused on comedies and dramas, and the latter two added movies. Across this decade, white males increased steadily from 81% to 88% of the television male character population, and black males fluctuated from 6% in 1971 to 9% in 1980, with no change recorded between 1975 and 1980. Both increases came at the expense of other minorities who decreased from 13% in 1971 to 3% in 1980. The pattern was parallel for females. In 1971, 84% were white, and 91% were white in 1980; black females fluctuated at a lower level from 5–6% across the decade; others dropped from 10% to 2.5%. Thus, whites expanded their domination in these television content areas, blacks were below their population percentages, and all others were negligible.

A second decade-long study (1969–1978) is from the University of Pennsylvania cultural indicators project (Gerbner & Signorielli, 1979). In the peak year of minority representation (i.e., 1977), all nonwhites comprised 14% of the television characters in prime time drama and were males by a 3–1 margin. Across the decade, they average 11% per year, with 8% male, but there is a systematic increase from 1969 through 1972, followed by small decreases in the next 2 years, a sharp drop in 1976, and then the peak in 1977.

Their breakdown by racial grouping of the nonwhites is equally informative. Blacks averaged 8% of all characters, Hispanics 3%, Orientals 2.5%, and Native Americans less than 1%. For all groups, the male domination was at least 3:1. There was no change across the decade for Hispanics and Native Americans, and a 1–2% gain for blacks.

From a 1979 program sample, Weigel, Loomis, and Soja (1980) report that blacks appeared in half the dramas and half the comedies studied, figures that paralleled estimates made by Roberts (1971). But such gross measures (i.e., the mere appearance in a show) mask the nature of those appearances, at least in terms of time. Black appearances filled 8% of the total human appearance time on those shows. And those appearances were concentrated in very few shows; 75% of the total time blacks were visible occurred in just 18% of the shows. Further, the black characters were six times as likely to be presented in comedies as in dramas.

These three studies are in relatively strong agreement. By 1980, 8 of every 100 prime time television characters were likely to be black, with 3 to 4 characters of other races observed. Black females were infrequent, and other nonwhite females were essentially absent.

These appearances by minority characters in prime time television do not carry over into the daytime. On soap operas, less than 3% of speaking characters have been identified as nonwhite (Greenberg, Neuendorf, Buerkel-Rothfuss, & Henderson, 1982).

Roles.   Seggar et al. (1981) examined role significance among black and white characters between their 1975 and 1980 studies. White males showed sizable gains in both major and supporting roles and had trivial changes in minor and bit parts. Black males gained only slightly in the latter two categories and dropped more than 50% in major and supporting roles, from 9% to 4.4% and 12% to 4.5%, respectively. White females gained 10% in major roles, whereas black females decreased in major and supporting roles even more sharply than black males; in 1980, they comprised 2.4% of the major female roles, and 2.7% of the supporting roles.

The particular setting of cross-racial interactions studied by Weigel et al. (1980) indicated that blacks and whites were cast together in predominantly egalitarian situations in at least 70% of the episodes they examined. However, only 13% of the interactions could be rated as displaying personal friendliness and/or mutual respect.

The discontinuity in the annual head count of nonwhites reported by Gerbner and Signorielli (1979) is even more striking in terms of major character portrayals, which averaged 10% per year (3.5:1 male). There were increases in even-numbered years and decreases in odd-numbered years until 1976, when a downward trend continued. In the most recent year presented (1978), nonwhites filled less than 5% of the major roles, although they had 13% of all roles; nonwhite females had 1% of the major roles, the same as 10 years earlier.

Gerbner and Signorielli elaborated role analyses for specific racial groups. Major roles for blacks and Hispanics paralleled their presence in prime time, comprising 8.5% and 2.5%, respectively. This study collapses what Seggar et al. (1981) break into major and supporting roles, and the figures are equivalent. Again, the most recent data for this analysis show a substantial drop (to 6.5%) in major roles for blacks from immediate past seasons. Whatever increase there was in nonwhite characters over portions of the decade occurred as minor characters.

This study also reported that nonwhites were as likely to be married and as likely to be involved in romantic episodes as were whites. However, the importance of family life to the characters was found to be much higher among nonwhite males and females. This reflects their relative containment in situation comedies, in contrast to more action-oriented programs. Nonwhite characters were consistently less serious than whites in prime time drama; two thirds of the white characters were portrayed in serious roles, compared to half of all nonwhite characters and less than half of the nonwhite females. Nonwhite characters were more likely depicted as good guys and equivalent to whites in their presence as bad guys. Success and failure occurred in equal portions as well. Among major characters these patterns persisted.

In occupational roles, nonwhites were less often portrayed in white collar and professional roles (although all were overrepresented in these roles when compared to U.S. census information) and more often portrayed in blue collar and service jobs.

Age results paralleled earlier research as well. One third of the white males were under 35 in age; three fifths of the nonwhites were in that age group. The same discrepancy existed for females, who overall are consistently younger than males on television. Nonwhite teen-agers were twice as frequent as white ones.

Cross-race Portrayals.   A promising approach to content and structural analysis of race on television is examining within-show characterizations of both races. For example, to what extent do direct comparisons between blacks and whites paired with (against?) each other on the same show provide findings not discernible from the total television racial composite, as provided by demographic comparisons alone? Young viewers with a need for more concrete referents may be particularly susceptible to observing how two racial groups interact and behave in the same context (i.e., the same show). A few such studies have emerged only recently. From a conceptual view, they begin to tackle the issue of whether impact is more likely to emerge from dynamic, interactive images of the races as contrasted with the more static models describable from head count and role attribute investigations.

Reid (1979) compared the behaviors of black and white characters on 10 half-hour comedies. The comedies selected were groupings of black-dominated, white-dominated, and racially mixed shows, all with at least one regular black character. Across a dozen different behaviors examined, the only one to yield racial differences was that black characters sought recognition for their deeds more often. Further analyses by sex of the characters indicated that black males did not differ from white males on any of the behaviors studied, whereas black females were less achieving (e.g., in initiating plans), were less succorant, more boasting, and more dominant—behaviors all indicative of a continuing black female stereotype. And black females appeared almost exclusively on the black-dominated shows.

Reid then analyzed the behaviors of the white characters across the three show types. Whites appearing on black-dominated situation comedies were more deferent and less autonomous, less nurturing, and less succorant than counterpart whites on white-dominated comedies. Whites on the former were generally less pleasant characters; they were more aggressive, dependent, and negative in their attitude toward others.

Another attempt to look at same-show characterization of the two races compared the 100 blacks found in a week's sample of programs with a sample of 100 whites from the same shows (Baptista-Fernandez & Greenberg, 1980). The blacks were systematically younger (two thirds were 23 or younger), less frequently employed, and funnier. Half the blacks were in comedies compared to one third of the whites, and the blacks were either in programs that were virtually all-black or were isolated blacks on otherwise white shows. Half the blacks and none of the whites appeared on shows with four or more black characters. In behavioral comparisons across these characters, the whites had eight conversations with other whites to every one with a black character, although there were only five times as many white characters. Blacks interacted with whites three times as often as the reverse. Both talked equivalently and primarily of domestic matters in these shows, but whites discussed business issues and crime more often; blacks discussed no specific topic more often than whites. There were no significant differences in the extent to which each group gave, sought, or received advice, information, or orders.

A study of race relations on prime time television focused on examining content variables that reflected social psychological determinants of interracial friendliness and prejudice reduction across racial lines, for example, equal status, cooperative interactions, supportive social norms, and interpersonal intimacy (Weigel et al., 1980). A 1-week prime time sample of drama, situation comedies, and movies yielded a total of 91 cross-racial interactions (1.5 per hr), and these were compared with a random sample of 60 white-white interactions. A principal finding is that only 2% of the human appearance time involved cross-racial interactions. Thus, although television is not entirely white, it continues to be subdivided into episodes in which blacks and whites seldom encounter one another.

In terms of variables that foster positive race relations, the study determined that black-white interactions were more interdependent than white-white relations with respect to both common goals and interpersonal cooperation. However, relationships between blacks and whites were also characterized by less shared decision making, narrower, more formal relationships, less intimate personal relationships, and almost no romantic relationships. Friendships and nonwork relationships were more common in white-white interactions. Blacks and whites discussed problem alternatives in but 13% of the possible situations, compared to 56% of the white-white decisions. Black-white interactions occurred almost exclusively in job-related contexts, compared to half of the white-white relationships. Thus, cross-racial relationships are infrequent and relatively formal. Blacks and whites can work together but do not maintain the same degree of voluntary, individualized relationships that whites do. For the most part, blacks and whites appear on different shows; when they do appear together, they largely maintain that separateness.

Although not an analysis of same-show behavior, another promising approach is examining larger units of behavior, such as families or work units. Do black families and family members behave differently than whites? Rarely would these families appear together, with some notable exceptions (e.g., *The Jeffersons*). Nevertheless, whether the portrayals of black and white families are comparable or different provides the basis for potential social learning hypotheses, as would work units consisting of either mixed racial membership (e.g., *Hill Street Blues*) or the same racial composition.

Across a week of television, one can see a black family on four or five shows and a white family eight times as often (Greenberg & Neuendorf, 1980). The dominant black family type consists of a single parent plus children; the primary white family type has two parents and one or more children. One could find the latter composition perhaps in one show a season featuring blacks. The single black parent tends to be a mother. Black families seldom have kinfolk, consisting almost entirely of nuclear family members, whereas as many as one fifth of the white family members would be cousins, uncles, in-laws, and other relatives. As for family interaction, black sons have had larger roles than daughters and white children. Overall, black males were more active in family interactions than white males, although the most active role pair in both black and white families was husband-wife. The major behavioral difference between black and white families was that of conflict, accounting for one sixth of the interactions in the former and one tenth in the latter. In white families, conflict was evenly distributed among role members; in black families, it was centered in the wives and among siblings. These are substantial differences and provide a potentially important basis for what young viewers may think they know about how black and white families are composed, interact, and behave.

News

By the early 1970s, blacks were becoming more visible in the news, and studies suggested more egalitarian coverage and presentation. Blacks were found in 13% of news-magazine pictures by Stempel (1971), and in 25% of network television newscasts by Baran (1973), although primarily in nonspeaking roles on segments dedicated to busing, segregation, and other civil rights issues. In 1977, the U.S. Commission on Civil Rights was claiming that there were few black television news correspondents and that they seldom handled lead stories. I find no more recent evidence to refute this claim, although it would be appropriate to examine the roles played by black news correspondents on local television stations.

In a more recent and extensive study, Chaudhary (1980) examined the newspaper coverage of black and white elected officials during 1974 and 1976 elections in 19 metropolitan cities in which the black population exceeded 200,000. News coverage on election day and for every other day up to 10 days before each election was analyzed across 2,780 items about elected officials. White elected officials received significantly more coverage on election day and 2 days before the election, and they received more favorable placement on the front page and inside front page above the fold, where most of the election stories were located. However, black elected officials received longer stories, averaging 300 words compared to 225 for white officials. There were no differences in terms of headline size, photo coverage, or story type. However, there were substantial divergences among the 19 newspapers, indicating that local editorial policy may play a major role in the equity of coverage of black and white candidates.

Chaudhary had coders rate the degree of positive and negative bias in each story, $r = .84$ between coders, and determined that most items for both sets of candidates were coded as neutral. However, the distribution of stories was such that significantly more negative stories appeared for black elected officials than for whites. This study highlights the importance of examining how blacks are covered, in addition to whether they are covered.

One systematic examination of the newspaper coverage of a second minority, Mexican Americans, was located. In six southwestern U.S. cities with Hispanic residents comprising 20–65% of the population, a 2-week sample of local daily newspapers was analyzed in terms of locally written Hispanic news, sports, editorials, photos, and bulletin listings (Greenberg, Heeter, Burgoon, Burgoon, & Korzenny, 1983a). All sites filled their local newshole with local Hispanic news stories in proportion to the percentage of Hispanics in their community, although 75% of these stories qualified solely because they contained a Spanish surname. There were four such stories per issue each day. However, news stories that focused primarily on Hispanics averaged only 10% of the local news. Local Hispanic sports stories filled more of the local sports newshole (42%), averaging two stories a day, with virtually all qualifying because the story contained one or more Spanish surnames. Sports coverage was markedly different by site, with the newshole proportion ranging between 18–77%. Bulletins (e.g., births, deaths, community events) indicated an underrepresentation of Mexican Americans. Overall, bulletin representation was one half or less of the proportion of the Hispanic population. Hispanic photos filled 19% of the total local photo newshole, or about 2 in 10 photos, with 1 in 10 on the front page. The primary photo content was that of soft news and sports (82% of all photos), with crime accounting for only 2%. Editorial page content carried one Hispanic referent every other issue, filling 13% of the local editorial page. Half the items identified were

Hispanic-authored letters to the editor on non-Hispanic issues; 33% of the items dealt with minority issues, 33% with other hard news issues, and 14% with crime.

Again, the newspapers varied greatly in their coverage of Mexican Americans across the sites and across the different types of news items. Stories primarily on Hispanics were rare in both the news and sports sections. Editorial page coverage was slight. Whether the coverage is adequate seems to depend on the individual newspaper and whether the criterion is that of prominence, representativeness, or content emphasis.

A follow-up study (Heeter et al., 1983) compared local Hispanic news coverage across newspapers, radio, and television on these same criteria. Local Hispanic community leaders believed that there was an overemphasis on crime and negative news, a shortage of positive news, and that the media just did not cover Hispanic events and individuals as much or as prominently as non-Hispanic activities. They also believed that radio offered the most local coverage and that television coverage was minimal (Korzenny, Griffis, Greenberg, Burgoon, & Burgoon, 1983). On a typical day, news that involved Hispanics averaged a little more than one-half page of text in the daily newspaper, 1 of 5 min. devoted to local news on the top-rated radio station, and a little more than 3 of the 14 min. of news on the major local evening television news show. Hispanic reports on both broadcast media were longer than non-Hispanic reports. As for content emphasis, more than one third of the radio stories about Hispanics dealt with crime, in contrast to less than half that figure in the other two media. Newspapers were most varied in the content issues covered. No Hispanic studio newscasters were reported for either radio or television. Radio news stories were far more likely to qualify solely because they contained a Spanish surname. Overall, local radio gave less of its newshole and focused more on crime and name dropping. Newspapers gave newshole and television gave time equivalent to Hispanic population proportions; newspapers covered many more kinds of issues for more varied reasons; television coverage was present and was at least as strong as radio. These results are in sharp contrast to the expressed beliefs of Hispanic community leaders in the study sites.

Advertising

The portrayal of blacks in print advertising has been sparse indeed. Early studies from the 1940s through the mid-1960s indicated not more than 3% usage of blacks in major magazine advertising, with their few appearances as entertainers, athletes, and servants (Colfax & Steinberg, 1972; Kassarjian, 1969; Stempel, 1971). An increase to 5% presence in magazine advertisements was identified by Cox (1969-1970) for the last half of the 1960s, yet in 1978, Bush, Resnick, and Stern (1980) again reported 2%. Seeking ads in 27 issues of *Time, Newsweek, Sports Illustrated,* and *U.S. News & World Report* between 1975 and 1980,

Soley (1983) found but 29; 2 had black females, 3 had both sexes, and the remainder had black males only. In an interesting analysis for the 10 years ending in 1977, Reid and VandenBergh (1980) specifically examined ads that presented a product or service new to the advertisers in *Time, Cosmopolitan, Reader's Digest*, and *Ladies' Home Journal*. Of the total 8,700 ads examined, only 59 (less than 1%) contained any black characters. There was no apparent trend across the years. Furthermore, in this small subset, only one sixth characterized the black in a major role. To the extent there was increased usage of blacks in print advertising, they did not introduce new products.

In an experimental study of female responses to black advertising models, controlling for facial features, hair style, and skin pigmentation, Kerin (1979) examined perceived product quality and suitability among black and white subjects. The black respondents associated quality most dominantly with Negroid facial features, and the white respondents with Caucasoid facial features. As for suitability, black and white subjects agreed that maximum suitability derived from models who clustered congruent or stereotypic characteristics, Negroid features with Afro hair styles, and Caucasoid features with wavy hair styles. Several experiments have all reported that white respondents do not respond negatively to the use of black models in ads (e.g., Block, 1972; Schlinger & Plummer, 1972).

Soley (1983) moved from the laboratory to the field to assess responses to advertising containing black models. Armed with a sample of ads with black male models and control sets of ads with white males, he compared Starch readership scores. These measures took into account whether the ad was merely seen, whether the name of the advertiser was read, and whether half or more of the copy was read. In sum, the ethnicity of the model made no difference in ad readership. The absence of blacks from advertising is bias on the part of the advertiser and/or the client, and not the consumer.

As for broadcast advertising, a sharp increase from 5–11% in black television models was identified from the mid- to late 1960s (Dominick & Greenberg, 1970), with a further increase by the mid-1970s (Bush, Solomon, & Hair, 1977). In both print and broadcast ads, these studies show that blacks tended to appear in "crowd scenes" with whites rather than alone or with other blacks. Atkin and Heald (1977) found that one-fifth of Saturday morning commercials contained black characters.

Using a prime time sample of 63 hours in 1978, Weigel et al., (1980) used time-on-air as their key measure of minority presence. Whites were visible in the ads 97% of the time and blacks were visible 8.5% of the time, with 5% of the time containing cross-racial appearances. Further, cross-racial interactions in the ads occurred slightly less than 2% of the time. Overall, 75% of the commercials were entirely white, and blacks appeared in less than 20% of the product commercials. In a poignant comparison, they note that all-black commercials comprised less than 2% of the items, whereas animated commercials without any human appearances occurred twice as frequently as that figure.

Blacks have yet to make major inroads in print advertising, and the importance of their presence in television advertising may have been overstated by merely counting faces. Certainly, the data verify that there are more black faces, but they get less time, are less visible, may be buried in a sea of faces, and rarely interact with whites.

Children's Television

In a series of reports for Action for Children's Television, Barcus (1975, 1978) and Barcus and Wolkin (1977) identified the presence of white, black, and other minority characters in weekday and weekend programs and in advertising directed at children. Then, in 1981, drawing a more extensive sample of programs from television stations in the Boston area, he compiled an elaborated description of what is available on television about minorities for child viewers (Barcus, 1983).

Head Counts. In the mid- to late 1970s, weekday programming for children yielded a 3% black population of television characters and 1–4% of other minorities; weekend programming was consistently higher, at 7% for blacks and 4–8% for other minorities. This difference can be attributed largely to the extensive use of syndicated programs on weekdays by local stations, many originating in an earlier decade when blacks were less likely to be part of any television program; weekend programming was largely network offerings. Blacks fared better in commercials during the late 1970s, at about 7% inclusion, whereas other minorities did not exceed 2%. If the stiffer criterion is invoked as to whether a black was a spokesperson on any ads during children's programming, the answer is no. In contrast, blacks were featured in no less than 10% of the public service announcements, and during one sample period, reached 23%.

According to Barcus (1983), blacks evidenced little gain in children's programming. They were 3.6% of 1,145 characters in 1981, whereas all other minorities combined totaled 4% on programs targeted for children. Blacks were clearly cast (perhaps stifled) among much younger characters. On these programs, 25% of all blacks were children (compared to 11% of all whites), 20% were teen-agers (13% for whites), 15% were middle-aged (34% for whites), and none were elderly (4% for whites), with the remainder as young adults. The other minorities more closely paralleled the white age distribution.

Gerbner and Signorelli (1979) report one specific analysis of minority character representation in weekend network programming for the period 1970–1976. The underrepresentation of nonwhites found in prime time is exacerbated on the weekends. The proportions of weekend black characters (6.5%) and of Hispanic characters (1%) are smaller than during prime time; the ratio of black males to females is larger (8:1), with females constituting less than 1% of the weekend characters. Orientals were overrepresented (2.7%) among weekend characters, and Native Americans were negligible (total of five males).

Black characters on weekend programming for children were consistently younger than white characters. More than 40% were teen-agers, compared with 25% among white characters. At the opposite end of the age continuum, the situation was reversed. Elderly blacks could be counted on one hand across 10 television seasons.

Weigel and Howes (1982) used appearance time rather than head count to assess the presence of blacks on children's programs, examining 15 hrs of Saturday morning network programming. They determined that 6.6% of program time contained black appearances, quite comparable to the 7% character population in weekend shows reported by Barcus during the late 1970s. They elaborate on this by identifying the kind of Saturday morning "ghetto" that exists: 48% of the total black appearance time was in just one program, and 85% was in but five shows.

Taken together, cross-racial interactions totaled just 1% of the children's programming sampled, yielding only 38 consistently brief and separate interactions. This pool was insufficient to analyze how the races got along with each other; children's programming was not a basis for fostering interracial goodwill through vicarious experience unless you chose to view the single show in which black-white and white-white interactions were equally cooperative and interdependent.

Earlier, we indicated that the presence of blacks and Hispanics in weekend programs is smaller than in prime time. This discrepancy continued in terms of major characters, wherein the proportion of major characters in each racial grouping is even smaller than their representation in the character population; that is not the case for minority characters in prime time programming (Gerbner & Signorelli, 1979).

Roles.   Barcus (1983) then moved from head counts to role depictions of blacks and other minorities on children's programs. He found that blacks were as often cast as heroes as were whites, and more so than other minority characters. They were less likely to be villains and more likely to be major characters. However, blacks constituted 2% of all major characters overall.

Blacks continue to be employed less often than whites, with one third of the former and one half of the latter clearly indicated as job holders. However, more than half of those employed, whether black or white, were in professional and managerial jobs, twice the proportion of other minorities in those jobs. It is the other minorities who have replaced blacks in the lower social classes on television. Barcus found the black social class distribution on these programs equivalent to that of whites and substantially higher than presented for other minorities.

Barcus further examined the goals of all major dramatic characters and classified them as basically self-goals (self-indulgence, wealth, power) or altruisitic goals (friendship, patriotism, justice). For whites, blacks, and other minorities, altruism comprised two thirds of the goals sought. Only animal characters, e.g.,

Bugs Bunny, overindulged themselves. The primary means used to seek goals were violence, personal hard work and intelligence; whites displayed these more than minority characters. Ethnic characters attempted to use personal charm more than did nonethnic characters.

Barcus' final analysis began to examine personality traits of minority and majority characters. Beset by small samples, the findings can at best be considered suggestive. The most intriguing conclusion is that ethnic heroes and villains tend to be more extreme than nonethnics; they are either superheroes or archvillains, given more extreme judgments on 10 of 12 personality scales.

Little data are presented dealing with program type. However, a concluding paragraph in Barcus' (1983) analysis of minorities is worth citing: "Cartoon-comedy programs contain the most blatant ethnic stereotypes. These programs . . . frequently provide cruel stereotypes of ethnic minorities. And cartoon comedies alone amount to nearly one-half of all program time in children's TV" (p. 115).

On weekend daytime programs, one third of the characters were serious, and the remainder at least partly comical. But black characters were even more likely to be comical than whites. This finding applies only to males, inasmuch as the total number of black female characters identified across 10 years was 15 (Gerbner & Signorielli, 1979).

Content and Character Perceptions and Preferences

In the midst of substantial new research on identification, role-model preferences, and content orientations, there lurk assumptions—some implicit and some tested—about social learning and social effects. These are examined in this section.

Dates (1980) reverified that black high school students had a stronger preference for black television shows (e.g., *Good Times*) than did white youngsters. The viewing of white situation comedies does not differ by race. The major focus of her study was the extent to which black and white youngsters identified with, thought favorably of, and perceived greater realism in black and/or white television characters. The black youngsters consistently rated black characters more positively; they rated white characters equally with white students. The same finding held for the other two variables: perceived reality and personal identification. Blacks exceeded nonblack students in both estimates for black television characters, with no stable differences between black and white responses to white characters.

Dates also demonstrated no particular relationship between her measure of racial attitudes and character perceptions. Among blacks, the correlations were nil; among whites, there tended to be a positive relationship between racial attitudes and black character evaluation.

Black and white television newscasters in New York City were evaluated by black and white high school students (Kaner, 1982) in terms of competency and social distance (as potential neighbors and as potential kin). The black students rated the newscasters of both races the same, whereas white students rated same-race newscasters higher on all attributes, particularly on the social distance estimates. The investigator's assessment of racial attitudes in terms of open-mindedness was not related to the evaluations, nor was frequency of viewing television news.

Elementary school children exhibit the same tendency to select same-race characters as their favorites (Eastman & Liss, 1980). When limited to identifying one favorite television character (during a season in which 85% of all characters were Anglo), 96% of the Anglo youngsters chose same-race characters as their favorites (Eastman & Liss, 1980). When limited to identifying one favorite television character (during a season in which 85% of all characters were Anglo), 96% of the Anglo youngsters chose same-race characters, compared to 75% of the black and 80% of the Hispanic youth. When limited to one favorite television program, the minority youth cited a minority-dominant show.

When not limited to a single character, the pattern of same-race selection becomes even more striking. Blacks and whites are equally likely to identify with white television characters. Across 26 white TV characters, 17% of the black youths and 16% of the white youths said they want to be like the character; relatively few white or black children want to be like most of the white models available to them on television. But, black youths are more than three times as likely to identify with black characters. Note these findings from Greenberg and Atkin (1982):

Percentage Wanting to Be Like:	Blacks	Whites
Freddy Washington	57%	27%
Lamont Sanford	45	13
J. J. Evans	45	19
Bill Cosby	43	15
Thelma Evans	43	7
George Jefferson	41	8
Dee Thomas	37	17
Louise Jefferson	30	6
Roger Thomas	28	11
James Evans	29	4
Mrs. Thomas	22	5
Florida Evans	21	3
Average	(37%)	(11%)

Even the scarce black females on television listed above draw strong identification scores (31% vs. 7%) among the black youth.

Experimental work supports minority role models in television programs as an effective means of enhancing interracial perceptions. Allsopp (1982) experimentally introduced two situation comedies, one with a predesignated negative black portrayal and another with a positive portrayal. The negative portrayal induced more positive attitudes among fourth- and fifth-grade black and white children; the positive portrayal decreased negative stereotyping among black youngsters. It is ambiguous as to whether any portrayal is better than none or if distinctively positive portrayals are necessary.

Experimental work also supports the ratings' data that minority viewers watch more minority programming, when available. Liss (1981) made two 10-min excerpts from situation comedies (one black dominant and one white dominant) simultaneously available to third and sixth graders. Blacks watched the black situation comedy for 7.5 min; whites watched the same-race show for 8 min.

The program preference of black elementary school children is situation comedies, which should be no surprise because that program type contains the majority of black characters. Hispanics, for whom no program types contain substantial same-race role models, prefer some program types together with Anglos and others with blacks, particularly children's shows and cartoons, where racial differences may be less important or less threatening (Eastman & Liss, 1980). The favorite program type among Anglo children was action-adventure shows; it constituted 67% of the favorite shows for Anglo boys compared to 27% for blacks and 3% for Hispanics. This program type subsumes prime time shows that have the most violence. That is important in relationship to a finding by Zuckerman, Singer, and Singer (1980) that elementary school whites with more negative stereotypes (less competent and less obedient) of blacks spent more time watching violent TV shows. The white children who spent more time watching shows with black characters, and who watched less violence, had more positive images of blacks. Only these two television viewing variables were significant correlates of racial prejudice; no demographic or family variables were significant in gauging racial prejudice.

Hispanic youngsters (second through fourth grades) were asked for their favorite television program and favorite characters in research concerned with reactions to television violence (Loughlin, Donohue, & Gudykunst, 1982). The children identified more violent than nonviolent shows and more violent than nonviolent characters. For boys, there was a significant relationship between what they themselves would do in these situations and what their favorite character would do.

Study of media content preferences, across several media, for Hispanic and Anglo youngsters in the fifth and tenth grades is reported by Greenberg, Heeter, Burgoon, Burgoon, and Korzenny (1983b). Although low in absolute level of content preference, Hispanic youths showed a consistent preference for Spanish-relevant content on television, in movies, on radio, and even for more news stories about Mexico and Latin America in the newspapers. Media use gratifications from this content also differed among the groups of youngsters. Newspapers were read more for diversion and for social learning purposes by the Hispanic youngsters; social learning and seeking advice were similarly different in the television gratifications. Hispanic youngsters believed more strongly that the portrayals of both Mexican Americans and blacks on television were more realistic than did Anglo youth, and they were far more likely to believe that local media and network television portrayed Mexican Americans more often doing good things than did the Anglos. Again, there seems to be a desire to see any Hispanic faces or hear any Hispanic voices in the media that are largely void of such appearances and an abundant belief in the fairness and equity of media presentations.

Studies among blacks continue to confirm this reality perception (Greenberg & Atkin, 1982). Black youths consistently believe that the television portrayals of blacks and nonblacks are more real-to-life. Typically, 40% of the blacks would agree that television's presentation of black men, women, teen-agers, dress, and language are realistic, compared to 30% for whites. An even greater discrepancy exists when the content referents were not black (e.g., doctors, wives and husbands, parents).

Additionally, black youngsters approach television more vigorously with the stated motivation to learn something they can apply in their daily lives. An early study (Greenberg, 1972) indicated that white youngsters depended on television as a major source of information about black youth. Within this survey, several hundred black preteens and teens claimed that television taught them most of what they know about jobs (47%), how men and women solve problems (42%), how parents and children interact (57%), how husbands and wives interact (45%), and how teen-agers act (48%). Corresponding percentages for white respondents averaged 33% (Greenberg & Atkin, 1982). Whites learn more about blacks from television; blacks claim to learn about both whites and themselves.

In turn, the impact on black self-esteem in general and racial self-esteem in particular of black programs on black fourth and fifth graders has recently been assessed by McDermott and Greenberg (1985) conjointly with the impact of peer and parental communication about the positive characteristics of black people. Parental communication and the regularity of watching black shows were both related to the black students' self-esteem; parental and peer communication were related to racial esteem, with exposure falling just short of significance. On the other hand, when respondents were subdivided into those with more and less positive attitudes toward black television characters, the correlations between exposure and both self and racial esteem were significantly larger for those with more favorable perceptions. Strong correlations were found between program exposure and attitudes toward both black adult and child television characters. Thus, black youngsters used the televised portrayals to reflect upon themselves, or alternatively, black youngsters holding stronger self-esteem estimates orient to such programming. The previously reported mediating variable test suggests the former as a more persuasive argument.

What do white youth who choose to watch black television programs on a regular basis learn? Is it program content or predispositions that form the basis for selectively exposing themselves to television programs heavily featuring black characters? From a sample of fourth-, sixth-, and eighth-grade white children, Atkin, Greenberg, and McDermott (1983) explored the consequences of black program exposure on a variety of belief areas. Frequent exposure to programs starring blacks was significantly associated with the motivation to watch television to find out how different people talk, dress, behave, and look, with higher estimates of the numbers of blacks to be seen in various roles in the real world, and with self-reports that television teaches them most of what they know about blacks. Show exposure was not related to real-life evaluations of black people in terms of attractiveness, strength, activity, or to discrepancies in these attributes between black and whites. Exposure was related to perceptions of funniness among black television characters. Those traits were all related to what the youngsters perceived the characteristics of TV blacks to be and with the strength of their identification with black characters.

The white youngsters' interpretation of black television character traits is closely related to parallel beliefs about the real world. Although this correlation may result in part from selective distortion of the televised portrayals, it is likely that the incoming perceptions exert a stronger influence. Thus, for some sets of beliefs, content is important; for others, predispositions clearly have a greater role. In this manner, television serves both to reinforce what is learned outside the television situation and offers the possibility of new information, where little or none was available. Finally, direct contact with blacks in real life did not diminish or enhance any of these findings. The interface of vicarious and non-vicarious interactions with minority group members has yet to be clarified in any reported research.

DISCUSSION

Analysis of media content has been the forte of researchers who examine minorities and the media. Field and experimental studies remain too infrequent. Perhaps it is easier to sort out once again how many types of people there are in different kinds of television shows or news articles. Maybe it is easier still to train reliable coders to assess image characteristics and role attributes. For whatever reason, the research on minorities and media is still heavily reliant on content analysis and subsequent speculation rather than on the demonstration of the impacts of that content.

Surely there have been some gains in the kinds of content analyses provided. Rather than finding only head counts, we now find studies that explore sensitively and intensively the role behaviors of the characters on television programs, studies that look specifically at the kinds of interactions that occur between the races within programs, studies that examine alternative content areas (e.g., children's television) and studies that have some theoretical basis in prior research. Nonetheless, there remains the gulf between what content projects and what viewers perceive, observe, and learn. This gulf reflects the paucity of social effects research on these kinds of issues: (a) What available images of blacks and other minorities on television are perceived by majority and minority viewers? (b) Do these perception translate into behavioral postures toward minorities? (c) What is the intersection of what is learned from the media about minorities with what is learned from direct, nonvicarious contact with minorities? (d) Is it the bulk of portrayal emphasis that is learned, or are there critical portrayals or programs that are more significant to large numbers of viewers? For example, are there key portrayals that stand out above the average occurrence obtained from counting a sample week or month of programming? Are 10 exposures to *The Jeffersons* paramount for some and two exposures to *Hill Street Blues* sufficient for others to form or alter attitudes as to possible or appropriate behavioral interactions between blacks and whites?

All these studies ignore the multichannel environment now accessed by more than 40% of the homes in this country via cable, subscription television, or satellite. There is a likelihood that more than half the homes will be so accessed before the 1980s end, and projections of 75–80% by the end of this century are not considered whimsical. Network television audiences are being diverted; estimates of viewing nonnetwork channels range from 30–50% of total viewing time, depending on season, offerings, and so on. Some portion of this comes at the expense of the commercial networks. Cable systems with 24–36 channels now serve more of the population than systems with fewer channels. One black satellite network and two Hispanic satellite networks are available and adopted in areas serving large minority communities.

Let me exemplify how this contextual change may affect what we think we know about minorities and the media, particularly in terms of the imagery of minorities. Take the case of Music Television (MTV). This cable-only channel is heavily viewed by preteens and teen-agers; it is credited with stirring a large-scale impetus in record and album sales when that market was drifting downward. MTV excluded black performers and black groups during its introductory period. Activist groups and critics identified this shortcoming to little avail. Then, the Michael Jackson phenomenon struck, his videos became featured on MTV, a single video ("Thriller") became a national phenomenon, and suddenly, the network discovered that black performers would be both popular and successful for it. MTV viewers are not yet saturated with black performers, but clearly, this is another major piece of content from which young viewers may derive impressions about one segment of the black population (whether for good or for bad has yet to be assessed).

The multiplicity of offerings in the new communication environment makes more complex the explication of possible effects. There are more images to choose from, and more content is available. Clearly, subsequent research on media and minorities cannot focus so heavily or solely on either network or local station offerings. They still constitute the primary load of viewing time, but they no longer monopolize. This again raises the question of whether it is conceptually rich to count each presence as equivalent to every other presence. I think not. Analytic procedures must take into account the importance of specific portrayals or content for individual viewers, without assuming that all such specificity is idiosyncratic. The mix of messages seems to caution against some overall summary of minority portrayals as cultivating in a given and singular direction.

There must be some additional caution. In both child and adult programming, the races are separated more than they are together. Half the programs still contain no minorities, and a television diet can easily be constructed with selective nonexposure. Hispanics remain a rare event in any programming from the networks and clearly are not found on reruns or on soaps. Only blacks have achieved a noticeable presence, and these studies indicate that that sheer presence is confounded by concentration on few programs, little cross-race interaction, and so forth.

In these ways, it appears that bias is more subtle in programming than might otherwise be thought. When there were no minorities on television, one could claim open discrimination. Their neglect in daytime and commercial children's shows remains open to that claim. Given the presence of blacks for more than a decade on a regular basis in prime time programming, and their slight incursion on daytime and weekend shows, counting heads is no longer particularly useful either for social research or for social equity. What blacks do and in what context are clearly more important observational points. There appear to be two extreme uses: concentrating blacks in a few programs (solely comedies) and isolating them in the midst of waves of nonblacks in both programming and advertising. Neither yield much in the way of cross-race interaction as potential models for viewers. Evidence suggests that the black characters are not rejected by white viewers and that shows are not rejected because of their inclusion; the evidence is very consistent that black models in advertising are not considered inferior to white models. There may be no overwhelming enthusiasm among whites, but latent or manifest fears that such models will detract from programming or from commercials seem unwarranted.

In contrast, there is considerable evidence that blacks, young and old, are very likely to watch shows with blacks, and this viewing is accompanied by a strong sense of identification. Give the minority viewer a show laced with a subset of minority characters, perhaps even one, and that character is a favored model target, perhaps somewhat independently of how positive the portrayal is.

Thus, programers have nothing to lose and something to gain by casting minority characters, perhaps even in pairs, rather than as singletons or in large groupings.

Where are the other minorities? What inhibits network programming from utilizing Hispanic actors and actresses in some more consistent pattern? If anything, there appears to be a slackening of their presence during the decade in which they rapidly approach blacks in terms of sheer population numbers. There is a distinct generation gap among Hispanics. Parents still orient themselves to their cultural heritage in Latin and South America; their offspring turn more to the culture in which they find themselves. For parents, experiences with Spanish-language media are more important and certainly would be more satisfying if they are seeking Spanish images. They are prime candidates for subscribing to Hispanic-based cable satellite networks. But the youngsters are part of the new media, and their inability to find contemporary Hispanic images, at least on television, is ironic given the institution's laggard response to the expressed needs of black Americans. While this chapter was in the process of being published, a new Norman Lear show, *A.K.A. Pablo*, premiered and failed. It continued Lear's attempts to satirize ethnic stereotypes in the hope of fracturing them. The best guess is that responses to this program would have followed the interpretations of Archie Bunker in *All in the Family*. Bigots watching the show will be reinforced in their negative impressions, interpreting the actions of the bigoted character literally; less prejudiced viewers, who are far more numerous, can be expected to recognize their own prejudices more clearly, to reduce the strength or centrality of their own ethnocentrism, and perhaps even to alter some prejudicial perceptions (Tate & Surlin, 1976; Vidmar & Rokeach, 1974; Wilhoit & de Bock, 1976).

Programs specifically designed to attack stereotypes and to catalyze more favorable affect toward minorities can be successful. Both field surveys and controlled experiments with *Sesame Street* (Gorn, Goldberg, & Kanungo, 1976) have demonstrated that for minorities, and recent research on *Freestyle* (Williams, LaRose, & Frost, 1981) did so for sex roles as well. However, few such programs are available. In most programs, race messages occur solely on the basis of the character's presence and behavior, and one must infer or ascribe racial overtones, feelings, and attitudes. This is likely to remain the normative media presentation. Thus, it is prudent for programmers to be sensitized to just what kinds of imprints these portrayals have for both black and white viewers, especially young people. They turn to television to learn about life, to learn about people, and to learn more about themselves. There is ample evidence that most characterizations of minorities stand out for them, in part because of their infrequency. And they recall them, and react to them affectively and cognitively. There may then be some obligation to provide more variety in black presentations and to move to other minorities with similar attempts at heterogeneity. Not all can expect to emulate Norman Lear's ability at satire.

A more exact research agenda could begin to identify some strains not present or insufficiently pursued to date. A clear absence from the literature exists as to the impact of television programming and other media content on minority perceptions of the majority world. Research interests in the minority perceptions of self, and majority responses to minority groups, have omitted the flip side of one of those coins. What expectations about whites emerge from their portrayals, as judged by minority viewers? Inasmuch as whites seldom interact with blacks or anyone else on television, what do blacks assess as appropriate self-behaviors when with whites, and what do they expect from them? What inferences do blacks derive about wealth, power, jobs, sex roles, or even the possibility of changes in interracial relations?

Inasmuch as there are relatively few black-dominated shows telecast in a given season, more intensive examination of just what goes on during those shows over multiple episodes may provide some clues as to their potential influence. This suggests an approach to content beyond those lauded elsewhere in this paper. What themes occur in the programs? What value statements are made by major characters? How are problems resolved? Do these occur consistently across episodes? If so, they are prime candidates for learning and modeling among regular viewers.

The issue can be reversed. The selection process of both blacks and whites who regularly watch one or more of the few shows featuring minorities can be probed. How did they choose to watch this show? What attributes of the show make it worth watching on a regular basis? Is it solely race for black viewers? Is race an unlikely response from regular, nonblack viewers? Indeed, is it some character or two that piques the fancy of the viewer? What are the character attributes that lead to return viewing? Are those attributes common across favorite shows or across favorite characters on different shows? If one wants to build a case for more minority characterizations, that argument is better made from success than failure. Such rhetoric warrants similar probing into least favorite minority characters and rejected shows. What did they have or do that turned off minority and/or majority viewers?

Do Hispanics resent blacks because blacks are visible on television whereas Hispanics are not? Or is there some doubly vicarious identification with another minority on television? Both arguments could be made and are worth testing. Without same-ethnicity role models, with whom does the young Hispanic choose to identify and, more important, with what attributes and for what reasons? Does identification with Anglo role models diminish cultural identity? Would available Hispanic role models solidify cultural identity?

No study has yet made an assessment of what should be at the crux of this research area: Do behaviors toward role holders change, and is that change consistent with either the general thrust of television portrayals or with the specific behaviors of a particular character? Do blacks alter or shape their behavior toward whites on the basis of anything they see on television, and vice versa? The studies conducted examine attitudes, beliefs, postures, and self-assessments, but they do not explore the physical or verbal behaviors of intergroup relations.

Comprehensive research is absent. We must patch together findings from separate studies conducted in disparate circumstances. Where is the research program that begins with current available content, systematically examines that content, moves to field work (preferably in a multiwave design), and supplements that concurrently with key experimental studies? Wholistic research has seldom been done without substantial federal incentive (e.g., the Surgeon General's research program on televised violence). Until that time, we must continue to fit together a puzzle without knowing how many pieces we are playing with and without a cover drawing that depicts the finished product.

It is worth repeating Barrow's (1975) observation that "we know virtually nothing about either the short- or the long-term effects of television on minority children . . . If I were to place all of our knowledge in a thimble, I would probably still have room for my thumb." Today the thimble is full; a carafe now may be an appropriate goal.

REFERENCES

Allsopp, R. N. (1982). *Portrayals of black people on network television and the racial attitudes of elementary school children: An experimental study.* Unpublished doctoral dissertation, New York University.

Atkin, C., Greenberg, B., & McDermott, S. (1983). Television and race role socialization. *Journalism Quarterly, 60*(3), 407–414.

Atkin, C., & Heald, G. (1977). The content of children's toy and food commercials. *Journal of Communication, 27*(1), 107–114.

Baptista-Fernandez, P., & Greenberg, B. (1980). The context, characteristics and communication behavior of blacks on television. In B. Greenberg (Ed.), *Life on television* (pp. 13–21). Norwood, NJ: Ablex.

Baran, S. (1973). Dying black/dying white: Coverage of six newspapers. *Journalism Quarterly, 50*(4), 761–763.

Barcus, E. F. (1975). *Weekend children's television.* Newtonville, MA: Action for Children's Television.

Barcus, E. F. (1978). *Commercial children's television on weekend and weekday afternoons.* Newtonville, MA: Action for Children's Television.

Barcus, E. F. (1983). *Images of life on children's television.* New York: Praeger.

Barcus, E. F., & Wolkin, R. (1977). *Children's television: An analysis of programming and advertising.* New York: Praeger.

Barrow, L. (1975, November). *Nonregulatory policy research.* Speech presented at the Research on Television and Children and Youth Conference, Reston, VA.

Block C. (1972). White backlash to Negro ads: Fact or fantasy. *Journalism Quarterly, 49*(2), 253–262.

Bush, R., Resnick, A., & Stern, B. (1980). A content analysis of the portrayal of black models in magazine advertising. In R. Bagozzi et al. (Eds.), *Marketing in the 80's: Changes and challenges.* Chicago: American Marketing Association.

Bush, R. F., Solomon, P., & Hair, J., Jr. (1977). There are more blacks in TV commercials. *Journal of Advertising Research, 17*, 21–25.

Chaudhary, A. (1980). Press portrayal of black officials. *Journalism Quarterly, 57*(4), 636–641.

Colfax, D., & Steinberg, S. (1972). The perpetuation of racial stereotypes: Blacks in mass circulation magazine advertisements. *Public Opinion Quarterly, 35*, 8–18.

Comstock, G., & Cobbey, R. R. (1979). Television and the children of ethnic minorities. *Journal of Communication, 29*(1), 104–115.

Cox, K. (1969–1970). Changes in stereotyping of Negroes and whites in magazine advertisements. *Public Opinion Quarterly, 33*, 603–606.

Dates, J. (1980). Race, racial attitudes and adolescent perceptions of black television characters. *Journal of Broadcasting, 24*(4), 549–560.

Dominick, J., & Greenberg, B. (1970). Three seasons of blacks on television. *Journal of Advertising Research, 10*(2), 21–27.

Eastman, H., & Liss, M. (1980). Ethnicity and children's preferences. *Journalism Quarterly, 57*(2), 277–280.

Gerbner, G., & Signorielli, N. (1979). *Women and minorities in television drama (1969–1978)*. Philadelphia: Annenberg School of Communication, University of Pennsylvania.

Gorn, G., Goldberg, M., & Kanungo, R. (1976). The role of educational television in changing the intergroup attitudes of children. *Child Development, 47*, 277–280.

Greenberg, B. (1972). Children's reactions to TV blacks. *Journalism Quarterly, 49*(1), 5–14.

Greenberg, B. S., & Atkin, C. (1978). *Learning about minorities from television: A research agenda.* Paper presented at a conference on Television and the Minority Child, Center for Afro-American Studies, University of California at Los Angeles.

Greenberg, B., & Atkin, C. (1982). Learning about minorities from television: A research agenda. In G. Berry & C. Mitchell-Kernan (Eds.), *Television and the socialization of the minority child* (pp. 215–243). New York: Academic.

Greenberg, B., Heeter, C., Burgoon, J., Burgoon, M., & Korzenny, F. (1983a). Local newspaper coverage of Mexican Americans. *Journalism Quarterly, 60*(4), 671–676.

Greenberg, B., Heeter, C., Burgoon, M., Burgoon, J., & Korzenny, F. (1983b). Mass media use, preferences and attitudes among young people. In B. Greenberg, M. Burgoon, J. Burgoon, & F. Korzenny (Eds.), *Mexican Americans and the mass media*. Norwood, NJ: Ablex.

Greenberg, B., & Neuendorf, K. (1980). Black family interactions on television. In B. Greenberg (Ed.), *Life on television* (pp. 173–182). Norwood, NJ: Ablex.

Greenberg, B., Neuendorf, K., Buerkel-Rothfuss, N., & Henderson, L. (1982). The soaps: What's on and who cares? *Journal of Broadcasting, 26*(2), 519–535.

Heeter, C., Greenberg, B., Mendelson, B., Burgoon, J., Burgoon, M., & Korzenny, F. (1983). Cross media coverage of local Hispanic American news. *Journal of Broadcasting, 27*(4), 395–402.

Kaner, G. (1982). *Adolescent reactions to race and sex of professional television newscasters.* Unpublished doctoral dissertation, New York University.

Kassarjian, H. (1969). The Negro and American advertising: 1946–1965. *Journal of Marketing Research, 6*, 29–39.

Kerin, R. (1979). Black model appearance and product evaluations. *Journal of Communication, 29*(1), 123–128.

Korzenny, F., Griffis, B. A., Greenberg, B., Burgoon, J., & Burgoon, M. (1983). How community leaders, newspaper executives and reporters perceive Mexican Americans and the mass media. In B. Greenberg, M. Burgoon, J. Burgoon, & F. Korzenny (Eds.), *Mexican Americans and the mass media*. Norwood, NJ: Ablex.

Liss, M. (1981). Children's television selections: A study of indicators of same-race preference. *Journal of Cross Cultural Psychology, 12*(1), 103–110.

Loughlin, M., Donohue, T., & Gudykunst, W. (1982). Puerto Rican children's perceptions of favorite television characters as behavioral models. *Journal of Broadcasting, 24*(2), 159–171.

McDermott, S., & Greenberg, B. (1985). Parents, peers and television as determinants of black children's esteem. In R. Bostrom (Ed.), *Communication yearbook* (Vol. 8). Beverly Hills, CA: Sage.

Poindexter, P. M., & Stroman, C. (1981). Blacks and television: A review of the research literature. *Journal of Broadcasting, 25*(2), 103–122.

Reid, P. T. (1979). Racial stereotyping on television: A comparison of the behavior of both black and white television characters. *Journal of Applied Psychology, 64*(5), 465–489.

Reid, L., & VandenBergh, B. (1980). Blacks in introductory ads. *Journalism Quarterly, 57*(3), 485–489.

Roberts, C. (1971). The portrayal of blacks on network television. *Journal of Broadcasting, 15*(1), 45–53.

Schlinger, M. J., & Plummer, J. (1972). Advertising in black and white. *Journal of Marketing Research, 9,* 149–153.

Seggar, J. F., Hafen, J., & Hannonen-Gladden, H. (1981). Television's portrayals of minorities and women in drama and comedy drama, 1971–80. *Journal of Broadcasting, 25*(3), 277–288.

Soley, L. (1983). The effect of black models on magazine ad readership. *Journalism Quarterly, 60*(4), 686–690.

Stempel, G. (1971). Visibility of blacks in news and news-picture magazines. *Journalism Quarterly, 48*(2), 337–339.

Tate, E., & Surlin, S. (1976). Agreement with opinionated TV characters across culture. *Journalism Quarterly, 53*(2), 199–203.

Vidmar, N., & Rokeach, M. (1974). Archie Bunker's bigotry: A study in selective perception and exposure. *Journal of Communication, 24*(1), 35–47.

Weigel, R., & Howes, P. (1982). Race relations on children's television. *The Journal of Psychology, 111,* 109–112.

Weigel, R. H., Loomis, J., & Soja, M. (1980). Race relations on prime time television. *Journal of Personality and Social Psychology, 39*(5), 884–893.

Wilhoit, G. C., & de Bock, H. (1976). All in the Family in Holland. *Journal of Communication, 26*(1), 75–84.

Williams, F., LaRose, R., & Frost, F. (1981). *Children, television and sex-role stereotyping.* New York: Praeger.

Zuckerman, D., Singer, D., & Singer, J. (1980). Children's television viewing, racial and sex role attitudes. *Journal of Applied Social Psychology, 10*(4), 281–294.

10 Policy Options for Early Election Projections

Percy H. Tannenbaum
University of California at Berkeley

The mass media in general, and television in particular, have often been blamed for more than their share of many of society's woes (e.g., violence, poor health, improper role modeling, etc.). There has also been considerable concern about how the media have influenced our natural political life by playing a leading role in setting, and possibly distorting, the national political agenda; by usurping the functions more conventionally performed by political parties; by distorting the electoral process with undue emphasis on style and appearance but less on the issues of the day; by overemphasizing the horserace characteristics of presidential primaries, and the like.

Some of these concerns stem from more or less deliberate media decisions, but others are more incidental if not accidental. That is, they are a byproduct of a situation where the media, in the act of doing their own thing anyway, come up against established practices and thereby create a conflict between certain desired behavior (at least on the part of certain political authorities) and the actual media behavior in question. In such cases, the established, desired practice or the media behavior must change or coexist in an uneasy relationship. Because political and media institutions are both well-entrenched, rather protected enclaves, there is resistance to change. Thus, mutual coexistence, with periodic flare-ups and calls for reform, becomes the dominant modus operandi. Add to that an element or two of new technology or untoward political events and you have the makings of a rather volatile situation.

The issue of early election night projections—essentially, the widespread dissemination of an election outcome before all voting is completed—stems from the inopportune confluence of several independent factors, not all within our control. In the main arena of national elections, the problem would abate: (a) if the country were within a single time zone; (b) if the means for making projections (i.e., the raw data and computer programs) were less well developed technically; and (c) if the main disseminators (i.e., the national broadcast networks and their affiliates) could be persuaded to forego their competitive zeal and refrain from such early forecasts within their regions of coverage while local voting was still in progress. As it is, however, we have had several instances—most immediately, the 1980 presidential election—in which information about the pending electoral result was available in most parts of the nation well before voting had ceased. This is seen as a blemish, real or potential, on our electoral system—more so in the western states, where the issue is naturally more prominent, but also as a matter of democratic principle. It has spawned a number of research studies, along with numerous proposals for reform in Congress, the press, and various public interest groups, boosted by the findings of several public opinion surveys.

Attention has focused on three kinds of possible consequences of the practice of premature projections. An early apprehension when the issue first surfaced was its effect on the presidential race itself. (The first bill to deal with the problem was introduced by Senator Barry Goldwater in 1961, well before he emerged as the GOP candidate in 1964.) Some proponents for reform were concerned with a possible bandwagon effect, whereby otherwise reluctant voters are prompted to rush out to vote for the apparent victor. Other observers speculated on the possibility of an underdog effect generating a sympathy vote for the apparent loser (indeed, there was some indication of this in favor of John Anderson in 1980). Although it is highly unlikely that the practice could affect who actually wins an election—the networks seek to be accurate as well as timely—it is possible that the margin of victory could be affected, converting an otherwise close election into mandate, or vice versa. In any event, evidence for one or the other effect—or even both, in which case they might partially cancel each other out—is absent in the research to date.

A more major concern is with the effect of early projections on voter turnout. Faced with a fait accompli in the form of a definite winner, some would-be voters might come to regard their vote as having no affect on the outcome anyway, so they might as well not vote. In 1980, there were some reports to this effect—even to the degree of some otherwise willing voters leaving poll queues upon hearing the news—along with charges of "disenfranchised voters." Such hyperbole aside, turnout is taken as a serious issue in its own right, especially in a country that takes pride in its democratic procedures but which already lags far behind other Western nations in turnout (at least, when it is calculated on initial age-eligible voters). Voting participation in the United States has steadily declined since 1960 and is now estimated to be only slightly over 50%.

To be sure, when the turnout question is addressed in the context of the early projection issue, it involves only a relatively small proportion of the total voter pool. The resulting critical mass of vulnerable voters may vary from one location to another and from one election to another; thus, size in a given instance is difficult to estimate properly. Jackson and MaGee (1981) found an effect on turnout of 6–11% in 1980; Wolfinger and Linquiti (1981) found 2–3% in the 1972 election. But for reasons detailed in a recent book on this subject (Tannenbaum & Kostrich, 1983), such results should not be taken as final and general. Nevertheless, any such effect deserves attention if only because it tends to make an already bad situation that much worse and if the inherent political as well as economic costs did not outweigh the apparent benefits.

The third misgiving stems from the turnout issue and is even more significant. It relates to the fact that numerous other elections—congressional, statewide, local, and those for various initiatives and referenda—are usually held along with the presidential race. Thus, to the degree that early projections reduce turnout in the main election, they may also do so for these other elections. Furthermore, in a governmental system where winner takes all and where a majority of 1 has the same legislative impact as 100, small differences in elections can have larger political consequences later on. This allows for a far more insidious if unintended byproduct of the network projections and provides a major rationale for examining various means of reducing their potential effect, including possible judicial intervention.

Some 2 dozen (the number depends on how fine a point of differentiation one wishes to draw between them) alternatives for potential intervention have been suggested. These include an assortment of bills introduced for congressional action, often the same ones reinstated in one congressional session after another. Others require state rather than federal action, and still others represent nonlegislative procedures that emerge from an analysis of the issue. They address one or several of the main loci for possible intervention—the data base for making projections, either early election returns or so-called exit polls, or the degree and timing of their dissemination. These options are best examined in terms of their legal, organizational, economic, and political feasibility, as well as their effectiveness and possible side effects.

EARLY RETURN ALTERNATIVES

Over the past few decades various bills have been introduced in Congress that were directed at eliminating or reducing the probable harmful effects of early election forecasts. Some even passed in the Senate but were never considered by the House. The fact that none ever became law is a good indication of their lack of political feasibility. The fact that they were repeatedly introduced, often accompanied by hearings of the appropriate subcommittees, testifies both to their political resilience and to their probable motivation to reach the folks back home more than to the realities of making national policy.

These alternatives have several elements in common:

1. They are basically directed at encouraging (at least, not discouraging) higher voter turnout. Curiously, although such a purpose also implies an effect on simultaneous state and local elections, this has not been identified as a concurrent problem.

2. They are designed to restrict the use of early returns in making the projections. In this sense, they may well be a case of too little too late, given the increasing use of exit polls in recent years. However, because all three networks claim to use early returns to some degree (apparently more by ABC, least by NBC) and because exit polls are less reliable both intrinsically and in providing misleading results (e.g., the 1981 New Jersey gubernatorial election and the 1982 California races for Governor and U.S. Senator), they deserve some attention.

3. They propose to do so through simultaneous closing hours for voting throughout the country, either in themselves or in combination with other means of encouraging more turnout.

Simultaneous Poll Closings

Uniform closing times have the advantage of insuring no early returns per se because such returns are available only after polls close. However, to close all polls at the same time and yet allow sufficient voting hours at convenient times of the day require rather awkward adjustments in some part of the country. The variety of methods suggested involves manipulating voting hours, voting days, or both, which in turn invites the question of congressional (as opposed to state) authority and control. Although the legal authority is somewhat ambiguous in the case of presidential elections, the court would probably rule in favor of such congressional power should a dispute arise.

Later Closings in the East.   Uniform balloting can be achieved if all states in the eastern part of the country stayed open later in order to conform to voting hours in the west. One version of this strategy would require all polls to close at 11 p.m. EST (8 p.m. PST), except for Alaska and Hawaii, which would be free to set their own hours.

Although this alternative could be reasonably effective, it suffers on the grounds of regional inequity in the distribution of costs and benefits. The Pacific states would gain the most and yield the least. But some change in voting hours would be required elsewhere in the country and, with them, varying degrees of recruitment difficulties, higher administrative costs, and sheer inconvenience, not the least being the need for individuals in the east to stay up well after midnight to find out the outcome of local and presidential races. As a result, this version has lacked sufficient political support, and it seems unlikely that the situation will change in Congress.

Earlier Closings in the West.   The reverse situation is to maintain the status quo in the Eastern states (except that they share the same closing time) and have the rest of the country close polling places earlier. A recent variation of this approach called for a uniform 9 a.m.–9 p.m. EST voting period in the United States, with some adjustments to accommodate Hawaii and Alaska.

This version displaces the inequities of the earlier proposal but comes off even worse overall. The lack of flexibility serves to restrict evening voting after work in the Pacific states and, correspondingly, the prework morning vote in the east, both probably decreasing turnout even more. Although more equitable in relative costs and benefits, this method is liable to be counterproductive in terms of its main purpose.

Extended Voting Period

Simultaneous poll closings within a single, limited voting period (e.g., 12 hrs) are bound to introduce some inequities and accompanying costs. A seemingly successful strategy to reduce the inequities is to expand the voting period while maintaining the uniform closing requirement. There would be more time to vote (thus presumably increasing turnout), the later voting hours would count for less of the total vote, and projections based on early returns would still be controlled for by the simultaneous closings.

Twenty-Four Hour Voting.   This version of the foregoing general strategy surfaces every so often. But for our purposes in terms of the projection issue, it is unlikely that this procedure will have a substantial effect. Allowing for more total time might increase turnout somewhat, but not substantially if it extends well beyond the daylight hours. It might serve to curb projections, but only if voting was concentrated in the later hours and if polls were to close before the start of prime time television in the east (e.g., 6 p.m. Monday to 6 p.m. Tuesday instead of a midnight to midnight Tuesday).

Either way, this proposal runs into difficulty in terms of administrative burden and cost. Keeping polls open around the clock involves at least doubling poll workers and hence more training time, recruiting difficulties, security (especially for the hours near midnight), and costs on the order of 75% higher. Election officials, who comprise a rather formidable self-interest group in this area, are adamantly opposed to such an option (especially when it is presented as a means of controlling early projections), and their clout can make a difference.

Modified 24-Hr Voting.   A more flexible, but also more complex, variation is not to insist on a consecutive 24 hrs for voting but to allow for 12 or more hrs within the total 24-hr period. Thus, one bill introduced in the aftermath of the 1980 election called for a 10 p.m. EST uniform closing time and for the polls to be open for at least the 6 hrs immediately preceding (i.e., 4–10 p.m. EST, or 1–7 p.m. PST) and for 6 or more of the preceding 18 hrs. Somewhat similar to the late eastern closing indicated earlier, it is more flexible in terms of opening time and in its allowance for staggered voting, even extending across 2 days. The eastern states could readily adapt by opening a bit later on Tuesday (e.g., 9 or 10 a.m.), with the Pacific states by accepting the 1-hr earlier closing (i.e., a 7 a.m.–7 p.m. PST voting day). Again, Alaska and Hawaii would be forced to make the most awkward adjustments, but at least with some choice.

This proposal contains most of the virtues and problems associated with the eastern late closings remedy. The fact that it allows more discretion to the individual states has some advantages, but that flexibility also suggests that local election officials will have a greater say. As they generally eschew new organizational, administrative, and economic costs, they have argued for the maintenance of the status quo.

Two-Day Voting.   The foregoing alternative suggests that differential inequities can be offset in part by splitting the voting period over 2 days. In principle, this allows for a proper number of voting hours at the most convenient day-light time and still conserves the desired simultaneous poll closing time. Thus, in one such option, all polling would shut down by 8 p.m. EST Tuesday, but states in other time zones could make up the lost hours (e.g., 3 hrs on the west coast) by having the polls open the same number of hours on Monday, leaving the choice of specific hours open to the state (e.g., 5–8 p.m. in California).

The extent to which this would affect turnout is unclear. One possible drawback is that it might encourage more exit polling on Monday night so that they would be available and broadcast before the heavier Tuesday voting begins. In addition, those states using the Monday option would face relatively high additional costs (e.g., up to 50% in Los Angeles county) because of the demands for overnight security, ballot transportation, and other administrative burdens.

Holiday Voting

If part of the reason for reduced turnout is that voting hours are restricted for many people, then having the balloting take place on an existing or a newly created holiday could contribute to a higher turnout rate. Presumably, this greater participation would take place throughout the day, thus making fewer individuals vulnerable to possible early projection effects. Some American observers note that other democracies with such a voting procedure also have high turnout and, accordingly, they are inclined to make a causal attribution between the two.

Sunday Voting.   This is the most common alternative employed in other Western countries. It has been proposed on more than one occasion for the U.S., most recently on an experimental basis covering several forthcoming elections, combined with the uniform closing provision. It called for a 9-hr 12 a.m.–9 p.m. EST voting day throughout the country on the first Sunday after the first Monday in November. Its proponents argue that turnout will increase dramatically, but others suggest that American recreational patterns are distinct enough not to affect turnout appreciably. Of course, the reduction in total voting hours to 9 could cut into turnout, but the sponsors reason it that should be enough time on what is a day of leisure for most of the population.

Although changing from a weekday to a Sunday does imply higher costs in the form of overtime pay for regular election personnel, the increase is within manageable limits (5–10% is one estimate), but in these days of fiscal stringency, it cannot be dismissed entirely. The effect on projections is uncertain other than the fact that the more ballots that are cast early during an election period, the greater the inducement for the networks to use exit polls to make their forecasts all the earlier.

The Sunday voting proposal has a uniform closing that may be awkward for some states, but it can be incorporated into the 2-day voting scheme. Thus, a Saturday-Sunday sequence is a conceivable alternative to the Monday-Tuesday schedule, and it might be preferred because it spreads the voting over the 2 days of the week when the most people are at leisure. But again, the added costs of 2-day voting have to be dealt with, not to mention the break with tradition in both day of week and number of days.

Weekday Holiday.   In some countries with high turnout rates, election day is a national holiday. This practice would allow us to keep the first Tuesday after the first Monday in November as election day, still with a fixed closing time (8 p.m. EST across the country, in one recent version). This maintains the presumed advantages of the Sunday option but does not deal with the issue of costs to the national economy effectively.

That depends in part on the specific type of holiday that is declared, either nationally or on a state-by-state basis. A paid mandatory holiday would be welcomed by employees but attacked by employers because they would have to bear the main burden. Conversely, an unpaid holiday would not sit too well with workers. Either way, productivity will suffer and, although we do have other holidays and this one may be as worthy as the next, it is not likely to be readily accepted. This may be reason enough to put the idea to rest, given a normal inertia against tampering with the existing system.

Delay the Release of Returns

If each of the alternatives involving manipulating voting hours and closing times involves one or more critical problems affecting its acceptability, an alternative is to manipulate when the returns become available. In their zeal to control the projection issue, or at least to grab some headlines back home, some members of Congress have proposed delaying the release of the voting results until all polls are closed, possibly as late as midnight or even the next morning.

The main value of such a proposal is control of the data without interfering with individual states and their voting hours. But several problems probably offset that advantage. Legally, there is a conflict over congressional power to control release of election findings, which is derived from a series of Supreme Court decisions relating to the congressional right to enforce its own regulations and extend that right to presidential elections, with First Amendment provisions. Even if the legal battle is won, there are still questions of differential inconvenience in different parts of the country (e.g.,is it fair to keep politically interested easterners awake all night in order to please residents of the Bering Straits?), different administrative cost effects (depending on whether voting machines, precinct-level counting, computerized systems, etc. are used), and media opposition. This adds up to strong resistance, rendering an essentially simple, effective scheme politically dubious, along with the other congressional initiatives.

EXIT POLLS

Not only are the various strategies for handling early election returns difficult to implement, they may also be beside the point because the networks seem to be relying more on exit polls in state and national elections. Exit polls have accordingly become a central focus in the early projection policy question, in large part because much earlier forecasts can be made than with actual vote returns. Indeed, all the previous options are meaningless if exit polls are applied on a more intensive and earlier basis. Their failure to predict accurately in several recent state-level elections may make the networks hesitant to rely solely on exit polls, but the odds are clearly toward still more use, unless the networks can be persuaded otherwise.

Those persons so moved by the early projection issue to consider legislative or judicial attempts to eliminate or control exit polls face a formidable barrier: The collection (not to mention the dissemination) of any such materials is clearly protected under the First Amendment and is liable to survive any such test. Thus, a straightforward ban on interviews with voters on election day would be summarily dismissed, even if it was ever passed into law, as would the related strategy of making such polls too expensive and cumbersome to conduct (e.g., through high licensing fees or taxation). The critical test in all such cases is the so-called clear-and-present danger doctrine, in which the deciding criteria are the gravity of the problem, the likelihood that it will arise, and the extent to which freedom of speech is infringed. These are difficult to establish in the case of exit polls as such.

CONTACT AT POLL SITES

Most states have laws restricting contact with voters within some distance (most often 100 ft, but with some variation) of the precinct locations. Although their main intention is to prohibit close-in electioneering activity on arriving voters, they conceivably apply to departing voters as well. Inasmuch as the particular margin appears arbitrary, the restrictive zone could in principle be enlarged to interfere with collecting data from a proper sample and thus render the projections based on such data less reliable. (The proposed state of Washington legislation contain just such a provision to extend the present 100-ft limit to 300 ft.)

The essence of this approach lies in its value as a deterrent—to get the networks or others to drop using exit polls or at least to rely on them less—under the guise of a criminal statute to be enforced legally. The main shortcoming of such a proposal is that it will have difficulty passing a serious court test because of its transparent intent. Although several state statutes governing behavior at voting booths have been upheld by the courts, a federal law applying solely to exit polling would be difficult to justify as an exception to the First Amendment. It would not take much legal skill to show how such a law was deliberately designed to circumvent a constitutional right, and broadening the law to disguise its exclusive intent would probably generate even more hostility. Nevertheless, the behavior of individual judges is difficult to predict in individual circumstances, and an issue of this type, involving as it does another cherished principle, could conceivably get through.

Exit Poll Boycotts

Exit polling is a rather fragile form of survey research. It conventionally uses a random selection of precincts and a relatively small sample of voters (often 25–30) within a precinct to represent an individual state. The common practice is to ask respondents to complete a sample ballot of the type they had filled in a few minutes earlier, perhaps containing several additional opinion items, along with their principal demographic characteristics. The accumulated data, taken at various times on election day, are phoned into the network election unit headquarters for computer treatment, allowing for a compilation of the state vote in the main races, voting trends by different population subgroups, various comparisons with previous voting behavior, and so forth.

As with all surveys, the critical ingredient is the respondent, perhaps more so in this case because of relatively small precinct samples. If enough respondents do not cooperate fully and honestly at a given precinct, it can appreciably throw off the precinct representation, and if that occurs in enough precincts, it can result in misleading estimates of the state vote. Thus, one line of attack for those who wish to undermine the continual reliance on exit polls is to convince a sufficient number of voters either not to cooperate at all or, better still (i.e., from the intervener's standpoint), to misrepresent their vote on the sample ballot. If this is done selectively rather than across-the-board, it can cause even more problems.

Clearly, this is a questionable, improper activity for a governmental agency to undertake. Although federal and state governments have sponsored large-scale educational campaigns for various health practices and the like, a government-sponsored boycott is another matter. A more modest approach (e.g., requiring that prior to the interview respondents be read a "Miranda statement" of the possible uses and consequences of exit polls) might be more acceptable, but just how effective that would be is unclear. Any such proposal is of dubious constitutionality because of potential interference with a First Amendment right and will undoubtedly draw the opposition of the broadcast media and survey researchers, thus rendering it unfeasible. Its main political appeal (viz., that it is not a coercive measure but one that relies on public support to be effective; an operational referendum in effect) is inadequate to overcome its inherent shortcomings.

This strategy can nevertheless be pursued outside the legislative realm through the efforts of some well-intended, established (e.g., the League of Women Voters) or newly created organization (e.g., a consortium of groups cosponsored the recent appeal to the networks along with LWV). That would remove a number of potential legal barriers, but it requires a very substantial organizational effort with appropriate funding to be effective. All these ingredients are in relatively short supply. Boycotts have a mixed record in this country, partly for this reason.

MEDIA INTERVENTIONS

The problem with early election night projections is not so much with the data base, but with when the projections are released and disseminated. The problem would disappear if the networks, and any other such outlets, would withold their release until all voting had ceased. More to the point, it is not necessary that the networks exercise centralized control, but that their affiliates and independent stations delay broadcasting the projections until the polls are closed within their respective areas of coverage. When all is said and done, projections constitute a local rather than a national problem in terms of their potential impact.

Canada provides a most appropriate comparison. It has almost as many time zones as the United States. In addition, the voting pattern in Canadian federal elections makes the earlier eastern vote critical for projection purposes. If the Liberal party does not carry a vast majority of the seats in the Maritime Provinces, and especially in Quebec and Ontario, it has virtually no chance of being the ruling party in Parliament. Canada handles the problem by initiating a centralized national broadcast feed when polls close in the eastern zone, but there is a regulation prohibiting stations from joining in on the feed until voting ends in their time zone. Although there are periodic accidental lapses, the system works rather well, without any hue and cry about freedom of speech being circumvented (although that may change now that Canada has a Bill of Rights in the works) or the public's right to know being curtailed. It is readily accepted by all concerned as part of the price for having a geographically large and widespread country with a desire for uncontaminated elections.

So why don't we have such a system in the United States? In fact, why don't local stations voluntarily delay the broadcast of exit poll findings until voting has ceased in their area? After all, virtually every night of the year, west coast programming has a routine 3-hr delay in the rebroadcast of news and prime time programming to capture large audiences. The answers are many and varied, and none are totally satisfactory, but two stand out: (a) a readiness to invoke the First Amendment—in effect, a readiness to hide behind the First Amendment's provisions—at the slightest suggestion of external interference; (b) a sense of professionalism, of knowing on one's own what is newsworthy and the right thing to do, which is mutually reinforced all through the industry but especially in the news departments. It is not that the industry is totally free of all external constraints. Willingly or not, it has generally followed a code of conduct, but one that was self-imposed rather than government dictated. And they have, whether they admit it openly or not, succumbed on more than one occasion to strictures from large advertisers, certain special interest groups, and their perception of public opinion. On this particular issue, however, they continue to deny any evidence of an adverse effect (the evidence is not that robust, to be sure, but they have none to counter it) and to plead that not issuing early projections is inconsistent with traditional journalistic standards and their responsibility to report as accurately and quickly as possible.

The key issue is what to report. The traditional defense of network brass before congressional committees and the like is that it is their duty to the public to report crucial news—the facts, the truth—when they know it. The election of a President is certainly a key news event, but early election projections do not constitute the event in this case. They are not necessarily the fact or the truth, but rather mere speculations regarding the outcome. It is shameful that the networks defend such a practice on so flimsy a basis. It is both unseemly and outright arrogant.

Such a holier than thou position is often employed when the media defend other practices to disguise a more fundamental motive, namely, to make a decent profit in a highly competitive business, all of it fueled by advertising rates closely linked to program ratings and the demographic makeup of their audiences. But that, curiously, does not appear to be the case here. Network and station ratings on election night tend to parallel those for the regular evening news, and it is unlikely that audience memories linger over 2 or 4 years on the basis of which station was first with the winner. Rather, it is more a case of professional pride among the network election units and the news divisions to which they belong, along with the vicarious thrill among other network units and affiliates of shouting "We're Number 1" in this, the Super Bowl of the news game.

Clearly, left to their own devices, the media are apt to continue doing their own thing in their own way. The election coverage issue thus represents a clash between the right of a free press and the right to free elections, an issue that parallels the clash between a free press and a fair trial. The media have not yielded on the latter issue, and they are not apt to change their ways on the election question. That leaves relatively few options worth exploring.

Legal Control

Although Congress possesses the inherent right to protect the democratic process, its power to coerce the media into compliance on content is totally limited by the First Amendment and the way it has been interpreted by the courts. Regulatory control by the Federal Communication Commission is equally farfetched as far as an outright ban on projections is concerned. The more modest proposals of enforcing a delay in the broadcast of projections, or even only on those based on exit polls, run into difficulties in trying to meet the clear-and-present danger test. The latter case, in particular, could pose an interesting legal situation, which is too questionable to decide ahead of time. But probably, the case is moot enough, and the present opposition strong enough to nullify the chances of the passage of such a bill in the first place.

Nevertheless, the introduction of these bills and other such legislation could have the effect of getting the networks and their affiliates out of their protective cocoon. They help place the issue where the advocates of reform feel it belongs: on the media side of the court with the pressure on them to defend current practice more directly or else accede to the demand. Other such efforts might include passing congressional resolutions, especially so-called concurrent resolutions, to express a shared sentiment of outrage. (Such a resolution was in fact introduced in 1964 by then Senator Pierre Salinger, but it did not pass.) The purpose, again, is to offer a rebuke and to build up enough strong opposition to persuade the media that election night projections just are not worth the effort.

By the same token, a lawsuit introduced by a losing candidate in a close race on the grounds that the forecasts interfered with a free and open election could have a similar effect. Such a suit would bear the heavy burden of establishing that it was the projections, as such, that were responsible for the margin of difference, but the sheer publicity of such a case could make the networks and local stations sit up and take more notice. Possibly more effective would be to request a preelection injunction against the broadcast of any projections while polls are still open, especially if such an appeal was nonpartisan and made by the major party candidates for, say, a House of Representatives seat. A number of such suits, spread across different types of districts in several states, might be enough to make the industry back off.

Voluntary Restraint

The key to it all is voluntary action on the part of the networks and their affiliates. In many ways, they are powerful, but they are also vulnerable to persuasive appeals and various overt and covert pressures. For all their posturing and spirited defense, this issue is not all that important for them to engage in a major battle.

At this point, pressure from several major advertisers could help make the difference. Though boldly independent, the networks are nevertheless sensitive enough to advertiser preferences not to rock the boat excessively and not to provoke unduly. If some advertisers can be mobilized to complain and even take action against violence on television, they could probably be persuaded to take on the equally or more worthy cause of purer elections.

Such indirect efforts require sophisticated organizational skills and no little amount of funding if they are to succeed. They also demand strong involvement in the cause and the motivation to do something about it, ingredients that may be the least readily available. Negative sentiment about network practices appears to be widespread in the aftermath of an election, but it is shallowly distributed and tends to fade between elections. Publications and broadcasts dealing with the problem may help pave the way but are rarely sufficient to launch major efforts for change.

STATE-LEVEL ACTION

Because the main effects of election night projections may be felt more at the local levels of government, some sort of state action becomes justified. Most of the interventions outlined at the federal level can be undertaken at the state level with similar consequences. However, there are several measures that can be introduced within a state that might make a difference in the potential contamination of election night forecasts.

Voting Hour Changes

For starters, states presently have control over voting hours for different elections. Although several of the proposals for adjusting voting hours are unfeasible nationally due to regional inequities, fewer such constraints operate within a single state. Thus, if Californians see it as advantageous to reduce the 3-hr gap with the east coast, they could easily choose to have an earlier closing time. A full 3-hr cut would be counterproductive, but a 1-hr change from 8 p.m. to 7 p.m. is reasonable. Similarly, declaring election day a national or state holiday might require a great deal of political effort to gain approval, but if it is applied only within California, letting other states do as they will, it would be more feasible.

Time Changes

As noted in the case of earlier poll closings, potential changes in this area come in the relatively large units of an hour rather than in minutes. A fairly simple procedure for reducing the gap still another hour stems from the fact that November elections days (the first Tuesday after the first Monday) are close to the conventional dates for reverting to standard time from summer Daylight Savings Time (the last Sunday in October). It thus turns out that if the changeover can be delayed by a suitable gap in time (no more than 2 weeks if one persists on Sunday as the change day), another full hour can be gained. The change could be initiated only on election years or annually to make it less conspicuous.

There are a number of controversial factors associated with such a step (e.g., congressional approval to depart from the Uniform Time Act must be obtained, travel schedules would be out of sync for a short spell, etc.), but none are insurmountable. Thus, it is quite feasible as a partial step. It does not solve the problem, but reducing the gap by a full hour with such a simple step should not be dismissed too lightly, especially when combined with 1-hr earlier closing.

Pressure on Local Stations

The 2-hr savings just noted come at the expense of the state citizenry giving up some convenience. If the other major party in the election coverage would contribute their bit, a compromise solution would be in the making. If all the California radio and television stations object to a 3-hr delay in carrying the national election coverage, they might agree to a 1-hr delay, thus accommodating the full 3-hr time gap.

More generally, the fact that the stations are local institutions with personnel living in local communities makes them potentially more responsive to local concerns. Because a large number of stations is involved, with widely overlapping coverage areas, any attempt at enforcing a 3- or even 1-hr delay must be done collectively rather than individually. But that all stations have a local community base and are organized into one or more statewide associations makes them, again in principle at least, more susceptible to state action (again, including resolutions of sentiment) and local political appeals.

Mail Ballots

No discussion of election procedural changes in California would be complete without acknowledging the growing use of absentee ballots in all types of elections and the conduct of some local elections (most recently in San Diego and Berkeley) solely with mail ballots. Confirmed by the state courts as valid, such voting procedures are expected to become more common for various local elections (because of potential cost-saving and greater participation rates) and may expand to the statewide level if the legislature can be assured that proper safeguards for a secret ballot can be provided. In addition, the development of new telecommunication technologies makes electronic voting a distinct possibility.

The relevance of these procedures to the problem at hand is that they can take place before national or other voting occurs and are thus immune from the potential effects of premature forecasts and the like. For example, a mail ballot may allow a week or more for submission with a fixed postmark due date and hour corresponding to regular poll closing hours. Such voting is seen as less demanding of voter time and effort and hence as a means of increasing turnout. The fact that it can be directed along partisan lines (as was the organized use of absentee ballots with potential Republican voters in the close election of California Governor George Deukmejian in 1982) makes it a more controversial topic among political activists in both major parties.

Of course, if the media were still intent on being "first with the most," they could adapt their polling methods to get readings of absentee mail ballots as they now do with exit polls. But the methodology is likely to be less precise (especially in terms of the sample of actual voters), and the results therefore more tenuous. Such imperfections, however, have not deterred premature, and at times incorrect, projections in the past, and they are not likely to do so in the future unless the networks and their affiliates can be persuaded otherwise.

In the end, the problem with early projections is less a matter of structural changes in the electoral system as it is with deliberate practices controlling their dissemination. Hence, any effective changes have to come from the broadcasting quarter. In our system, it is difficult if not impossible to force networks to do it. So they must be convinced by other means, or the problem will continue.

ACKNOWLEDGMENTS

Materials for this chapter are derived from my recent book (with Leslie Kostrich), *Turned on TV/Turned-off Voters* (1983). More elaborate treatment of the various policy alternatives can be found there. An earlier version of the present paper was prepared for the Harvard/American Broadcasting Companies Symposium on "Voting for Democracy," held in September, 1983, in Washington, DC.

REFERENCES

Jackson, J., & McGee, W. H. (1981). *Election reporting and voter turnout.* Ann Arbor: University of Michigan, Report of the Center for Political Studies.
Tannenbaum, P. H., & Kostrich, L. S. (1983). *Turned-on TV/Turned-off voters: Policy options for elections projections.* Beverly Hills, CA: Sage.
Wolfinger, R. E., & Linquiti, P. (1981, February/March). Tuning in and turning out. *Public Opinion,* pp. 56–60.

11 The Lens of Television and the Prism of Personality

J. Mallory Wober
Independent Broadcasting Authority

An American in Ethiopia (Korten, 1971) once analyzed 129 indigenous folk tales and found that their themes portrayed life as a contest providing few opportunities for cooperation. Although the fictional person resorts to deception or revenge to survive in a hostile cultural climate, Korten further claimed "that the imagery of the Ethiopian stories is generally consistent with actual social behavior in Ethiopia is well supported by a wide variety of studies" (p. 220). Korten compared the Ethiopian tales with their American parallels in print, implying that the latter both reflected and fostered a more mellow and cooperative society. Today, however, it is more usual to examine the content of television fiction to explore its possible reflective or formative roles in personality portrayal and development.

The Ethiopian study is an example of several that formed an uneasy hybrid discipline examining links between culture and personality. From an anthropological perspective, the emphases were on the power of culture to influence individuals at all levels of functioning including their fundamental psychological structures. On the psychological side, a powerful tradition of behaviorism fit in with this idea of individual responsiveness to external stimuli; but there was some reluctance in identifying constructs such as personality, which would generate behavior autonomously rather than merely accept a refractive role in modifying responses to external initiatives.

In the culture and personality field, there were ideological difficulties and conflicts that absorbed energies which would have been more fruitfully spent in refining definitions, the measures of cultural variables, and their potential psychological counterparts. It fit a socialist case to believe in the power of the environment to mold humans, and sociologists opposed "psychological reductionism," which might undercut their theories and the programs that aspired to combat racism, educational, and third world disadvantages. Some psychologists (Argyle 1972; Mischel 1968) took the view that personality measures were unstable, predicted little, and were of little scientific importance. Later, though, it was acknowledged (Hampson 1982; Tapp 1981) that individual differences at a fundamental structural level, however elusive they were to detect, would not be dispensed with and would remain useful in understanding human behavior.

The behaviorist tradition is easy to detect in mass communication studies. Wherever one reads of subjects "exposed to" screen materials, it is likely that these human billiard balls are conceived of as responding principally to external events, without displaying autonomous initiative in seeking the cue. Writers may overtly deny they have a "Kodak" model of the observer in which exposure imprints messages received from a sender; yet the idiom reveals a tradition of approach that minimizes the role of the individual in seeking and modifying stimuli. Some explanation is needed for the low profile that the subject of personality has had in media studies, and the behaviorist approach may constitute a part of the phenomenon. In Comstock's (1975) review, 208 key studies were assembled on psychological processes in television and human behavior, but only 1 used the word *personality* in its title. Comstock concentrates on processes rather than on constructs, but several of the lines of enquiry he introduces lead up to, without naming and engaging with, personality structures. Murray (1980) has no entry for personality in the index to his bibliography. Gordon and Verna (1978) have 11 entries out of over 2,700 in their bibliography, 4 of which are non-American, 3 are unpublished doctoral dissertations in the United States, and 2 are socialization studies not particularly focused on television. Certainly, many studies deal with measures and processes in the realm of personality, but there has clearly been a reluctance to identify this domain explicitly in American research on television.

In general, it may be that as personality is a construct that is comparatively static in its structural nature, it has not appealed to the more dynamic ethos of much American research. Yet personality has obviously been researched both in America and Europe, and a variety of theories and constructs have been generated. Although personality studies are not yet in the position of those of cognitive development, with a fashionable and coherent body of theory and evidence, some thought on their fundamental nature points to the conclusion that adequate, let alone full, understanding of how individuals interact with mass media will not be reached without a good account of those individuals' fundamental attributes.

Some personality constructs have been explicitly studied as such, and offered for use in media studies. Thus, Rubin and Peplau (1975) explain that belief in a just world is "an attitudinal continuum," but they also see it as a "pervasive cognitive tendency" prevalent in cultural forms (e.g., religion and stories justifying the exalted status of heroes and leaders), serving an adaptive purpose (allowing one to trust others and to invest work with a belief in ultimate reward), and inculcated in childhood. As such, built into the underlying psychological structure of the individual, it is sensible to label (depth of) belief in a just world (not that Rubin and Peplau do so) as a personality construct. They point out that television dramas, nearly always ending in punishment for the bad guy and success for the good, teach just world beliefs, and they even plead for a contrary emphasis to help reflect reality.

There are, however, two potentially powerful personality theories that could be of considerable use in television studies, but which have not yet been exploited for this purpose. The better known of these is the theory of psychological differentiation (Witkin & Berry, 1975). Differentiation involves specialization of "areas" of functioning, such as a sharpening of the distinctness of the self from others, but it also involves development of integration between experience and expression in different areas, when necessary. Greater differentiation is linked to specific experiences in childhood, broadly involving encouragement to take responsibility, to make a separation from dependence on the mother, and to develop internal mechanisms for impulse control. Research in several countries shows that conformist and authoritarian environments do not foster differentiation.

Differentiation theory suggests that youngsters who are heavy viewers, probably as a result of weaker parental control and guidance, and who see a considerable amount of happy-ending fiction are less likely than lighter viewers to become highly differentiated. Curiously, although differentiation is established through social experiences (e.g., parental control or its absence) and cultural lessons (e.g., television fiction), it has commonly been assessed not with attitude or personality but with cognitive tests. High differentiation is indicated by high scores on tests such as Kohs Blocks, Raven's Matrices, or Embedded Figures. Although Witkin and Berry state that differentiation proceeds equally in all aspects of an individual's functioning, Witkin, Dyk, Faterson, Goodenough, and Karp (1962) earlier asserted that verbal intelligence was not one of these aspects. So those who find that heavy viewing hampers reading development (Morgan & Gross, 1980) or vocabulary and composition skills have a separate case from differentiation theory.

In a less differentiated direction of the construct continuum, there is a condition termed *field dependence*. This is associated with greater identification with the social field or relevant others and produces a hypothesis that, given alternative company, field-dependent people will socialize more and hence watch television less. The theory is complex and allows different and even opposite hypotheses to be generated, given certain variations in the relevant conditions; hence, it is not particularly easy to corroborate experimentally. Nevertheless, it is a wide-ranging theory with considerable potential in explanatory power for integrating observations across a variety of levels.

Witkin's work in bridging cultural, cognitive, and personality domains is paralleled by a second theory, developed by Gittinger (cited in Marks & Greenfield, 1984), a psychologist employed for several years by the CIA. Gittinger uses the subtests of the Wechsler Adult Intelligence Scale (WAIS) to assess attributes that are normally thought of as occupying the separate realm of personality. Infants are seen as inheriting a position on each of three primitive dimensions, which can be located with an individual's scores on the appropriate WAIS subtests. Subsequent socialization may reinforce or may alter these initial positions, and the new or basic statuses can be located by scores on three other subtests. Finally, the self that outsiders encounter may be different from the basic profile, and this contact level is assessed with three more subtests. Overriding all of this is a dimension of activity level measured by the digit symbol subtest. Gittinger's theory affords a complex description of personality and accommodates both inherited and acquired characteristics in a way that resembles modern interactionist personality theory. A conspicuous weakness is the absence of a convincing reason to explain why the particular WAIS subtests function as proposed.

Both Witkin's and Gittinger's theories use the Block Designs test as an index of something other than a cognitive skill. Gittinger describes high scorers as regulated (as opposed to flexible), whereas Witkin sees them as more highly differentiated. Both systems appear well suited to explorations of patterns of selectivity in viewing, and a suitable operationalization of viewing selectivity, with other dimensions controlled or partialed out, would vindicate one system over the other.

This brief glance at some unconventional personality theories indicates not only that well-recognized constructs (e.g., belief in a just world, neuroticism, extroversion, authoritarianism, etc.) should be employed in unraveling the reasons for and the consequences of mass media use, but that much that is unfamiliar remains to be harnessed in this field. We know that television is a pervasive presence for nearly all from early childhood. A recent estimate (Heeter, D'Alessio, Greenberg, & McVoy, 1983) gives an average of over 7 hrs a day spent in the presence of screen fare, and this may have a variety of influences ranging from the replacement of other activities (e.g., outdoor sport, reading) and the effects they might otherwise produce to direct influences upon cognitive or attitudinal structures.

Where influence may occur during childhood socialization and bear upon psychological structures which then endure and make themselves manifest in recognizable ways, we are witnessing effects on the construction of personality. These processes are dealt with by other contributors to this book (Berkowitz, Reeves, Tan). In the United States and Britain, television became a common domestic possession in the mid-1950s. People born close to 1950 or thereafter and who are now in their mid-30s and under can thus be termed the television generation. For these people it is useful to try to assess the role television may have played in their early socialization. But having become what they are, it is of equal interest in quite another direction to explore what they make of television as they see and use it now. This whole realm of issues, of what the individual makes of television currently, applies equally to those now aged 35 and over, the pretelevision generations.

The personalities of the pretelevision generation were for the most part formed without the experience of this medium, and personality can be used as an independent variable in exploring their patterns of viewing behavior and reaction. For the new television generation, their personality attributes are both dependent variables, reflecting their socialization experience with the medium, and independent variables in the same way as for older people. The dangers of conceptual and procedural confusion that can attend the careless use of the terms independent and dependent variables are thus nicely anticipated, where a single entity can take both roles.

In practice, the pitfalls can be seen to have trapped several investigators. Most recently, Carlson (1983) decided that the independent variable in his study of public school pupils was an index of crime show viewing; the dependent variable was a Civil Liberties Support Scale (similar in rationale, with an opposition between due process and crime control, to that which underlies the dimension of beliefs in a just world). Carlson found that heavier viewers have lower support for civil liberties than do lighter viewers and concluded that television experience influences these young viewers. This is entirely possible, but it is also conceivable (as Carlson indicates in an aside) that self-selection may mean that preadults who are anti-civil libertarian appear to prefer crime shows. Carlson's study is not really equipped to demonstrate whether personality determines patterns of television use, or vice versa, but his frames of thought and exposition are principally in the second direction. It illustrates that caution is needed in making such inferences with television-generation samples. An older group with more firmly established personality structures might have helped shed light on the question.

This review concentrates on two perspectives involving personality. One concerns the possible role of personality factors in influencing patterns of medium use; linked with this is the exploration of how personality may influence perceptions of television as an institution and of its contents. The second perspective sees personality as an important feature of the context into which messages and experience are received. Personality attributes work here so as to vary the form or intensity of incoming material. An analogy is of a two lens refractive telescope. Whereas some writers have thought of television as a window and others refer to it as a mirror reflecting reality, I present it as a first lens that refracts reality toward perceivers. They in turn receive the television portrayal through a second refractive device, the prism of personality structure, so that the messages finally reach consciousness having undergone at least two changes from their original reality.

Underlying this treatment is a conception of personality as a fundamental structural aspect of the individual, established early in life by an array of surrounding influences, of which television is but one. Thereafter, personality is less accessible to change. What can be changed most easily is knowledge. Attitudes are also reasonably plastic. It is not always clear what distinguishes a personality measure from an attitude measure. The former should be of broader relevance (e.g., authoritarianism), which has been laid down in explicable circumstances for which there has been some theoretical and empirical support. Attitudes are more particular expressions of feeling linked with origins in personality, but subject to much external influence. Linked to personality structures are biological structures with psychological relevance, such as the somatotypes, which correspond to profiles of metabolic rate and arousal needs, and the two sexes, which overlap in their psychological characteristics, even though the differences are not always culturally determined.

There are two exceptions to this view of personality as relatively inaccessible to change once it is established. One involves a sustained attack by a coherent source of influence upon the individual, preferably of a kind in which the subject is highly aroused. Such a case may be a barrage of pornography (e.g., Zillmann & Bryant, 1983), after which profound changes have been detected. The other possibility is that a particularly appropriately aimed shaft of information may fall through chinks in the outer defenses and hit a vulnerable part of the underlying personality structure so that a substantial rearrangement of elements may occur. Examples include sudden religious or political conversions. Television as currently organized, however, is seen to deliver enjoyment much more than impact, and when programs have strong impact, they are more often benevolent than disturbing (Wober & Reardon, 1983). The difficulty of changing attitudes, let alone underlying personality, is demonstrated by the studies of *Roots* (Surlin, 1978) and *The Day After* (Wober & Gunter, 1984), in which the tendency for some selective recruitment of viewing occurred. Those who approve the message tend to have viewed more than those who disapprove, and their convictions are reinforced modestly by what they see.

PERSONALITY AND PATTERNS OF VIEWING

The principal founts of data on viewing have been generated by market researchers, Nielsen and Arbitron in the United States and Audits of Great Britain in the United Kingdom and several other countries. Numerous surveys are done for advertising agencies and their clients, and in all these cases, the researchers need to represent the population at large to account efficiently for as much of the variation as possible in the phenomena measured. Age, sex, and socioeconomic class fulfill these requirements well enough to guide attempts to influence subsequent behavior (e.g., purchasing products or watching more TV). These dimensions are easily assessed by interviewers who use them to assemble their quotas. However, in themselves, demographic indices do nothing to explain why perceptions or behavior proceed as they do.

In universities, research goes beyond mere measurement and seeks explanations of behavior, but funding does not exist for large-scale and continuous data collection, so projects relating patterns of viewing behavior to psychological variables have tended to be piecemeal. Webster and Wakshlag (1983) note that academic researchers have often come close to identifying personality explicitly as an antecedent of viewing behavior, in the uses and gratifications tradition. But neither most of those researchers (Blumler, 1976) nor Webster and Wakshlag themselves take uses as springing not just from needs, but from the personality constructs which are the sources of these needs. Webster and Wakshlag (1983) also point out that many studies fail to make a proper distinction between program preference and program choice . There are three separate phenomena that must be distinguished analytically and operationally: (a) preferences or attitudes concerning what particular programs or types people would like to view; (b) actual viewing behavior; and (c) program appreciation, again a retrospective attitude concerning what has been viewed. Wober (1983a) has shown that although there have been strong ideological temptations to identify actions with attitudes, these three phases of the relation between viewers and programs have not always been parallel.

The data from which these distinctions have been distilled are generated not by market or academic researchers but by researchers in a broadcasting control organization, the Independent Broadcasting Authority (sometimes likened to "the FCC—with teeth"). The IBA staff is required to provide information on public attitudes concerning the programs and advertisements broadcast, and it has been doing this by regular weeklong diary measurements of appreciation (using a 6-point scale of viewer interest and/or enjoyment). These data are analyzed into seven program types and show patterns of appreciation and patterns of viewing by sex, age, and class. Although the industry takes the program as its data base unit, wanting to know its audience size, composition, and appreciation, the researchers have treated the individual viewer as an alternative data base unit. In this way, the average number of items viewed, per program type, per individual is known. By including additional questionnaires, it is possible to collect experience, attitude, or personality measures and then relate these to viewing behavior and appreciation scores.

When the addiction research unit at London's Maudsley Hospital became interested in smokers' explanations for their smoking, they came to the IBA for data on the audience for an antismoking program. It was suggested to the addiction researchers that smoking might be partly explained as fulfilling a need for external stimulus, as might heavy television viewing; extroversion was a possible common underlying factor. From a questionnaire accompanying a week's viewing diaries, it was indeed reported (Eiser, Sutton, & Wober, 1978) that heavier television viewers were also heavier smokers.

This finding spurred further exploration of viewing patterns in relation to personality (Wober, 1980b). From a viewers' panel in London, it first emerged that people with greater feelings of external control over their fortunes tended to view more fiction and information than did internal controllers (no differences existed with comedy and light entertainment). This correlation suvived the partialing out of age, class, and a measure designed to assess Gerbner's theory of mean world perceptions (see Chapter 2 this volume). Both mean-world perceptions and measures of selfish aggression and satisfaction with one's lot, though they initially showed significant correlations with amounts of viewing, did not sustain these links once the locus of control measure was partialed out. Now, either viewing models personality among adults, or personality determines viewing behavior. The former is less plausible because personality structures are forged at a fundamental level during a plastic stage in individuals' growth; hence, support is given to the latter explanation.

As part of a 20-year three-wave study in England, Himmelweit and Swift (1976) had similarly shown that heavier amounts of television viewing occurred among people with feelings of powerlessness and those who had high authoritarianism scores. Although the viewing estimate by personal claim on a 3-point scale is now known to be less satisfactory than diary measures, there is a multiple regression predictor of 0.4 between background, outlook, and media taste at the earlier waves of the study and amount of television viewing at the later stage. The background measures included personality, and although these predictors of later viewing patterns were not as strong as were prior preferences, they were nevertheless significantly linked, and the sequential design of the study suggests the direction of causality from personality to behavior. A similar two-wave study by Atkin, Greenberg, Korzenny, and McDermott (1979) among 227 fourth, sixth, and eighth graders measured aggression values for each of 29 programs. Those with aggressive characteristics at the first testing were more likely to view violent material a year later than were those initially low on aggression.

Cook, Kendzierski, and Thomas (1983) in discussing the longitudinal study of Milavsky, Kessler, Stipp, and Rubens (1983), reported similar findings by a Chicago research group that repeat those referred to earlier. These cross lagged correlation studies, which link personality dispositions measured earlier with viewing behavior patterns recorded later, do not eliminate the parallel possibility that viewing violent material may have a harmful effect in reinforcing aggressiveness. Both processes are probably in action, as Himmelweit and Swift imply in pointing to a critical period in adolescence when emerging personality structures match media experiences to their needs and reinforce these characteristics.

During the Falklands conflict (Wober, 1982b), questionnaires were added to routine IBA appreciation diaries to monitor viewers' experience of the conflict as portrayed on television. As well as levels of authoritarianism, viewers' expectations of how broadcasters should cover the conflict (e.g., whether they might stress patriotism or a more universalist pacifism) were recorded. The personality characteristic of high authoritarianism was linked with the more temporal attitude of expecting broadcasters to be patriotic, and the former also related to heavier viewing of the news coverage. However, weight of viewing of news coverage did not relate to expectations of patriotism in style. Because viewing did not relate to these expectations, it could not cause an attitude formation, and it is even less likely that it could create a personality structure at a deeper level. This again leads to the interpretation that it is the inner attribute that determines the more superficial viewing behavior.

Recalling the study of Ethiopian folk tales, I now turn to Hendry and Thornton (1976) in Scotland who assessed whether each of 204 adolescents saw life as a game of power, as one of strategy, or as a game of chance. Likewise, 24 well-known programs were each cast into one of the three categories. Weights of overall viewing as well as that of the items on the special list were assessed, and measures of neuroticism and extroversion were taken. Light viewers were more likely to be strategists than potents or fortunists, and strategists were lower on extroversion than were the potents or fortunists, which adds to other evidence that greater externality is associated with, probably helps determine, and is then reinforced by heavier viewing.

Working with a sample of 2,302 15-year-olds, Hendry and Patrick (1977) found that lighter viewers were less neurotic but more extroverted, and heavier viewers had lower school achievement scores. These findings are at odds with those of the previous study regarding personality. It is possible that more docile teen-agers are heavier viewers, less sociable, and partly because of this, reflect these attributes in lower extroversion and higher neuroticism scores. As Himmelweit and Swift observed, the ways in which internal and external factors inter-relate depend on ages and norms of behavior, which differ as people grow older. Nevertheless, Hendry and Patrick's study is a major one. Their results are significant for both girls and boys and require assimilation into a general theory dealing with personality and viewing.

Elsewhere, in a study of similar size, Eastman (1979) interviewed 1,795 adults asking them 250 questions each! One set of questions covered the uses made of television and the reasons for them; another set exhausted the area of what market researchers call life styles analysis. This battery was factor analyzed and yielded 14 factors including: leader, mover, messy/clean housekeeper, swinger, and brand-name shopper. The television-uses battery revealed 12 patterns. The two sets of data were then merged in canonical correlations, a procedure that examines the extent to which items in each set of variables are related to others within their own set and, notwithstanding such mutual within-set relationships, whether items within one set relate significantly to any in the other set. The outcome is that people who use television for pleasure and distraction tend to try many new products, have a lot of debts, and look for bargains. In contrast, Eastman (1979) found that the reader is not likely to use television for escape, arousal, distraction or pleasure. Less firmly, she reported that those who use television for information are not movers and may not be swingers or messy housekeepers; they may be parents and bargain shoppers.

Although this kind of study presumably requires and satisfies commercial financing, it appears at the same time to be highly proficient technically but shallow conceptually. Whether a messy housekeeper is always a messy housekeeper or not probably depends on the existence of any underlying (personality) attribute that would link this particular behavior to others. It is tempting to see this as a brittle exercise in the externals of behaviorism, which is shy about seeking unifying structures beneath the psychological surface.

A smaller though better study (Gandy, 1981) involved 227 black college students who gave their frequencies of and reasons for watching television and responded to Rokeach's value indicators (which ask subjects to rate personal qualities they would like to possess and exhibit). Students who placed a high value on politeness were likely to report heavier viewing of programs such as *20/20, Saturday Night Live,* or *White Shadow*; others highly valuing self-respect were more likely to include *Benson* among their top 10 programs. This program-by-program analysis interestingly pointed to differences between items that normally would be grouped together because of their formats, such as the comedies *Soap* and *MASH*, but which corresponded to different personal characteristics among viewers. Gandy concludes that Rokeach's value measures are better predictors of viewing than are traditional uses and gratifications measures, such as reasons for viewing including companionship, escape, arousal, and relaxation.

Two IBA studies have examined the possibility that sensation seeking is an identifiable characteristic that might relate either to amounts or to patterns of viewing behavior. Thus, it might be expected that high sensation seekers would be found to watch relatively more action adventure or less soap opera; in addition, sensation seekers might be more inclined to welcome technical innovations, such as satellites with new channels and video recorders, or broadcasting innovations, such as a new independent (commercially financed) channel. A sensation-seeking scale was compiled with questions drawn from Zuckerman, Kolin, Price, and Zoob (1964) and others which tapped sensory routes involving smell and taste that are not usually included in such scales. Factor analyses in two separate samples taken a year apart (Wober, 1981b, 1982a) revealed five distinct factors on both occasions: three revolved around one sense each—smell, taste, and hearing—and one linked preferences for calmness and stability (including one visual item, liking for a tranquil picture) and another linked preferences for novelty (including the other visual item, liking for a startling picture). In the first study, canonical correlations produced two significant collections of variables. In one, preference for the noise and bustle of the city (in contrast to the peace and quiet of the country) was related to heavier viewing of information programming as well as to an agreement that nuclear generation of electricity was acceptable. High total viewing was linked not to high sensation seeking but to a preference for stability and calm. This relationship remained significant when the mutually interrelated measure of age was partialed out.

In the second study, one collection of significantly related variables suggests that those who like noise and bustle tend to watch more comedy, more soap opera, and perhaps more sport; they also like novelty. A separate canonical variable links those who watch more news, more soap opera, less drama, and less comedy with a preference for stability, calmness, and conventional food tastes. Although the two studies are not identical in outcome, they both show that aspects of sensation seeking do relate to patterns of viewing recorded by diary across a whole week. Differences between surveys may relate to differences in scheduling across the weeks, to the season and year of field work, or to cultural differences between London and Scotland. Further work may clarify some of these questions.

Progress in the identification of personality constructs that may link with and eventually determine viewing patterns requires a commendation, a caution, and two constructive suggestions. The commendation is that the exercise has considerable ideological significance. If mature viewers determine their own viewing diets, they are less likely to be regarded as passive recipients of influences. This does, of course, leave the question as to the possible influences of screen fare on the young. The caution is that underlying personality attributes work their way toward influencing behavior past a variety of external influences and intervening variables that can modify their effects. Therefore, modest, null, or even contradictory findings should not be severely discouraging.

One positive proposal is that studies should try to use several scales at a time so that combinations of attributes rather than single descriptions can be used to discriminate between kinds of viewers and their different patterns of behavior in the use of television. The second area in which more development is required is in the definition of program type. IBA studies have used screen types based on cluster analyses of similarities perceived between programs that were done over a decade ago (see Wober, 1983a). Though this taxonomy retains a good correspondence with institutional structures of program making and critical reviewing, internal studies suggest that the broad category of comedy and light entertainment probably contains two or three differently functioning subtypes. Other potential splits of current type specifications are also indicated. In order to reveal the functional distinctions of new program types, it is necessary to have a good instrument for recording viewing behavior, as well as sophisticated statistical techniques. Fortunately, the IBA's weekly appreciation diaries provide the first condition, though the quality of analysis brought to bear upon it from now onwards remains to be assessed. There is little doubt, however, that more sensitive procedures would yield rich and positive results. It is a pity, therefore, that this means of research has now been discontinued.

PERSONALITY AND THE PERCEPTION
OF TELEVISION AND ITS CONTENTS

In 1972, David Newell of the BBC wrote that little was known about how viewers' own characteristics modified their perceptions of what they saw on the screen. A few studies (e.g., Zagona & Kelly, 1966) had shown that enjoyment of an unorthodox film was inversely related to dogmatism scores for example. Newell reported a major new experiment in which 1,000 questionnaires had been distributed to fresh samples just after each of 13 violence-containing programs had been shown. From those who had seen the designated items, 98 people were further interviewed in depth and given personality scale questions. Newell (1972) claimed that a viewer's standing in terms of fearfulness, aggressiveness, social extroversion and, to a lesser extent, neuroticism, all affected his perceptions of violence in the target programmes to some extent; he also reported that it was the fearful, non-aggressive and the introverted who tended to express greater concern. This claim was accepted by Brody (1977) who referred to a modest relationship having been found. Himmelweit, Swift, and Jaeger (1980) also referred to "the view frequently expressed that perception of violence is so greatly influenced by subjective factors that little reliance can be placed on such perceptions" (p. 91). Unfortunately, from the figures provided, which add up to 82 rather than 98 subjects, little reliance should be placed on such research conclusions. No tests of significance were given, but the largest chi-square is 3.1, suggesting that more fearful people may be more inclined to perceive violence as more potent (but failing to reach acceptable significance). The extroversion result is clearly null, chi-square $= 0.6$. The first exploration in this field, although originally described as fulfilled, must be considered to have failed to demonstrate the expected results. Newell states, however, that pressures to meet a deadline precluded a full calculation and analysis of all the data.

Interest in the topic was kept up by Himmelweit et al. (1980), who used a sample of over 1,000 adults on a BBC volunteer viewing panel. These people were asked to make 10 judgments on each of 20 program titles. In addition, there were other scales of attitudes toward television and measures of the self as powerless or efficacious and of the importance attached to each of five goals: concerning living up to one's standards, being successful, leading a quiet life, opportunity for self-expression, and having a desire to understand society. One of the prime determinants of preferences for different types of programs was the weight of viewing overall, a relationship that persisted even when effects of education and social status were partialed out. Although the older and less educated felt enriched through television, and more dependent on it, those who valued a quiet life, conformity, and saw themselves as powerless were more involved in their viewing. Interpreting these results in the perspective of an associated but longitudinal study, Himmelweit et al. (1980) inferred that "it is the social environment, the skills and outlook of the individual which help shape the response both to the presence of television in the home as well as to its content. Television does not influence basic goals and values" (p. 87).

There is one difficulty with this conclusion, however. The raters did not judge the programs as they were seen, but their titles. The program given the highest rating for "liking" was the news, but regular and copious measurement of appreciation of programs (Wober, 1983a) shows that different newscasts and editions thereof can vary in appreciation index by 10 or 15 points, and the best newscasts typically are not liked distinctly better than the best rated comedy programs (as Himmelweit et al.'s results imply). In short, there is likely to have been an element of social desirability in the rankings that formed the dependent measures and susceptibility to such influence is clearly, in field dependence and other personality theories, linked with such basic goals and values as measured in this project.

Newell's technique for measuring reactions to actual viewing is available only to large broadcasting organizations, and a lone researcher has to narrow down this phase of data collection. Aiming to compensate with immediacy what could not be afforded in size of sample, Robinson (1980) observed that several American investigators asked subjects to recall, rather than immediately observe, screen material. Further, these studies (including that of Greenberg & Gordon, 1972) had not explored what about the programmes was perceived as violent, nor had the viewer attributes been analyzed in greater detail than sex, age, class, and race (though sex, for one, may be a reliable index of certain personality states, e.g., greater field dependence among women). Robinson therefore assembled a video tape carrying 3 practice and 44 test segments, each 10 sec long and showing different kinds of violence. Subjects were 258 students, who supplied data on their patterns of media use and attitudes. Using a measure of viewer training based on course experience in television and film criticism and production, there were low but significant correlations between amount of training and a tendency to attribute less violence to the sample scenes. Media training is not something that reconstructs the personality, so it is hazardous to infer from these results much more than that a mild ideological desensitization to violence has been acquired through professional familiarity. In fact, Robinson (1980) concluded that "the viewer characteristic which has the clearest relationship to usage of specific violence criteria is sex. Females see more violence generally and rate segments typical of all assessment criteria except humour as more violent than do males" (p. 20).

Although Himmelweit et al. (1980) note they "could not find any studies . . . which canvassed in any depth the public's response to entertainment programmes" (p. 69), this neglects several such studies done at the IBA which began to explore, as Robinson and others had done, the relationship between viewer attitudes and perception. *The Naked Civil Servant* was a docu-drama about a homosexual, and a survey (Independent Broadcasting Authority, 1976) showed that women were more likely than men to have sympathized with the main character, although people of both sexes say they understood his problems equally. To be sure, the viewer attribute here identified was only sex, but in regard to the portrayal of homosexuals' problems, it is fair to infer that it is at a personality level, rather than at some neutrally biological level, that the differences between women's and men's perceptions are located. A subsequent survey (Independent Broadcasting Authority, 1978) looked at perceptions of *The Champions*, a drama about disaffected teen-age soccer fans who, in failing to get into a vital match, curse and swear about their plight. On the day after the program, 1,000 interviews yielded 154 adults who had watched. Everybody evaluated items, some expressing sympathy for soccer fans, and others expressing hostility. There was no difference in attitudes toward fans between those who had seen the play and those who had not, but among those who did see it, there was a tendency for people who were more permissive about violence among football supporters to accept favorable descriptions of the programme (amusing, enjoyable, exciting), whereas those who were punitive about fans tended to be hostile about the programme (exaggerated, stupid, disgusting).

In the same vein, Wober (1978) investigated attitudes toward the drama series, *Edward and Mrs. Simpson*, a portrayal of the brief reign of Edward VIII and his abdication following his decision to marry the American divorcee, Wallis Simpson. One measure that tapped an underlying personal attribute among viewers was of reality shift (see Tate, 1977), and Hedinsson and Windahl (1984), that is, the feeling that the characters as portrayed must have been exactly like the originals (as against a detached view of such authenticity). A second measure that might go deeper than one of attitude was privacy concern. Reality shift is theoretically similar to field dependence and was found to relate to liking the series in particular, although it had no relation to general appreciation levels for all programs viewed or for drama programs (other than *Edward and Mrs. Simpson*) seen that week. Privacy concern, which assessed support for the idea that the privacy of others should not be breached in drama portrayals, was not related, when age was partialed out, to amount of viewing of the series, nor was it related to liking the series or to reality shift. Closer to the self, "privacy need" was next measured (Wober 1980a) by a simple 5-point scale asking people how important privacy was for themselves ("things like getting dressed, having a bath, etc."). Privacy need was related to the propensity to take offense at bad language on the screen, and so was personal religiousness. But partial correlations eliminating the effect of religiousness showed that privacy need was independently related to sensitivity about broadcast bad language. Later, Durkin (1983) showed that two religious programs, *House Communion* and *This Is the Day*, appealed differently according to viewers' privacy needs. Those liking privacy more strongly preferred the former program and had less approval for the second than was shown by people for whom privacy was less important. Data are available, as yet unpublished, which suggest that privacy need is a structural personality feature similar to, but also different from, introversion and found more markedly among old and among lower social class adults.

A later study explored perceptions of the portrayal of a broad range of phenomena on television and compared these perceptions with a number of measures, including personal characteristics which may lie at a level somewhat deeper than attitudes, though not yet recognizably being assimilated to any of the more well-founded dimensions of personality. The study concerned the portrayal of women on British television (Wober, 1981c). Here, the quasi-personality measures involved responses to questions on how women ideally should be. There were seven items describing how women ought to lead their lives ranging from "women should be judged on what they can do more than how they look" to "women should generally want to be mothers." In general, there were some weak but positive and significant correlations between feelings about how women should be and perceptions of how they actually are portrayed in daily life serials and situation comedies. In this study, however, the perceptions of television content were images and relatively distant from the experience of viewing actual programs or program segments, a drawback which is not shared by the next series of studies.

The background for the research to be described is of some interest and relevance. A long awaited report (Belson, 1978) had asserted that violence on the screen caused imitation among viewers; considerable pressure then fell upon the broadcasters to reduce the amount of violence shown. But what was the relevant amount of violence? The American example was to count "objective" acts of aggression on the screen (Gerbner, 1972). It was argued in Britain, however, that some objective violence may not be perceived as anything harmful or might be discounted for various reasons (too foreign, too staged, or whatever). Therefore, a researcher was employed to investigate the feasibility of perceptual methods of assessing violence content (Gunter, 1983a). Moreover, a dimension of inquiry that he was asked to include was concerned with variance among viewers.

A Canadian study by Fouts (1976) surveyed 308 children in Calgary, using many measures including some of aggressive disposition, activity levels, and introversion. Fouts did not do enough to reduce ambiguity due to multicollinearity but concluded nevertheless, from his mental assessment of the array of results, that the most influential variables on viewers' perceptions of violence, the reactions of victims, and the consequences for victims were sensitivity to psychological forms of aggression and introversion. Introverted children saw alternatives to violence and perceived subtle forms of violence on television, whereas extroverted children stereotyped criminals. Although these conclusions raise questions to which the theories of Witkin and Gittinger offer opportunities of resolution involving alignment between socialization experiences and the establishment of structures of personality or cognitive style, they also suggest complex problems for the administrative assessment of broadcast violence.

If adults with different characteristics assessed violence differently, there would either have to be several assessors, representing a range of personality attributes distributed in the population, or the assessors would have to be those with the most delicate susceptibilities or chosen at some point on the range of susceptibility that had been administratively determined as appropriate. Himmelweit et al. (1980) had already magnified the supposed consequences of BBC research, stating that subjective factors would make it too complex to assess violence content with any practicality; if explored again in detail, the difficulty of assessing violence subjectively might be reaffirmed. This is, indeed, what has happened.

In one study (Gunter 1985), 40 viewers rated brief scenes on each of eight scales. Ratings were then related to scores on the Eysenck Personality Inventory (EPI). One purpose of the procedure was to establish the relative seriousness of different kinds of violence (shootings, fist-fights, cartoon violence), and a hierarchy duly emerged. The other purpose, more relevant here, was to explore personality differences in perception. Canonical correlations were run and revealed that more neurotic people are more likely to find British crime and western scenes violent than are less neurotic viewers; a similar pattern, to a lesser extent, is found among people with higher psychoticism scores. More neurotic people are less likely to judge American crime scenes and even cartoon extracts as more frightening than are less neurotic people. However, having identified British and western violent scenes as more potent, more highly neurotic people also find these kinds of material more frightening, and American crime and westerns more personally disturbing and likely to disturb people in general. Findings such as these may help explain why pressure groups and defenders of freedom of expression develop their opposing positions; they may be composed of people who differ in underlying personality attributes. This hypothesis invites a project to collect EPI (or similar scale) scores from members of such groups, but it does not dismiss two further problems, one dealing with research and the other administrative.

The research task is based on the fact that Gunter's and Robinson's fertile findings of links between personality and perception are based on short scenes taken out of their broader context. Other researchers using perception measures based on entire programs have found it more difficult to demonstrate such links. Therefore, further experiments are needed in which perceptions of larger numbers of short scenes are then related to perceptions of whole programs (necessarily, for logistic reasons, involving fewer materials). Either the personality measures would fail in general to relate to impressions of whole programs, in which case the administrative problem would be simpler and less selective panels could be used to assess violence content, or the perceptions of the two levels would be parallel, in which case judges would have to be selected with attention to their personality attributes.

One study in which viewers saw whole programs (Diener & Woody, 1981) used several personality measures, including sensation-seeking scales, a sex-role inventory, and parts of Jackson's Personality Research Form. People then saw two 1-hr episodes of adventure shows and judged them on violence, humor, and other dimensions. Although two sensation-seeking subscales showed that people low in experience seeking and disinhibition on the whole seemed to like television programs better, with correlations significant beyond the 0.01 level, the authors concluded that their personality measures did not predict reported program liking. They sensibly comment that there may not have been enough variance among groups of psychology students. Larger and more representative samples are therefore advisable.

The interaction of the perception of dramatic content structures with the personality of viewers was pursued in Gunter's (1985) next procedure. Using the same methods, the focus turned to the consequences of the violence portrayed. Significant canonical variables now showed that although neuroticism and extroversion levels had no links with the extent to which different consequences (fatality, degree of injury) affected perceived strength of violence, psychoticism levels were weakly implicated. High scorers perceived harmful violence as less violent and more humorous than did lower scorers on the psychoticism scale. The findings support the stereotype of the psychotic condition, but there are two reasons for caution. One is that the numerous links between neuroticism and, to a lesser extent, extroversion that emerged with regard to genre imply some recognition of the broader contextual significance of such categories. Such a contextual sensitivity should therefore reveal similar personality and perception relationships, though these did not appear. Second, the same question of contextual location means that the consequences of violence discerned in brief incidents could be modified considerably by their place in whole programs. This reinforces the case that linking experiments are needed to tie perceptions at the atomic and at the molar levels together.

The third currently available report in this series (Gunter & Furnham, 1984b) varies the genre from which extracts were taken and looks at the forms of violence, namely, shootings, fist fights, explosions, and stabbings. Half the scenes of each type of violence were taken from British crime series and half from westerns. The personality variables under examination were indexed by four subscales of the Buss-Durkee self-endorsed Hostility Inventory. This assesses reported use of assault, indirect hostility, irritability, and verbal aggression and has been shown by Petzel and Michaels (1973) to distinguish between high- and low-hostility subjects. The former tend to see a violent rather than a nonviolent picture when both were presented in binocular rivalry. Canonical correlations showed that tendencies to indirect hostility and verbal aggression linked with perceptions of British crime excerpts as less violent, though more humorous and exciting; the same people with leanings to symbolic violence in themselves considered American excerpts as less realistic, frightening, disturbing, and as more suitable for children.

Several major linkages were found between measures of personal hostility and perceptions of different forms of violence in this third study (Gunter & Furnham, 1984b). People who are physically violent themselves are likely to consider stabbings and fist fights as less violent, frightening, and disturbing; they consider shootings and explosions as more violent than do more peaceful people. Those whose aggressive impulses turn toward more symbolic outlets tend to find shootings and explosions as less violent and stabbings and fist fights as more potent than is felt by people who do not rate themselves highly on the uses of symbolic violence. It would be of interest to see what people who are high on both physical and symbolic violence (if they exist) feel about screened portrayals.

It would also be useful to have not just the loadings on canonical correlates with which to judge the directions of relationship between variables, but also the mean scores so as to view the levels of scores on all these measures.

Finally, in this series of reports, Gunter and Furnham (1984a) describe links between scores on the Bem Sex Role Inventory and perceptions of screened excerpts of violent scenes. High masculinity scores were linked with the view that males attacked by females provided a more violent and disturbing spectacle than women being attacked by men. Those with high feminity scores found women as victims more violent and disturbing than men as such. These relationships held good separately among men and women viewers. This may indicate the importance of psychological sex as the effective aspect of the biological criterion in influencing perceptions of television or other content.

Turning from violence to the political field, in a study of Party Political Broadcasts (PPBs), Wober and Svennevig (1981) incorporated items of Rotter's scale of internal versus external feelings of control over one's fortunes into their analysis. Although scores on this scale related to age, sex, class, and overall weight of viewing suggest that something real was being measured, they did not relate to the amount of PPBs claimed to have been viewed. Because there is a relationship between PPB viewing and knowledge of political matters, it may be argued that people with a desire to acquire political information to increase their feeling of participation view the PPBs more heavily. The absence of a relationship between the locus of control scores and a composite index of the utility of party politicals (nine scales, including informative, easy to understand, etc.), and of amount of PPBs viewed, weakens this argument, however.

On the other hand, in weakening the interpretation of selective recruitment of viewers for the PPBs, it reinforces the opposite case for interpreting heavier viewing of PPBs as having caused or contributed to better knowledge. The Rotter scale was also used by Cross (1981) who studied the role of direct sound recordings of Parliament on radio and television (in sound only, with still photograph visuals). Cross used a laboratory-style approach by playing extracts to groups of people (up to 300 in all) and collecting their reactions to these samples, as well as a wide range of personal and attitudinal information. People with greater feelings of personal efficacy (internal control) showed a higher appreciation of the repartee in the Parliamentary material, tended to approve of its presentation, and had a better comprehension of what they heard. Here again, a personality measure reveals links between perceptions and the content of extracts, but it is difficult to parallel such relationships when whole program measures have been used.

It may be useful to close this section with reference to the study conducted during the Falklands war (Wober 1982b). Viewers were sent a week's diary to record their viewing experience, plus questions including authoritarianism items, others to assess their preferences on how the conflict should be portrayed (i.e., patriotically or with a pacifist outlook), and other items to assess how the actual coverage was perceived. Both at the level of simple and of canonical correlations, people who expected patriotic broadcast coverage tended to approve of Independent Television's newscasts, but not those by the BBC. The effect was slightly more marked with regard to coverage of the fighting and the families of servicemen, and slightly less marked in the case of coverage of diplomacy. The canonical correlation excluded authoritarianism from links with perception of coverage quality. Thus, the deeper personality measure did not relate to assessments of content, whereas preferences on how the conflict should be portrayed, which may be a less deeply rooted structure, did relate to such assessments.

Most recently, a survey of viewers of *The Day After* (Wober, 1984b) has shown that low authoritarianism was linked to a stronger approval of the action in showing the film and to a greater tendency to see it as balanced and fair. Those who thought the film biased toward the cause of the antinuclear camp were by a clear majority high authoritarians. A locus of control measure yielded no relationships with evaluations of the program.

It can be concluded that personality factors influence how adults perceive segments of screen fare; there is some, though notably weaker, evidence that the same is true for aspects of programs seen as wholes. Because much of the work has focused on violence, there is a need for studies to look at other issues. The political field is a large and important one to develop. That of taste and decency, and of appropriate personality constructs such as privacy need, is another. Bridging studies are required to establish (or reject) links between the more atomistic effects shown with segmentary materials and the broader effects that may be established with entire programs or even with program types. Further attention needs to be given to working with measures, even abbreviated ones, of established personality constructs, of which a number, including those that link personality and cognitive psychology, have not yet begun to be harnessed.

PERSONALITY AND PERCEPTION
OF TELEVISION'S PORTRAYAL OF THE WORLD

We have already seen that personality probably affects how viewers assess television in itself. But because actuality programs are not there merely for their superficial value, but as accounts of something else, the question arises as to whether viewers differ in how they accept or filter television's account of the world. Although Gerbner (Chapter 2, this volume) has maintained that fiction programming also affects Americans' images of reality dealing with perceptions of old people, women, homosexuals, and the meanness of the social environment, he has not yet explored images of men, ethnic minority groups, or views of non-American reality.

Diversifying the format of Gerbner's studies was a survey by Wober and Gunter (1982b) in which 322 adults completed viewing diaries and answered questions tapping Gerbner's "fear of victimization" or "mean world" concept, as well as others indexing Rotter's (1966) Locus of Control and two further personality dimensions. The simple outcome was that when the mean world scores were held constant by partial correlation, the relationships between locus of control and the amount of viewing of fiction and information programming each remained significant. When the locus of control scores were held constant, the relationships presented in simple correlation between fear of victimization and amounts of viewing dropped into insignificance. The most efficient interpretation of these results is that an underlying disposition of personality (feelings of external control over one's fate) causes both heavy viewing and a fear of victimization. The relationship of heavy viewing to fear of victimization is thus likely to be an epiphenomenon of the common origin of the two expressions of the one personality construct. It may not be television viewing that constructs a fearful view of the world as much as an underlying personality disposition that produces this feeling.

The next step was to carry out a further survey (Gunter & Wober, 1983) in which 488 adults provided both viewing diaries and questionnaires covering mean world and anomie items adapted from Gerbner, as well as two items from Rubin and Peplau's Just World scale. Twenty multiple classification analyses (MCA; a form of analysis of variance controlling for the effects of chosen variables, in this case, age, sex, and class) were computed to relate amounts of viewing of four separate program categories and overall viewing with each of the personality and perception measures. Only two MCAs were significant, and these showed that people who viewed more action adventure or programs from the United States tended to have stronger just world beliefs. It is a matter of interpretation whether belief in a just world is a deeply embedded construct that can be regarded as a feature of personality, and longitudinal data would be required to substantiate this. But if this is so, then it indicates that an underlying optimism may be one reason why fear of victimization is not an outcome of heavy television viewing in general, or of information or fiction viewing in particular. This not only confirms but expands on the original demonstration (Wober, 1978) that British viewers were not disposed to a paranoid view of the world as a result of their television viewing.

Within the same series of papers, Wober and Gunter (1982a) looked at perceptions of the elderly as they are in real life and as they are portrayed on television in relation to the viewing that people generally do. It was argued that perceptions of the real-life nature of the elderly are likely to tap underlying personality-type dispositions, while perceptions of television portrayals are what is under scrutiny now. Results indicate that the belief that the elderly should be treated with respect correlated significantly with the perception that this was how they were portrayed in actuality programming; feelings that old people are very cheerful in real life correlated with perceptions that they are portrayed as such for all program types. Even when the mutual relationships with own age and class were partialed out, the links between perception of old people on television and their real-life nature remained significant, both for the respect and for the happy items.

Parallel to this is a set of results relating perceptions of women as they are in real life, and as depicted in soap operas, with the amount of soap operas viewed each week (Wober, 1981c). For two characteristics—that women are quarrelsome with other women and keen on romantic affairs with men—there was a low degree of endorsement that these were true in real life. There was only a marginally significant or nonsignificant relationship between these answers and the amount of soap opera viewing. For two other characteristics—that women at some time want to be mothers and that they are very interested in jobs and careers—there was a high degree of endorsement that these are true in real life and more significant relationships between answers on these items and amounts of soap opera viewing. Thus, a positive disposition toward women's identity was matched in and reinforced by soap opera viewing.

The British studies on the Gerbner hypothesis have been presaged and followed by others from Canada and Europe. Having shown (Surlin & Tate, 1976) that viewer personality was instrumental in shaping responses to the meaning and content of the program *Archie Bunker*, with dogmatic people more likely to agree with the prejudiced views of the main character, Tate (1976) reported a survey in Saskatoon in which five measures of personality and social perception were related with those of viewing television. One scale was adapted from Gerbner and labeled fortress mentality; a second, labeled the Pollyanna scale, resembled that of just world beliefs; a third tapped the perceived realism of television programming. It demonstrated that heavy watching of crime dramas did not relate to a fortress mentality or to any higher degree of perceived realism. Overall weight of viewing did relate to perceived reality of content, and also positively to personal authoritarianism, but not to Pollyanna perceptions, to a fortress mentality, or to anomie. Tate's interpretation is that although weight of viewing is not implicated in forming a view of the world, authoritarian viewers already believe the world is full of danger and evil, and they do not need television to tell them that. Tate concludes that authoritarians desire to control and censor television. Such viewers agree with fortress mentality because it corresponds with their belief system.

An Icelander with a colleague in Sweden has advanced technically with a study involving 1,000 children in each of three waves of observation, in 1976, 1978, and 1980 (Hedinsson & Windahl, 1984). They measured the degree of involvement with television (similar to Wober's reality shift) and included a measure of perception of real-life violence as well as a retribution index (tapping the extent to which people feel wrongdoing should be punished) and questions on occupational aspiration. Multiple classification analyses were carried out to relate total television viewing separately for fifth and ninth graders with personality and other measures. At the fifth grade, there were only two dependent variables (retribution and number of people estimated in the United States) that each revealed a linear relationship with viewing volume; by the ninth grade, there were four out of five such patterns, suggesting that a process of personality formation had occurred in the intervening years. However, the retribution measure (or vindictiveness, which is recognizably a more fundamental personal property than the others) did not have a significant linear relationship with television involvement, as it had with amount of viewing in each grade. Because the time spent watching television does not relate systematically to the adolescents' perceptions of violence, but involvement does link with such perceptions of real-life violence as portrayed on television (and a similar though weaker pattern exists with occupational aspirations), the authors see the dispositional interaction with television, rather than the simple exposure to it, as the important mediator of views of the world.

Two recent studies present further evidence that personality may be important in shaping a view of the world as seen on television. In the first study (Wober, 1984a), viewers in two regions were asked to estimate the numbers of people of ethnic minority origin seen in drama on television. Parallel samples were asked to estimate the proportions of such groups living in their own areas and living in the United Kingdom. One region is known to have a relatively high concentration of ethnic minority immigrants; the other region has fewer. People in the two regions did not differ with regard to two estimates of Irish and West Indian minority members seen on television, nor did they differ in their estimates of the numbers of such people living in the country as a whole, an impression to which television might theoretically contribute some influence. What did relate to the estimates of numbers of ethnic minority citizens was the viewers' own authoritarianism levels. Therefore, there is the prism of personality through which the vision of reality is turned. However, when age, class, and authoritarianism measures were partialed out, there still remained some positive relationships between the amount of drama viewed and estimates of the number of ethnic minority individuals living in the United Kingdom. This provides evidence of the lens or of the curved mirror of television, which refracts rather than simply reflects an aspect of reality.

The second study with relevant evidence (Wober, 1984b) concerns a television series called *The Nation's Health*. A drama of four episodes with a strong flavor of documentary realism, it was also cynical about many aspects of the health service and those who run it. A sample of viewers answered questions on their degree of confidence in getting good treatment should they enter a hospital, their feelings of control over their own health, and whether the world is a just one or not. They reported how many episodes of *The Nation's Health* as well as *Angels* (a nurse-based, benevolently oriented soap opera) and *Where There's Life* (a lighthearted medical talk show) they had seen. Locus of control over health and just world beliefs provided the strongest correlations (having partialed out the effects of sex, age, and class) with levels of confidence in hospital treatment. Here again, the substrate of personality is perhaps the most durable determinant of perceptions of external reality. These perceptions also touch upon television's portrayal in that there are very small but significant correlations linking viewing of *The Nation's Health* with lowered confidence in hospital treatment; the correlations are near zero with locus of health control and just world measures, and negligible between viewing *Angels* and the personality and perception variables. Thus, television viewing may, at least in the short term, have some effect on our perceptions of some features of external reality.

Finally, it is worth mentioning a study that involves a variable that is by no means one of personality, but nevertheless designates a deep and underlying predisposition that can affect social perception and behavior. This index is of religion among people in Northern Ireland. A survey in connection with two programs on Ireland (Wober, 1981a) put seven attitude questions to participants including four on perceptions of television portrayal and, through that, of the reality behind it. The same survey was repeated soon afterwards in Yorkshire, where people learn of events in Northern Ireland largely via the mass media. In Northern Ireland, Catholics were more inclined than Protestants to agree that "the future of Northern Ireland looks very bleak" and to reject the idea that "in real life Northern Ireland is not as violent as TV suggests"; in Yorkshire, both Catholics and Protestants agreed equally on the first proposition, but Protestants particularly rejected the second more strongly. The interpretation of these results strongly suggests that two influences are at work. One is proximity to the society being reported; people in Yorkshire are more pessimistic about Northern Ireland than are people who actually live there. Second, religious affiliation affects pessimism or optimism of those who are in Northern Ireland more than it does in Yorkshire.

CONCLUSIONS

There is much flux in the field of personality theory and measurement, but there is also considerable opportunity to identify links between disparate approaches and to unify definitions of constructs that have been developed by different workers in separate fields. From the confluence of social anthropology and psychology comes the idea, and much evidence, that culture and socialization processes influence personality formation in youth, which in turn, through adult behavior, carries forward the culture. Television is now a principal channel or purveyor of culture, and as such, it can be studied as one determinant of personality among the young, as well as something that interacts with personality among older people.

Methods of studying television and personality have often left much to be desired. Analytic clarity is required to distinguish between: (a) measures of favorite programs; (b) broad estimates of viewing amount and distribution, which involve perceptual judgments of behavior that are likely to involve distortion; and (c) diary procedures of notation and close recall as soon as possible after viewing behavior occurs. In general, except for simple purposes of broad comparisons, in which case cruder assessments may suffice, diary or even metered diary measurement of viewing behavior is preferred; this should also ensure that whole programs or even groups of programs are used to assess viewing experience rather than partial extracts, which raise difficult assessment problems of particular material in the broader context. Likewise, the field of personality measurement, rather than inferential indices, such as religious affiliation or attitude and even value measures that may go somewhat deeper, which may have been used when other measures were not opportune, well-established or newly developed and validated personality constructs, should be preferred and harnessed. A number of these, such as extroversion, neuroticism, locus of control, and variants of anomie, have been explored; others remain to be investigated. These include the needs for achievement, affiliation, and privacy; preference for delayed versus immediate gratification; and the cognitively based hierarchical interactionist theory of Gittinger and the psychosocial differentiation into field-independence construct of Witkin.

From what has been done so far, it appears promising that more relationships will be found among adults that link personality dispositions with the perception and assimilation of programs experienced as wholes and with the perception of themes such as the portrayal of women and men and of old and young people in general. Next, it may be just as possible to show links between personality attributes and total amounts, or of distributions of patterns (among program types) of viewing behavior. Third, though this will be more difficult to apportion because of problems of multicollinearity, it is likely that through its interactions with viewing experiences, personality will be seen to contribute to the shape of perceptions and attitudes concerning the world portrayed by television. This interactionist assertion will certainly not aspire to minimize television as an influence because some say, with Klapper (echoing Kennedy?), that one should ask not what television does to one, but what one does with television. Instead, at least with adults, it will be seen that viewing experience and personal predispositions usually reinforce each other in affirming perceptions, attitudes, and even reflexively, personality structures. Yet it will remain of interest to reveal instances where television is effective without, or even against, prior dispositions in altering attitudes. Such discoveries, if rigorous enough, will be rare prizes sought after by researchers.

REFERENCES

Argyle, M. (1972). *The social psychology of work*. London: Allen Lane.
Atkin, C., Greenberg, B., Korzenny, F., & McDermott, S. (1979). Selective exposure to television violence. *Journal of Broadcasting, 23,* 5–13.

Belson, W. A. (1978). *Television violence and the adolescent boy*. Farnborough, England: Saxon House.

Blumler, J. G. (1976). The role of theory in uses and gratifications studies. *Communication Research, 3*, 243–260.

Brody, S. (1977). *Screen violence and film censorship: A review of research* (Home Office Study No. 40). London: Her Majesty's Stationery Office.

Carlson, J. M. (1983). Crime show viewing by pre-adults: The impact on attitudes toward civil liberties. *Communication Research, 10*, 529–552.

Comstock, G. (1975). *Television and human behavior: The key studies*. Santa Monica, CA: Rand.

Cook, T. D., Kendzierski, D. A., & Thomas, S. V. (1983). The implicit assumptions of television research: An analysis of the 1982 NIMH report on television and behavior. *Public Opinion Quarterly, 47*, 161–201.

Cross, J. (1981). *Audience responses to the sound broadcasting of Parliament*. London: Independent Broadcasting Authority.

Diener, E., & Woody, L. W. (1981). Television violence, conflict, realism and action. *Communication Research, 8*, 281–306.

Durkin, K. (1983). *Viewers' reactions to the House Communion programme*. Canterbury: University of Kent Social Psychology Research Unit.

Eastman, S. T. (1979). Uses of television viewing and consumer life styles: A multivariate analysis. *Journal of Broadcasting, 23*, 492–500.

Eiser, J. R., Sutton, S. R., & Wober, M. (1978). Can television influence smoking? Further evidence. *British Journal of Addiction, 73*, 291–298.

Fouts, G. T. (1976). Effects of television on children and youth: A developmental approach. Ontario Report of the *Royal Commission on Violence in the Communications Industry (Vol. 6)* Ottawa: Queen's Printer.

Gandy, O. H. (1981, April). *Is that all there is to love? Values and program preference*. Paper presented at the conference on Culture and Communication, Temple University, Philadelphia.

Gerbner, G. (1972). Violence in television drama: Trends and symbolic functions. In G. A. Comstock & E. A. Rubinstein (Eds.), *Television and social behavior: Vol. 1. Media content and control*. Washington, DC: U.S. Government Printing Office.

Gordon, T. F., & Verna, M. E. (1978). *Mass communication effects and processes: A comparative bibliography, 1950–1975*. Beverly Hills, CA: Sage.

Greenberg, B. S., & Gordon, T. F. (1972). Social class and racial differences in children's perception of televised violence. In G. A. Comstock & E. A. Rubinstein (Eds.), *Television and social behavior: Vol. 1. Media content and control*. Washington, DC: U.S. Government Printing Office.

Gunter, B. (1985). *Dimensions of television violence*. Aldershot, England: Gower Press.

Gunter, B., & Furnham, A. (1984a). Androgyny and the perception of television violence as perpetrated by males and females. *Australian Journal of Psychology*.

Gunter, B., & Furnham, A. (1984b). Perceptions of television violence: Effects of programme genre and type of violence on viewers' judgments of violent portrayals. *British Journal of Social Psychology, 23*, in press.

Gunter, B., & Wober, M. (1983). Television viewing and public trust. *British Journal of Social Psychology, 22*, 174–176.

Hampson, S. E. (1982). *The construct of personality*, London: Routledge & Kegan Paul.

Hedinsson, E., & Windahl, S. (1984). Cultivation analysis: A Swedish illustration. In G. Melischek, K. E. Rosengren, & J. Strappers (Eds.), *Cultural indicators: An international symposium* (pp. 389–405). Vienna: Verlag der Osterreichischen Akademie der Wissenschaften.

Heeter, C., D'Alessio, D., Greenberg, B. S., & McVoy, D. S. (1983, May). *Cableviewing*. Paper presented at the International Communication Association Conference, Dallas, TX.

Hendry, L. B., & Patrick, H. (1977). Adolescents and television. *Journal of Youth and Adolescence, 6*, 325–336.

Hendry, L. B., & Thornton, D. J. E. (1976). Games theory, television and leisure: An adolescent study. *British Journal of Social and Clinical Psychology, 15,* 369–376.

Himmelweit, H., & Swift, B. (1976). Continuities and dicontinuities in media usage and taste: A longitudinal study. *Journal of Social Issues, 32,* 133–156.

Himmelweit, H., Swift, B., & Jaeger, M. J. (1980). The audience as critic: An approach to the study of entertainment. In P. Tannenbaum (Ed.), *The entertainment functions of television* (pp. 67–106). Hillsdale, NJ: Lawrence Erlbaum Associates.

Independent Broadcasting Authority. (1976, January). *The Naked Civil Servant: Audience Reactions to the programme and to the use of the warning symbol.* London: Author.

Independent Broadcasting Authority. (1978, April). *Attitudes towards The Champions.* London: Author.

Korten, D. C. (1971). The life game: Survival strategies in Ethiopian folktales. *Journal of Cross Cultural Psychology, 2,* 209–224.

Marks, J., & Greenfield, P. M. (1984). How the CIA assesses weaknesses: The Gittinger personality system. *Psychology News, 35,* 1–6.

Milavsky, J. R., Kessler, R. C., Stipp, H. H., & Rubens, W. S. (1983). *Television and aggression: A panel study.* New York: Academic.

Mischel, W. (1968). *Personality and assessment.* New York: Wiley.

Morgan, M., & Gross, L. (1980). Television viewing and reading: Does more equal better? *Journal of Communication, 30,* 159–165.

Murray, J. P. (1980). *Television and youth: 25 years of research and controversy.* Stanford, CA: Boys Town.

Newell, D. S. (1972). *Studies of the functions served for viewers by selected programmes containing violent sequences, in violence on television: Programme content and viewer perception.* London: BBC Audience Research Department.

Petzel, T. P., & Michaels, E. J. (1973). Perception of violence as a function of levels of hostility: Levels of hostility. *Journal of Consulting and Clinical Psychology, 41,* 35–36.

Robinson, D. C. (1980, May). *Young adults' assessment of dramatic television violence.* Paper presented at the International Communication Association Conference, Acapulco, Mexico.

Rotter, J. B. (1966). Generalized expectancies for internal versus external control of reinforcement. *Psychological Monographs, 80,* (Whole No. 609).

Rubin, Z., & Peplau, L. A. (1975). Who believes in a just world? *Journal of Social Issues, 31,* 65–89.

Surlin, S. H. (1978). "Roots" research: A summary of findings. *Journal of Broadcasting, 22,* 309–320.

Surlin, S. H., & Tate, E. D. (1976). All in the Family: Is Archie funny? *Journal of Communication, 26,* 61–68.

Tapp, J. L. (1981). Studying personality development. In H. C. Triandis & A. Heron (Eds.), *Handbook of cross cultural psychology.* Boston: Allyn & Bacon.

Tate, E. D. (1976). A typology of viewers. In *Report of the Royal Commission on Violence in the Communications Industry* (Vol. 6). Ottawa: Queen's Printer.

Webster, J. G., & Wakshlag, J. J. (1983). A theory of television program choice. *Communication Research, 10,* 430–446.

Witkin, H. A., Dyk, R. B., Faterson, H. F., Goodenough, D. R., & Karp, S. A. (1962). *Psychological Differentiation,* New York: Wiley.

Witkin, H. A., & Berry, J. W. (1975). Psychological differentiation in cross cultural perspective. *Journal of Cross Cultural Psychology, 6,* 4–87.

Wober, M. (1978). Television violence and paranoid perception: The view from Great Britain. *Public Opinion Quarterly, 42,* 315–321.

Wober, M. (1979, March). *Edward and Mrs. Simpson: Explorations of the significance of the series for the public.* London: Independent Broadcasting Authority, Audience Research Department.

Wober M. (1980a, February). *Offence and defence in the home.* London: Independent Broadcasting Authority, Audience Research Department.

Wober, M. (1980b, September). *Patterns of personality and of televiewing.* London: Independent Broadcasting Authority, Audience Research Department.

Wober, M. (1981a, December). *Broadcasting and the conflict in Ireland.* London: Independent Broadcasting Authority, Audience Research Department.

Wober, M. (1981b, December). *Pyramids or chariots?—The satellite question.* London: Independent Broadcasting Authority, Audience Research Department.

Wober, M. (1981c, September). *Television and women: Viewing patterns and perceptions of ideal, actual and portrayed women's roles.* London: Independent Broadcasting Authority, Audience Research Department.

Wober, M. (1982a, December). *All set for channel 4?* London: Independent Broadcasting Authority, Audience Research Department.

Wober, M. (1982b, August). *The Falklands conflict: Further analysis of viewers' behaviour and attitudes.* London: Independent Broadcasting Authority, Audience Research Department.

Wober, M. (1983a). Assessing the patterns and experiences of viewing television. In S. H. Irvine & J. W. Berry (Eds.), *Human assessment and cultural factors* (pp. 539–559). New York: Plenum.

Wober, M. (1983b, May). *A twisted yarn: Some psychological aspects of viewing soap operas.* Paper presented at the Independent Broadcasting Authority Convention, Dallas, TX.

Wober, M. (1984a). *Citizens of ethnic minorities: Their prominence in real life and on television.* London: Independent Broadcasting Authority Research Reference Paper.

Wober, M. (1984b). *The Nation's Health.* London: Independent Broadcasting Authority Research Reference Paper.

Wober, M. (1984c). *The Day After: British viewers' attitudes.* Paper presented at the World Association for Public Opinion Research, Lake Delavan, Wisconsin.

Wober, M., & Gunter, B. (1982a). Impressions of old people on TV and in real life. *British Journal of Social Psychology, 21,* 335–336.

Wober, M., & Gunter, B. (1982b). Television and personal threat: Fact or artifact? A British survey. *British Journal of Social Psychology, 21,* 239–247.

Wober, M., & Gunter, B. (1984). *The Day After: The audience view.* London: Independent Broadcasting Authority Research Reference Paper.

Wober, M., & Reardon, G. (1983). *Enjoyment and strength of impression.* London: Independent Broadcasting Authority, Research Working Paper.

Wober, M., & Svennevig, M. (1981, October). *Party political broadcasts and their use for the viewing public.* London: IBA/BBC Audience Research Departments.

Zagona, S., & Kelly, M. (1966). The resistance of the closed mind to a novel and complex audio visual experience. *Journal of Social Psychology, 70,* 123–131.

Zillmann, D., & Bryant, J. (1983). Pornography, sexual callousness and the trivialization of rape. *Journal of Communication, 32,* 10–21.

Zuckerman, M., Kolin, E. A., Price, L., & Zoob, I. (1964). Development of a sensation seeking scale. *Journal of Consulting Psychology, 28,* 477–482.

12 Activity in the Effects of Television on Children

Robert P. Hawkins, Suzanne Pingree
University of Wisconsin—Madison

Television effects research since the mid 1970s has increasingly recognized the child viewer as an active rather than passive participant. The notion that children are active in their use of television is now so widespread that it is tempting to consider it the base assumption of a new dominant paradigm in effects research (Pingree & Hawkins, 1982). Unfortunately, researchers mean so many different things by "active" that it is not clear what this dominant paradigm is. For example, active viewer can denote the locus of control in the communication transaction, as in Anderson and Lorch's (1983) work on active monitoring of television by preschool children. The activity of viewers as they approach television with various purposes and needs is also central to the theoretical perspectives of the uses and gratifications approach (cf. Blumler, 1979; Levy & Windahl, 1984). Or activity can refer to comprehension strategies such as learning to focus on central instead of incidental events (Collins, 1982). For Salomon (1983), in contrast, activity refers to the amount of mental effort invested during viewing. Dervin (1982) intends a much more substantial shift of paradigms from sender centered to receiver centered, in which "effects" is a misnomer for subjectively defined and controlled construction of meaning. The same recognition of the possibility of systematically different responses to the same message is present in research motivated by cognitive developmental theories proposing qualitative developmental differences in cognition (cf. Wartella, 1979).

These meanings for activity have very different implications for television effects. Some merely posit variability between individuals, others reject the idea of effects altogether, and still others are initially tangential to effects. In this chapter, we propose to elaborate on meanings of activity as they are applied to television use and suggest how these different meanings imply different kinds of effects.

We first make a key distinction in the various meanings of activity, namely, between those meanings that center around different kinds of cognitive activities employed while processing television and those meanings that refer to the overall amount of cognitive effort that viewers apply to processing television. There is sufficient research to show that both are important in cognitive effects of television, but the research also suggests that they are important in quite different ways.

However, neither the kinds of cognitive activities employed nor the amount of effort applied can be examined separately. Cognitive effort makes sense only as applied to some processing activity; cognitive processing activities make a difference in the effects of television depending on how much effort is applied. Thus, our model of individual cognitive processing in television effects on children (Fig. 12.1) shows cognitive activities as affecting children's attention to television, information constructed as a result of that attention, and meanings constructed from that information. Cognitive effort is applied to those cognitive activities and is hypothesized to determine the amount they affect attention, retention, and construction. We return to this model in more detail later, but first we elaborate on cognitive activities and effort.

COGNITIVE ACTIVITIES

Much of our knowledge about the kinds of cognitive activities that are involved in message processing comes from studies of how and how much children comprehend the television they watch. Researchers have been very active in this

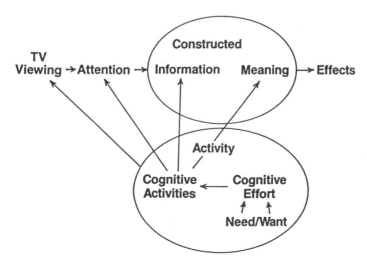

FIG. 12.1 A model of activity in television use and effects.

area (see reviews by Collins, 1982; Pingree & Hawkins, 1982), and recent work has also given young children credit for more abilities than previous research by reducing the task demands for comprehension and processing measures (e.g., Smith, Anderson, & Fischer, 1985). This research also allows us to break cognitive activities during viewing down into a number of components children (and presumably adults as well) employ in processing television messages. A list of such activities follows, along with a brief summary of evidence for the necessity and use of each.

Segmenting

Television presents sounds and images continuously, although adult viewers are accustomed to using a variety of cinematic devices and dramatic conventions to break action into meaningful chunks of related actions. In one study comparing break points placed in the same film by respondents of different ages, adults and ninth-grade children segmented by combining scenes. Third-grade children generally made use of these adult break points, but also broke the program at many other points, including breaking within a scene (Wartella, 1978). Breaking a program into many segments should tend to produce memory and processing overloads because the larger number of discrete units may make relating scenes more difficult.

Focusing

Because the sheer number of things a viewer could notice and remember is so very large, another logically necessary activity is to focus on important or useful information and to ignore most of the incidental information. Even if effects are not defined from a sender's perspective, some sort of focusing seems inescapable, although the definition of what is important or unimportant may vary.

There are a number of studies showing that after 8–10 years, the mix of central and incidental items learned shifts so that a decreasing share of total learning is incidental to following the plot (Calvert, Huston, Watkins, & Wright, 1982; Collins, 1970; Hawkins, 1973). Some of the tests of alternative explanations in these and other studies suggest that young children lack strategies favoring the selection and encoding of plot-relevant content while filtering out irrelevant detail. Young children thus seem equally open to all that television presents, whereas older children are selective. However, given some recent work suggesting that preschool children can reproduce more of a television story using dolls than they are given credit for with recognition tests (Pingree et al., 1983; Smith et al., 1985) this conclusion bears reexamination.

Reading Formal Features

In recent years there has been a great deal of attention to what several researchers have called the "formal features" of television—visual effects, movement, and editing; audio compression, sound effects, and music; and formally defined information content or entropy (cf. Rice, Huston, & Wright, 1982; Watt & Welch, 1983). Huston and Wright (1983) propose that formal features can play three roles in young children's television viewing: (a) maintenance of attention through the orienting response to change, (b) marking significant content for children's monitoring strategies through learned associations between features and content, and (c) signifiers of some of the meaning gained from the television program. In the third case, formal features require a cognitive activity that might be called *reading*, that is, applying learned or constructed interpretations to the formal features.

We are beginning to gain some idea of the range and types of features that can be assigned meaning as one processes television (Huston & Wright, 1983; see also Anderson & Smith, 1984, on "montage"), but we have as yet only a vague understanding of the extent to which each of these different features is used or how they are integrated into an overall meaning when they complement or contradict each other. More important for the study of children and television, we need considerable work on how children learn that formal features are potentially meaningful and then learn particular meanings for individual features or combinations of features. Experience with television seems important, but we do not know how much experience, at what ages, and with what relationship to nontelevision experience. Smith et al. (1985) showed even preschool children assigning meaning to formal features in very short animations.

Using Time

In a sense, the time order of events in a program is just another formal feature, and children's use of time in processing television and making sense of it is again the reading of formal features. However, time order seems especially difficult for children and thus deserves some special consideration. For example, Leifer et al. (1971) found that preschool children could not sequence even three central scenes from a 20-min film of a familiar fairy tale they had just seen, and 7-year-olds did very poorly when the sequence contained five or more central events. Even when children are old enough to begin integrating motives for and consequences of aggressive acts (third grade), the additional temporal distance provided by inserting an intervening commercial seriously disrupted their abilities (Collins, 1973).

Part of this poor performance with time may be due to problems of memory overload in long sequences and testing that is too demanding, as suggested by studies in which young children were able to keep events in order (Smith et al.,

1985). However, there are also some indications that young children's difficulties with time may be a more fundamental disinclination to use time, even if not an inability. Collins, Wellman, Keniston, and Westby (1978) found that second graders' comprehension was essentially unaffected by editing that jumbled the order of scenes within a television program, and fifth and eighth graders were less able to draw the inferences, many of which depended on the time order of events.

Drawing Inferences

Much that is crucial to gaining adultlike comprehension of a television program is never presented explicitly, but instead requires the viewer to draw inferences based on what is available in the program. Thus, we might observe two actions and draw a connection such as causation or motivation between them. Often these meanings are intended by the sender and are only implied for reasons of narrative economy and because the producer can safely assume that all adults will draw the intended inference. Thus, we are left to infer spatial relationships, the passage of time, character perspective and motivation, causation, and consequences throughout television programming.

With children, however, such assumptions seem questionable. Collins in particular has done a number of studies showing that children do less well with implicit than explicit central content (Collins et al., 1978; Collins, Sobol, & Westby, 1981; see Collins, 1983, for a fuller review). That the ability (or inclination) to draw inferences is the root of some of this difficulty is revealed by analyses showing that second graders did not draw the expected inference even when they knew the relevant explicit information; fifth and especially eighth graders will draw the appropriate inferences as long as they have learned the necessary explicit information.

On the other hand, preschool children were able to reconstruct implicit material using dolls (Smith et al., 1985). Filling in events not shown was fairly easy for 4- and 7-year-olds, and inferring the passage of time from camera techniques was most difficult (with character perspective and location intermediate), but even for time inferences, more than a third of the youngest children reconstructed the action correctly. Several factors could be responsible for the very different results. First, the poor inference results were with recognition tests, and the good results were with doll reconstructions. Second, many of Collins' inferences were about relatively abstract things such as motives, goals, and consequences of action, whereas the inferences in Smith et al. were very concrete. Third, the inferences children drew in the Smith study seemed to be based largely on the formal features presented, while Collins' inferences tended to draw more on general world and television knowledge. Thus, we see no contradiction from these very different results. In fact, what they make clear is that the number and range of inferences useful in comprehending television are very great indeed and that this cognitive activity is very central.

Drawing on Other Knowledge

Although some inferences require drawing conclusions based on formal features, others require the application of one's knowledge about television and the world in general. A number of researchers have proposed that this application of knowledge often proceeds via scripts or schemata, that is, organized prototypic expectations of individuals, objects, and event sequences (Bower, Black, & Turner, 1979; Schank & Abelson, 1977; Wyer & Srull, 1981). These schemata are hypothesized to serve as a framework for new information, as mnemonic aids, and as guides to the interpolation of missing actions, motivations, and plans. Scripts and schemata seem to be very handy tools for organizing experience, but they can also be a source of error, as when Collins and Wellman's 7-year-olds were judged to make schema-driven or stereotypic errors (1983).

All these activities seem necessary in one form or another to achieve comprehension of television as the sender intended it. Of course, comprehending artificially simplified television might not require each one, but regularly broadcast television watched by children seems to need them all. But what about meanings not intended by the sender? By "constructed information and meaning" in our model, we endorse the receiver perspective of granting independence and subjectivity to viewers in constructing meanings that may be quite different from what the sender intended.

For the cognitive activities listed, this distinction between sender-intended meaning and individually defined variations in meanings seems irrelevant. All of the activities seem necessary to attend to television, acquire facts, and construct meanings, regardless of what those meanings are. But several other activities are part of processing television subjectively, which have nothing to do with achieving adult-defined comprehension. We propose three, largely without evidence, because their role in adult-defined comprehension research is only as intervening variables enhancing or inhibiting effects, not as processing activities in their own right.

Evaluating Information

One viewer activity that probably has considerable impact on the meanings they construct is assigning values and affect to bits of information taken from the television content. These values then form part of the meaning constructed and may also influence application of other cognitive activities.

Making Connections

Another activity in assigning meaning to television is making comparisons between the television content being viewed and past real-life and television experience. This activity is more general, subjective, and less tied to regularities than the application of schemata. That is, although schema application deals with recognizing the immediate as representative of some generalization, making connections refers to an activity such as distinguishing between reality and fantasy portrayals, but it could also include connections that are much more isolated and unpredictable. Nevertheless, such associations are a potential starting point for considerable analytic thought.

Stimulation

Finally, an activity in response to television may be independent or creative thought. Such thought may begin with connections and continue to create meanings and relations that seem to an outside observer to be entirely independent of the television viewing experience. Including them here is thus rather far from comprehending television in the usual (adult-defined) sense, but because we are discussing cognitive activities in processing television, the inclusion seems appropriate.

This list is not exhaustive; there probably are some other cognitive activities in processing television, especially in the latter group of subjective activities. Nonetheless, the number and variety of activities used in processing television are large, and the activities are interrelated in complex ways, such that the interactions are themselves as important for understanding television as any activity alone.

COGNITIVE EFFORT

In addition to the cognitive activities used in processing television messages, activity has meant the amount of effort applied to processing. Thus, we can describe more or less effort applied to focusing processes, more or less effort applied to comparison processes or evaluative processes, and so on. Recently, researchers have made some serious attempts to measure amount of cognitive effort, using operationalizations centering around attention, brain waves, reported amount of thinking while viewing, and results of cognitive effort.

Attention

Attention probably has been used more than other operationalizations of cognitive effort, especially as an intervening variable that locates cognitive processes between message reception and effect. For example, two studies show that survey attention measures (questions such as "How much attention do you pay to television news?" which can be answered "a great deal," "some attention," or "don't pay much attention") contribute their own predictive power beyond that of exposure measures for political effects of mass media (Chaffee & Choe, 1979; McLeod, Leutscher, & McDonald, 1980).

However, self-report measures of attention may not be a particularly accurate way to measure cognitive effort. In the first place, they assume that people are self-aware or that their attentiveness is salient enough to answer such questions meaningfully. But more problematic, survey questions about attention may be asking for traitlike responses, when effort is likely to be much more situational. That is, the assumption that effort is applied consistently across viewing situations (whether these situations are conceptualized as different kinds of television content or different personal contexts for the viewer) may provide a misleading average.

Researchers have also operationalized attention as visual orientation to the television screen. Much of this research began by focusing on attributes of television content that would capture and maintain children's attention so that maximum learning would take place (Anderson & Levin, 1976; Lesser, 1974; Rice et al., 1982), but this approach has little to do with what we mean by cognitive effort.

More recent work by Anderson and his colleagues, however, begins to make an argument for visual attention as an indicator of cognitive activity. Their research suggests that even very young children strategically direct their visual attention to content that is comprehensible (Anderson, Lorch, Field, & Sanders, 1981; Lorch, Anderson, & Levin, 1979). From these results and others (Anderson & Lorch, 1983), they argue that children learn that some formal features of television signal significant messages and that comprehensibility is a prime factor in determining significance for young children. It is not clear at present what proportion of children's attention is passively captured by salient formal features of television and what proportion is actively directed the the child. But to the extent that attention reflects the child's monitoring, it also provides an indirect indicator of the amount of prior cognitive activity directing that visual attention.

The problem with visual attention as a measure of cognitive effort is that although it is sometimes necessary to watch carefully while applying effort, it may often be equally or more useful to look away. For example, if some aspect of television content stimulates viewers to think about the relationships between ideas, very hard thinking about these ideas might be better accomplished if viewers divert their attention from television either physically (moving their eyes away) or psychologically (putting their eyes out of focus and "clicking out"). Thus, amount of visual attention by itself may partially capture what we mean by cognitive effort, but it could also represent no effort at all.

Brain Waves

The use of electroencephalographic (EEG) recordings made while viewing television constitutes another major attempt to measure cognitive activity. This approach is based on research suggesting that the alpha portion of EEG is an inverse indicator of the amount of cognitive activity (Greenfield & Sternbach,

1972). EEG has the advantage of being measured continuously in both amplitude and duration so that the researcher can associate variations in activity with variations in content; in contrast, dichotomous visual attention measures may indicate nothing more active than an orienting response. It also has the advantage of measuring activity within the brain rather than using some exterior indicator that may or may not be related to cognitive activity.

However, it is not clear at present exactly what EEG means (it probably is also sensitive to the orienting response) or how variations in EEG relate to reasonable outcomes of cognitive effort. Although some researchers appear to be finding EEG patterns that are potentially exciting (see, e.g., Reeves, Thorson, & Schleuder, chapter 13 in this volume), research linking EEG with effort and other indicators of activity is just beginning.

Thinking While Viewing

Some researchers have attempted to measure quantity of cognitive effort during viewing by asking about it directly. Salomon (1983) has suggested the construct of amount of invested mental effort (AIME) in nonautomatic elaboration of material as a measure of the amount of mindful or deep processing of television content. For example, he argues that AIME increases "when a unit of material cannot be easily fitted into existing schemata" (p. 187). When respondents are questioned about the amount of AIME they generally expend with media and with various types of media content (adventure, news, science, etc.), it has been found to be associated with greater learning (Kane & Anderson, 1978; Salomon, 1983).

Results of Cognitive Effort

As with visual attention, it may be possible to infer amount of cognitive effort from the results of effort. That is, for some kinds of cognitive activities (e.g., focusing, segmenting, inferring, etc.), those children whose performance is superior most likely devoted more effort to those activities at some previous point. For example, Pingree (1983) studied fifth, sixth, and seventh graders' ability to infer television content that was not explicitly presented in the program. She predicted that children who scored high on this ability would also be the most affected by implicit social reality messages on television because of their greater ability to draw inferences.

Surprisingly, the children who did less well at the inference task seemed most affected. High scoring children were consistently unaffected by social reality messages. Pingree suggests that what was measured as inference-making ability may have reflected the results of prior cognitive effort. A similar argument can be used to explain Pingree's (1978) and Reeves' (1978) results with children's perceptions of reality. For both studies, perceptions were directly related to beliefs, although perceived reality had been hypothesized to work only as an intervening variable. What had been conceived of as an indicator of children's beliefs about television's portrayal of reality might also have located prior cognitive effort of other sorts.

Most of these measures of cognitive effort are fairly unsatisfactory. Self-report measures are likely to be unreliable, are likely to elicit responses about usual behaviors when responses in specific situations and contexts would be more valuable, have tended thus far to measure activity while viewing and to ignore activity related to television content during nonviewing periods, and have assumed that subjects are aware of their cognitive effort level so that they can report those levels accurately. Unobtrusive measures (e.g., visual orientation and EEG) probably measure much more and much less than cognitive effort. What looks like effort may be effort, or it may be something less rich and interesting. In addition, for visual orientation at least, some effort is almost certainly taking place where that measure would suggest no effort, that is, when people aren't looking.

Finally, no measure is specific enough for precise predictions about outcomes. All of these are measures of effort in a general sense: "How hard were you thinking just then?" We need measures of cognitive effort applied to each type of cognitive activity so that some sense can be made of how this effort and activity are being used by children (and adults). We also need measures of whether effort is being applied to several activities simultaneously and/or to the integration or mastery of these activities. In other words, cognitive activity and cognitive effort will be more useful as explanatory variables to the extent that measures of both activities are specific.

IMPLICATIONS FOR EFFECTS

We began this chapter by suggesting that researchers have been using activity to mean many things, thus leading to some confusion about whether contradictory results represent true conflicts or just unfortunate disagreements over definitions. Now that we have distinguished between cognitive activities and cognitive effort and suggested many specific activities, the semantic disagreements are less troublesome, but trying to describe and predict the effects of television is still complex. We begin by returning to our model of individual cognitive processing in television effects (Fig. 12.1) and explaining our intentions in more detail.

One usage of activity has not been dealt with directly so far, although we think it is implied throughout. This is the general philosophical approach of emphasizing the relative power and independence of receivers of mass communications. It does not necessarily mean discarding traditional conceptualizations of effects as changes or differences (or the lack of change or difference) in learning, attitudes, or behavior resulting from using television. What it does require, however, is not making the assumptions of determinism about effects and of isomorphism of messages and effects. That is, one should avoid the magic bullet assumption that message reception will necessarily produce change, but one should also avoid the more subtle assumption that any given message will produce a particular sort of effect (e.g., assuming violent content produces aggressive behavior rather than fear, desensitization, or revulsion).

We do not want to argue that messages have no influence or that there is no predictable relationshp between television messages and the changes that result. Our models of television effects need to predict subjectivity and audience independence while still allowing for substantial similarity of effects on occasion. For television effects on children (and perhaps for adults as well), we propose a model of individual cognitive processing in such effects (Fig. 12.1) that bases variability largely on the intermediate result of comprehension, that is, information and meaning constructed from viewing.

We show these as two separate intermediate products for simplicity, but label them both as constructed to suggest a continuum of multiple levels of depth. One might be tempted to separate the facts retained from the meanings constructed, but this would bias toward an objectivist assumption about just what facts are there and tend to ignore individuality in selecting and interpreting these facts. Still, there is a real sense in which construction can vary from relatively unprocessed segmentation, selection, and reading formal features to constructions that are highly processed by multiple activities and far removed from the original perceptions. We want these intermediate products to express a continuum of levels or amount of construction in which individual variation is possible from the beginning, but in which subjective variability in interpretation becomes successively more probable with greater processing.

The placement of television viewing at the left of Fig. 12.1 (i.e., at the beginning of the model) does not reflect causal priority; it is simply the beginning of a cognitive processing model. Actually, the amount and kind of television viewing a child does are themselves the product of many antecedents, including most of the other elements in our model (see also Rubin, Chapter 14 in this volume).

Activities, Effort, and Effects

In applying this model for research on effects, we see two broad research agendas. The first concerns the ways in which cognitive effort applied to these various activities changes the intermediate and traditional effects of viewing television. Because cognitive activities work in different ways for viewers' processing of television, the application of more or less effort to them may have different outcomes. Some cognitive effort while viewing may increase learning, comprehension, or the isomorphism between television content and viewer beliefs or behaviors. In other cases, cognitive effort may decrease learning from television or increase the likelihood of beliefs opposed to those presented on television.

Alternatively, active thinking while viewing may sometimes lead to creative and diverse beliefs that would seem to have little to do with television content (see Hawkins & Pingree, 1982, and Pingree, 1983, for fuller discussion of these ideas as applied to social reality effects). With the distinction between cognitive activity and cognitive effort, we should be ready to specify programs, outcomes, and populations for which we are willing to make each of these kinds of predictions.

Individual hypotheses can be thought of as residing at intersections of a matrix in which the rows are the various kinds of cognitive activities and the columns are various effects of viewing television, including predictions about intermediate products such as getting the meaning the sender intended or constructing one with considerable variation. One might then predict that as greater effort is applied to such processes as segmenting, focusing, drawing inferences, reading formal features, or using real-world knowledge, the likelihood of constructing the sender's intended meaning increases. This could be elaborated by restricting such a prediction to early, less-processed constructions and predicting greater likelihood of variation from the sender's intention with increased effort for higher level constructions, and for the application of effort to activities such as evaluation, making connections, or stimulation. Or one might predict that individualistic meanings are more likely a result of some types of activity than others, such as applying real-world knowledge, and less so from reading formal features.

Or one could predict, although it would be difficult to test, the level to which construction proceeds based on the activities brought into play and the amount of effort devoted to them. Predictions could also be made about the effects of energy expended regardless of activity or, in some cases, of activities regardless of the amount of energy expended (i.e., hypothesizing that the effects of an activity are dichotomously present or not). All such predictions should then move to more traditional effects on attitudes, behavior, social agendas, and so on, with the intermediate products themselves still tested and treated as intervening variables.

Competence and Performance

A second broad research agenda needs to deal with factors that determine children's application of effort and activities to processing television. Here we see three subagendas. One deals with the ability to perform and coordinate cognitive activities, and the other two appear in the model as factors influencing the amount of cognitive effort applied. To discuss these, we would first like to distinguish between competence and performance in processing television. Chomsky was very careful to point out that his phrase-structure and transformational grammars were theories of linguistic competence, describing what people knew about language and not theories of linguistic performance, describing how people actually behave in producing and decoding language (1965). A similar distinction may be crucial in describing people's real-life processing of television because what people actually do may often be less than they could do optimally.

Coordinating Abilities

One problem for children lies in the distinction between individual competencies and the competence to coordinate a variety of activities. Research on children's comprehension has for years cataloged the abilities young children do not have that lead to their difficulties with television. However, recent research on comprehension (Pingree et al., 1983; Smith et al., in press) suggests that even preschool children have many abilities they were thought to lack and can do many of the cognitive activities we outlined. At the minimum, these studies show that preschoolers can focus, segment, use time, and draw inferences (at least in some fashion). However, for a period of years thereafter, children's application of these abilities is uncertain and uneven, probably reflecting other limitations on their abilities.

Processing television requires children or adults to apply, not just a few, but many different cognitive activities, all of which seem necessary and useful. Thus, one major problem for children processing television, and an important topic for research, is just how one coordinates all the different activities that go into processing television, and how one integrates and organizes the products of these various activities.

What Viewers Need to Do

Problems in coordinating and using cognitive activities may also influence competence-performance by changing the amount of effort viewers need to apply. While children are learning to coordinate their cognitive activities, they need to deal with information overload, a problem that is familiar from studies of distraction and division of attention.

Commercial television shows provide a fairly rich stimulus environment, and several varieties of overload could thus limit cognitive effort applied to various comprehension activities. The richness of the stimulus—many things happening at once—provides many distracting features that can lead to dead ends, during which crucial features have been ignored (e.g., is that car in the background going to turn this way and enter the plot or go on past and out of view forever?). With sufficient processing capacity, both foreground and background action can be monitored, but if capacity is exceeded and if the wrong choice is made, comprehension (adultlike meanings) will be downgraded.

A related overload may have to do with capacities of working memory and may operate in studies where children as old as 8 comprehend less when related facts are separated by a commercial instead of immediately following one another

(Collins, 1982). Full-length television programs may simply separate facts needing integration too far apart in time.

In addition, although recent studies were able to show that very young children could do a number of the cognitive activities we posited, they do not tell us about the cognitive capacity implications of having to do many of them more or less simultaneously. The constant switching between activities and integration of these cognitive activities may provide the overload for children.

A key idea here is *automaticity*. With experience, processing cinematic conventions becomes highly automatic and makes very little demand on cognitive resources. Thus, as processing television becomes more automatic, the demands of each individual interpretation become reduced, and cognitive resources are available for parallel processing and other aspects of comprehension.

Another factor that may be related to automaticity is the concept of schema or scripts as organized, prototypic expectations of individuals, objects, and event sequences. Earlier, we discussed how applying schema may be an important cognitive activity in processing television, but in addition, their application to the problem of processing television is expected to reduce the cognitive demands of that processing, both by allowing low-effort, top-down interpretation of the television stimulus and by allowing high-probability predictions that make focusing and segmenting more efficient. Context cues and schema for television programs probably give adult viewers the advantage of predicting whether to attend or not. Thus, schema application can make it easier for effort to be applied to other cognitive activities.

Schank and Abelson (1977) suggest that children younger than 4 years are basically in the process of acquiring scripts. Thereafter, they argue that scripts and schemata become more elaborated, easier to instantiate, and more flexible each time they are instantiated. Although subsequent research has demonstrated that even younger children have scripts for familiar event sequences such as eating dinner (Adams & Worden, 1983; Nelson & Gruendel, 1981), it is clear that they have some difficulties manipulating and applying them. Thus, we would expect relatively little benefit to cognitive capacity of script use early in their acquisition, but progressively greater reductions in processing demands through their use with continued experience.

What Viewers Want to Do

A third set of factors that can affect performance has to do with motivations or orientations toward the viewing task. Children (or adults) may approach their viewing situation with more or less interest, involvement, intent, or something like a cognitive set that motivates them to put forth more or less effort than they would otherwise apply. In research with children and adults, Salomon (1983) found evidence that stereotyping of television affects effort invested. He found less variance in his respondents' feelings about their own abilities, in the amount of energy they said they invested in processing, and in the depth they attributed to their response to television compared to the same material in print form. His results also suggest that the more stereotyped the perception of the medium, the less effort was invested in it.

Other factors in the viewing situation can change effort expended. Reasons for viewing and the viewer's relative effort in approaching the choice of what to view may contribute to more or less effort in processing. When "to relax" or "I just like it" are important reasons for viewing, for example, we suggest that cognitive activity will be lower. In a study of the relationship between effort in the decisions to view and what to view and active television processing while viewing, Rouner (1983) found partial support for this hypothesis. Rouner used college students' self-reports of decisional effort and found some relationships between this effort and a set of measures that would seem to locate cognitive effort while viewing.

Both formal and content features of the television program being watched will be more or less easy to process, but we hypothesize that such features may also be more or less motivating as well. For example, one can argue that some television genres, primarily soap operas and mysteries, inherently motivate more effort in solving their puzzles, keeping track of secrets and clues, and making predictions about character actions (Cantor & Pingree, 1983). Similarly, sports fans may devote exceptional energy to some sports viewing in comparing athletes' performances statistically and in predicting plays.

We also suggest that some situations are motivating for greater expenditure of energy in and of themselves. These situations actually act on individual expectations and reasons for viewing, but we mention situations separately to emphasize that the process begins externally to the individual. For example, viewing with others (e.g., parents) instead of alone could lead to greater effort through mechanisms such as modeling of interest and attention, instantiation of family values (Atkin & Greenberg, 1977), or to less effort through diffusion of the need to keep up with the plot. Or, viewing in competition with other activities could lead to less effort in viewing, although there is some reason to believe that dividing attention actually calls up more effort (Turnure, 1970).

CONCLUSION

The concept of activity is generating a great deal of activity in research on television effects on children (and for effects research generally). To alleviate some of the resulting confusion, we have differentiated between the cognitive activities applied in processing television and the cognitive effort applied to these activities. In so doing, we have also presented a model of how these various elements play a part in the effects of television, and we have proposed several research agendas implied by the combination of concept distinctions and their places in the model.

We want to reemphasize the need to keep distinct the different types of cognitive activity in processing television, as well as to keep clear the difference between effort and activities. This is not to say that these concepts can only be studied individually and in isolation. On the contrary, a large part of our research problem is to deal with a real multiplication of concepts theoretically and operationally.

Finally, we want to reemphasize the receiver-oriented perspective, which gives receivers credit for independence and the ability to construct meanings. In adopting such a perspective, one need not give up all similarity of meanings and effects. Prediction is still possible. But prediction does need a sensitivity to the receiver, and that means increasingly greater care in conceptualizing and operationalizing the products or effects of mass communication. In so doing, we need to distinguish in fairly detailed ways between products at different stages or levels of construction.

All of this multiplication and specification of concepts necessarily multiplies the number of testable hypotheses as well. Our hope is that these more specific hypotheses will also be more powerful.

REFERENCES

Adams, L. T., & Worden, P. E. (1983, April). *Script development and memory organization.* Paper presented at the meeting of the Society for Research in Child Development, Detroit, MI.

Anderson, D. R., & Levin, S. R. (1976). Young children's visual attention to attributes of television. *Child Development, 47,* 806–811.

Anderson, D. R., & Lorch, E. P. (1983). Looking at television: Action or reaction? In J. Bryant & D. R. Anderson (Eds.), *Children's understanding of television* (pp. 1–33). New York: Academic.

Anderson, D. R., Lorch, E. P., Field, D. E., & Sanders, J. (1981). The effects of TV program comprehensibility on preschool children's visual attention to television. *Child Development, 52,* 151–157.

Anderson, D. R., & Smith, R. (1984). Young children's TV viewing: The problem of cognitive continuity. In F. J. Morrison, C. Lord, D. F. Keating (Eds.), *Advances in applied developmental psychology,* (Vol. 1, pp. 115–163). New York: Academic.

Atkin, C. K., & Greenberg, B. S. (1977). *Parental mediation of children's social behavior learned from television.* Unpublished manuscript, Michigan State University, Department of Communication, East Lansing.

Blumler, J. (1979). The role of theory in uses and gratifications research. *Communication Research, 6,* 9–36.

Bower, G., Black, J. B., & Turner, T. J. (1979). Scripts in memory for text. *Cognitive Psychology, 11,* 177–220.

Calvert, S. L., Huston, A. C., Watkins, B. A., & Wright, J. C. (1982). The relation between selective attention to television forms and children's comprehension of content. *Child Development, 53,* 601–610.

Cantor, M. R., & Pingree, S. (1983). *The soap opera.* Beverly Hills, CA: Sage.

Chaffee, S. H., & Choe, S. Y. (1979, April). *Communication measurement in the March 1979 NES pilot study.* Paper presented at the meeting of the American Political Science Association, Washington, DC.

Chomsky, N. Y. (1965). *Aspects of the theory of syntax.* Cambridge, MA: MIT Press.

Collins, W. A. (1970). Learning of media content: A developmental study. *Child Development, 41,* 1133–1142.

Collins, W. A. (1973). The effect of temporal separation between motivation, aggression and consequences: A developmental study. *Developmental Psychology,' 8,* 215–221.

Collins, W. A. (1982). Cognitive processing in television viewing. In D. Pearl, L. Bouthilet, & J. Lazar (Eds.), *Television and behavior: Ten years of scientific progress and implications for the eighties* (Vol. 2, pp. 9–23). Washington, DC: U.S. Government Printing Office.

Collins, W. A. (1983). Interpretation and inference in children's television viewing. In J. Bryant & D. R. Anderson (Eds.), *Children's understanding of television* (pp. 125–150). New York: Academic.

Collins, W. A., Sobol, B. L., & Westby, S. (1981). Effects of adult commentary on children's comprehension and inferences about a televised aggressive portrayal. *Child Development, 52,* 158–163.

Collins, W. A., & Wellman, H. (1983). Social scripts and developmental changes in representations of televised narratives. *Communication Research, 9,* 380–398.

Collins, W. A., Wellman, H., Keniston, A., & Westby, S. (1978). Age-related aspects of comprehension and inference from a televised dramatic narrative. *Child Development, 49,* 389–399.

Dervin, B. (1982). Mass media: Changing conceptions of the audience. In R. E. Rice & W. J. Paisley (Eds.), *Public communication campaigns* (pp. 71–88). Beverly Hills, CA: Sage.

Greenfield, N. S., & Sternbach, R. A. (1972). *Handbook of psycho-physiology.* New York: Holt, Rinehart & Winston.

Hawkins, R. P. (1973). Learning of peripheral content in films: A developmental study. *Child Development, 44,* 214–217.

Hawkins, R. P., & Pingree, S. (1982). Television influence on constructions of social reality. In D. Pearl, L. Bouthilet, & J. Lazar (Eds.), *Television and behavior: Ten years of scientific progress and implications for the eighties* (Vol. 2, pp. 224–247). Washington, DC: U.S. Government Printing Office.

Huston, A. C., & Wright, J. C. (1983). Children's processing of television: The informative functions of formal features. In J. Bryant & D. R. Anderson (Eds.), *Children's understanding of television* (pp. 35–68). New York: Academic.

Kane, J. M., & Anderson, R. C. (1978). Depth of processing and interference effects in the learning and remembering of sentences. *Journal of Educational Psychology, 70,* 626–635.

Leifer, A. D., Collins, W. A., Gross, B. M., Taylor, P. H., Andrews, L., & Blackmer, E. R. (1971). Developmental aspects of variables relevant to observational learning. *Child Development, 42,* 1509–1516.

Lesser, G. (1974). *Children and television: Lessons from Sesame Street.* New York: Random House.

Levy, M. R., & Windahl, S. (1984). Audience activity and gratifications: A conceptual clarification and exploration. *Communication Research, 11,* 51–78.

Lorch, E. P., Anderson, D. R., & Levin, S. R. (1979). The relationship of visual attention to children's comprehension of television. *Child Development, 50,* 722–727.

McLeod, J., Leutscher, W., & McDonald, D. (1980, August). *Beyond mere exposure: Media orientations and their impact on political processes.* Paper presented at the meeting of the Association for Education in Journalism, Boston, MA.

Nelson, K., & Gruendel, J. (1981). Generalized event representations: Basic building blocks of cognitive development. In M. Lamb & A. Brown (Eds.), *Advances in developmental psychology* (Vol. 1, pp. 131–158). Hillsdale, NJ: Lawrence Erlbaum Associates.

Pingree, S. (1978). The effects of nonsexist television commercials and perceptions of reality on children's attitudes about women. *Psychology of Women Quarterly, 2,* 262–277.

Pingree, S. (1983). Cognitive processes in constructing social reality. *Journalism Quarterly, 60,* 415–422.

Pingree, S., & Hawkins, R. P. (1982). What children do with television: Implications for communication research. In B. Dervin & M. Voigt (Eds.), *Progress in communication sciences* (Vol. 3, pp. 225–244). Norwood, NJ: Ablex.

Pingree, S., Hawkins, R. P., Rouner, D., Burns, J., Gikonyo, W., & Neuwirth, C. (1984). Children's reconstruction of a television narrative. *Communication Research, 11,* 477–496.

Reeves, B. (1978). Perceived TV reality as a predictor of children's social behavior. *Journalism Quarterly, 55,* 682–689, 695.

Rice, M. L., Huston, A. C., & Wright, J. C. (1982). The forms and codes of television: Effects on children's attention, comprehension, and social behavior. In D. Pearl, L. Bouthilet, & J. Lazar (Eds.), *Television and behavior: Ten years of scientific progress and implications for the eighties* (Vol. 2, pp. 24–38). Washington, DC: U.S. Government Printing Office.

Rouner, D. L. (1983). *Individual and environmental determinants of television viewing behavior.* Unpublished doctoral dissertation, University of Wisconsin, Madison.

Salomon, G. (1979). *Interaction of media, cognition, and learning.* San Francisco: Jossey-Bass.

Salomon, G. (1983). Television watching and mental effort: A social psychological view. In J. Bryant & D. R. Anderson (Eds.), *Children's understanding of television* (pp. 181–198). New York: Academic.

Schank, R., & Abelson, R. (1977). *Scripts, plans, goals, and understanding.* Hillsdale, NJ: Lawrence Erlbaum Associates.

Smith, R., Anderson, D. R., & Fischer, C. (1985). Young children's comprehension of montage. *Child Development, 55.*

Turnure, J. E. (1970). Children's reactions to distractors in a learning situation. *Developmental Psychology, 2,* 115–122.

Wartella, E. (1978, August). *Children's perceptual unitizing of a televised behavior sequence.* Paper presented at the meeting of the Association for Education in Journalism, Seattle, WA.

Wartella, E. (1979). Children and television: The development of the child's understanding of the medium. In D. Wilhoit & M. de Bock (Eds.), *Mass communication review yearbook* (Vol. 1, pp. 516–553). Beverly Hills, CA: Sage.

Watt, J. H., & Welch, A. J. (1983). Effects of static and dynamic complexity on children's attention and recall of televised instruction. In J. Bryant & D. R. Anderson (Eds.), *Children's understanding of television* (pp. 69–102). New York: Academic.

Wyer, R., & Srull, T. (1981). The processing of social stimulus information: A conceptual integration. In R. Hastie, T. Ostrom, E. Ebbesen, R. Wyer, D. Hamilton, & D. Carlston (Eds.), *Person memory: The cognitive basis of social perception* (pp. 227–300). Hillsdale, NJ: Lawrence Erlbaum Associates.

13

Attention to Television: Psychological Theories and Chronometric Measures

Byron Reeves, Esther Thorson, Joan Schleuder
University of Wisconsin—Madison

Psychologists wince when reminded of William James' (1890) dictum, "Everyone knows what attention is." Mass communication researchers would be equally disturbed if we said, "Everyone knows what attention to television is." In fact, attention to television involves a wide range of stimuli, assumptions, theories, levels of analysis, and methods. In this paper, we suggest reasons for this diversity and for the absence of programmatic development in research. In a brief historical overview, past approaches to the study of television attention are contrasted with recent research innovations. We argue that research questions increasingly involve processes that are covert and that these questions require close examination of relevant psychological studies. Specifically, two areas of the psychological research literature relevant to television are reviewed: information processing and neural functioning. For each, a pilot experiment that uses a television stimulus is reported.

MASS COMMUNICATION APPROACHES TO ATTENTION RESEARCH

A newcomer to mass communication research might expect to find an accumulated wealth of information about attention to television. The object of study (the television screen) is an obvious and fixed starting point, and its physical characteristics have, except for improvements like color, larger screens, and better resolution, remained essentially unchanged. But unfortunately, for a number of reasons, there has not been programmatic growth in research on attention. First, a physical definition of television was never of prime interest. To social scientists, the medium was not defined in terms of fluorescent light, camera angles, spatial frequency, pacing, or zooms and pans, even though artists responsible for producing messages were sensitive to these features. For most researchers, television was content: violence, sports, news, and so forth. This definition was more relevant to social policy, effects analysis, and television executives attempting to attract larger audiences. There have been minor, short-lived psychological considerations of communication technologies per se mainly limited to issues regarding children, for example, possible eye damage from exposure to flickering light in the case of film, loud noise from radio and recorded music, fluorescent radiation from television, and overdeveloped hand-eye coordination from the new computer games (Wartella & Reeves, 1983).

A second reason relates to research agendas. It is natural to ask first the questions that researchers are most capable of answering. This is not only true for individual scholars, but also of research fields, where collections of researchers tacitly formulate agendas and provide leadership by example. The expertise brought to media studies, although interdisciplinary, was not as much related to psychology, especially a psychology of the mind and mental processes, as it was to the social psychology of attitudes and group processes, and the sociology of the mass audience. In retrospect, it is remarkable that the use of reaction-time (RT) measures, sensory tasks, masking, secondary-task procedures, and brain electrical potentials did not emerge as staples of psychological communication research. These techniques were used extensively and successfully throughout the century in research attempting to answer questions similar (at least in hindsight) to those being asked in mass communication. These methods had been used to explore determinants of selective attention, recall and recognition of information, and motivations for information processing. But the procedures did require a measurement expertise (or maybe just equipment) that hindered their use in communication. Social psychology promised that for many questions, introspective techniques were adequate to examine relationships between mind and behavior, and questionnaires, whether used in field surveys or as dependent measures in experiments, were the most reasonable first choice.

Two important developments in mass communication research suggest that the situation is changing. First, there is now a clearer distinction between research questions that are psychological versus sociological. This distinction has had the effect of pushing theory more into the domains of traditional level disciplines, psychology in the case of questions about attention to television. Second, though less important, several techniques used in psychology are now more accessible and feasible for use in mass communication research.

There can be little doubt that questions about attention have changed dramatically during the 30 years of television research. In early studies, attention to television was usually assumed and not thought of as a process to be studied. Attention was considered a necessary precondition for learning or attitude change, or for any other type of behavioral effect, and direct measurement of it seemed superfluous because attention could be inferred if effects were found. The information recalled was assumed to be that which was selected for attention and processing. Most often, attention was measured by merely asking people if they watched a program. There was a heyday of emphasis on selective attention (Donohew & Tipton, 1973; Sears & Freedman, 1971), but this referred more to a choice between competing message sources (usually newspapers) or analysis of the reasons for deciding to use one medium rather than another (Comstock, Chaffee, Katzman, McCombs, & Roberts, 1978). In these cases, selective attention was more a surrogate concept for the entirety of mental processing rather than the first part of a series of mental exercises that would determine the information available for subsequent processing.

When researchers examining cognitive development (but trained in communication) became interested in children's attention to television, the concept became explicitly mental, sharing important features (if not measures) with similar concepts in psychology.[1] But this new approach was born as much of pragmatic as of theoretical concerns. Studies of media effects showed that prosocial as well as antisocial acts could be learned from television (Bandura, 1977; Stein & Friedrich, 1972). This naturally led to the creation of effective educational programs that would attract and hold children's attention long enough for good things to be processed and learned. At the same time, popular books voiced concerns that children spent too much time passively watching television (Mander, 1978; Winn, 1977). Fear surfaced that television seized and held viewer attention with constant sensory stimulation, fast-paced scene changes, and other tricks of the trade.

This was a significant departure from past concerns related to theory and policy for two reasons. Most obviously, the shift emphasized the form and structure of television in addition to content. Concepts like pacing, movement, and zooms were thought to be as responsible for effects as violence, politics, and advertising. Second, and more important, these issues caused researchers to look at television viewing and attention to messages as an event that not only varied between people at a single point in time, but as a process that varied within individuals over time. This was an important contribution, but unfortunately, questions focused almost exclusively on developmental issues.

Most research tried to determine the program attributes that caused children to attend to television rather than to distractions such as toys or slides shown simultaneously. Episodes of *Sesame Street* or *The Electric Company* served as stimulus messages, and attention was defined exclusively as visual selection (Alwitt, Anderson, Lorch, & Levin, 1980; Anderson & Levin, 1976; Anderson, Levin, & Lorch, 1977; Krull & Husson, 1980; Ward & Wackman, 1973; Wartella

---

[1]There were some attempts to have people orally describe the amount of attention given to certain media and content within a medium, and these measures were more successful than questions about mere exposure (see Hawkins, Ibok, & Pingree, 1983, for a review).

& Ettema, 1974; Watkins, Huston-Stein, & Wright, 1981).[2] Attention was measured by a hidden observer who pushed a button (connected to a real-time recording device) when a child's eyes were directed toward the television screen and
released the button when the child looked away. Although the televised messages
have varied across studies, this eyes-on-screen measure has dominated.

In summary, the recent research on children's cognitive processing has had
important effects on mass communication research. This literature has clearly
defined attention as a psychological, cognitive process that varies within individuals over time. Attention is an important beginning of a sequence of mental
events that culminates in the encoding and storage of information and ultimately
in its use. This approach has led to three new questions about the psychology
of attention to television. First, it has caused researchers to redefine the television
stimulus and ask, in addition to questions about semantic content, what effects
structural features and symbol systems have on attention. A second question
asks which aspects of television attention are under the voluntary control of the
viewer and which, if any, are involuntary and controlled by the stimulus. Finally,
there are questions about the relationship between attending to television and
comprehension and learning.

Although these questions are relatively new to mass communication research,
they are not new in psychology. At first glance, psychological research appears
filled with as many different conflicting conceptualizations, research tasks, and
methods as exist in mass communication. These apparent differences, however,
should not be taken as evidence of a research area in disarray. In fact, a current
assessment of attention research suggests there has been cumulative development
and commonality of assumptions in the research conducted over the last 100
years (Posner, 1982). This observation is made even though research has progressed in three distinct areas, labeled by Posner as introspection, information
processing, and neural processes. Two of these areas are emphasized in this
review: theories of information processing and research about the orienting reflex.

INFORMATION-PROCESSING APPROACHES
TO ATTENTION RESEARCH

Although experimental studies of attention in psychology have been carried on
for more than 100 years (Norman, 1976), information-processing concepts of
attention were initiated by British researchers in the 1950s (Broadbent, 1958;
Cherry, 1953; Moray, 1959). Early studies used a task called *shadowing* (Cherry,
1953). Subjects were required to repeat aloud, or shadow, a message heard in
one ear while a second message was presented simultaneously to the other ear.
Not surprisingly, people could recall more of the shadowed information. To

---

[2]Detailed reviews of these studies can be found in Bryant and Anderson (1983).

explain this, Broadbent (1958) hypothesized that people were severely limited in how much information they could acquire at one time. According to Broadbent's model, a filter located in an early part of the system could be tuned to only one input channel (e.g., a single intensity, frequency, or sensory modality). Stimuli in untuned channels could register in a preattentive store, but only information that passed through the filter could reach long-term memory and be recalled.

Broadbent's filter theory explained early findings in the shadowing studies, but additional experiments soon demonstrated that limitations on attention were not so simple. Treisman (1960) showed that people could follow meaning shifts across sensory channels, recognizing, for example, "Dear Aunt Sally," even when "Aunt" was presented in a different ear (or sensory channel) than "Dear" and "Sally." Norman (1969) showed that if people were stopped in the middle of a shadowing task, they could recognize both the shadowed and the unshadowed messages. In fact, there were numerous demonstrations that the filter was not tuned to a single input (e.g., Corteen & Wood, 1972; MacKay, 1973).

A number of models were proposed to account for the new results. Deutsch and Deutsch (1963) and Norman (1968) suggested there was an attentional filter but that it operated only after stimuli had been processed sufficiently to be recognized. These late-filter models, however, had trouble explaining why people, when asked to shadow one channel but also respond to designated targets in another channel, were still much more accurate for the shadowed information (Moray & O'Brien, 1967; Treisman & Geffen, 1967). These findings led to a third model that incorporated aspects of each previous idea. Treisman (1960) proposed that Broadbent's filter was not an all-or-nothing gate, but rather one that amplified some inputs and attenuated others. Treisman also said that the channel tuned to a filter could be either physical, as in Broadbent's model, or meaningful, as in the Deutsch–Norman model.

In 1973, Kahneman proposed that attention was not a filter mechanism, but a capacity for arousal and performance of mental work. Arousal could vary in total amount, and it could be allocated in different ways to a range of tasks, but it was always guided by four processes. The first involved enduring dispositions that guided involuntary attention to novel, moving, or meaningful stimuli. Momentary intentions, a second process, guided voluntary attention. For example, when people were requested to attend to messages presented only to the left ear, they would voluntarily direct attention to that ear. A third process was controlled by attention demands. Attention was allocated to tasks in relation to the effort required to perform them. When the need for attention exceeded capacity, people would simply stop performing a task. When two activities demanded more capacity than was available, only one would be completed. The fourth process involved the effects of arousal. When arousal was low, selectivity was also low, and irrelevant cues were accepted uncritically. When arousal was high, selectivity and performance improved because irrelevant cues were rejected.

With further increases, however, relevant cues were again ignored and perform-ance deteriorated.

Attention Tasks

Ideas about attention have continued to change, but before summarizing the most current research, it is important to note that each different theoretical statement in the literature is intimately associated with a particular measurement paradigm. Six categories of tasks have been prominent in the psychological literature. Each task is potentially relevant to the study of attention to television, and some have already been applied, but usually in altered form.

The *vigilance task* requires people to wait for an event (e.g., an electronic blip on a radar screen) and to respond as quickly as possible when it occurs. For example, Mackworth (1950) had people watch a clock second hand and press a key whenever it made a 2-sec jump. Typical of most vigilance findings, he found that performance was quick and accurate for about half an hour, but thereafter, major response errors occurred. Given the long periods that people spend watching television, it would seem useful to examine viewing behavior as a vigilant attentional process.

There are already suggestions in the mass communication literature that vig-ilance decreases during a single viewing period, although the results are limited to child audiences. Husson and Krull (1983), for example, determined that attention, measured as the amount of time children had their eyes on the screen, decreased over a 1-hr period and, more important, that visual complexity was negatively related to attention during the first 30 min, but unrelated in the final half hour. This suggests that not only may vigilance change over time, but the visual features affecting attention may be differentially influential depending on when they occur in a viewing period. Husson and Krull caution that analyses that do not account for this trend, or nonstationarity, will be biased.

A second kind of task involves *presentation of simultaneous sources of stim-ulation* along with instructions to attend to only one. The shadowing task belongs to this category.These tasks seem natural for the study of television, itself a source of simultaneous inputs. To what extent do people select only the audio or only the video portion of the television message? How does the integration of the two channels affect selection? Do different viewing motivations bias attention in favor of one channel?

The simultaneous inputs need not be separate channels in a single presentation (audio and visual information in the case of television). It would be possible to require simultaneous attention to two separate programs on different television sets. This task could be used to correlate primitive and semantic cues in programs with the selection of a particular screen, assuming people were instructed to attend to both presentations as much as possible. A version of this task, used in psychology to study selective looking, parallels more exactly the original audio-shadowing experiments. Subjects are presented with two video-taped episodes simultaneously, in full superimposition, and are asked to attend to one and ignore the other (Becklen & Cervone, 1983; Neisser & Becklen, 1975). People are able to accomplish the task with high accuracy even though the visual jumbling is a less likely natural occurrence than simultaneous auditory inputs.

The *dual-processing task* also involves simultaneous sources of stimulation, but people are required to process both signals. The earliest task was the split-span experiment (Broadbent, 1954) in which people were given pairs of stimuli, one to each ear, and were asked to report both. In the secondary task paradigm, there is an ongoing primary task, such as following a pursuit rotor, listening to a story, or reading, accompanied by a second task, such as an occasional flash or tone to which people must also respond. Dual-processing tasks have been particularly useful for investigating the attentional cost of complex primary tasks (e.g., Posner & Snyder, 1975), and for this reason, we have conducted a pilot television study using this method (reported in a later section).

Attentional preparation tasks vary in detail but in general involve giving people cues or primes before stimulus occurrences. Individuals are then asked about the cue's effect on processing. Semantic priming studies (e.g., Becker, 1980; Ratcliff & McKeon, 1978) examine how words with semantic relationships to a target differentially affect response time to the target. Cuing studies (e.g., LaBerge, 1975) present primes that carry different probabilistic information about an upcoming target and examine the effects of that preinformation on attentional preparation.

Television can be thought of as a continuous process of priming or cuing. This is true whether an announcer overtly prepares viewers for upcoming visuals or more subtle visual cues are used to promote attention (or to indicate that attention is unnecessary). There have been some attempts to study the effects of priming on attention, but once again, the research comes from the literature on children and television. For example, Palmer and McDowell (1979) tested the ability of separation devices that occur between regular programs and commercials to signal or cue children that a commercial is about to appear. These devices had little effect on kindergarten and first-grade children, but this same strategy could be used to study the sequencing of other visual devices (e.g., pans, zooms, audio silence, screen luminance, pacing) and their ability to prime attention for subsequent program content. Other questions could be asked about the effects of uncued or abrupt scene changes on attention and the circumstances under which cuing increases processing efficiency.

In *perceptual intrusion tasks*, stimuli are arranged so that people cannot avoid attending to a particular stimulus dimension. The classic task in this category is the Stroop test (1935). People are asked to call out the ink color used to print color names. Inhibition occurs when the word and color do not match (e.g., *red* printed in blue ink). Facilitation occurs when word and color do match (*red* printed in red ink). The original hypothesis was that the color words were attended to involuntarily; hence, there were inhibition or facilitation effects. It was also hypothesized that involuntary reading carried no attentional cost and was therefore performed automatically (Keele, 1972; Posner & Snyder, 1975). Although the second hypothesis has been questioned (Kahneman & Chajczyk, 1983), the paradigm still is an interesting one for television viewing. One application could involve inconsistencies (or consistencies) between semantic content and the formal structure of presentations. For example, there may be intrusive effects of fast-paced editing on intimate scenes or slow pacing for scenes meant to convey action.

Attention switching tasks form the sixth category. In these tasks, subjects must change their focus from one stimulus to another without changing their overt orienting responses, such as eye position (e.g., Sperling & Reeves, 1980). Alternatively, subjects may expect to process one stimulus but actually receive another (e.g., LaBerge, 1975). These tasks are recent innovations and would seem to be of particular importance to the television viewer. Attention is often internally guided from one aspect of the message to another, for example, from music, to dialogue, to actors, even to whether a better program is on a different channel. How fast can viewers switch attention? Is there an intrinsic pattern to the switching? Do some people switch more often than others, depending on viewing motivation? Do some programs provoke more or less switching?

Present Theorizing About Attention

In spite of several experimental paradigms, there is some consensus about how attention works. Posner (1982) argued that four basic ideas about attention are consistent with all theories and data. First, mental operations related to attention require time to perform. The amount of time required to think about and make decisions and the sequencing of mental events required to perform tasks will correspond to fixed qualities of stimuli and discretionary strategies of individuals. Second, mental events occurring closely in time are processed successively. The amount of interference one task produces for attention to another is used as a measure of the common capacity they require. Third, internal events can be studied by observing the amount of facilitation or inhibition they cause. This process is hierarchically influential such that higher levels of the nervous system inhibit lower levels and control central attention. Fourth, attentional processing favors stimulus change. An orienting reflex biases people toward fresh or novel sources of stimulation. Posner argued that these results are also consistent with the studies of conscious experience and neural processing.

Within information-processing research, the agreement covers basic assumptions as well as theoretical models. For example, the early distinction between filter and capacity limitations on attention has faded, and following the lead of Navon and Gopher (1979, 1980), new models combine structural and capacity concepts of limitation (e.g., Kahneman & Chajczyk, 1983; Moore, 1981). Navon and Gopher (1979) have suggested that attention requires mechanisms that are used differently depending on the task to be performed. These mechanisms are limited in number, as is the capacity required to use them. Their model predicts that the nature of attentional tasks will determine whether they can be performed simultaneously, without costs to each other. This approach is similar to the distinction between automatic versus controlled processing (Shiffrin & Schneider, 1977), the cost-benefit analysis of Posner (1978), and the classic British studies of attention. Further, it is consistent with the physiological work of attention theorists who have proposed a principle of functional cerebral distance (e.g., Kinsbourne & Hicks, 1978). Brain control centers that are highly connected will conflict if they are independently engaged in unrelated activity.

A second area of progress concerns the information-processing level of attentional limits. There has been movement away from Broadbent's equating of attention and consciousness toward the idea that early input to the human system includes more stimulation than is experienced consciously. The bottleneck appears to be the capacity for conscious attention. Several studies support the existence of an unlimited preattention system (Marcel, 1983; Neisser, 1967; Shaffer & LaBerge, 1979) or preperceptual storage (Averbach & Coriell, 1961; Massaro, 1975), in which unconscious processing occurs. Neisser (1967) suggested that processing at this level consists of monitoring movement and governing innate or well-learned body movements. Kahneman, Treisman, and Burkell (1983) represent preperceptual processing as unique memory traces that are episodic in nature, temporary and addressable by either spatiotemporal coordinates or physical attributes of stimuli. They call these preattentive representations *object files* and suggest that they operate automatically and outside consciousness, but under a system of costs and benefits similar to conscious attention. There is then evidence for two kinds of attentional processing: the conscious semantic "display board of the mind" (Shiffrin & Schneider, 1977; Johnston & Dark, 1982) and the automatic, unconscious, and preattentive type. This distinction is also made in the orienting literature, discussed in a later section.

A Pilot Television Information-Processing Study

Although many of the information-processing paradigms and models have interesting implications for television research, we selected the secondary task for use in a pilot application. The secondary task has been suggested as one suitable for investigating real-world processing (Posner, 1982), and there have been studies of attention to textual messages that imply applicability to complex stimuli such as television (Britton, Holdredge, Curry, & Westbrook, 1979; Britton, Westbrook, Holdredge, 1978). Britton et al. (1978) showed that, as expected, people read difficult passages more slowly than easy ones and remembered less about them. Nevertheless, responses to a periodic click (the secondary task) were more rapid in the difficult text condition. Britton et al. eliminated the hypothesis that higher arousal and interest in the difficult text lead to the RT advantage and suggested as an alternative that easy reading "fills cognitive capacity" to a greater extent than does difficult reading and slows RT to the click.

Another explanation is possible. As noted earlier, Posner (1982), Kinsbourne and Hicks (1978), and Navon and Gopher (1979) cite evidence that tasks will interfere with each other inversely to their similarity. There is also evidence that when subjects process language at a meaningful level there is motor encoding of relevant responses. The motor encoding occurs simultaneously with the stimulus encoding (Brady & Levitt, 1966; Brown, 1968; Lang, 1979; Shaw, 1940). Motor encoding that occurs with simple messages is similar to the motor requirements of the RT task and, consequently, may interfere more with the secondary task.

The task developed for the pilot test was comparable to the one used by Britton et al. (1979). The primary question was whether the visual and auditory complexity of short messages affected viewer attention. Simple auditory detection was used as the secondary task. We predicted that RT to the secondary task would be faster for complex visuals than for simple ones. We also predicted that memory, as in Britton's study, would be poorer for complex than simple messages.

A second question was whether elimination of the visual channel (the audio only, *AO*, condition) would lead to fewer processing demands and, hence, less decrement in performance on the secondary task. To test this, half the subjects heard but did not see the messages while performing the secondary task. Faster RTs were expected in the AO condition than in the audio plus visual (AV) condition. Results in the predicted directions would demonstrate the applicability of the secondary task to television and show that the psychological processes involved in television watching and reading are comparable.

The stimuli were 30-sec television commercials. Initially, 32 commercials were included to represent four combinations of audio and visual complexity: auditory simple, visual simple; auditory simple, visual complex; auditory complex, visual simple; and auditory complex, visual complex. To select the commercials, pretest subjects were asked to view each one and then to rate either audio or visual complexity on a 100-point scale. One third of the subjects only heard the commercials, one third only saw them, and one third were exposed to both channels. The averaged ratings from these groups were used to select four commercials from each category.

Of the 40 subjects tested individually, 20 only heard the commercials (AO) and 20 both heard and viewed them (AV). In both conditions, subjects were presented with 2 practice commercials followed by the 16 experimental ones, presented in random order. Four tones occurred in randomly selected locations in each commercial, no two closer than 4 sec apart. Subjects were instructed to attend closely to the messages and press a RT button as fast as possible after hearing the tones. They were also forewarned that there would be a comprehension test for each commercial. AO subjects were given a verbal recognition test after each commercial, and AV subjects were given both a verbal and a visual recognition test. The verbal test questions each provided six similar versions of a phrase from each message. Subjects had to select the one they heard. The visual recognition test (presented on video tape) provided six similar visual frames from commercials, and subjects had to indicate whether or not they had seen each frame in the commercial just viewed.

Although analysis of variance failed to show a significant main effect of viewing condition (AO vs. AV), the mean RTs in the AO condition were faster than those in the AV condition for each of the 16 commercials. This showed that the addition of visual information added an attentional burden to television watching, slowing response to the secondary task.

The effects of stimulus complexity can be seen in Fig. 13.1 and 13.2. Auditory complexity did not affect RT, but complex visual commercials led to significantly faster RTs than did simple ones, $F(1,38) = 11.60$, $p < .002$. There was no interaction between viewing condition and the effects of visual complexity.

Subjects who only heard the commercials were affected by visual complexity identically to those who both heard and saw them. It is difficult to see how a visual stimulus that was not present could affect processing. One hypothesis is that the AO subjects were "imaging" the unseen visuals, thus allowing visual complexity to have an effect, but not causing as much of an attentional burden as actually seeing the commercials (since the AO condition was still faster than the AV condition). This hypothesis is consistent with Lang's (1979) model of how linguistic events are stored. Greater subject involvement should lead to more integration of present information with past experience. This result is also consistent with Britton and Tesser's (1982) contention that simple tasks lead to

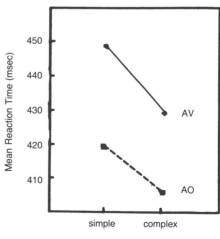

FIG. 13.1 Reaction time as a function of visual complexity and viewing condition.

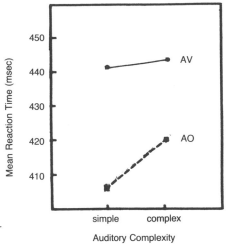

FIG. 13.2 Reaction time as a function of auditory complexity and viewing condition.

slower RTs because people bring more prior knowledge into conscious attention, exhausting a limited resource. If simple material is indeed more involving, unseen simple visuals should slow RT more than unseen complex visuals. Investigation of this possibility awaits further research.

Figures 13.3 and 13.4 show the performance scores. Consistent with expectation, the phrases from auditory-complex commercials were more poorly recalled, $F(1,19) = 7.25, p < .01$, and video frames from visual-complex commercials were more poorly recognized, $F(1,19) = 39.12, p < .001$. No interactions were significant.

The results of the pilot study are encouraging. They are consistent with the application of the secondary task to reading (Britton et al., 1978), indicating some validity for the procedure as a measure of attentional demands during television viewing. The results also suggest additional questions. First, is greater secondary task interference from visually simple messages the result of simple motor encoding of the visual portion of the messages? We plan to study this by varying the modality of the secondary task and manipulating level of processing (e.g., using a discrimination task instead of detection). Second, is the effect of unseen visual complexity due to the nature of image encoding by the AO subjects? This could be investigated by instructing the subjects either to image more or to image less, as has been done in other psychological experiments (Paivio, 1971). Finally, why is there no effect of auditory complexity on the secondary task when the effect on performance is significant? This may occur because auditory encoding is less active than visual processing and therefore interferes less with auditory detection. We plan to study this by asking people to rate the involvement of the two channels separately.

In summary, the study of attention from an information-processing perspective

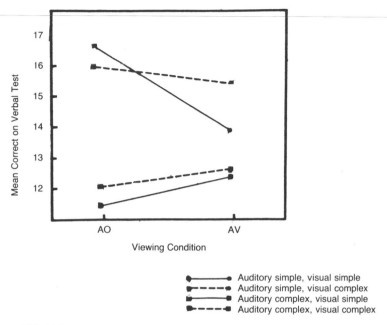

FIG. 13.3 Verbal performance as a function of viewing condition and auditory and visual complexity.

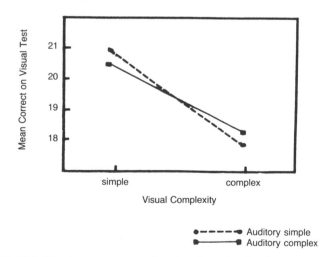

FIG. 13.4 Visual performance as a function of visual and auditory complexity.

is useful and feasible. The literature is rich in theory and method, many of which are relevant to applied questions about attention to television. A second area of research applicable to the same questions concerns orienting responses, and not only have media researchers failed to capitalize on this literature, but so have many psychologists. In the next section, we attempt to point out overlap between the two areas, but for the most part, the research and researchers have been separate. The studies are, however, full of similar concepts and conclusions, even if expressed with unique vocabularies.

ORIENTING RESPONSE APPROACHES
TO ATTENTION RESEARCH

Loud bangs and bright flashes are hard to ignore, especially when unexpected. For good reason, we immediately adjust our posture toward novel stimuli. This orientation, or "what-is-it?" reaction, first described by Pavlov (1927), prepares people to deal with novelty by making them more sensitive to incoming stimuli and helping to mobilize the body for action, if necessary. In the most basic sense, these orientations serve as a guide to attention, alertness, and vigilance. Since the 1950s, the growing literature about the orienting response (OR) has been concerned with human attention to audio and visual stimuli, and orienting reactions have even been hypothesized to affect attention to television (Singer, 1980; Zillmann, 1982). But before reviewing applications to television research, what exactly is the OR and what stimuli elicit it?

Apart from simply turning toward the source of a novel stimulus, it is now clear that the orienting reaction involves several other physiological changes (Lynn, 1966). There is an increased ability to detect light and sound. Irrelevant ongoing reactions are temporarily arrested, and general muscle tonus increases (indicated by increased electrical activity in the muscles). There is increased cortical arousal (faster and lower amplitude EEG activity) and galvanic skin reactions. Also, blood vessels to the limbs constrict while those to the brain dilate, presumably to facilitate cortical processing. Although there are individual differences in the magnitude and sometimes even the presence of these responses, each has a higher probability of occurrence immediately after the presentation of novel and unexpected stimulation.

A critical feature of the OR is that the magnitude of reaction is not equal for repeated stimulations. A process of habituation occurs, which shows decreased response to the same stimulus after repetition. This is clearly adaptive, otherwise we could spend a great deal of life orienting. Outside the laboratory, for example, the process of habituation has been used to explain how inner city residents adapt to unusually high levels of urban noise (Glass & Singer, 1972).

Although there are disagreements about the specifics of habituation as applied to the OR in humans (Graham, 1973), seven results summarize the substantial literature (Thompson, Berry, Rinalai, & Berger, 1979):

1. Repeated stimulation results in a decrease in OR (usually a negative exponential).

2. After stimulation is stopped, spontaneous recovery occurs.

3. Long-term habituation can occur (e.g., habituation to repetitions of a stimulus over the course of several minutes could affect the rate of habituation to the same stimulus presented several hours or days later).

4. Habituation is directly proportional to stimulus frequency (i.e., shorter intervals between stimuli will increase the rate of habituation).

5. Habituation is inversely proportional to stimulus intensity (i.e., more intense stimuli will cause slower habituation).

6. Habituation exhibits some degree of stimulus generalization.

7. Presentation of a different stimulus can cause *dishabituation*, which itself habituates with repetition.

How Does the Orienting Response Work?

Unlike the information-processing models that deal with mental black boxes or computer analogies for cognitive processes, the OR paradigm proposes an intervening physiological mechanism that accounts for attention. The most influential model of the OR and attention was proposed by the Russian psychologist Sokolov (1960, 1963). He suggested that the cortex compares all incoming information with expectations based on previous inputs or models. If the incoming stimulus does not match a preexisting cortical model, then the reticular system, a more basic amplifying system for arousal, activates the cortex, which in turn produces an OR, attention, and a new cortical model. However, if a stimulus matches the cortical model, the reticular system is inhibited, and nothing happens but passive perception. The basic principle is a match–mismatch rule governed by the cortex.

Sokolov's model, though simple and elegant, is somewhat incomplete. First, he does not say much about how the cortex accomplishes the matching other than to suggest a general feature analysis system. Second, more recent studies indicate that habituation to mismatch, predicted accurately by Sokolov, may not be a single dimension of reaction (Groves & Thompson, 1970; Thompson et al., 1979). Dual-process theories of habituation propose that repeated stimulation results in the development of two separate processes: habituation and sensitization (or dishabituation). Because the OR involves lower thresholds for sensory input, new stimuli, introduced during the process of habituation, can be sensed independently of the habituation process, but the recovery process will continue as if no habituation had occurred. In spite of these problems, Sokolov's theory has received considerable support in laboratories in the United States, Russia, and

Europe, and it remains a reasonable explanation for the brain's processing of novelty and allocation of attention.

What Causes the Orienting Response?

Novelty is the overriding characteristic that elicits the OR, although other stimulus features make it more probable, stronger, and/or more resistant to habituation (van Olst, Heemstra, & Kortenaar, 1979). Probabilistic determinants of the OR other than novelty are surprise and predictability. In addition to the detection of match and mismatch, this could include discovery of an unexpected stimulus change or a resequencing of stimuli that have previously been presented in a certain order. Sensory determinants refer to the intensity and duration of stimuli as well as features such as tone, frequency, and color. Structural determinants of the OR are characteristics of the stimuli such as complexity, number of elements, asymmetry, and information value.

Television certainly has its share of novel sights and sounds, and consequently, it would seem reasonable to assume that television could cause ORs. Theories of the OR, however, are based on experimental studies that concentrate on isolatable and manipulatable pure forms of stimuli, mostly single laboratory surprises like loud tones played several times in sequence and without other confusion in the background. This allows a precise determination of physiological reaction to a specific stimulus and also detailed information about habituation. Unfortunately, this situation bears little resemblance to the structural complexity and overtly meaningful information available on television. Only recently have researchers begun to analyze television messages with specific reference to orienting demands and habituation, although the discussions have been cursory, hypothetical, and related mostly to child audiences and educational programming. No data on television and cortical arousal have as yet been reported in the mass communication literature.

Singer (1980) claims, however, that television can elicit the OR and that many programs for children (e.g., *Sesame Street*) continually exploit it by purposefully designing messages in favor of constant change. These changes—in the form of scene shifts, extreme acoustical changes, and unexpected motion—cause the OR and appear frequently enough to make habituation impossible. Singer also suggests that the same strategy is used to capture attention in adult programming. Writers of adventure shows, for example, realize they must introduce action with conversation and other plot developments or risk losing their audience. Further, Singer claims that constant orienting is detrimental to learning and understanding. Although others acknowledge that television can cause ORs, they do not think that performance is jeopardized either because the OR may directly facilitate learning (Zillmann, 1982; Zillmann & Bryant, 1981) or because viewers are as likely to follow meaningful characteristics of stories as they are to be passively manipulated by message structure (Anderson & Lorch, 1983).

There are few ecological reasons to orient to the screen (television is not something to eat, nor is it likely to pose a physical threat to viewers), but this lack of adaptive value may not preclude an OR. In fact, a careful reading of the stimulus descriptions that elicit the OR suggests that television (and film) may be uniquely structured to facilitate that response. Primitive features of message structure, especially edits, zooms, and movement, are instances of perceptual mismatch that are unlikely events in the real world. It is difficult to image, for example, a more abrupt mismatch than a visual edit occurring within 1/30 of a second. It is rare that we blink and have a substantial portion of our visual field change.

An important question is whether features like scene changes and the onset of movement remain a determinant of the OR and attention when they are translated to the television screen. It may be impossible (at least unconsciously) to divorce perception of television forms from perceptions in the real world, even though the television set remains stationary. The ecological significance of attention to movement in any domain may override an inclination to consider television as a unique stimulus, incapable of producing physical threats or opportunities.

A Pilot Study of Orienting to Television

We tested ORs in relation to primitive visual cues on television by examining brain electrical activity recorded via electrodes attached to the scalp (Reeves et al., in press). The recording is called the electroencephalogram (EEG). The frequency spectrum and amplitude of this activity change as a function of internal and external variables, and when greatly amplified, the aggregation of these signals can serve as an index of covert mental processing. The dominant frequency of the EEG is alpha (8–12 cycles per sec). The amount of alpha present in the EEG varies inversely with the amount of mental activity or cortical arousal. Alpha can be recorded from most places on the scalp, although it is most prominent in the occiput or rear of the head.

EEG assessment provides a valuable method for assessing the OR in relation to quickly moving stimuli such as television. First, the alpha frequency has long been known to vary inversely with mental arousal (Doyle, Ornstein, & Galin, 1974; Gevins et al., 1979; Mulholland & Runnals, 1962), and there is substantial evidence that alpha rhythms change during ORs such that lower alpha amplitudes indicate greater cortical arousal (Lynn, 1966). There is also evidence that these changes occur in relation to television messages and that the alpha reaction habituates after repeated stimulation (Mulholland, 1973). Second, unlike eye fixation methods used in past television research to measure overt attention to the screen, brain wave measures can be used to assess covert attention. Also, they do not require conscious reports by viewers, they react quickly, and they can be recorded over small time units to allow examination of causal sequences between the structural features of messages and attention.

A test of ORs produced by television was accomplished using continuous alpha recordings taken during the second half of a 1-hr viewing period. Occipital and central alpha levels for 26 subjects were recorded and averaged for each half-second interval of programming (television commercials) and were then correlated with the presence or absence of edits and movement. The video was analyzed frame by frame to determine the exact location of these features.

The time series for three sample messages are plotted in Fig. 13.5. Each horizontal line represents a 30-sec message (60 time units). The points in the message where edits occurred are shown by vertical arrows, and the portions with moving objects or people (not camera movement, e.g., zooms and pans) are shown by the broken lines above each series. It is possible to determine visually two important features of each series. First, each contained a considerable amount of autocorrelation. This indicated that alpha variation followed relatively smooth changes rather than abrupt fluctuations. Second, alpha was positively related to the passage of time for one message, indicating that attention decreased as the message progressed.

The hypothesis that alpha would respond to edits and movements (evidence of an OR) was tested by regressing alpha on two time series coded to indicate

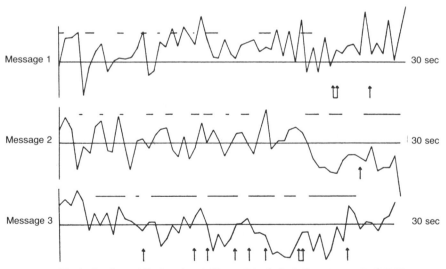

The broken lines at the top of each 30-sec series indicate the presence or absence of movement in the visual channel of the message.

The vertical arrows indicate the location of edits

FIG. 13.5 Aggregated alpha values plotted every half second for three 30-sec messages (from Reeves et al., in press).

the presence or absence of movement and edits. The regression equations were computed on the residuals for each alpha series after accounting for regular variation in alpha (autocorrelation and nonstationarity). The analyses showed that a significant portion of the variance in alpha (45–70%) could be predicted with the covariates, movement, and scene changes. By comparing predictions at different lagged pairings of the visual cues and alpha, it was determined that alpha dropped immediately after each cue and continued to drop for approximately 1.5 sec.

The regression analyses showed that it was possible to predict alpha variation using two crude measures of visual structure, but the data did not show clearly that television cues caused a rapid alpha drop followed by gradual recovery. This could have been caused by constant dishabituation or interruption of the recovery by other cues that also elicited an orientation. Careful examination of each series in Fig. 13.5 shows that a movement sequence or edit often ended and another began within the time expected for recovery (2 to 20 sec). This interference is in addition to other unknown characteristics of television messages that could disrupt habituation.

A second analysis controlled for these influences (Fig. 13.6) . The mean value of alpha for all segments where movement began or an edit occurred was plotted over seven time points. Alpha values were excluded at subsequent time points if a second movement sequence or edit was encountered. The vertical axis at $t + 0$ represents onset of the stimulus cue. A pattern of rapid alpha drop followed by a gradual recovery is evident. Taken together, these analyses indicate that it is possible for primitive visual elements of television to elicit an OR and that withdrawal of the stimulus will cause spontaneous recovery.

The Orienting Response and Meaningful Stimuli

Another important determinant of the OR is signal value or stimulus relevance. ORs are stronger and more resistant to habituation for meaningful stimuli. This feature has often been ignored or dealt with only in relation to arbitrary, conditioned, laboratory stimuli that are otherwise neutral (e.g., flashes and tones). However, signal value can also refer to permanent qualities of information (e.g., one's name) or to stimuli that have momentary significance either because of instructions from an experimenter (e.g., "pay attention to the tone when it occurs") or receiver-determined significance (e.g., information critical for completing a task).

Sokolov (1963) introduced the concept of *signal stimulus*, although his reference was primarily to stimuli that were conditioned to elicit certain reactions. For example, if subjects were required to press a button after hearing a tone, the tone would then become a conditioned stimulus for a specific reaction. Later research questioned whether every stimulus change automatically resulted in an

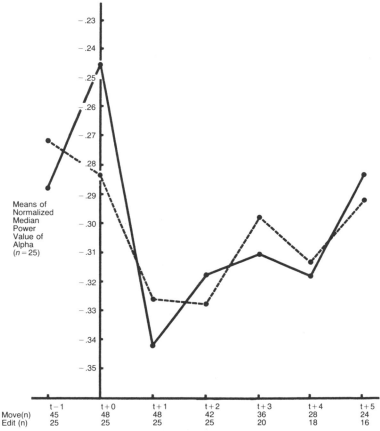

Number of half-second time units before and after the beginning (t + 0) of movement and edits

FIG. 13.6 Reaction of alpha to the beginning of movement (dotted line) and edit placements (solid line) (from Reeves et al., in press).

OR apart from conditioning. According to Bernstein (1969), following the detection of a mismatch there must still be an evaluation of the relevance of the change. He proposed that this evaluation, occurring instantly, meant that the OR was more a "what does this mean?" response rather than simply a response designed to determine "what is it?" or "what has to be done?"

The addition of meaning to a list of stimulus features that elicit the OR is critical. First, it allows for voluntary selective attention to significant stimuli that are not loud bangs or bright flashes. It has even been suggested that ORs can be generated internally at people's discretion (Maltzman, Langdon, & Feerey, 1970). Second, allowing for an active role of the receiver helps sharpen the distinction between automatic processing and more advanced, selective, and resource-limited processing. This distinction is critical not only in the OR literature; it has also been defined in cognitive psychology as a distinction between controlled and automatic processing (Shiffrin & Schneider, 1977) and between episodic and semantic memory (Tulving, 1970). The similarities in findings from these unconnected studies were summarized by Pribram (1979): "There is good evidence to believe that all these distinctions refer to the same two types of learning mechanism: the controlled, context-dependent, episodic, which is a manifestation of the frontolimbic function, and the automatic, context-free, semantic, which refers to the posteriolateral cerebral convexity" (p. 11). There are numerous synonyms for automatic and controlled, to be sure, but the major conclusion should not be lost. The organism and the stimulus can control attention and, hence, memory and performance. Theories that ignore one in favor of the other will be incomplete. The most important question is not whether people are active or passive processors. But when they are either or both, how does each process work, and with what consequence for retention of experience and later performance?

These prescriptions seem especially appropriate for current communication theories that attempt to juxtapose competitively active and reactive models. Although syntheses have been suggested (e.g., Anderson & Lorch, 1983; Bryant, Zillmann, & Brown, 1983; Krull & Husson, 1979), most reports of research about attention to television begin with a historical note saying that the reactive models of the past have been replaced with a realization that viewers are actively attempting to make sense of television content quite independently of visual and auditory gimmicks. The recent OR literature proposes that the kind of stimulation occurring on television may determine whether attentional control is voluntary or involuntary. Some primitive stimuli command involuntary responses, as shown in the EEG reactions to edits and movement. Most of these stimuli (also including pans, zooms, loud and sudden noise, etc.) derive their attentional value through the evolutionary significance of detecting movement. Other kinds of stimulation do not demand attention, but instead allow the viewer to select or not, presumably depending on internal events. This category consists mainly of the semantic content of programming. Content that is interesting, meaningful, or important to the viewer will draw attention voluntarily.

The Orienting Response and Information-Processing Models

Aside from Pribram's brief synthesis of research areas, there has been little cross-referencing between the OR and information-processing literatures, even though there are several places in OR research where cognitive concepts are used (the reverse is seldom true). In fact, OR studies are often associated mistakenly with behaviorist rather than cognitive psychology. There are, however, at least a few attempts at integration of cognitive and OR models that may be useful in elaborating the active–passive distinction in mass communication research.

Information-processing formulations usually involve hypothetical processing centers, but as Pribram noted, they are highly similar to physiological mechanisms that explain the OR. The basic proposition of a combined model is that autonomic properties of the OR initiate processing in a central channel, which is reponsible for attention, but with limited capacity and resources (Ohman, 1979). An important limitation of processing is that only a small set of total memory is available at one time. This is short-term memory. The unavailable information is the long-term memory store (LTS). The short-term store (STS), which decays in seconds, may operate similarly to the neuronal model of immediate experience proposed by Sokolov (1960). If preattentive mechanisms (designed to merely identify a stimulus) fail to find a match in STS, then an OR is elicited, and the stimulus is admitted into the central channel for further processing. A search for similar representations in long-term memory then begins, resulting in new information in the STS. The STS could then consist either of the most recent stimuli perceived or of information designated as significant by the receiver.

The idea that information in STS determines match or mismatch, and subsequently attention and memory, has implications for habituation. This is especially true for information that is familiar and periodically presented in a similar way (e.g., information on television). Once again, the magnitude and probability of an OR is determined by a match of current input with the contents of STS. But STS could be determined by either immediate past experience (usually the previous several seconds) or by previous experience in similar situations, beliefs about the task at hand (if any), instructions given by another person, or internally generated strategies. This suggests that habituation could occur over the long term (from day to day) as well as during shorter periods (i.e., during a single session of viewing television).

The Orienting Response and Performance

Both OR and information-processing models propose only interventions between input, and memory and performance, although the expectation is clear that the interventions should be related to information retention and action. In fact, most researchers view the OR as a prerequisite for learning and hold that more intense and persistent ORs are positively related to enhanced performance in tasks demanding attention (Waters, McDonald, & Koresko, 1977). The OR has been associated with increased ability to detect signals (Blakeslee, 1979), and habituation of the OR is a predictor of errors in signal detection (Mackworth, 1969; Maltzman, 1967). There is even evidence that people who habituate slowly perform better on audio and visual tasks than those who habituate quickly (Coles & Gale, 1971; Crider & Augenbraun, 1975).

It is difficult, however, to speculate on how these measures of performance relate to television viewing, where ORs may occur frequently (at least in fast-paced programming) and dishabituation could be a persistent event. It now seems likely that elements of television presentations can elicit ORs, but their effect on performance is still uncertain. There is evidence that program segments containing many primitive cues (i.e., a large amount of visual complexity associated with bright flashes) enhance information acquisition for children (Zillmann & Bryant, 1981; Zillmann, Hezel, & Medoff, 1980). There is also evidence that high cortical arousal during viewing is related to an increased ability for adults to recall and recognize information (Rothschild, Thorson, Hirsch, Goldstein, & Reeves, 1983). These results run counter to Singer's suggestion that ORs impede performance by precluding rehearsal and reflection.

Most of the foregoing data and discussion, however, are related to multiple ORs for entire programs, program segments, or 30-sec messages. There is no evidence about ORs and memory for information presented immediately after an eliciting cue. We have suggested elsewhere that recall and recognition should be better for content that appears within seconds after the onset of an OR (indicated by a rapid fall and gradual recovery of alpha), but as yet this relationship is untested (Reeves et al., 1984).

SUMMARY

In the literature about the psychology of attention, readers are confronted with dichotomies that describe unique forms of mental processing. Attention, depending on situation and task, is either active or passive, conscious or unconscious, automatic or controlled, voluntary or involuntary, mindful or mindless, overt or covert, cortical or autonomic, data driven or subject driven, top down or bottom up, and so on. These distinctions are based on stimuli and tasks designed to demonstrate each condition separately. The single most important contribution of the psychological literature may be to remind us that television viewing can never be one or the other. Television as a psychological stimulus is too complex; it is viewed in too many different situations, for too many different reasons, in combination with too many other activities to ever represent a stimulus located precisely in one category and never in the other. The important research questions should be those that help explain when each type of process operates, how the process works, and how the processes are responsible, either in combination or interaction, for memory and performance.

A second contribution of the psychological literature is to remind us that in spite of the apparent complexity of television, we have constrained the scope of research about attention. This has resulted primarily in a reliance on self-reports about conscious attention. The development of observational procedures to measure visual orientation was important because it advanced the study of attention beyond a verbal ability to express a cognitive process. But even these measures depend on counting an overt reaction. Apart from popular discussions of subliminal persuasion and hypnotic trances, mass communication researchers have been reluctant to acknowledge covert and unconscious features of attention to the screen. The original data reported in this review indicate the possibility and potential theoretical value of examining attention at this level.

The two methods proposed—a performance measure of reaction time to a secondary task and a neural measure of mental activity—in combination with more traditional introspective methods, complete Posner's (1982) triadic approach to the study of attention. It is important to emphasize that the approaches are additive rather than competitive. Each is likely to make contributions at a different level of analysis. There is little reason to believe that one source of information will be more important than another or that theory at one level will be totally reducible to theory at a lower level. As Neisser (1967) warned, we should not view psychology as something to do until electrophysiologists get around to solving all of the problems. But it is appropriate to view information at one level as a constraint (rather than as a determinant) of operations at a higher level.

Finally, psychological theories should continue to provide useful definitions of media. Many definitions of television, for example, emphasize professional occupations, corporate organizations, regulations, and especially content rather than characteristics of the technologies and their symbol systems that might affect mental processes. Psychological questions require psychological definitions. The theories reviewed here suggest that it is the structure, in addition to the meaning, of television messages that causes variance in attention. And it is the form, not the content, of television that is unique. This has been persuasively argued by others (e.g., Salomon, 1979) and is appropriately the basis of future study.

ACKNOWLEDGMENTS

The authors would like to thank the following students at the University of Wisconsin—Madison for their assistance in collecting data reported in this paper: Brian Deith, Annie Lang Derryberry, Marian Friestad, Roz Pearson, and Michael Shapiro.

REFERENCES

Alwitt, L. F., Anderson, D. R., Lorch, E. P., & Levin, S. R. (1980). Preschool children's visual attention to attributes of television. *Human Communication Research, 7,* 52–67.

Anderson, D. R., & Levin, S. R. (1976). Young children's attention to *Sesame Street. Child Development, 47,* 806–811.

Anderson, D. R., Levin, S. R., & Lorch, E. P. (1977). The effects of TV program pacing on the behavior of preschool children. *AV Communication Reviews, 25,* 159–166.

Anderson, D. R., & Lorch, E. P. (1983). Looking at television: Action or reaction? In J. Bryant & D. R. Anderson (Eds.), *Children's understanding of television* (pp. 1–33). New York: Academic.

Averbach, E., & Coriell, A. S. (1961). Short term memory in vision. *Bell-System Technical Journal, 40,* 309–328.

Bandura, A. (1977). *Social learning theory.* Englewood Cliffs, NJ: Prentice-Hall.

Bauer, R. T. (1973). *Television and the public.* New York: Holt, Rinehart & Winston.

Becker, C. A. (1980). Semantic context effects in visual word recognition: An analysis of semantic strategies. *Memory & Cognition, 6,* 493–512.

Becklen, R., & Cervone, D. (1983). Selective looking and the noticing of unexpected events. *Memory & Cognition, 6,* 601–608.

Bernstein, A. S. (1969). To what does the orienting response respond? *Psychophysiology, 6,* 338–350.

Blakeslee, P. (1979). Attention and vigilance: Performance and skin conductance response changes. *Psychophysiology, 16,* 413–419.

Brady, J. P., & Levitt, E. E. (1966). Hypnotically induced visual hallucinations. *Psychosomatic Medicine, 28,* 351–353.

Britton, B. K., Holdredge, T. S., Curry, C., & Westbrook, R. D. (1979). Use of cognitive capacity in reading identical texts with different amounts of discourse level meaning. *Journal of Experimental Psychology: Human Learning and Memory, 5,* 262–270.

Britton, B. K., & Tesser, A. (1982). Effects of prior knowledge on use of cognitive capacity in three complex cognitive tasks. *Journal of Verbal Learning and Verbal Behavior, 21,* 421–436.

Britton, B. K., Westbrook, R. D., & Holdredge, T. S. (1978). Reading and cognitive capacity usage: Effects of text difficulty. *Journal of Experimental Psychology: Human Learning and Performance, 4,* 582–591.

Broadbent, D. E. (1954). The role of auditory localization in attention and memory span. *Journal of Experimental Psychology, 47,* 191–196.

Broadbent, D. E. (1958). *Perception and communication.* London: Pergamon.

Brown, B. B. (1968). Visual recall ability and eye movements. *Psychophysiology, 4,* 300–306.

Bryant, J., & Anderson, D. (Eds.). (1983). *Children's understanding of television: Research on attention and comprehension.* New York: Academic.

Bryant, J., Zillman, D., & Brown, D. (1983). Entertainment features in children's educational television: Effects on attention and information acquisition. In J. Bryant & D. R. Anderson (Eds.), *Children's understanding of television* (pp. 221–240). New York: Academic.

Cherry, E. C. (1953). Some experiments on the recognition of speech, with one and two ears. *Journal of the Acoustical Society of America, 25,* 975–979.

Coles, M. G., & Gale, A. (1971). Physiological reactivity as a predictor of performance in a vigilance task. *Psychophysiology, 8,* 594–599.

Comstock, G., Chaffee, S., Katzman, N., McCombs, M., & Roberts, D. (1978). *Television and human behavior.* New York: Columbia University Press.

Corteen, R. S., & Wood, B. (1972). Autonomic responses to shock-associated words in an unattended channel. *Journal of Experimental Psychology, 94,* 308–313.

Crider, A., & Augenbraun, C. B. (1975). Auditory vigilance correlate of electrodermal response habituation speed. *Psychophysiology, 12,* 36–40.

Deutsch, J. A., & Deutsch, D. (1963). Attention: Some theoretical considerations. *Psychological Review, 70,* 80–90.

Donohew, L., & Tipton, L. (1973). A conceptual model of information seeking, avoiding, and processing. In P. Clarke (Ed.), *New models for mass communication research* (pp. 243–268). Beverly Hills, CA: Sage.

Doyle, J. C., Ornstein, R., & Galin, D. (1974). Lateral specialization of cognitive mode: II. EEG frequency analysis. *Psychophysiology, 11,* 567–578.

Gevins, A. S., Zeitlin, G. M., Doyle, J. C., Yingling, C. D., Schafler, R. E., Callaway, E., & Yeager, C. L. (1979). Electroencephalogram correlates of higher cortical functions. *Science, 16,* 665–667.

Glass, D. C., & Singer, J. E. (1972). *Urban stress: Experiments on noise and social stresses.* New York: Academic.

Graham, F. K. (1973). Habituation and dishabituation of responses unnervated by the autonomic nervous system. In H. V. S. Peeke & M. J. Herz (Eds.), *Habituation: Behavioral studies* (Vol. 1, pp. 163–218). New York: Academic.

Groves, P. M., & Thompson, R. F. (1970). Habituation: A dual-process theory. *Psychological Review, 77,* 419–450.

Husson, W., & Krull, R. (1983). *Theoretical implications of non-stationarity in children's attention to television.* Paper presented at the meeting of the International Communication Association, Dallas.

James, W. (1890). *The principles of psychology.* New York: Holt.

Johnston, W. A., & Dark, V. J. (1982). In defence of intraperceptual theories of attention. *Journal of Experimental Psychology: Human Perception and Performance, 8,* 407–421.

Kahneman, D. (1973). *Attention and effort.* Englewood Cliffs, NJ: Prentice-Hall.

Kahneman, D., & Chajczyk, D. (1983). Tests of automaticity of reading: Dilution of Stroop effects by color-irrelevant stimuli. *Journal of Experimental Psychology: Human Perception and Performance, 9,* 497–509.

Kahneman, D., & Treisman, A. (1983). Changing views of attention and automaticity. In R. Parasuraman & R. Davies (Eds.), *Varieties of attention* (pp. 29–61). New York: Academic.

Kahneman, D., Treisman, A., & Burkell, J. (1983). The cost of visual filtering. *Journal of Experimental Psychology: Human Perception and Performance, 9,* 510–522.

Keele, S. W. (1972). Attention demands of memory retrieval. *Journal of Experimental Psychology, 93,* 245–248.

Kinsbourne, M., & Hicks, R. E. (1978). Functional cerebral space: A model for overflow, transfer and interference effects in human performance: A tutorial review. In Jean Requin (Ed.), *Attention and performance VII* (pp. 345–362). Hillsdale, NJ: Lawrence Erlbaum Associates.

Krull, R., & Husson, W. G. (1979). Children's attention: The case of TV viewing. In E. Wartella (Ed.), *Children communicating: Media and development of thought, speech, understanding* (pp. 83–114). Beverly Hills, CA: Sage.

Krull, R., & Husson, W. G. (1980). Children's anticipatory attention to the TV screen. *Journal of Broadcasting, 24,* 36–47.

LaBerge, D. (1975). Acquisition of automatic processing in perceptual and associative learning. In P. M. A. Rabbit (Ed.), *Attention and performance V* (pp. 50–64). London: Academic.

Lang, P. (1979). A bio-informational theory of emotional imagery. *Psychophysiology, 16,* 495–512.

Lynn, R. (1966). *Attention, arousal and the orientation reaction.* London: Pergamon Press.

MacKay, D. G. (1973). Aspects of the theory of comprehension, memory and attention. *Quarterly Journal of Experimental Psychology, 25,* 22–40.

Mackworth, J. F. (1969). *Vigilance and habituation.* Baltimore, MD: Penguin.

Mackworth, N. H. (1950). *Researches on the measurements of human performance* (Special Report Series No. 268). England: Medical Research Council.

Maltzman, I. (1967). Individual difference in "attention": The orienting reflex. In R. M. Gange (Ed.), *Learning and individual differences* (pp. 94–112). Columbus, OH: Merrill.

Maltzman, I., Langdon, B., & Feerey, D. (1970). Semantic generalization without prior conditioning. *Journal of Experimental Psychology, 83,* 73–75.

Mander, J. (1978). *Four arguments for the elimination of television.* New York: Morrow.

Marcel, A. J. (1983). Conscious and unconscious perception: Experiments on visual masking and word recognition. *Cognitive Psychology, 15,* 197–237.

Massaro, D. W. (1975). *Experimental psychology and information processing.* Chicago: Rand McNally.

Moore, D. (1981). *The behavioral measurement of information load.* Unpublished manuscript, University of Florida.

Moray, N. (1959). Attention in dichotic listening: Affective cues and the influence of instructions. *Quarterly Journal of Experimental Psychology, 11,* 56–60.

Moray, N., & O'Brien, T. (1967). Signal-detection theory applied to selective listening. *Journal of the Acoustical Society of America, 42,* 765–772.

Mulholland, T. (1973). Objective EEG methods for studying covert shifts of visual attention. In F. J. McGuigan & R. A. Schoonauer (Eds.), *The psychophysiology of thinking* (pp. 109–151). New York: Academic.

Mulholland, T., & Runnals, S. (1962). A stimulus-brain feedback system for evaluation of alertness. *Journal of Psychology, 54,* 69–83.

Navon, D., & Gopher, D. (1979). On the economy of the human processing system. *Psychological Review, 86,* 214–255.

Navon, D., & Gopher, D. (1980). Task difficulty, and dual-task performance. In R. S. Nickerson (Ed.), *Attention and performance* (pp. 297–315). Hilldale, NJ: Lawrence Erlbaum Associates.

Neisser, U. (1967). *Cognitive psychology.* New York: Appleton-Century-Crofts.

Neisser, U., & Becklen, R. (1975). Selective looking: Attending to visually specified events. *Cognitive Psychology, 7,* 480–494.

Norman, D. A. (1968). Toward a theory of memory and attention. *Psychological Review, 75,* 522–536.

Norman, D. A. (1969). Memory while shadowing. *Quarterly Journal of Experimental Psychology, 21,* 85–93.

Norman, D. A. (1976). *Memory and attention.* New York: Wiley.

Ohman, A. (1979). The orienting response, attention, and learning: An information processing perspective. In H. D. Kimmel, E. H. van Olst, & J. F. Orlebeke (Eds.), *The orienting reflex in humans* (pp. 443–471). Hillsdale, NJ: Lawrence Erlbaum Associates.

Paivio, A. U. (1971). *Imagery and verbal processes.* New York: Holt, Rinehart & Winston.

Palmer, E. L., & McDowell, C. N. (1979). The program commercial separators in children's television programming. *Journal of Communication, 29,* 197–201.

Pavlov, I. P. (1927). *Conditioned reflexes.* Oxford: Clarendon.

Posner, M. I. (1978). *Chronometric explorations of mind: The third Paul M. Fitts lectures.* Hillsdale, NJ: Lawrence Erlbaum Associates.

Posner, M. I. (1982). Cumulative development of attentional theory. *American Psychologist, 37,* 168–179.

Posner, M. I., & Snyder, C. R. R. (1975). Facilitation and inhibition in the processing of signals. In P. M. A. Rabbit (Ed.), *Attention and performance V* (pp. 669–682). London: Academic.

Pribram, K. H. (1979). The orienting reaction: Key to brain re-presentational mechanisms. In H. D. Kimmel, E. H. van Olst, J. F. Orlebeke (Eds.), *The orienting reflex in humans* (pp. 3–20). Hillsdale, NJ: Lawrence Erlbaum Associates.

Ratcliff, R., & McKeon, G. (1978). Priming in item recognition: Evidence for the propositional structure of sentences. *Journal of Verbal Learning and Verbal Behavior, 17,* 403–407.

Reeves, B., Thorson, E., Rothschild, M. L., McDonald, D., Hirsch, J., & Goldstein, R. (in press). Attention to television: Intrastimulus effects of movement and scene changes on alpha variations over time. *International Journal Of Neuroscience.*

Rothschild, M. L., Thorson, E., Hirsch, J. E., Goldstein, R., & Reeves, B. (1983). *EEG activity and the processing of television commercials.* Unpublished manuscript, University of Wisconsin.

Salomon, G. (1979). *Interaction of media, cognition, and learning.* San Francisco: Jossey-Bass.

Sears, D., & Freedman, J. (1971). Selective exposure to information: A critical review. In W. Schramm & D. Roberts (Eds.), *Process and effects of mass communication* (pp. 209–235). Champaign-Urbana: University of Illinois Press.

Shaffer, W. O., & LaBerge, D. (1979). Automatic semantic processing of unattended words. *Journal of Verbal Learning and Verbal Behavior, 18,* 413–426.

Shaw, W. A. (1940). The relation of muscular action potentials to imaginal weight lifting. *Archives of Psychology, 50,* 247.

Shiffrin, R. M., & Schneider, W. (1977). Controlled and automatic human information processing: II. Perceptual learning, automatic attending, and a general theory. *Psychological Review, 84,* 127–190.

Singer, J. (1980). The power and limitations of television: A cognitive-affective analysis. In P. J. Tannenbaum (Ed.), *The entertainment functions of television* (pp. 36–42). Hillsdale, NJ: Lawrence Erlbaum Associates.

Sokolov, E. N. (1960). Neuronal models and the orienting reflex. In M. A. B. Brazier (Ed.), *The central nervous system and behavior* (pp. 187–276). New York: Josiah Macy Jr. Foundation.

Sokolov, E. N. (1963). Higher nervous functions: The orienting reflex. *Annual Review of Physiology, 25,* 545–580.

Sperling, G., & Reeves, A. (1980). Measuring the reaction time of a shift of visual attention. In R. S. Nickerson (Ed.), *Attention and performance* (pp. 347–360). Hillsdale, NJ: Lawrence Erlbaum Associates.

Stein, A. H., & Friedrich, L. K. (1972). Television content and young children's behavior. In J. P. Murray, E. A. Rubinstein, & G. A. Comstock (Eds.), *Television and social behavior* (Vol. 2, pp. 202–317). Washington, DC: U.S. Government Printing Office.

Stroop, J. R. (1935). Studies of interference in serial verbal reactions. *Journal of Experimental Psychology, 18,* 643–652.

Thompson, R. F., Berry, S. D., Rinalai, P. C., & Berger, T. W. (1979). Habituation and the orienting reflex: The dual-process theory revisited. In H. D. Kimmel, E. H. van Olst, & J. F. Orlebeke (Eds.), *The orienting reflex in humans* (pp. 21–60). Hillsdale, NJ: Lawrence Erlbaum Associates.

Treisman, A. M. (1960). Contextual cues in selective listening. *Quarterly Journal of Experimental Psychology, 12,* 242–248.

Treisman, A., & Geffen, G. (1967). Selective attention and cerebral dominance in perceiving and responding to speech messages. *Quarterly Journal of Experimental Psychology, 19,* 1–17.

Tulving, E. (1970). Short term and long term memory: Different retrieval mechanisms. In K. H. Pribram & D. Broadbent (Eds.), *The biology of memory* (pp. 7–10). New York: Academic.

van Olst, E. H. (1971). *The orienting reflex.* The Hague: Mouton.

van Olst, E. H., Heemstra, M. L., & Kortenaar, J. (1979). Stimulus significance and orienting reaction. In H. D. Kimmel, E. H. van Olst, & J. F. Orlebeke (Eds.), *The orienting reflex in humans* (pp. 521–547). Hillsdale, NJ: Lawrence Erlbaum Associates.

Ward, S., & Wackman, D. (1973). Children's information processing of television advertising. In P. Clarke (Ed.), *New models for communication research* (pp. 119–147). Beverly Hills, CA: Sage.

Wartella, E., & Ettema, J. S. (1974). A cognitive developmental study of children's attention to television commercials. *Communication Research, 1,* 69–88.

Wartella, E., & Reeves, B. (1983). Recurring issues in research on children and media. *Educational Technology, 23,* 5–8.

Waters, W. F., McDonald, D. G., & Koresko, R. L. (1977). Habituation of the orienting response: A grating mechanism subserving selective attention. *Psychophysiology, 14,* 228–236.

Watkins, B. A., Huston-Stein, A., & Wright, J. C. (1981). Effects of planned television programming. In E. L. Palmer & A. Dorr (Eds.), *Children and the faces of television: Teaching, violence, selling* (pp. 49–70). New York: Academic.

Winn, M. (1977). *The plug-in-drug.* New York: Viking.

Zillmann, D. (1982). Television viewing and arousal. In *Television and behavior: 10 years of scientific progress and implications for the 80s: Vol. 2. Technical reviews* (pp. 53–64). U.S. Dept. of Health and Human Services.

Zillmann, D., & Bryant, J. (1980). *Uses and effects of humor in educational television.* Paper presented at the Third International Conference on Experimental Research in TV Instruction, St. John's, Newfoundland, Canada.

Zillmann, D., Hezel, R., & Medoff, N. (1980). The effect of affective states on selective exposure to televised entertainment fare. *Journal of Applied Social Psychology, 10,* 323–339.

14

Uses, Gratifications, and Media Effects Research

Alan M. Rubin
Kent State University

The goal of most mass communication research is to explain the impact of mass communication. Instead of assuming that media directly influence the recipients of messages, however, uses and gratifications researchers view the media as sources of potential influence amid other sources. Media consumption has been the primary focus of uses and gratifications research. The perspective presumes that: (a) we need first to understand audience needs and motives for media behavior before we can explain the effects of the media; and (b) an understanding of audience consumption patterns enhances an explanation of media effects.

The rationale for these presumptions is found in some basic tenets of uses and gratifications. These include the overriding belief that individuals differentially select and use communication vehicles to gratify or satisfy felt needs. Media and communication channel use is motivated behavior that performs certain functions for the individual users. People, not the media, are most influential in the relationship. Within this process, individuals are influenced by a host of social and psychological factors, and the media compete with other forms of communication for attention, selection, and use. The approach emerges from a mediated view of mass communication influence that underscores the role of sociological and psychological factors in mitigating mechanistic media effects.

According to Fisher (1978), the psychological perspective to communication study shifts the focus of inquiry from the mechanistic perspective's interest in the effects of the mass media on receivers to a determination of how audience members use the media, "that is, what purposes or functions the media serve for a body of active receivers" (p. 159). Uses and gratifications researchers are not disinterested in questions of media effects. To the contrary, as adherents of the psychological perspective, they seek to explain the effects of the mass media "in terms of the purposes, functions or uses (that is, uses and gratifications) as controlled by the choice patterns of receivers" (Fisher, 1978, p. 159). Uses and gratifications, then, also is concerned with the functions of mass communication for the individual.

THE FUNCTIONAL APPROACH

Uses and gratifications research generally focuses on the consuming behaviors of media audience members; these behaviors have consequences for individuals and social systems. In addition to the psychological perspective's focus on individual use and choice, a pragmatic perspective of communication is useful for depicting the interrelationships among the parts of a social system. From a pragmatic perspective of communication, "The interdependent relationships among components can be described according to the three interrelated elements of structure, function, and evolution" (Fisher, 1978, p. 198).

The concepts of *function* and *functionalism* shed some light on the workings of mass communication in a social system beyond the individual. Function entails the relationships among and the interdependence of subsystems and systems (Timasheff, 1967). For example, functions of television news in a free enterprise system include informing the citizenry and selling products, among others. Functionalism considers the structure (relationships) and activities (behaviors) of units or elements of a system and the functions (consequences) of these activities for the system. The conduct of these activities or behaviors is believed to be purposive and may be thought of as having positive (functional) or negative (dysfunctional) consequences for social systems.

A view of systemic relationships among individuals, the media, and society emerges from a functional or pragmatic approach to mass communication study. It is assumed that component subsystems are interrelated and integrated within the complete system. For example, individuals are related to one another via group memberships, groups are interconnected with each other and societal structures, individual and group behavior is influenced by social structure and norms, media are affected by audience use and by societal components such as advertising, regulation, and the like, societal components are influenced by the media and audiences, and so on. Alterations in any subsystem affect the workings of the complete system.

Functionalism and Mass Communication

Mass communication functional schemes provide explanations for the media behavior of individuals within social systems that contrast with more mechanistic media effects research. In general, media effects studies seek to isolate a set of factors (e.g., source or message characteristics) for the purpose of explaining or predicting the effects of a message on receivers. Principal characteristics of mechanistic media effects research are: a common view of a passive and reactive audience; a focus on short-term, immediate, and measurable changes in the thoughts, attitudes, or behaviors of individuals; and an assumption of more direct media influence on audience members.

A variety of psychological and sociological factors has been suggested to intervene between the sender and receiver. The phenomenistic approach of Klapper (1960) questioned the validity of mechanistic media perspectives and proposed that psychological and social influences intercede between the media message and an individual's response so that, in most instances, mass media messages that are intended to persuade really reinforce existing attitudes. These mediating factors include individual predispositions and selective perception processes, group norms, message dissemination via interpersonal channels, opinion leadership, and the free enterprise nature of the mass media in some societies.

Such views are consistent with a functional view of mass communication which maintains that: mass communication is not a necessary or sufficient cause of audience effects; mass communication is only one source of influence in the social and psychological environment; and the media perform certain activities for individuals, groups, and society and, by so doing, have various consequences (i.e., functions or dysfunctions).

Since the 1940s, three predominant functional or quasi-functional views of mass communication have included inventories of media activities, functional analysis, and uses and gratifications. The first two orientations are identified in the following subsection; uses and gratifications (linked to the psychological perspective to explain individual media behavior) is described in the next main section. Following a description of the uses and gratifications paradigm, criticisms, research investigations, and media uses and effects research linkages are considered.

Media Activities and Functional Analysis

An inventory of media activities proposed by Lasswell (1948) stresses the functions of mass media content instead of audience uses of content. It indicates that by performing various societal activities—surveillance of the environment, correlation of parts of the environment, and transmission of social heritage—the media have effects that are common for members of society. A fourth activity—entertainment—was added to this scheme by Wright (1960) to analyze mass communication functionally.

Wright (1960) synthesized Lasswell's (1948) notion of media activities using Merton's (1968) view of functions and consequences of activities within a system. According to Wright's framework for functional analysis, the investigator inquires about the manifest and latent functions and dysfunctions of mass-communicated surveillance, correlation, cultural transmission, and entertainment for the individual, group, society, and cultural system. Functional analysis, then, focuses on the activities of a system and their consequences. When considering the individual as a system, as in uses and gratifications research, elements of the system could include needs, motives, values, attitudes, interests, desires, tastes, behaviors, and the like.

The work of Lasswell (1948) and of Lazarsfeld and Merton (1948) exemplifies early studies of media functions. In addition to Lasswell's posited functional activities of the mass media (i.e., surveillance, correlation, and transmission), Lazarsfeld and Merton proposed two functions and one dysfunction of the mass media: a status conferral function, an ethicizing function, and a narcotizing dysfunction.

These works were followed by a host of investigations that proposed various functions that one or more of the media serve for individuals or society. For example, Horton and Wohl (1956) suggested that television viewing provides a sense of parasocial interaction with media personae for viewers. Pearlin (1959) surmised that individuals are given the opportunity to escape from unpleasant life experiences via television viewing. Mendelsohn (1963) concluded that mass media entertainment reduces the anxiety in people that mass media news creates. Stephenson (1967) argued that the most significant function of television lies in its play or pleasurable aspects. McCombs and Shaw (1972) viewed agenda setting as an important function of mass communication in an election campaign. Himmelweit, Oppenheim, and Vince (1958) found that television functions for children as a time filler and as a vehicle of information, excitement, escape, and identification. And Schramm, Lyle, and Parker (1961) concluded that television meets children's fantasy needs better than their reality needs and performs a social function as a medium of entertainment, escape, and information.

USES AND GRATIFICATIONS INQUIRY

These studies of mass media functions were surrounded by research that focused on audience motives for using media or selected content. Research that focuses on the audience is guided by the belief that the essence of functionalism is that something is best defined by its use. Klapper (1963) argued that mass communication research "too frequently and too long focused on determining whether some particular effect does or does not occur" (p. 517). He observed that mass communication research had found few clear-cut answers to yes–no questions of media effects and called for an expansion of uses and gratifications inquiry.

Klapper (1963) saw the need to use functional analysis to extend uses and gratifications research by identifying the elements of the media situation (the process of use, the content, and the medium) that provide the gratification, the consequences of the observed use, and the role of functional alternatives. Such an analysis would enhance an understanding of the role of mass communication in the lives of people. This view is consistent with that of Katz (1959) who suggested that a media message ordinarily cannot influence an individual who has no use for it. Uses and gratifications research, then, is virtually a marriage (or at least an engagement) of functionalism and the psychological perspective.

The Uses and Gratifications Paradigm

The principal elements of uses and gratifications models include the needs and motives of individuals for communication behavior, the social and psychological environment of people, the mass media, functional alternatives to media use, communication behavior, and the consequences of such behavior. Uses and gratifications often is thought of as an umbrella that encompasses several different models (Blumler, 1979; Windahl, 1981).

The primary components of such models have been identified by several investigators, especially Katz, Blumler, and Gurevitch (1974) and Rosengren (1974). Katz et al. (1974) stated that uses and gratifications focuses on: "(1) the social and psychological origins of (2) needs, which generate (3) expectations of (4) the mass media or other sources, which lead to (5) differential patterns of media exposure (or engagement in other activities), resulting in (6) need gratifications and (7) other consequences, perhaps mostly unintended ones" (p. 20).

Rosengren (1974) similarly maintained that uses and gratifications considers several elements and their interrelationships: (a) basic biological and psychological human needs; (b) personality and social characteristics of individuals; (c) the structure of society; (d) felt individual problems; (e) perceived problem solutions; (f) problem-solving or gratification-seeking motives; (g) media consumption; (h) other behavior; (i) patterns of gratifications and nongratifications; (j) effects on individual characteristics; and (k) effects on the structure of society (e.g., media, social, political, cultural, and economic structures).

Uses and gratifications research focuses on media consumption by individuals. It is guided by revised research questions that shift to a focus on what people do with the mass media instead of what the mass media do to people (Klapper, 1963). Typical uses and gratifications models also ask about the consequences or functions of media use.

Objectives and Assumptions of the Perspective

The logic of uses and gratifications rests on three objectives and five assumptions as outlined by Katz et al. (1974). The three objectives are: to explain how the mass media are used by individuals to gratify their needs; to understand the motives for media behavior; and to identify the functions or consequences that follow from needs, motives, and communication behavior. This latter objective obviously links uses and gratifications to functional analysis through the iden-tification of the consequences of individual behavior. As such, the units of analysis are individuals; the structures are the relationships between the individ-ual, the media, and the social system; the activities are media and other com-munication behavior; and the functions are the consequences of this pattern of behavior.

According to Katz et al. (1974), uses and gratifications is formulated on five suppositions. First, media use is goal-directed, purposive behavior. Individuals are active mass communication participants who select certain media or media content. Second, mass media are used by individuals in response to their felt needs. Media use expectations are produced from individual predispositions, social interaction, and environmental factors. The mass media are viewed in competition with other modes of communication (i.e., functional alternatives) for needs gratification. How well media use satisfies needs or motives varies with individuals. Third, the individual initiates media selection. Instead of being used by the media, individuals use the media and select media or media content to gratify their needs (Katz, Gurevitch, & Haas, 1973). This initiative mediates patterns and consequences of media use. Fourth, it is thought that, methodo-logically, individuals are able to articulate their own needs or motives for media use and communication behavior. Therefore, accurate information about media uses and gratifications can be gathered via audience self-report accounts. Fifth, value judgments about the cultural significance of media content or use should be suspended until media use motives and gratifications are understood.

The Evolution of Uses and Gratifications Research

Early gratifications investigations aimed to determine why people used or what gratifications people sought from certain media content. In this form, gratifi-cations research was seen by Lazarsfeld (1940) as a vehicle for determining the appeals of radio programs. Although they were not really guided by the broader needs-motives-uses-consequences paradigms of uses and gratifications, the stud-ies primarily were interested in exploring audience needs and motives as variables that intervene before media impact, instead of the persuasive effects of the media. Examples of these early gratifications investigations include the appeals of a radio quiz program for its listeners (Herzog, 1940), the gratifications obtained by women who listened to radio daytime serials (Herzog, 1944), and the reasons why people read the newspaper (Berelson, 1949).

This focus on individual needs, motives, and media uses largely was aban-doned in favor of studies of personal influence and media functions until after Katz's (1959) argument that media cannot ordinarily influence those who have no use for the media and Klapper's (1963) mandate for uses and gratifications study in mass communication.

Uses and gratifications research of the early 1970s began with a focus on the development of typologies of mass media gratifications. These structures of media use were related to various individual characteristics and to audience members' media attitudes and behaviors. The typologies depicted the seeking of gratifications as audience behavior before any media effects. Although the intent of such typologies was to explain the media consumption patterns of individuals, they do tell us something about the relationships among uses, gratifications, and media effects. These typologies provide some preliminary indications of such relationships between media uses and media effects research.

The goals of a research program of McQuail, Blumler, and Brown (1972) were: to categorize types of audience gratifications relevant to television content use; to classify audience members; to link social circumstances and viewer background with gratifications sought; to develop methods for measuring these relationships; and to generalize about the salience of satisfactions provided by television for different personality and demographic groups. In an initial study, McQuail et al. (1972) formulated a typology of media–person interactions, observing that individuals are motivated to use television for: diversion (escape and emotional release); personal relationships (companionship and social utility); personal identity (personal reference, reality exploration, and value reinforcement); and surveillance (e.g., acquiring news and information). They concluded that an escapist view of television use is unconvincing, that programs are multidimensional in appeal, and therefore, "the relationship between content categories and audience needs is far less tidy and more complex than most commentators have appreciated" (p. 162).

Rosengren and Windahl (1972) saw several relationships between the media and their audiences. For example, the interrelationships between individual and environmental possibilities to satisfy a given need can result in satisfactory or nonsatisfactory solutions to the perceived problem. Rosengren and Windahl labeled this the degree of *dependence* on functional alternatives. This dependence can lead to the use of functional alternatives that supplement, complement, or substitute for media use. These functional alternatives may be sought by individuals for various reasons or motives including change, compensation, escape, or vicarious experience. In addition, audience needs for interaction and identification can lead to media use that results in four types of relationships or degrees of *involvement*: detachment, parasocial interaction, solitary identification, or capture. Lastly, audience members' needs for interaction can be seen in terms of the degree of *reality proximity* of media content, ranging from noninformative, fictional content to informative, nonfictional content.

Rosengren and Windahl (1972) posited a relationship between degrees of dependence, involvement, and reality proximity. From an empirical study of these relationships, they reported that an individual's interaction potential leads to actual interaction, mass media consumption, and degree of involvement, that actual interaction leads to mass media consumption, and that mass media consumption leads to degree of involvement. They also argued that the two traditions of media effects and media functional studies must merge, that "functions are a certain type of effect," and that "it is quite possible to ask what effect a given use made of the mass media, or a given gratification obtained from them, may have" (p. 176).

Appraisal of the Perspective

Uses and gratifications has had almost a magnetic force in drawing criticism. Even though uses and effects studies have the same goal—to explain mass communication impact—some critics have been quick to berate the uses and gratifications perspective and its research. Most of the criticisms, although still repeated today (often without appropriate attention to post-1974 development), have been directed at the basic assumptions and early research investigations. The arguments of several critics can be briefly summarized and appraised.

Functionalism is viewed as a conservative orientation that fosters the status quo. As such, its method has been criticized as geared to stable, rather than dynamic, systems (Anderson & Meyer, 1975; Carey & Kreiling, 1974). Some see functional explanations as being supportive of system maintenance and stability instead of change. Such views have political and ideological overtones for both developed and developing societies. A major problem with this criticism is that it fails to address the orientation of functionalism that seeks to explain not only system maintenance and equilibrium, but also system dynamics, alterations, and consequences. A related criticism is that functional explanations sometimes result in oversimplified explanations of behavior, such as television functions as a vehicle of entertainment.

The individualistic orientation of uses and gratifications also has been criticized. As discussed previously, the focus of uses and gratifications study has been on individual consumption of mass media. Critics contend that this orientation makes it difficult to explain or predict beyond the individual unit (Becker, 1979; Carey & Kreiling, 1974; Elliott, 1974). Proponents, however, regard this as a strength of the perspective in that is geared to account for individual differences in media uses and effects. In addition, consistent findings across separate investigations and samples lend a degree of generalizability to research findings beyond the individual, the sample, and the investigation.

Early critics of the perspective argued that research is compartmentalized and that separate studies produce separate typologies of audience motives and functions (Anderson & Meyer, 1975; Swanson, 1979). The argument presented is usually that because different investigators have focused on different media uses or functions for different individuals of different backgrounds, a lack of integration and synthesis of research findings hinders conceptual development. Fisher

(1978) summarized this argument about pragmatic communication research that "reflects a proliferation of category systems for analyzing communicative functions and reflects the specific and unique interests of each investigator rather than a clear-cut paradigmatic inquiry into communicative phenomena performed by a substantial portion of the scientific community" (p. 232). Research since the mid-1970s has countered this criticism by developing systematic lines of conceptual inquiry.

Critics also have contended that the conceptual foundations of uses and gratifications are unclear and that adequate theoretical linkages have not been provided between the perspective's central components: background and environment, needs, motives, communication behavior, and consequences (Anderson & Meyer, 1975; Blumler, 1979; Elliott, 1974; Swanson, 1977, 1979). Systematic exploration of these components is required. For example, what conceptual framework might explain social and psychological needs that produce patterns of motives and audience behavior? What is the social origin of needs and motives? How do cultural and environmental factors contribute to the seeking, use, and consequences of communication sources and behavior or to the gratification of individual needs? Functional orientations identify a wealth of system units, relationships, and activities. It is limiting to suggest that the only appropriate means of study would be to consider all such elements and relationships in total. As have media effects investigations, uses and gratifications studies have tended to dissect a process and focus on some relevant parts and connections. Although this is highly appropriate for empirical investigations, it has resulted in some neglect for certain important relationships and theoretical linkages in much uses and gratifications research.

The use and meaning of principal terms and concepts have been criticized (Elliott, 1974; Swanson, 1977, 1979). Different investigators have applied different meanings to primary components of uses and gratifications paradigms, including motives, uses, gratifications, functions, and functional alternatives. This has resulted in some confusion about the objects and results of investigations. There is also some inconsistency about what constitutes antecedent, intervening, and consequent factors in such research. From most studies, though, it is possible to identify terms used in an equivalent fashion, such as needs, motives, gratifications sought, and uses, and on the consequent side, functions, consequences, gratifications obtained, and effects.

The notion of an active audience has been criticized both for what it assumes and how it has been measured (Blumler, 1979; Elliott, 1974; Swanson, 1977, 1979). Critics and proponents have argued that a universal and absolute view of audience activity is inappropriate. It is probably best to treat audience activity as a variable in its own right, instead of a descriptive and prescriptive condition of audience behavior (Blumler, 1979; Rubin, 1984; Windahl, 1981). Methodologically, audience members also have not been studied, in general, as active message consumers or processors, although certain ethnographic techniques might be more adept at doing so (Lull, 1980). Similarly, audience motives and communication behaviors typically have been measured via self-report instruments, the reliability and validity of which have been questioned. However, a few investigations have addressed these issues (Becker, 1979; Rubin, 1979, 1981a).

As mentioned before, uses and gratifications research has seemed to invite criticism. For several years now, many investigations have existed within the shadows of these criticisms or have been geared to addressing one or more of them, sometimes almost apologetically. Uses and gratifications research often has been on the defensive and, as such, has made efforts to address the critics. Similar criticisms, though, can be applied to media effects research. For example, the validity and reliability of measuring instruments are often suspect. Audiences are frequently and inappropriately treated as passive and reactive recipients of messages. The individual is typically the unit of analysis, and generalizations beyond the individual, when drawn, are questionable. Media effects research is often compartmentalized according to research interests and frequently lacks synthesis and integration for mass communication conceptual development.

In short, empirical research itself, regardless of research orientation, is subject to many of these criticisms. Obviously, empirical researchers often recognize these obstacles, but fortunately, have not ignored the need to try to explain the role and effects of mass communication despite these limitations. Some criticisms of uses and gratifications, as well as of media effects perspectives, are still valid to a degree. For example, uses and gratifications research has not yet achieved a true functional analysis as advocated by Klapper (1963). Many of the early criticisms, though, have been noted by researchers and considered in the design of later research studies. Substantial and systematic research efforts since the mid-1970s have addressed many of these criticisms, have provided valuable explanations of media consumption, and have enabled important implications to be drawn about mass communication uses and effects.

Contemporary Uses and Gratifications Studies

A series of studies illustrates responses to several of the previous criticisms. In particular, issues about compartmentalized typologies, measurement validity and reliability, individualistic restrictions, relationships between media uses and social-psychological factors, and audience activity have been addressed to varying degrees in uses and gratifications research since the mid-1970s.

For example, several studies adapted a similar set of television use scales and have produced a more systematic examination of mass communication (Bantz, 1982; Eastman, 1979; Greenberg, 1974; Palmgreen & Rayburn, 1979; Rubin, 1977, 1979, 1981a, 1981b, 1983). The original scales were developed by Greenberg (1974) for his investigation of television use by British children and adolescents. By analyzing the degree of concurrence with each of 31 reasons for watching television, several categories of motives for child and adolescent television use were determined: learning, habit, arousal, companionship, relaxation, escape, and to pass time. Greenberg noted that age was the most significant demographic correlate of the viewing motives and found several relationships among the motives and media behaviors, aggressive attitudes, and television attitudes.

A partial replication of this study was done in the United States (Rubin, 1977, 1979). The goals of the investigation were: to examine the associations between viewing motives and television attitudes, behaviors, and audience demography; to consider the compatibility between findings on American children and adolescents and those of Greenberg's (1974) study; and to address the issues of validity and reliability of viewing motive measures. The questionnaire contained measures of television viewing motives, viewing behaviors (level of viewing and program preferences), television attitudes (perceived realism and television affinity), and sociodemographic characteristics.

A pretest of the instrument reduced the number of viewing motive scales from 31 to 24. Factor analysis identified six reasons why children and adolescents watch television: learning, habit or pass time, companionship, escape, arousal, and relaxation. Viewing to pass time, for relaxation, and for arousal were the most salient motives. Various relationships were identified between viewing motives and demographics, television attitudes, and behaviors. For example, age was the most significant correlate of the viewing motives. Habitual or pass time viewing was linked negatively to watching news/public affairs programs and positively to television affinity and watching comedy programs. Viewing to learn was related positively to perceived realism of television. Viewing for excitement and for companionship was associated with watching action/adventure and comedy programs, respectively. These findings are quite similar to those of Greenberg (1974) and provide a clearer picture of television viewing behavior.

The instrument also included some repeated viewing motive items to check for test-retest reliability. This procedure indicated that responses to the tested viewing motive items were consistent for a subsample of the children and adolescents. In addition, before the presentation of the 24 viewing motive scales, the children and adolescents were asked to state their reasons for watching television. Both this open-ended question and the viewing motive scales reflected the ability of respondents (even children) to verbalize their reasons for using television; this is an important assumption of the uses and gratifications perspective. The responses to both the open-ended question and viewing motive scales showed a great degree of consistency about the salience of television use motives, establishing convergent validity of the measures.

A similar procedure was employed in a later study of a broader sample, ranging from children to older adults (Rubin, 1981a). The results of this investigation contributed to systematic development of this line of uses and gratifications research in contrast to the criticism of compartmentalized and individualistic results. The findings also affirmed the ability of people to verbalize their motives and the validity of measurement procedures.

Contemporary uses and gratifications investigations also exemplify systematic research development and responses to criticisms of the perspective. In particular, several specific and coherent research directions are obvious. Studies within and across these research programs have included several partial replications and a secondary analysis of research data. Both replication and secondary analysis contribute to conceptual development. These research directions are identified here, and the linkages of the results of such investigations to media effects research are drawn in the next section.

One research direction has been an analysis of media use motives, their interrelationships, and their associations with media attitudes and behaviors (Eastman, 1979; Rubin, 1977, 1979, 1981a, 1981b, 1983, 1984; A. Rubin & R. Rubin, 1982b). These studies have found consistent relationships and patterns of media use. A second direction has been a comparison of motives for media use across several media or categories of media content (Bantz, 1982; Elliott & Quattlebaum, 1979; Katz et al., 1973; Lichtenstein & Rosenfeld, 1983; Payne & Caron, 1982). A third research direction has been the examination of the social and psychological circumstances of media use (Adoni, 1979; Dimmick, McCain, & Bolton, 1979; Korzenny & Neuendorf, 1980; Lull, 1980; Miyazaki, 1981; A. Rubin & R. Rubin, 1982a; R. Rubin & A. Rubin, 1982). These works have considered various factors that might influence media consumption, including interpersonal interaction, social activity, mobility, life satisfaction, the family viewing environment, personality factors, and life position. One other research direction has been an analysis of the relationships between gratifications sought and gratifications obtained by individuals in their uses of certain media or media content (Galloway & Meek, 1981; Palmgreen & Rayburn, 1979, 1982; Palmgreen, Wenner, & Rayburn, 1980, 1981; Wenner, 1982). Not only do these studies consider whether the motives people have for using media are satisfied, but they also have proposed transactional, discrepancy, and expectancy-value models of media uses and gratifications.

MEDIA USES AND EFFECTS

As mentioned earlier, some researchers have proposed a merger or synthesis of uses and gratifications and media effects research (Rosengren & Windahl, 1972; Rubin & Windahl, 1982; Windahl, 1981). According to Windahl (1981), a primary difference between the two traditions is that whereas a media effects researcher "most often looks at the mass communication process from the communicator's end," a uses and gratifications researcher takes the active "audience member as a point of departure" (p. 176). Windahl argued that an emphasis on the similarities of perspectives is more beneficial to a synthesis than is a stressing of differences. As such, uses and effects are both seeking to explain outcomes of mass communication. Thus, uses and gratifications researchers typically include some sort of consequences in their paradigms and stress that media use may have outcomes such as dependence on a medium, influence of gratifications obtained on the structure of needs and preferences, behavioral alterations such as substitution or displacement, and societal effects such as the widening of knowledge and information gaps.

Uses and gratifications studies usually have tapped media effects that can be labeled attitudinal or predispositional. The state of affairs is hardly different for most media effects research. In particular, the consequences considered by uses and gratifications studies include levels of media use, content preferences, affinity, dependency, and perceptions of television realism. Researchers also have addressed uses and gratifications assumptions that have implications for the discussion of media effects.

Audience Activity

Although uses and gratifications research assumes audience activeness in media selection and use, the concept of audience activity is not easily defined. Blumler's (1979) argument that audience activity should be treated as a variable, not as an absolute, finds support in recent research.

For example, Levy and Windahl (1984) identified three different periods of audience activity for Swedish television users: previewing, during viewing, and postviewing. They noted different linkages between the activity variable and gratifications sought from television use. Whereas preactivity and entertainment media use were only weakly connected, preactivity and surveillance media use were strongly related. They argued that the viewers in their sample actively sought news exposure to gain information about their worlds, but they did not actively seek diversion.

This finding is similar to the results of several investigations in another research program (Rubin, 1981b, 1983, 1984; A. Rubin & R. Rubin, 1982b) that has attempted to consider motives for audience use as interrelated structures instead of independent and isolated factors. Methodological treatments in these studies have produced a consistent finding: Audience use of television can be described as primarily ritualized or instrumental in nature. Although instrumental television use might indicate audience utility, intentionality, and selectivity, ritualized television use might indicate utility but an otherwise less active audience condition (Rubin, 1984). Therefore, the universality of the uses and gratifications assumption of audience activity is called into question.

Ritualized and Instrumental Television Use

In general, ritualized television use means more habitual viewing of television for diversionary purposes; instrumental television use refers to seeking certain media content for more informational reasons. Ritualized use is related to watching some entertainment types of programming, and even more to greater exposure to television itself (i.e., higher viewing levels). Instrumental use typically correlates with news, talk, and magazine types of program viewing, but not with higher television viewing levels. Thus, ritualized and instrumental structures of motives for media use tell us something about media behaviors, namely the amount of media use and the types of content that are preferred.

These media use patterns also are largely supported by earlier studies that have looked at independent television viewing motives in relationship to television behaviors and attitudes. For example, several investigations have found that levels of television viewing are most strongly related to using television to pass time, and for habit, arousal, companionship, and entertainment reasons (Greenberg, 1974; Rubin, 1979, 1981a; A. Rubin & R. Rubin, 1981, 1982b).

Ritualized and instrumental television use reveals pertinent information about two media attitudinal effects: perceived realism of television content and dependence on a mass medium. Dependency has been partly studied as media attachment or affinity in several investigations. A general conclusion is that instrumental television use and perceptions of television realism are significantly related, as are ritualized television use and affinity with the television medium. Several studies have found significant positive correlations between using television instrumentally for learning or information seeking and how realistic television content is perceived to be, and between using television ritualistically or habitually for diversion or time consumption and how important watching television is felt to be (Greenberg, 1974; Rubin, 1979, 1981a, 1983, 1984; A. Rubin & R. Rubin, 1982b).

Affinity and realism also may serve as attitudinal predispositions that filter mass media and message selection and use. This is consistent with Swanson's (1979) argument that uses and gratifications researchers should be concerned with "the perceptual activity of interpreting or creating meaning for messages" (p. 42). Meaning would be affected by such attitudes as perceived realism and affinity that likely are to result from prior experiences with a medium and its content or messages. These predispositions should influence an individual's subsequent gratification-seeking behavior.

Ritualized and instrumental media use patterns have important implications for media influence beyond media behaviors and attitudes. Windahl (1981) argued that using a medium instrumentally or ritualistically should produce different effects or consequences. Windahl saw *effects* as the outcome of using media content, *consequences* as the outcome of media use, and *conseffects* as the outcome of both media and content use. The uses and dependency model of

Rubin and Windahl (1982) also posited different outcomes as the result of ritualized use of a medium and instrumental use of media content. Because uses and gratifications research stresses the role of many variables in the effects and social influence process, including societal structure, individual needs and motives, and functional alternatives, these variables may contribute to the different patterns of media use and to possible dependence on certain media or media content.

Dependency

The notion of dependency is derived in part from Rosengren and Windahl's (1972) ideas about the role of functional alternatives. Dependence on a medium may result from particular motives or strategies for obtaining gratifications and from the lack of or inability to use functional alternatives. Various social and psychological attributes of individuals (e.g., health, mobility, interaction, social activity, life satisfaction, and economic security) can influence the availability of functional alternatives, motives for media use, and dependency on a medium. For example, two studies have indicated a significant negative link between an individual's degree of self-reliance and dependence on television (A. Rubin & R. Rubin, 1982a; R. Rubin & A. Rubin, 1982).

This view sees dependency as a consequence of environmental context and restricted use of functional alternatives that produces a certain pattern of media use. Therefore, dependency can be seen as an antecedent and intervening factor in media use. In one study, Miller and Reese (1982) found that certain political effects (i.e., activity and efficacy) are more apparent through exposure to a medium when that medium is relied upon. They concluded: "Dependency on a medium appears to enhance the opportunity for that medium to have predicted effects" (p. 245). Dependency also might be viewed as a consequence of media use; thus, one result of motives that produce extended use of a medium might be greater reliance on that medium for information or diversion. In this manner, dependency that precedes, accompanies, or results from media use also could lead to greater potential media effects on an individual's attitudes and behaviors.

The relationship between dependency and functional alternatives also leads to a broader conceptualization of uses and gratifications as a vehicle for interfacing interpersonal and mass communication. For example, according to Rubin and Rubin (1985), "More resourceful interpersonal communicators will possess a wider availability of alternative channels, a broader conception of the potential channels, and the capacity for using more diversified message- and interaction-seeking strategies" (p. 39). Similarly, Lull's (1980) typology of the social uses of television also makes it obvious that the way in which media are used by people has important implications for media effects. The two principal social uses of television, according to this scheme, are structural and relational. An individual might use television structurally as an environmental resource (e.g., for companionship) or as a behavioral regulator (e.g., for punctuating time). Or an individual might use televison relationally for communication facilitation such as an agenda for conversation, for affiliation or avoidance such as conflict resolution, for social learning such as behavioral modeling, or for competence or dominance such as role reinforcement. Obviously, different uses of television should have different consequences for the individual and the interaction.

Uses and Effects Models

Several models have been introduced whose purpose is to explain media uses and effects. The models typically concern the linkages of media use motives, media behaviors, media content, and other factors in the mass communication process. As McLeod and Becker (1974) have written, "A reasonable synthesis of the hypodermic and limited effects models, in which the exposure characteristics of the message *combine with* the orientation of the audience member in producing an effect, may be able to escape the unwarranted simplicities of each of the parent models" (p. 141). They argued that such a transactional model would "recognize the erroneousness" of either the "content equals effect" or the "audience intention equals effect" position. They also noted that such a transactional model might be additive, with "the gratification contribution supplementing that due to exposure," or interactive, with "an exposure effect being contingent on the presence of a gratification condition" (p. 141).

McLeod and Becker (1974) found support for the additive model because gratification and exposure variables contributed independently and noninteractively to political effects, such as campaign issue accuracy and campaign interest. Wenner (1982) also found support for an additive model because the addition of media gratifications to a hierarchical regression model containing media exposure variables accounted for further variance in explaining media dependency on television news and information programs. McLeod, Becker, and Byrnes (1974), though, noted interaction effects of media gratifications and exposure for agenda setting because "most of the gratifications seem to act as deterrents to agenda setting" (p. 161). Both additive and interactive explanations might be appropriate depending on the content and context of media use.

The uses and dependency model proposes another view of the synthesis of media uses and effects by placing audience consumption processes at the center of the systems approach of dependency theory (Rubin & Windahl, 1982). According to the model, societal structure, the media system, individual needs and motives, media use, the use of functional alternatives, and consequences of communication behavior might be continually altered by other components of the system. The model also depicts relationships between needs and motives, information-seeking strategies, media and functional alternative use, and media dependency such that, for example, needs and motives that produce narrow information-seeking strategies might lead to restricted use of and dependence on communication channels. Dependency, in turn, could lead to additional effects (e.g., attitude change) and would feed back to alter system components and relationships.

An expectancy value model has emerged from the gratifications sought and gratifications obtained research approach. According to Palmgreen and Rayburn (1982), behavior, behavioral intention, and attitude can be seen as a function of: "(1) *expectancy* (or belief)—that is, the probability that an attitude possesses a particular attribute or that a behavior will have a particular consequence—and (2) *evaluation*—that is, the degree of affect, positive or negative, toward an attitude or behavioral outcome" (pp. 562–563). The model is useful for predicting the seeking of gratifications from communication channels owing to the expectancy of a certain outcome. The links to effects research occur with the investigation of the outcome of such behavioral intention that can be interpreted in terms of the gratifications actually obtained (i.e., consequences), such as comprehension, attitude formation, or behavior. The model allows for consideration of expectancy and evaluative thresholds for particular behaviors and for comparisons of congruence of expectation and outcome.

USES, EFFECTS, AND THEORY DEVELOPMENT

Katz et al. (1974) wrote that "hardly any substantive or empirical effort has been devoted to connecting gratifications and effects" (p. 28). As discussed throughout the last section, this situation has changed somewhat since that time. Research since the mid-1970s has attempted to reformulate the presumption of audience activity, to refine the conception of audience gratification seeking, to relate gratification seeking to media behaviors and dependency to consider (to a limited extent) consequences beyond media exposure and attitudes, and to synthesize theoretical conceptualizations of media uses and media effects. However, despite the recent progress of uses and gratifications research regarding some questions of media effects, further effort is needed to link gratifications with specific attitudinal and behavioral consequences.

Blumler (1979) placed the problem of this lack of theoretical advancement in proper perspective: "We lack a well-formed perspective about which gratifications sought from which forms of content are likely to facilitate which effects" (p. 16). He noted that the research consistently observed three media use orientations that are in need of attention because of their likely effects. These include cognitive, diversion, and personal identity orientations or functions. Blumler hypothesized three propositions about media effects from these orientations: (a) information gain will be facilitated by cognitive motivation; (b) audience acceptance of perceptions of social situations in line with entertainment portrayals will be facilitated by diversion and escape motivations; and (c) reinforcement effects will be promoted by personal identity motivations.

The first of these hypotheses has received some empirical support. At a minimum, cognitive (instrumental) motivations appear to lead to news and informational program viewing (Rubin, 1981b, 1983, 1984; A. Rubin & R. Rubin, 1982b). Other studies have found links between surveillance or information-seeking motives and information gained during a political campaign (McLeod & Becker, 1974), about political candidates (Atkin & Heald, 1976), and about candidates' stands on issues (Garramone, 1983). The second and third hypotheses have not been tested directly, although the evidence on escapist motivations points away from perceiving television content to be particularly realistic (Palmgreen, 1984). Clearly, there is a need to consider Blumler's (1979) hypotheses further, as well as his call for theoretical advancement by investigating and establishing more direct links between media uses and media effects.

Since the late 1970s and early 1980s, uses and gratifications research has attempted to address such effects, connections, and theoretical omissions. However, the synthesis of media uses and effects still has a long way to go. The goal of uses and gratifications research remains to explain media effects. However, single-variable causal explanations are limiting and suspect. The more proper view of many factors contributing to effects has offered no shortcuts. Uses and gratifications research has considered the gratifications of human needs and motives by using the mass media. We have gained a more exacting comprehension of the audience as variably active consumers and participants in the mass communication process. Still needed is a clearer picture of the relationships between media and personal channels of communication and sources of potential influence. The continuing step is to explore and explain the specific links among motives, attitudes, behavior, and communication effects.

REFERENCES

Adoni, H. (1979). The functions of mass media in the political socialization of adolescents. *Communication Research, 6,* 84–106.

Anderson, J. A., & Meyer, T. P. (1975). Functionalism and the mass media. *Journal of Broadcasting, 19,* 11–22.

Atkin, C. K., & Heald, G. (1976). Effects of political advertising. *Public Opinion Quarterly, 40,* 216–228.

Bantz, C. R. (1982). Exploring uses and gratifications: A comparison of reported uses of television and reported uses of favorite program type. *Communication Research, 9,* 352–379.

Becker, L. B. (1979). Measurement of gratifications. *Communication Research, 6,* 54–73.

Berelson, B. (1949). What 'missing the newspaper' means. In P. F. Lazarsfeld & F. N. Stanton (Eds.), *Communications research 1948–1949* (pp. 111–129). New York: Harper.

Blumler, J. G. (1979). The role of theory in uses and gratifications studies. *Communication Research, 6,* 9–36.

Carey, J. W., & Kreiling, A. L. (1974). Popular culture and uses and gratifications: Notes toward an accommodation. In J. G. Blumler & E. Katz (Eds.), *The uses of mass communications: Current perspectives on gratifications research* (pp. 225–248). Beverly Hills, CA: Sage.

Dimmick, J. W., McCain, T. A., & Bolton, W. T. (1979). Media use and the life span. *American Behavioral Scientist, 23*(1), 7–31.

Eastman, S. T. (1979). Uses of television viewing and consumer life styles: A multivariate analysis. *Journal of Broadcasting, 23,* 491–500.

Elliott, P. (1974). Uses and gratifications research: A critique and a sociological alternative. In J. G. Blumler & E. Katz (Eds.), *The uses of mass communications: Current perspectives on gratifications research* (pp. 249–268). Beverly Hills, CA: Sage.

Elliott, W. R., & Quattlebaum, C. P. (1979). Similarities in patterns of media use: A cluster analysis of media gratifications. *Western Journal of Speech Communication, 43,* 61–72.

Fisher, B. A. (1978). *Perspectives on human communication.* New York: Macmillan.

Galloway, J. J., & Meek, F. L. (1981). Audience uses and gratifications: An expectancy model. *Communication Research, 8,* 435–449.

Garramone, G. M. (1983). Issue versus image orientation and effects of political advertising. *Communication Research, 10,* 59–76.

Greenberg, B. S. (1974). Gratifications of television viewing and their correlates for British children. In J. G. Blumler & E. Katz (Eds.), *The uses of mass communications: Current perspectives on gratifications research* (pp. 71–92). Beverly Hills, CA: Sage.

Herzog, H. (1940). Professor quiz: A gratification study. In P. F. Lazarsfeld, *Radio and the printed page* (pp. 64–93). New York: Duell, Sloan & Pearce.

Herzog, H. (1944). What do we really know about daytime serial listeners? In P. F. Lazarsfeld & F. N. Stanton (Eds.), *Radio research 1942–1943* (pp. 3–33). New York: Duell, Sloan & Pearce.

Himmelweit, H., Oppenheim, A. N., & Vince, P. (1958). *Television and the child.* London: Oxford University Press.

Horton, D., & Wohl, R. R. (1956). Mass communication and para-social interaction. *Psychiatry, 19,* 215–229.

Katz, E. (1959). Mass communication research and the study of popular culture. *Studies in Public Communication, 2,* 1–6.

Katz, E., Blumler, J. G., & Gurevitch, M. (1974). Utilization of mass communication by the individual. In J. G. Blumler & E. Katz (Eds.), *The uses of mass communications: Current perspectives on gratifications research* (pp. 19–32). Beverly Hills, CA: Sage.

Katz, E., Gurevitch, M., & Haas, H. (1973). On the use of the mass media for important things. *American Sociological Review, 38,* 164–181.

Klapper, J. T. (1960). *The effects of mass communication.* New York: Free Press.

Klapper, J. T. (1963). Mass communication research: An old road resurveyed. *Public Opinion Quarterly, 27,* 515–527.

Korzenny, F., & Neuendorf, K. (1980). Television viewing and self-concept. *Journal of Communication, 30*(1), 71–80.

Lasswell, H. D. (1948). The structure and function of communication in society. In L. Bryson (Ed.), *The communication of ideas* (pp. 37–51). New York: Harper.

Lazarsfeld, P. F. (1940). *Radio and the printed page.* New York: Duell, Sloan & Pearce.

Lazarsfeld, P. F., & Merton, R. K. (1948). Mass communication, popular taste and organized social action. In L. Bryson (Ed.), *The communication of ideas* (pp. 95–118). New York: Harper.

Levy, M. R., & Windahl, S. (1984). Audience activity and gratifications: A conceptual clarification and exploration. *Communication Research, 11,* 51–78.

Lichtenstein, A., & Rosenfeld, L. B. (1983). Uses and misuses of gratifications research: An explication of media functions. *Communication Research, 10,* 97–109.

Lull, J. (1980). The social uses of television. *Human Communication Research, 6,* 197–209.

McCombs, M. E., & Shaw, D. L. (1972). The agenda-setting function of the mass media. *Public Opinion Quarterly, 36,* 176–187.

McLeod, J. M., & Becker, L. B. (1974). Testing the validity of gratification measures through political effects analysis. In J. G. Blumler & E. Katz (Eds.), *The uses of mass communications: Current perspectives on gratifications research* (pp. 137–164). Beverly Hills, CA: Sage.

McLeod, J. M., Becker, L. B., & Byrnes, J. E. (1974). Another look at the agenda-setting function of the press. *Communication Research, 1,* 131–166.

McQuail, D., Blumler, J. G., & Brown, J. R. (1972). The television audience: A revised perspective. In D. McQuail (Ed.), *Sociology of mass communications* (pp. 135–165). Middlesex, England: Penguin.

Mendelsohn, H. (1963). Socio-psychological perspectives on the mass media and public anxiety. *Journalism Quarterly, 40,* 511–516.

Merton, R. K. (1968). *Social theory and social structure.* New York: Free Press.

Miller, M. M., & Reese, S. D. (1982). Media dependency as interaction: Effects of exposure and reliance on political activity and efficacy. *Communication Research, 9,* 227–248.

Miyazaki, T. (1981). Housewives and daytime serials in Japan: A uses and gratifications perspective. *Communication Research, 8,* 323–341.

Palmgreen, P. (1984). Uses and gratifications: A theoretical perspective. In R. N. Bostrom (Ed.), *Communication yearbook 8* (pp. 20–55). Beverly Hills, CA: Sage.

Palmgreen, P., & Rayburn, J. D. (1979). Uses and gratifications and exposure to public television. *Communication Research, 6,* 155–179.

Palmgreen, P., & Rayburn, J. D. (1982). Gratifications sought and media exposure: An expectancy model. *Communication Research, 9,* 561–580.

Palmgreen, P., Wenner, L. A., & Rayburn, J. D. (1980). Relations between gratifications sought and obtained: A study of television news. *Communication Research, 7,* 161–192.

Palmgreen, P., Wenner, L. A., & Rayburn, J. D. (1981). Gratification discrepancies and news program choice. *Communication Research, 8,* 435–478.

Payne, D. E., & Caron, A. H. (1982). Anglophone Canadian and American mass media: Uses and effects on Québecois adults. *Communication Research, 9,* 113–144.

Pearlin, L. I. (1959). Social and personality stress and escape television viewing. *Public Opinion Quarterly, 23,* 255–259.

Rosengren, K. E. (1974). Uses and gratifications: A paradigm outlined. In J. G. Blumler & E. Katz (Eds.), *The uses of mass communications: Current perspectives on gratifications research* (pp. 269–286). Beverly Hills, CA: Sage.

Rosengren, K. E., & Windahl, S. (1972). Mass media as a functional alternative. In D. McQuail (Ed.), *Sociology of mass communications* (pp. 166–194). Middlesex, England: Penguin.

Rubin, A. M. (1977). Television usage, attitudes and viewing behaviors of children and adolescents. *Journal of Broadcasting, 21,* 355–369.

Rubin, A. M. (1979). Television use by children and adolescents. *Human Communication Research, 5,* 109–120.

Rubin, A. M. (1981a). An examination of television viewing motivations. *Communication Research, 8,* 141–165.

Rubin, A. M. (1981b). A multivariate analysis of *60 Minutes* viewing motivations. *Journalism Quarterly, 58,* 529–534.

Rubin, A. M. (1983). Television uses and gratifications: The interactions of viewing patterns and motivations. *Journal of Broadcasting, 27,* 37–51.

Rubin, A. M. (1984). Ritualized and instrumental television viewing. *Journal of Communication, 34*(3), 67–77.

Rubin, A. M., & Rubin, R. B. (1982a). Contextual age and television use. *Human Communication Research, 8,* 228–244.

Rubin, A. M., & Rubin, R. B. (1982b). Older persons' TV viewing patterns and motivations. *Communication Research, 9,* 287–313.

Rubin, A. M., & Rubin, R. B. (1985). Interface of personal and mediated communication: A research agenda. *Critical Studies in Mass Communication, 2,* 36–53.

Rubin, A. M., & Windahl, S. (1982, May). *Mass media uses and dependency: A social systems approach to uses and gratifications.* Paper presented at the convention of the International Communication Association, Boston.

Rubin, R. B., & Rubin, A. M. (1982). Contextual age and television use: Reexamining a life-position indicator. In M. Burgoon (Ed.), *Communication yearbook 6* (pp. 583–604). Beverly Hills, CA: Sage.

Schramm, W., Lyle, J., & Parker, E. (1961). *Television in the lives of our children.* Stanford, CA: Stanford University Press.

Stephenson, W. (1967). *The play theory of mass communication.* Chicago: University of Chicago Press.

Swanson, D. L. (1977). The uses and misuses of uses and gratifications. *Human Communication Research, 3,* 214–221.

Swanson, D. L. (1979). Political communication research and the uses and gratifications model: A critique. *Communication Research, 6,* 37–53.

Timasheff, N. S. (1967). *Sociological theory: Its nature and growth* (3rd ed.). New York: Random House.

Wenner, L. A. (1982). Gratifications sought and obtained in program dependency: A study of network evening news programs and *60 Minutes. Communication Research, 9,* 539–560.

Windahl, S. (1981). Uses and gratifications at the crossroads. In G. C. Wilhoit & H. deBock (Eds.), *Mass communication review yearbook* (Vol. 2, pp. 174–185). Beverly Hills, CA: Sage.

Wright, C. R. (1960). Functional analysis and mass communication. *Public Opinion Quarterly, 24,* 605–620.

15

Exploring the Entertainment Experience

Dolf Zillmann
Indiana University

Jennings Bryant
University of Houston

Entertainment is a ubiquitous phenomenon. No culture of which we have an adequate accounting has been entirely without it. As soon as the struggle for survival left human groups with sufficient time for relaxation, some form of communicative activity in which dangers and threats and their mastery and elimination were represented seems to have come into being (e.g., Hauser, 1953; Kühn, 1962–1963; Malinowski, 1948). By the time permanent records were left for posterity, cultures had developed well-defined rites. These rites, to be sure, served the maintenance of social structure and postmortem welfare. In large measure, however, they also served the cause of amusement, merriment, gaiety, fun, and joyous enlightenment. In other words, they served the cause of entertainment.

If entertainment is crudely defined as any activity designed to delight and, to a smaller degree, enlighten through the exhibition of the fortunes or misfortunes of others, but also through the display of special skills by others and/or self, it becomes clear that the concept encompasses more than comedy, drama, and tragedy. It engulfs any kind of game or play, athletic or not, competitive or not, whether witnessed only, taken part in, or performed alone. It subsumes, for instance, musical performances by self for self or others, of others for self, or with others; similarly, it subsumes dancing by self, of others, or with others.

Given such a broad conceptualization, entertainment happenings must have been obtrusive enough to catch the attention of those inclined to understand social phenomena. And they did. Plato, through the dialogue between Socrates and Protarchus in *Philebus*, reflected on the delight derived from learning about the fortunes and misfortunes of others. He approved of some conditions for delight, but he morally condemned many others. In so doing, he set a trend:

Entertainment was to be judged in moral terms, a judgment that tended to give it little social merit and that detracted from studying its function in a neutral fashion. Surely, there were less value-laden analyses. Aristotle, in his *Poetics*, furnished an account of the workings of drama that could stand as a model of morally detached description. Western thinking about entertainment and its usefulness continued in a moral vein, however. Barring sacral contexts, Christian philosophers failed to see any redeeming value in singing and dancing, in merriment and gaiety. Those who reflected about the nature of joy and, in particular, amusement and laughter detected nothing but evil. Hobbes, for example, thought that laughter "is incident most to them that are conscious of the fewest abilities in themselves; who are forced to keep themselves in their favour, by observing the imperfections of other men" (p. 125). Pascal is usually singled out (e.g., Lowenthal, 1961) as the Christian philosopher who condemned entertainment in the strongest possible terms. Pascal (1941) thought that humans have an "instinct which impels them to seek amusement" and that this impulsion "arises from the sense of their constant unhappiness" (p. 50), and he obviously deemed entertainment an unacceptable means of relief from such unhappiness. But the avenues toward salvation that he favored were not accepted by many others. Montaigne tends to be credited (e.g., Mendelsohn, 1966) with the opposing, "modern" conception of entertainment as an effective and acceptable means for relief from discontent and the unavoidable stress of daily life. Though he endorsed the unhappiness premise as well, he thought merriment and enlightenment through entertainment, transitory as they may be, were bona fide blessings. In emphasizing the recreational value of entertainment, Montaigne is said to have anticipated Freud's (e.g., 1930/1960a, 1915/1960b, 1919/1963a, 1908/1963b) views in these matters. Freud's thinking essentially parallels that of Montaigne, indeed. Persons are viewed as suffering the blockage of uncounted pleasure impulses (not to mention their suffering from numerous profound apprehensions and fears), and the need to repress them is seen to open the door for indirect gratification. Many of these indirect gratifications are projected as attainable through entertainment, and the numerous mechanisms said to accomplish this (e.g., identification with another person who is being gratified) have remained the mainstay in a deluge of popular speculations about how entertainment works.

Much of what Freud proposed seems to have been uncritically and carelessly adopted and adapted to entertainment. It was accepted as gospel that provided unfailing post facto "explanations." Freud had lavishly illustrated his theorizing with examples from drama (e.g., the Oedipus complex). His mechanisms were thus linked to drama. However, Freud did not propose any formal theory of drama or drama appreciation, nor did he articulate specific, testable hypotheses that could have spawned psychological research in this area. The situation is very different for humor. Freud's (1905/1960c) treatise on that subject entailed highly specific mechanisms and, presumably because of it, produced a flurry of research on humor appreciation. Freud's publication, it seems, made the study of humor acceptable, though not entirely respectable, among psychologists. Research on drama and related entertainment forms, on the other hand, has simply remained somewhat suspect for serious and profession-conscious psychologists, despite valiant efforts toward its recognition by investigators such as Berlyne (1971, 1973).

Whereas psychological research into the entertainment experience stagnated and really failed to get underway, communication researchers started to probe the uses and gratifications of what the mass media offered (e.g., Blumler & Katz, 1974; Katz, Gurevitch, & Haas, 1973; Palmgreen & Rayburn, 1982). Although the realization that radio and television are primarily media of entertainment was slow in coming (cf. Tannenbaum, 1980) and the acknowledgement of this fact continues to disillusion numerous irrepressible media idealists, the specifics of what is being consumed for what reason started to be investigated. The assessments were exploratory and largely nontheoretical. The technique was the interview, and the instrument was mainly the questionnaire. Media users reported their perceptions of why they consumed what they consumed, and they did so in unstructured or moderately to highly structured interviews (e.g., Blumler & Katz, 1974).

Assessments of this sort provided valuable insight into the entertainment consumers' beliefs about their motives for choosing this and that, as well as about their distaste for some material. The consumers' perceptions are not necessarily veridical, however, in the sense of reflecting correctly the actual motives that govern their entertainment choices. Consumers may be unaware of the actual determinants of their choices, and should they have reliable introspections of these determinants, they may be unable to articulate them. In addition, they may have cause to distort—in efforts at projecting a favorable image of themselves—whatever they know and can articulate. For these reasons, it would seem prudent to consider many of the survey findings concerning people's motives for consuming entertaining fare suggestive rather than conclusive. The motives projected on the basis of consumers' introspections could be treated as hypotheses that are yet to be subjected to testing that circumvents the problems and limitations associated with introspective assessments. Such testing is known, of course, as behavioral research.

In the study of communication phenomena, the behavioral approach has been successfully employed for decades by psychologists and communication researchers alike. Research has concentrated on persuasion (e.g., Rosnow & Robinson, 1967), interpersonal communication (e.g., Berscheid & Walster, 1969; Miller, 1966), nonverbal communication (e.g., Harper, Wiens, & Matarazzo, 1978; Knapp, 1978), and on the impact of asocial (e.g., Donnerstein, 1980; Geen, 1976) and prosocial messages (e.g., Rushton, 1979). Oddly enough, until recently nobody saw fit to apply the behavioral approach to the study of why people enjoy whatever they enjoy by way of entertainment. Only recently has research been published that probes the determinants of enjoyment and enlightenment in a behavioral fashion and is designed to test proposals deriving from survey research on motives as well as from motivation and emotion theory generally.

In this chapter, we attempt to provide an overview of what has been accomplished in this behavioral exploration of entertainment consumption and its immediate affective effects. The reader who is interested specifically in the perceptions of what makes consumers choose whatever they choose is referred to up-to-date reviews of the pertinent research by Atkin (1985) and Rubin (Chapter 14, this volume). We briefly inspect the exploration of entertainment choices and then turn to theory and research concerning the enjoyment of entertaining messages.

SELECTIVE EXPOSURE TO ENTERTAINMENT

In making entertainment choices, people can be very deliberate. A particular program might have attracted their attention, they may have decided to watch it, and they may be determined to turn to it once it becomes available. Such deliberate choices appear to be the exception, however. The choice of entertainment is usually made "on impulse." The program that holds the greatest appeal at a given time and under given circumstances, for whatever particular reasons, is likely to be picked. The factors that determine this appeal tend to be unclear to the respondents. It would be the rare exception for respondents to engage in formal and explicit evaluative comparisons of the choices before them. It is more likely that they make these choices rather "mindlessly," without using reliable and never-changing criteria in their appeal assessments and ultimately in their choices. Once the proposal is accepted that most entertainment choices are made spontaneously, rather than calculated like business deals, it can be projected that these choices are situationally variable and serve ends which respondents need not be and probably are not aware of.

Excitement Versus Relaxation as Ends

Entertaining fare can produce considerable excitement in respondents (cf. Zillmann, 1982). Such excitement manifests itself in obtrusive sympathetic dominance in the autonomic nervous system, among other things, and it produces intense affective reactions. Hedonically speaking, these reactions can be positive or negative, depending on the respondents' idiosyncratic appraisals of what transpired.

Television's capacity to produce excitement is obviously greater for persons experiencing low levels of excitation than for persons already experiencing high levels. To the extent that this capacity might influence entertainment choices, it should do so more strongly for people who suffered through a hapless day characterized by monotonous and boring chores than for people who were confronted with uncertainty, competition, and other pressures—in short, people who suffer from overstimulation and stress.

Under the assumption that levels of excitation that vary within a normal range (i.e., nonextreme levels) constitute a necessary, though not sufficient, condition for an individual's feelings of well-being, it has been proposed (Zillmann & Bryant, 1985b) that entertainment from television or elsewhere might be employed to regulate excitation. Understimulated, bored persons should be eager to expose themselves to exciting television fare. Even if the material is not intrinsically pleasant, such exposure should be pleasantly experienced because it brings these persons back to levels of excitation that are more closely linked to feeling good. If the materials are intrinsically enjoyable, all the better. Thus, for understimulated, bored persons, exposure to exciting television programs can be seen as having the benefit of returning them conveniently (i.e., with minimal effort and safely) to a hedonically superior and, hence, desirable state. Put bluntly, entertainment consumers of this kind should be appreciative of each and every arousal kick that television or any other medium provides (Tannenbaum, 1980).

But entertainment not only has the capacity to excite. It can soothe and calm as well (cf. Zillmann, 1982). This capacity may benefit those who are uptight, upset, annoyed, angry, mad, or otherwise disturbed. All these experiences are associated with sympathetic hyperactivity, and those who experience such hyperactivity obviously would profit from exposure to nonexciting, relaxing entertainment fare because this exposure would lower these persons' excitation and return it to more desirable levels. Stressed persons, then, would do well to avoid exciting fare and to seek out materials capable of calming them down.

Intuitive Grounds

Television's excitation- and mood-altering effects are not in doubt. But can it be assumed that, in selecting programs for viewing, people make choices that serve excitatory homeostasis? Do people do what is good for them spontaneously and without reflection? Can it be assumed that bored persons prefer exciting materials over relaxing ones and that stressed persons display the opposite preference? It can, indeed, based on the premise that bored persons experience relief when watching exciting programs, that stressed people experience relief when watching relaxing programs, and that the experience of relief constitutes negative reinforcement that shapes initially random choice patterns into mood-specific entertainment preferences.

The proposal that people form mood-specific preferences (i.e., behave as if they had a tacit understanding of what is good for them under particular affective circumstances) has been supported by experimental research (Bryant & Zillmann,

1984). Subjects were placed into states of boredom versus stress and then, ostensibly in a waiting period, allowed to watch television as they pleased. Their choice was among three exciting and three relaxing programs. Time of program consumption was unobtrusively recorded. The data revealed that exciting programs attracted bored subjects significantly more than stressed subjects and that relaxing programs attracted stressed subjects significantly more than bored subjects. Effects of self-determined exposure on excitation were assessed as well, and it was found that almost all subjects had chosen materials that helped them to escape effectively from undesirable excitatory states. In fact, almost all subjects overcorrected, that is, bored subjects ended up above base levels and stressed ones below base levels of excitation. The few bored subjects that failed to behave in line with expectations elected to watch relaxing fare and, as a result, remained in a state of subnormal excitation.

Affective Relief as an End

The tacit understanding of the benefits that accrue to consuming entertainment fare is not limited to exciting and calming materials, but extends to other message characteristics. Experimental research has provided evidence that people select programs that are involving to different degrees as a function of their affective states. Choices are such that persons who would affectively benefit from distraction (i.e., rid themselves of a bad mood) tend to select highly absorbing fare. Those with less need for distraction show less appetite for this kind of material (cf. Zillmann & Bryant, 1985b). And those confronted with acute problems from which distraction through entertainment cannot offer any escape or prompt relief (e.g., anger from provocation that demands corrective action) tend to stay away from entertainment altogether, at least temporarily (Christ & Medoff, 1984).

In seeking mood changes for the better (i.e., in terminating bad moods, in switching over into good moods, or in facilitating and extending good moods), humor and comedy appear to play a special role. To those in acute need of some cheering up, merriment and laughter must be assumed to hold considerable appeal. Generally speaking, entertainment that seems capable of stimulating positive affect immediately and frequently should be the pick of those suffering from the blahs. These people should be strongly inclined to choose comedy and its kin over alternative, competing offerings.

An investigation that makes this point most compellingly has been conducted with women at different stages in the menstrual cycle (Meadowcroft & Zillmann, 1984; see also Zillmann & Bryant, 1985a). On the premise that the premenstrual syndrome is created mainly by the rapid withdrawal of progesterone and estrogen that afforded anesthetizing protection earlier, it was argued that premenstrual and menstrual women should suffer from bad moods, if not from feelings of depression. As a result, these women should experience the greatest need for relief through merriment and laughter. Midway through the cycle, when estrogen levels are elevated and progesterone levels rise, this need should be less pronounced, if existent at all. As there is little that premenstrual and menstrual women can do about their misery, comedy of any kind offers a most convenient way out and, consequently, should become highly attractive.

To test this proposition, women were asked to select programs they would enjoy watching. They chose from among known situation comedies, action dramas, and game shows. Their position in the cycle was ascertained afterward. On the basis of the latter information, the women were placed into 4-day phase groups throughout the cycle, thus allowing the tracing of programs chosen for consumption as a function of hormonal conditions. In confirmation of the hypothesis, it was found that premenstrual and menstrual women are indeed significantly more eager to expose themselves to comedy than are women in other phases of the cycle. At midcycle, the women exhibited comparatively little interest in comedy and showed appetite for drama instead. On gloomy days, then, comedy becomes hyperattractive. If the behavior of the premenstrual and menstrual women is any indication, all people who are down on their luck may be expected to seek, and obtain, mood lifts from comedy.

But comedy is not by necessity a mood improver. Television comedy, in particular, is laden with teasing and demeaning happenings, even with considerable hostility (Zillmann, 1977). Material of this sort is unlikely to amuse persons who have recently been targets of similarly debasing actions because exposure to the material will tend to reinstate the unpleasantness and the annoyance from the treatments in question. Acutely angry persons, for example, cannot expect favorable mood changes from comedy that dwells on hostile actions. Angry persons thus would be well advised to refrain from exposure to such comedy, though not from other forms of comedy. Experimental research again shows that people behave as if they had tacit knowledge of these effects. Provoked, angry persons were found to refrain from watching hostile comedy and turn to alternative offerings (Zillmann, Hezel, & Medoff, 1980).

Interestingly, children as young as 4 and 5 years of age are already capable of using television fare to improve their mood states. In an experiment by Masters, Ford, and Arend (1983), boys and girls of this age were placed into a nurturant, neutral, or hostile social environment and then provided with an opportunity to watch children's television programs. In the neutral condition, the subjects received the same treatment from an adult supervisor as did a same-gender peer. In the nurturant or good-mood condition, the supervisor repeatedly criticized and belittled the peer; by implication the subject was doing fine. In the hostile or bad-mood condition, the supervisor continually and obtrusively admired and praised the subject's companion. Subjects in this condition were thus made to feel unimportant, disliked, and rejected. Once the different affective states had been induced, the subjects were allowed to watch television for as long as they pleased. They were free to shut off the monitor on which only one program could be received. This program was either nurturant or neutral. The nurturant one was composed of segments from *Mister Rogers' Neighborhood.* Mr. Rogers was highly supportive at all times, making nurturant comments like "I really like you," and "You know, you are a nice person." The neutral program consisted of new shows for children that presented world events devoid of emotional content. The time the children elected to watch one or the other program served as a measure of exposure.

The effects were clear-cut and as expected for boys. Boys treated in a hostile manner stayed with the nurturant program more than twice as long as others. Boys in a good mood exhibited the least need for exposure to nurturant fare. In contrast, the mood treatment had no appreciable effect on exposure to the neutral program. For girls, the mood treatment had apparently failed. Girls confronted with the supervisor who treated them nonnurturantly coped with this situation by paying minimal attention to the discriminating treatment, and reliable exposure effects could not be observed.

Avoiding Discomfort

The boys in the study by Masters et al. (1983) may have found relief in the exposure experience and tried to extend that experience because it felt so good. The information that was offered in the television program was apparently comforting to those in acute need of being comforted. However, the program that proved comforting might be classified as education rather than entertainment. The question thus arises: Can pure entertainment provide comfort? Is it used to obtain comfort or, at least, to minimize and avert discomfort? The research-based answer is: surely!

How exposure to entertaining fare can provide comfort and help avoid discomfort in adult respondents has been discussed elsewhere (e.g., Zillmann, 1982; Zillmann & Bryant, 1985a). Here we concentrate on the spontaneous selection of entertaining programs and on the tendency in this selection to choose programs that are likely to minimize discomfort through avoidance of disturbing events and, at the same time, maximize comfort through the provision of pacifying information.

An experiment conducted by Wakshlag, Vial, and Tamborini (1983) shows these selection tendencies most clearly. Male and female adults were placed in a state of apprehension about becoming victims of crime, especially violent crime, and later given an opportunity to select entertaining drama for consumption. The differently apprehensive subjects chose from a list of film synopses. These synopses had been pretested and received scores for the degree to which a film was perceived as featuring violent victimization and/or the punitive restoration of justice. Measures of the appeal of violence and justice were obtained by summing the scores across the films that were selected.

The findings revealed strong gender differences in the appeal of both violent victimization and justice restoration. Females responded less favorably to violence than did males. At the same time, they were attracted more strongly than males to justice restoration as a salient theme of drama. Irrespective of these overall gender differences, both crime-apprehensive males and crime-apprehensive females proved equally sensitive to the drama dimensions under consideration. Acutely apprehensive persons selected drama that was lower in violent victimization and higher in justice restoration than did their nonapprehensive counterparts. Apprehensive persons thus exhibited the proposed tendency to minimize exposure to disturbing events. Moreover, they exhibited the proposed tendency to expose themselves to information capable of diminishing their apprehensions. The main message of television crime drama—namely, that criminals are being caught and put away, which should make the streets safer—apparently holds great appeal for those who worry about crime (cf. Zillmann, 1980).

The reader who is interested in a more complete accounting of the research on selective exposure is referred to a recent collection of exposés on that topic (Zillmann & Bryant, 1985a). The purpose of the discussion here is only to highlight recent behavioral research into selective exposure to entertainment and to indicate the emerging choice-controlling variables.

ENJOYMENT OF ENTERTAINMENT

Quite obviously, entertainment off the screen does not merely serve the regulation of arousal and associated affect or produce a contagion with merriment for persons in need of overcoming the blahs. Entertaining messages are capable of gratifying respondents because of unique intrinsic properties, along with the respondents' idiosyncratic appraisals of these properties. But what are these properties? What are the ingredients of good entertainment? And what properties spoil enjoyment?

The enjoyment of drama, comedy, and sports is influenced by a multitude of variables, many of which have received considerable attention (e.g., Goldstein, 1979; Jauss, 1982). But none seem to control enjoyment as strongly and as universally as do affective dispositions toward interacting parties, especially parties confronted with problems, conflict, and aversive conditions. The exhibition of human conflict in the raw has often been singled out as the stuff of which all good drama is made (e.g., Smiley, 1971). The focus on conflict constitutes only a starting point, however. The dramatic portrayal of intense conflict, in and of itself, does not with any degree of regularity, certainly not by necessity, lead to enjoyment reactions in the audience. Enjoyment depends not so much on conflict as on its resolution and on what the resolution means to the parties involved. It depends on how much those who come out on top are liked and loved and on how much those who come out on the short end are disliked and hated. Good drama, then, relies on positive and negative sentiments toward the parties in conflict and on the extent to which a resolution can be accepted by the audience. Indifference toward protagonists and antagonists is the antidote to good drama. Positive and negative affective dispositions toward the agents in drama are vital and must be created if drama is to evoke strong emotions, enjoyment included. There need be beloved heroes (regardless of how their definition might change over the years), and there need be villains whom the audience can love to hate.

Dispositions and Affective Reactions

The response side of what is commonly referred to as "character development" is affect. The portrayal of goodness in protagonists is to make them likable and lovable. Analogously, the portrayal of evil in antagonists is to make them dislikable and hateable. To the extent that any intended character development works, it produces positive and negative dispositions toward the agents of a play.

Character development is effective, generally speaking, because respondents bring empathy and, more important, moral considerations to the screen. What the agents in a play do matters the most. It is the basis for the audience's approval or disapproval of conduct. Such approval or disapproval is a moral verdict, of course. The fact that this is not generally recognized by respondents (and those who study their behavior) does not alter that circumstance. Approval of conduct is assumed to promote liking; disapproval is assumed to promote disliking. Affective dispositions toward protagonists and antagonists, then, derive in large measure from moral considerations (cf. Zillmann, 1980).

Once an audience has thus placed its sentiments pro and con particular characters, enjoyment of conflict and its resolution in drama depends on the ultimate outcome for the loved and hated parties. Positive affective dispositions inspire hopes of positive outcomes and fears of negative ones. Protagonists are deemed deserving of good fortunes and utterly undeserving of bad ones. Negative affective dispositions, on the other hand, activate the opposite inclinations: fear of positive outcomes and hopes for negative ones. Antagonists are deemed utterly undeserving of good fortunes and deserving of bad ones. Such hopes and fears are obviously mediated by moral considerations.

These hopes and fears lead respondents to empathize with the emotions displayed by protagonists. The joys as well as the suffering of liked characters tend to evoke concordant affect in the audience. Positive and negative affect is said to be "shared." In contrast, these hopes and fears prompt counterempathetic reactions to the emotions experienced by antagonists. The villains' joy is the audience's distress, and their suffering, their being brought to justice, and their getting their comeuppance is the audience's delight (cf. Zilllmann, 1983). These basic dynamics of affect in spectators are summarized in Fig. 15.1.

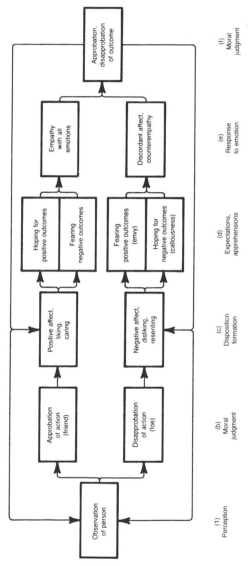

FIG. 15.1 Dynamics of affect from witness of others' actions (from Zillmann, 1983).

Although these dynamics of affect have been outlined in dichotomous terms, they should not be construed as merely dichotomous. They should be thought of as a dichotomous system underneath which continuous variables exist. Liking and disliking of characters are clearly matters of degree, and the projection of consequences for the enjoyment of events and final outcomes must take this into account. In more formal terms, the following predictions can be stated (cf. Zillmann, 1980):

1. Enjoyment deriving from witnessing the debasement, failure, or defeat of a party, agent, or object increases with the intensity of negative sentiment and decreases with the intensity of positive sentiment toward these entities.
2. Enjoyment deriving from witnessing the enhancement, success, or victory of a party, agent, or object decreases with the intensity of negative sentiment and increases with the intensity of positive sentiment toward these entities.
3. Annoyance deriving from witnessing the debasement, failure, or defeat of a party, agent, or object decreases with the intensity of negative sentiment and increases with the intensity of positive sentiment toward these entities.
4. Annoyance deriving from witnessing the enhancement, success, or victory of a party, agent, or object increases with the intensity of negative sentiment and decreases with the intensity of positive sentiment toward these entities.
5. Propositions 1 through 4 apply jointly. Consequently, all contributions to enjoyment and/or annoyance combine in total enjoyment or annoyance. In this integration of contributions, annoyance is conceived of as negative enjoyment, and contributions to enjoyment and to annoyance are assumed to combine in an additive fashion.

Predictions from this disposition model have been confirmed not only for the enjoyment of drama, but also for humor appreciation and the enjoyment of sports (Zillmann, Bryant, & Sapolsky, 1979; Zillmann & Cantor, 1976). Comedy can of course be construed as a form of drama that differs from drama proper only in that cues abound which signal that things are not to be taken too seriously (McGhee, 1979). Most tendentious jokes (i.e., hostile and/or sexual ones in which somebody is victimized) can also be construed as dramatic episodes—miniaturized ones, to be sure—in which there is conflict that is resolved in favor of a deserving party and to the detriment of a victim who had it coming. Setting someone up for the punch line is nothing other than making him or her deserving of the humorous knockdown.

The dispositional mechanics of enjoyment are most obvious in sports spectatorship. Sports fans have favorite players and teams. They also have players and teams that they detest with considerable intensity. Seeing a beloved competing party humble and humiliate a resented one obviously constitutes the ultimate in sports enjoyment. And the reverse outcome is the kind of event that can make grown men cry. It is clear, in addition, that indifference toward persons or teams in a contest is the kind of condition under which excitement and intense enjoyment cannot materialize. Surely, in the enjoyment of athletic events, there are many other factors that must be considered (Zillmann et al., 1979). But the dispositional mechanics seem of overriding significance in the enjoyment of dramatic confrontations of any kind.

On Thrills and Suspense

Upon cursory inspection, the enjoyment of suspenseful drama may strike one as being contradictory, even paradoxical. Such drama tends to be enjoyed despite the fact that for most of its duration the protagonist or protagonists (i.e., those dear to the audience) are seen in duress and in peril; they appear to be doomed (Zillmann, 1980). Over considerable periods of time, the heroes are tormented and about to be overpowered and destroyed by evil forces or extraordinary dangers. Dreaded, disastrous happenings are imminent—repeatedly, frequently, and in the latest action-packed raids on the audience, almost continually. How can anybody, under these circumstances, enjoy drama? The dominant affective experience should be one of empathetic distress. Surely, such distress is relieved at times when the feared and seemingly imminent events fail to materialize and, especially in the resolution, when in the grandest of fashions and usually against all odds, the protagonists overcome the dangers that threatened them and destroy the evil forces behind them, too. At times, of course, the resolution is less full-fledged, and the protagonists merely get away with dear life (e.g., the survivors of typical disaster movies). Contemporary horror movies tend to take that format also, as tormented ladies barely escape the chain saws, and the villains are spared for the sequel. Still, even in these resolutions that do not feature the annihilation of evil forces, there is cause for jubilation, and the resolution can be deemed satisfying.

Generally speaking, then, suspenseful drama exhibits much of the condition describable as "hero in peril," but it also offers a resolution that is satisfying, if only minimally so. The indicated paradox consists of the fact that such drama should evoke more empathetic distress than euphoria, at least in terms of time. It should be suffered more—or more accurately, longer—than it should be enjoyed. How can this formula work for nonmasochistic audiences?

One explanation is that the persons attracted to such drama are sufficiently understimulated and bored to appreciate any shake-up of their excitatory state (Tannenbaum, 1980; Zuckerman, 1979). If arousal levels are subnormal, excitatory reactions—even those derived from distress—can help return arousal to more pleasantly experienced levels. The safety and convenience of the exposure situation make it unlikely that levels rise to uncomfortable heights. Still, the immediate affective experience associated with any arousal kicks tends to be construed as negative in valence, and this seems to favor a more elaborate explanation.

According to the alternative account, residues of excitation from empathetic distress and/or from the response to the threatening stimuli persist through resolutions and intensify the euphoric experience that is evoked by these resolutions. As the magnitude of residual excitation is greater the more intense the distressful experience, it follows that the enjoyment of satisfying resolutions will be the more intensified the greater (and more immediate) the preceding distress reaction. The simple consequence of this is that suspenseful drama will be the more enjoyable, the more the audience is initially made to suffer, through empathy with the endangered protagonists and/or any duress induced by those dangers with which the protagonists struggled. Great enjoyment rides the back of great distress. Evidence for this relationship has been provided by numerous experimental investigations of suspenseful drama (Zillmann, 1980).

The intensification of the enjoyment of favorable final outcomes by residual excitation from preceding uncertainty and distress should apply to the appreciation of athletic performances, too. A liked team's victory after a close, tense game should be more enjoyable than a similar victory that was decided early in the contest. But research efforts at validating this have not yet been successful, owing to subjects' indifference toward unknown teams, which prevented the development of any appreciable degree of suspense (Sapolsky, 1980).

Tragic Events and Bad News

The phenomenon that is most puzzling as far as the prediction of enjoyment from the discussed disposition model is concerned is the apparent appeal of tragedy and news reports about disasters and the like. The persons who are witnessed suffering misfortunes and grievous occurrences are, as a rule, not resented and not considered deserving of tragic happenings. However, despite the fact that fiction often entails circumstances that make a tragic outcome more acceptable (e.g., the hero's so-called tragic flaw), it need not be assumed that the immediate affective reactions to the portrayal of tragic events are in any way positive. In all probability, these immediate reactions are negative, even intensely so. Tear-jerkers are, after all, known to jerk tears, and negative affect in response to newscasts on tragic events is not in doubt (Veitch & Griffitt, 1976). This makes the fascination with seeing the victimization of parties that are neither disliked nor deemed deserving of what happens to them all the more bewildering. Granted that tragic drama is not exactly the main course of popular drama, it does enjoy a considerable following that needs to be explained. The same applies, outside fiction, to the appeal of bad news in print and broadcast journalism, which is said to be ubiquitous and growing in popularity (Haskins, 1981). What needs might be satisfied by exposure to tragic happenings? And how can such exposure be gratifying, if it is gratifying in some way?

Some have postulated that the fascination with tragic events reflects morbid curiosity (Haskins, 1981). Others have suggested that responding sadly to the sadness of suffering people affords respondents an opportunity to celebrate their own emotional sensitivity (Smith, 1759/1971). Sobbing through a tear-jerker is proof to oneself that a valued social skill is abundantly present. Yet others have emphasized that exposure to tragic events invites social comparison, that respondents contrast their own situation with that of the suffering parties they witness, and that this contrasting eventually produces a form of satisfaction (Aust, 1984). Seeing misfortunes befall others and seeing them suffering from it thus may make viewers cognizant and appreciative of how good they have it. And as such positive feelings accrue to seeing tragedy strike, in reality or in fiction, tragedy becomes appealing despite the negative affect that is initially associated with it.

All these explanatory efforts remain conjecture at present. Research has failed to elucidate the response to the exhibition of tragedy in people's lives. Not only does it remain unclear why respondents are initially drawn to watching truly tragic events, but it remains particularly puzzling why exposure is sought repeatedly, as it seems likely that immediate responses were noxious and noxious experiences are generally avoided. Understanding tragedy and, in particular, the popularity of bad news thus poses a formidable challenge to entertainment research.

Audience Influences

Much of the consumption of entertaining messages occurs in particular social situations. Going to the movies is an event that usually involves friends or that happens in the context of dating (Mendelsohn, 1966). Going to see an athletic contest similarly tends to involve well-known others. Television fare is also consumed in the company of such others, but with one big difference: The television audience is limited to comparatively small numbers, in contrast to the backdrop of large audiences composed of unknown others at the movies or, especially, at athletic events.

Given these social circumstances, it should not be surprising to find that a considerable amount of speculation exists dealing with the consequences of specific social conditions for the enjoyment of the entertaining event, even with the consequences of the entertaining event for cohesion in the audience and for affective inclinations among members of that audience. Regarding the latter effect, Ovid (Artis amatoriae) was one of the first to propose that audience members' romantic passions might be enhanced by arousing, potentially violent, and bloody entertaining events. His intuition has actually received experimental support in recent years (e.g., White, Fishbein, & Rutstein, 1981). But many other socially relevant effects on the audience have remained unexplored, in spite of the fact that they are highly obtrusive on occasion. For instance, winning an Olympic hockey match against a powerful nation, especially when the victory comes unexpectedly, seems to have the capacity for uniting a nation in some not so tangible way and for a limited period. In a similar vein, entire communities become high-spirited cities of champions when they have a winning team or fall into gloom if their athletic entertainers fail to defeat the out-of-towners. Effects of this kind have received little attention by researchers. Rigorous exploration is difficult and, presumably for this reason, virtually nonexistent.

The exploration of the effects of social conditions of consumption on the enjoyment of entertaining events has met with greater success, but is quite incomplete nonetheless. The best documented phenomenon of this kind is the facilitative influence of others' laughter on the laughter of respondents (e.g., Chapman, 1973b; Chapman & Wright, 1976; Fuller & Sheehy-Skeffington, 1974; Smyth & Fuller, 1972). Even the canned laughter that accompanies comedy and humorous situations generally has been found to enhance laughter in child and adult audiences; moreover, it has been found to increase enjoyment in many, though not in all, instances (e.g., Chapman, 1973a; Cupchik & Leventhal, 1974; Leventhal & Cupchik, 1975; Leventhal & Mace, 1970). Persons responding to humor appear to take the reactions of others as a cue that signals the extent to which the events before them are laughable and, ultimately, enjoyable. The facilitative effect of others' laughter on laughter and enjoyment, then, seems to derive from the informational utility of the reactions of others rather than from a mechanical contagion that produces laughter which, through self-monitoring, eventually leads to a distorted appraisal of enjoyment. Such an interpretation is suggested by the finding that a model's laughter in response to particular stimuli tends to enhance an observers' laughter to these stimuli at a later time; that is, laughter is enhanced in the absence of the laughter of others that could function as an immediate stimulus for laughter in observers and thus serve contagion (Brown, Brown, & Ramos, 1981; Brown, Wheeler, & Cash, 1980).

Applause in response to musical performances functions analogously. As others' laughter makes humor appear funnier, others' applause makes music seem better. Hocking, Margreiter, and Hylton (1977), for instance, succeeded in planting numerous confederates into a nightclub, and members of the audience later evaluated the quality of the band and its music. This quality was deemed higher on nights when the confederates showed delight by applauding enthusiastically than on nights when they failed to do so.

Oddly enough, where the social facilitation of enjoyment is thought to be least in doubt—namely, in the cheering, quasi-hysterical crowds at athletic events—research has failed us, and we must continue to trust journalistic assertions (Hocking, 1982). Research on the effects of the social conditions under which athletic contests are watched on television has proven similarly uninformative. Audience size, for instance, could not be shown to exert an appreciable degree of influence on the enjoyment of a game (Sapolsky & Zillmann, 1978).

Audience size, in and of itself, may not have the impact that many feel it has. What people in the audience do, in contrast, seems to matter greatly. In many instances, the expression of particular emotions may well affect similar emotions in those amidst an expressive audience. The effects can be far more complicated, however, than any model of empathetic contagion and escalation would suggest.

A specific kind of influence of a companion's behavior on the enjoyment of drama has been demonstrated for horror movies. In an investigation by Zillmann, Weaver, Mundorf, and Aust (1984), subjects saw terrifying events from the latest horror flicks in the presence of an opposite-gender confederate who gave ample indication of being terrified in a distress condition, gave no indication of affective responsiveness in a neutral condition, or gave clear signs of taking things with the greatest of ease in a mastery condition. Following exposure to the materials, subjects reported their enjoyment.

Could their enjoyment be affected by these audience conditions and, if so, in what way? Those who believe in affective contagion might expect the terrified companion to enhance similar reactions in the subject and, because the object of horror movies is to terrify the audience, the film is deemed scarier and, hence, better and, hence, more enjoyable, at least in retrospect. It could also be conjectured that seeing horror with a terrified companion enhances enjoyment in those who enjoy being scared and/or seeing others scared and that it diminishes enjoyment in those who detest being scared and/or seeing others scared. But the findings are consistent with another model that is somewhat more elaborate, yet also more obvious.

On the premise that in our own and in most other societies young men are expected to master fear-arousing situations and, if scared, to deny such a response, whereas young women are allowed, if not encouraged, to express their distress freely, it can be argued that horror films, for better or worse, are a significant socializing institution. The horror genre provides a forum in which persons can confront terrifying happenings such as gruesome maimings and killings, and they can do so safely (i.e., without suffering bodily harm). Respondents can gauge their emotional reactions and in case these reactions should become overly intense, they can curb them by discounting the disturbing events as mere fiction. The reactions are thus always bearable, and thanks to excitatory habituation (cf. Zillmann, 1982), they should grow smaller with repeated exposure to similar stimuli.

Boys and young men apparently benefit most from such habituation. As their distress reactions diminish, they can more readily pretend not to be distressed at all. In fact, they should become proficient in denying any distress by expressing amusement or by similarly belittling the terrifying events before them. How better to exhibit mastery of terror than by waving it off with a smile? And what better companion for showing off this mastery than an apparently terrified female? The presence of such a female, compared to a less expressive one or, worst of all, one that exhibits mastery herself, should make the male feel great because (a) the movie is obviously scary, and (b) he is so cool about it that he could virtually comfort his disturbed companion. Young women, on the other hand, are not burdened with acculturation pressures toward callousness. They can live through and express their dismay. But as they do, an equally frightened male companion renders little comfort. He who effectively pretends not to be disturbed about the terrifying happenings is the one who radiates security, and a terrified female should feel inclined to seek comfort with him rather than with his more sensitive (or less callous) counterparts. The frightened maiden's desire to snuggle up on the macho companion is a cliché for horror movies.

If there is any truth to it, we can see why boys want to master, why girls want to scream, and why both parties want to go to such movies in the first place. We can see the implications of entertainment consumption for falling in love. But what about enjoyment of the movies themselves? Here it may be assumed that persons do not fully comprehend what it is that gives them pleasure. They do not neatly identify the sources of their enjoyment and trace different contributions. Rather, they are likely to come to a global assessment of how much they enjoyed a particular movie. Enjoyment that derives from the social circumstances of consumption tends to go unrecognized and is usually misattributed to the entertaining message.

According to this, young men should enjoy horror more in the company of an apparently frightened female companion than in the company of an unexpressive or mastering female. Young women, on the other hand, should enjoy horror more in the company of a mastering male companion than in the company of an unexpressive or distressed male. The experimental investigation (Zillmann et al., 1984) confirmed just that very strongly.

CONCLUDING REMARK

This brief introduction to research into the entertainment experience is necessarily incomplete. The interested reader is referred to the various cited summaries of research in particular domains (i.e., the exploration of enjoyment from suspense, comedy, horror, sports, etc.). But granted incompleteness, this exposition should make the point that it is most meaningful to treat the entertainment experience as an effect. It is, in fact, *the* effect of entertainment consumption. It is the primary effect that is sought out and pursued for the benefits that it entails— benefits such as being distracted from acute grievances, having boredom removed, being cheered up, being given great excitement, being helped to calm down, or being fed pacifying messages. Surely, many media analysts might be inclined to label the attainment of these benefits *escapism*. Heavy consumption of entertainment is indeed likely to be maladaptive in the sense that problems that could be resolved by appropriate action remain unresolved and may grow to calamity levels. The consumption of much entertainment does not fit such an account, however. Consumption is often not just not maladaptive; it can be highly adaptive. This is the case when consumption serves to improve on prevailing moods, affects, and emotions, shifting them from bad to good or from good to better, under conditions in which undesirable states cannot be eliminated and altered through well-targeted action. What should an individual who comes home exhausted from a long day's work in a steel mill or, for that matter, in an executive office do about this undesirable situation? And what can a woman in premenstrual pains do about the pain-inducing conditions? If entertainment consumption manages to calm them down, cheer them up, and get them ready for the next similarly trying day, is it fair to condemn such benefit as escapism? Would it not be more reasonable to accept such effects on mood and emotional well-being as recreational success?

But regardless of how media analysts might elect to characterize the effects in question, the fact remains that much entertainment is consumed to alter moods, affects, and emotions in the specified fashion; moveover, the fact remains that the desired effects come about with considerable regularity. De facto, then, the consumption of much entertainment has beneficial consequences. It is adaptive, recreational, restorative, and in this sense, therapeutic. This is not to say that all of entertainment necessarily has these effects or that massive consumption has benefits. Quite obviously, numerous, highly undesirable side-effects exist. This volume gives ample testimony to that. It is to say, however, that entertainment provided by the so-called mass media can provide highly beneficial emotional experiences that are truly recreational and may be uplifting. These effects of entertainment, presumably because of the ready condemnation of entertainment as cheap escapism, have received very little attention from researchers. We feel that some reevaluation is in order, and we hope that the exploration of the entertainment experience with its consequences for the emotional welfare of the consumers of entertaining fare will receive the attention that it deserves.

REFERENCES

Atkin, C. (1985). Informational utility and selective exposure to entertainment media. In D. Zillmann & J. Bryant (Eds.), *Selective exposure to communication* (pp. 63–82). Hillsdale, NJ: Lawrence Erlbaum Associates.

Aust, C. F. (1984). *The effect of "bad news" on respondents' satisfaction with their own situation.* Unpublished master's thesis, Indiana University, Bloomington.

Berlyne, D. E. (1971). *Aesthetics and psychobiology.* New York: Appleton-Century-Crofts.

Berlyne, D. E. (1973). The vicissitudes of aplopathematic and thelematoscopic pneumatology (or The hydrography of hedonism). In D. E. Berlyne & K. B. Madsen (Eds.), *Pleasure, reward, preference: Their nature, determinants, and role in behavior* (pp. 1–33). New York: Academic.

Berscheid, E., & Walster, E. (1969). *Interpersonal attraction.* Reading, MA: Addison-Wesley.

Blumler, J. G., & Katz, E. (Eds.). (1974). *The uses of mass communication: Current perspectives on gratifications research.* Beverly Hills, CA: Sage.

Brown, G. E., Brown, D., & Ramos, J. (1981). Effects of a laughing versus a nonlaughing model on humor responses in college students. *Psychological Reports, 48,* 35–40.

Brown, G. E., Wheeler, K. J., & Cash, M. (1980). The effects of a laughing versus a nonlaughing model on humor responses in preschool children. *Journal of Experimental Child Psychology, 29,* 334–339.

Bryant, J., & Zillmann, D. (1984). Using television to alleviate boredom and stress: Selective exposure as a function of induced excitational states. *Journal of Broadcasting, 28*(1), 1–20.

Chapman, A. J. (1973a). Funniness of jokes, canned laughter and recall performance. *Sociometry, 36,* 569–578.

Chapman, A. J. (1973b). Social facilitation of laughter in children. *Journal of Experimental Social Psychology, 9,* 528–541.

Chapman, A. J., & Wright, D. S. (1976). Social enhancement of laughter: An experimental analysis of some companion variables. *Journal of Experimental Child Psychology, 21,* 201–218.

Christ, W. G., & Medoff, N. J. (1984). Affective state and selective exposure to and use of television. *Journal of Broadcasting, 28*(1), 51–63.

Cupchik, G. C., & Leventhal, H. (1974). Consistency between expressive behavior and the evaluation of humorous stimuli: The role of sex and self-observation. *Journal of Personality and Social Psychology, 30,* 429–442.

Donnerstein, E. (1980). Pornography and violence against women: Experimental studies. *Annals of the New York Academy of Sciences, 347,* 277–288.

Freud, S. (1960a). Das Unbehagen in der Kultur. In *Das Unbewusste: Schriften zur Psychoanalyse* (pp. 339–415). Frankfurt: Fischer Verlag. (Original work published 1930)

Freud, S. (1960b). Das Unbewusste. In *Das Unbewusste: Schriften zur Psychoanalyse* (pp. 1–40). Frankfurt: Fischer Verlag. (Original work published 1915)

Freud, S. (1960c). *Jokes and their relation to the unconscious.* New York: Norton. (Original work published 1905)

Freud, S. (1963a). Das Unheimliche. In *Das Unheimliche: Aufsätze zur Literatur* (pp. 45–84). Frankfurt: Fischer Doppelpunkt. (Original work published 1919)

Freud, S. (1963b). Der Dichter und das Phantasieren. In *Das Unheimliche: Aufsätze zur Literatur* (pp. 7–18). Frankfurt: Fischer Doppelpunkt. (Original work published 1908)

Fuller, R. G. C., & Sheehy-Skeffington, A. (1974). Effects of group laughter on response to humorous material: A replication and extension. *Psychological Reports, 35,* 531–534.

Geen, R. G. (1976). Observing violence in the mass media: Implications of basic research. In R. G. Geen & E. C. O'Neal (Eds.), *Perspectives on aggression* (pp. 193–234). New York: Academic.

Goldstein, J. H. (Ed.), (1979). *Sports, games, and play: Social and psychological viewpoints.* Hillsdale, NJ: Lawrence Erlbaum Associates.

Harper, R. G., Wiens, A. N., & Matarazzo, J. D. (1978). *Nonverbal communication: The state of the art.* New York: Wiley.

Haskins, J. B. (1981). The trouble with bad news. *Newspaper Research Journal, 2*(2), 3–16.

Hauser, A. (1953). *Sozialgeschichte der Kunst und Literatur* (Vols. 1 & 2). München: C. H. Beck'sche Verlagsbuchhandlung.

Hobbes, T. (1968). *Leviathan.* Harmondsworth: Penguin. (Original work published 1651)

Hocking, J. E. (1982). Sports and spectators: Intra-audience effects. *Journal of Communication, 32*(1), 100–108.

Hocking, J. E., Margreiter, D. G., & Hylton, C. (1977). Intra-audience effects: A field test. *Human Communication Research, 3*(3), 243–249.

Jauss, H. R. (1982). *Aesthetic experience and literary hermeneutics: Vol. 3. Theory and history of literature* (M. Shaw, Trans.). Minneapolis: University of Minnesota Press.

Katz, E., Gurevitch, M., & Haas, H. (1973). On the use of the mass media for important things. *American Sociological Review, 38,* 164–181.

Knapp, M. (1978). *Nonverbal communication in human interaction.* New York: Holt, Rinehart & Winston.

Kühn, H. (1962–1963). *Vorgeschichte der Menschheit* (Vols. 1 & 2). Köln: Verlag M. DuMont Schauberg.

Leventhal, H., & Cupchik, G. C. (1975). The informational and facilitative effects of an audience upon expression and evaluation of humorous stimuli. *Journal of Experimental Social Psychology, 11*, 363–380.

Leventhal, H., & Mace, W. (1970). The effect of laughter on evaluation of a slapstick movie. *Journal of Personality, 38*, 16–30.

Lowenthal, L. (1961). *Literature, popular culture, and society.* Englewood Cliffs, NJ: Prentice-Hall.

Malinowski, B. (1948). *Magic, science and religion.* Garden City, NY: Doubleday Anchor Books.

Masters, J. C., Ford, M. E., & Arend, R. A. (1983). Children's strategies for controlling affective responses to aversive social experience. *Motivation and Emotion, 7*, 103–116.

McGhee, P. E. (1979). *Humor: Its origin and development.* San Francisco: Freeman.

Meadowcroft, J., & Zillmann, D. (1984, August). *The influence of hormonal fluctuations on women's selection and enjoyment of television programs.* Paper presented at the meeting of the Association for Education in Journalism and Mass Communication, Gainesville, FL.

Mendelsohn, H. (1966). *Mass entertainment.* New Haven, CT: College & University Press.

Miller, G. R. (1966). *Speech communication: A behavioral approach.* Indianapolis, IN: Bobbs-Merrill.

Montaigne, M. E. de. (1927). *The essays of Montaigne* (Vols. 1 & 2) (E. J. Trechmann, Trans.). London: Oxford University Press.

Ovid. (1947). *The art of love, and other poems* (J. H. Mozley, Trans.). Cambridge, MA: Harvard University Press.

Palmgreen, P., & Rayburn, J. D. (1982). Gratifications sought and media exposure: An expectancy model. *Communication Research, 9*, 561–580.

Pascal, B. (1941). *Pensées* (W. F. Trotter, Trans.). New York: The Modern Library.

Plato. (1892). Philebus. In B. Jowett (Ed. and Trans.), *The dialogues of Plato* (3rd ed., Vol. 4, pp. 519–645). New York: Macmillan.

Rosnow, R. L., & Robinson, E. J. (Eds.). (1967). *Experiments in persuasion.* New York: Academic.

Rushton, J. P. (1979). Effects of prosocial television and film material on the behavior of viewers. In L. Berkowitz (Ed.), *Advances in experimental social psychology* (Vol. 12, pp. 321–351). New York: Academic.

Sapolsky, B. S. (1980). The effect of spectator disposition and suspense on the enjoyment of sport contests. *International Journal of Sport Psychology, 11*(1), 1–10.

Sapolsky, B. S., & Zillmann, D. (1978). Enjoyment of a televised sport contest under different social conditions of viewing. *Perceptual and Motor Skills, 46*, 29–30.

Smiley, S. (1971). *Playwriting: The structure of action.* Englewood Cliffs, NJ: Prentice-Hall.

Smith, A. (1971). *The theory of moral sentiments.* New York: Garland. (Original work published 1759)

Smyth, M. M., & Fuller, R. G. C. (1972). Effects of group laughter on responses to humorous material. *Psychological Reports, 30*, 132–134.

Tannenbaum, P. H. (1980). An unstructured introduction to an amorphous area. In P. H. Tannenbaum (Ed.), *The entertainment functions of television* (pp. 1–12). Hillsdale, NJ: Lawrence Erlbaum Associates.

Veitch, R., & Griffitt, W. (1976). Good news–bad news: Affective and interpersonal effects. *Journal of Applied Social Psychology, 6*, 69–75.

Wakshlag, J., Vial, V., & Tamborini, R. (1983). Selecting crime drama and apprehension about crime. *Human Communication Research, 10*, 227–242.

White, G. L., Fishbein, S., & Rutstein, J. (1981). Passionate love and the misattribution of arousal. *Journal of Personality and Social Psychology, 41*, 56–62.

Zillmann, D. (1977). Humor and communication. In A. J. Chapman & H. C. Foot (Eds.), *It's a funny thing, humour* (pp. 291–301). Oxford: Pergamon.

Zillmann, D. (1980). Anatomy of suspense. In P. H. Tannenbaum (Ed.), *The entertainment functions of television* (pp. 133–163). Hillsdale, NJ: Lawrence Erlbaum Associates.

Zillmann, D. (1982). Television viewing and arousal. In D. Pearl, L. Bouthilet, & J. Lazar (Eds.), *Television and behavior: Ten years of scientific progress and implications for the eighties: Vol. 2. Technical reviews* (pp. 53–67). Washington, DC: U.S. Government Printing Office.

Zillmann, D. (1983, March). *Three-factor theory of empathetic delight and distress.* Paper presented at the NIMH Conference on Affect, Santa Barbara, CA.

Zillmann, D., & Bryant, J. (1985a). Affect, mood, and emotion as determinants of selective exposure. In D. Zillmann & J. Bryant (Eds.), *Selective exposure to communication* (pp. 157–190). Hillsdale, NJ: Lawrence Erlbaum Associates.

Zillmann, D., & Bryant, J. (Eds.). (1985b). *Selective exposure to communication.* Hillsdale, NJ: Lawrence Erlbaum Associates.

Zillmann, D., Bryant, J., & Sapolsky, B. S. (1979). The enjoyment of watching sport contests. In J. H. Goldstein (Ed.), *Sports, games, and play: Social and psychological viewpoints* (pp. 297–335). Hillsdale, NJ: Lawrence Erlbaum Associates.

Zillmann, D., & Cantor, J. R. (1976). A disposition theory of humour and mirth. In A. J. Chapman & H. C. Foot (Eds.), *Humour and laughter: Theory, research, and applications* (pp. 93–115). London: Wiley.

Zillmann, D., Hezel, R. T., & Medoff, N. J. (1980). The effect of affective states on selective exposure to televised entertainment fare. *Journal of Applied Social Psychology, 10,* 323–339.

Zillmann, D., Weaver, J., Mundorf, N., & Aust, C. F. (1984). *Companion effects on the enjoyment of horror.* Unpublished manuscript, Indiana University, Bloomington.

Zuckerman, M. (1979). *Sensation seeking: Beyond the optimal level of arousal.* Hillsdale, NJ: Lawrence Erlbaum Associates.

16 Setting the Parameters for Information Society Research

Jerry L. Salvaggio
University of Houston

The purpose of this chapter is to assess the state of research on the social and psychological side effects of the newer communications technology, referred to hereafter as *information society research.* Two criteria were used in selecting research studies to include. The first was that the study dealt with communications technology in particular, as opposed to technology in general. The second was that the research focus specifically on the potential social changes resulting from communications technology. Studies that deal with the impact on organizations (e.g., office automation studies) and the potential benefits of communications technology have been excluded.

It is instructive to examine the tradition from which information society research evolved. The study of the social consequences of communications technology is basically an outgrowth of the study of the consequences of technology in general. Research on the threat of technology traditionally has been rooted in the humanities. The first significant studies were published prior to 1950 (e.g., Huxley's *Brave New World*, 1932, Mumford's *Technics and Civilization*, 1934, and Orwell's *1984*, 1949). In 1964 Jacques Ellul's *Technological Society* appeared and has been extremely influential ever since. Less influential, though still significant, are two books published in the 1970s. Muller's *The Children of Frankenstein* (1970) and Teich's *Technology and Man's Future* (1977), both of which examined the nature of technological societies, attracted considerable attention and are still cited as important works. Most of these books described the kinds of technology which is now available and warned that totalitarian dystopias would evolve.

Research on information societies, then, evolved out of the humanistic tradition. As is seen later, this may account for the fact that information society research has not been well represented in the social sciences.

With the exception of a few studies, information society research emerged in the late 1970s concurrently with the advent of the well publicized QUBE cable system, the announcement of direct broadcast satellites (DBS), and the debut of videotex in England. By the mid-1980s, numerous books on communications technology had been published, but the majority focused on technology rather than social problems. This situation is even more lamentable when it comes to scholarly journals. The major journals in the field of communications have virtually ignored information society research. As of 1985, *Communication Monographs, Human Communication Research, Journal of Broadcasting, Quarterly Journal of Speech*, and *Journalism Quarterly* had yet to publish an article on the information society. Some of these journals have published articles on the use of technology, especially cable and satellite, but studies of the nature of information societies or of the major social problems associated with information societies are difficult to find. The most significant studies of communications technology and social effects are found in one communication journal, the *Journal of Communication*, and a variety of noncommunication journals and international journals including: *Telecommunications Policy, Information Age, Information, Economics and Policy, Transnational Data Report, Computer Compact, Daedulus, Computers and Society*, and several general journals in the humanities. Moreover, only a modicum of behavioral research on social effects has been published, as most of the behavioral scientists examining these issues have turned to the study of how technology is most effectively used in an organizational setting.

THE NATURE OF INFORMATION
SOCIETY RESEARCH

The social effects of communications technology (computer, cable, broadcast, telephone, satellite, and videotex communications) are quite different from the social effects of traditional mass communication systems. Most notably, the social effects of mass communications generally come through exposure to the media or lack of exposure. The social effects of many of the newer forms of communications technology, on the other hand, have more to do with transforming society as a whole. As an example, the social effect of videotex may be that more individuals will become involved in telecommuting or working at home connected to a computer at the office. Second, mass communication systems have had a significant effect on socialization through homogeneous reception. Examples are numerous and include the many television programs that have been broadcast live to more than one third of the world. The new technologies are likely to affect society indirectly through heterogeneous reception. As video cassette recorders (VCRs), cable systems with 40 or more channels, direct broadcast satellite, and home computers achieve a level of penetration equal to that of the television set, it will become increasingly rare that two individuals will have seen the same program the previous evening. Third, with mass media systems, the public as one comprehensive unit is the passive receiver of prepackaged programming. Most of the newer technologies, however, allow the viewer to respond and communicate with the system or with other individuals. Thus, information society research should focus on what happens to individuals and to societies when individuals are intricately tied into a communication and information system that allows them to: (a) view specialized programs, (b) retrieve information instantly, and (c) communicate directly in an electronic form with other individuals at great distances. Fourth, mass media research emphasizes content analysis as opposed to the communication system. Individuals in an information society are less likely to be affected by television content than by how they use the communications system and by how the system operator, the government, and the corporate world use the system. Thus, it follows that methodologies used to study mass media effects are less applicable in information society research.

PARAMETERS OF INFORMATION SOCIETY RESEARCH

It is profitable to offer a taxonomy of social problems that might fall under information society research.

Information Inequity.   In an information society, all individuals do not have equal access to information and/or information technology. The same can be said of world societies. As yet there are still many countries where fewer than 1 in 100 people has a telephone.

Social Control.   Historically, both governments and private sectors of society have attempted to control society through the use of the press, the church, the military, or whatever means are available. Speech, travel, religious affiliation, and participation in government are a few of the activities that one or more sectors of society might wish to control. Communications technology offers a potent force for potential control of societies.

Information Overload.   In the mid-1970s Alvin Toffler referred to the ever increasing body of information exposed to members of society. To stay informed, one must specialize in smaller and smaller areas of knowledge. The tendency to overspecialize presents a threat to the democratic process because fewer individuals are prepared to cope with more general, complex social problems.

Information Monopoly.   Many of the newer forms of communications technology are capital intensive. That is, they require the kind of capital to start that only a large corporation can afford. Knight-Ridder, for example, had to invest more than $25 million in its videotex experiment before offering the system commercially and it may be years before a modest profit is seen. Interactive cable systems are even more expensive. For this reason, most of the larger telecommunication systems are owned by only the largest multinational corporations. Moreover, many of these corporations own two or more different systems, such as interactive cable and broadcast television.

Information Censorship.   Censorship of information, especially by government, is clearly one of society's oldest social problems. Communications technology, however, offers more sophisticated means by which to monitor an individual's access and publication of sensitive information.

Pornography.   Soft- and hardcore pornography have traditionally been limited to theaters and adult arcades. With the advent of VCRs, cable and subscription television (STV), both hardcore and softcore programming have entered the American home.

Invasion of Privacy.   Computer, videotex, and interactive cable systems allow individuals to shop, bank, send electronic mail, and watch movies at home. But in order for these systems to operate, all data must be kept by the company offering the service. The possibility that this information will be sold or given to other organizations opens the way to numerous privacy issues.

Misuse of Information and Information Technology.   Most cases of misuse fall under the category of computer crime and computer hacking. Hackers frequently alter and destroy computer files that they have gained illegal access to, and computer criminals use information systems for embezzlement and fraud. An examination of the work that has been done in these areas would necessitate a monograph rather than a book chapter if the literature were thoroughly reviewed. An alternative would be a bibliography of publications that have touched on these issues. Rather than merely providing a list of the research, I have chosen to examine the areas of invasion of privacy, information inequity, and misuse of information in greater detail.

PRIVACY

The problem of privacy in an information society has been identified by numerous scholars in various disciplines, though seldom by communication scholars (e.g., Bamford, 1982; Blackhall, 1979; Breckenridge, 1970; Burnham, 1983; Donner,

1981; Garfield, 1979; Hiramatsu, 1983; Linowes, 1978; Marchand, 1980; McLuhan & Powers, 1981; Moses, 1981; Porat, 1978; Rose, 1983; Salvaggio, 1983a; Simon, 1982; Washburn, 1979; Westin & Baker, 1972; Wigand, 1982). Thus, it is difficult to argue against the notion believed by most experts that loss of privacy will be a major consequence of the growth of communications technology. There are numerous reasons for this pessimistic view.

First, there has been a proliferation of files in government and private computers. In 1982, 16 government departments had a combined total of 3,529,743,665 files on American citizens (*U.S. News & World Report*, 1982), an average of 15 files per citizen. The following organizations routinely collect data on individuals: hospitals, governmental agencies, law enforcement agencies, federal agencies dealing with organized crime and national security, credit agencies, employers, insurance companies, courts, banks, direct mail marketers, market research firms, car rental agencies, credit card companies, psychologists, lawyers, universities, schools, accountants, licensing boards, the Armed Services, cable companies, utilities, and many more. The types of information collected include: consumer, employment, education, financial, medical, psychological, criminal, legal, travel, and leisure activity.

Most alarming to those studying privacy issues is that communications technology will allow such organizations to collect, create, store, manipulate, trade, sell and distribute information in a far more efficient and detailed manner than ever before. Interactive cable systems, for example, collect data on movie viewing, home shopping, opinion polls, security, and so on for the purpose of billing and building demographic data. Videotex systems store information provided willingly by subscribers who request newspaper and magazine articles, government publications, airline schedules, encyclopedia articles, company profiles, and who also send and receive electronic mail.

A second privacy problem lies in the computer's ability to collect and correlate aggregate data and impose categories into which individuals can then be placed. An increasing number of corporations are using computer programs to identify possible drug abusers. Joseph H. Lodge, president of Corporate Security Advisors in Miami, has boasted: "We can look at information in personnel files and rate or rank each employee according to their drug use" (Faber, 1983, p. 19).

Other advances in communications technology make the possibility of a national identity card attractive because the card could save the government billions of dollars. Both Japan and Canada have also been tempted to issue a national identity card but eventually decided that the card was too sensitive politically. The use of the polygraph, which has become a new form of communication between employee and employer, poses a greater threat to individual privacy. As the polygraph is used today, employees and prospective employees have little choice but to submit to an exam that involves answering intimate questions having little to do with the nature of the employment. Approximately 500,000 individuals a year reportedly undergo polygraph tests. It has been estimated that if experts are correct and the tests are only 90% accurate, the remaining 10% would amount to 50,000 individuals possibly deprived of employment unfairly (*U.S. News & World Report*, 1982).

Research

Communication scholars have virtually ignored privacy issues despite the fact that communications technology is what makes unprecedented invasion of privacy possible. Work has begun, however, on defining the concept of privacy. Burgoon (1982) cites 11 definitions of privacy and concludes that they overlap and are confusing.

Research on how and why governments collect and abuse information on individuals is fairly well established. It has been determined that invasion of privacy is often a byproduct of good intentions. As criminal activity and military espionage increase, the need for greater surveillance increases. Donner (1981) argues that both government and private industry have a history of building files on citizens in the interest of national security.

The danger of too much surveillance has been discussed by numerous researchers. Gabor (1976) notes that computers and telecommunications are useful in reducing crime through surveillance but then suggests that the same technologies which allow us to watch the criminal also serve to allow others to watch us.

Research on the vulnerability of data banks suggests that safeguards are needed to prevent illegal entry and unethical use of the personal information (Diebold, 1973). Homet (1983) warns that data base technology is especially vulnerable to dictators and terrorists.

A different approach is to ask what national variables (political, economic, ideological, policy making) are most likely to lead to privacy problems. Salvaggio (1983a) points out that the United States is one of the few societies where a strong central communications policy-making organization does not exist. This makes the creation of privacy legislation difficult. As of 1985, there were no federal laws that applied to computer trespassing. In Japan and in Western European countries, the Ministry of Post and Telecommunications or similar organizations are capable of creating privacy policy.

Numerous research questions remain unanswered relative to communications technology and privacy. Do government and private industry need the amount of information collected on individuals to be effective? Which particular forms of communications technology are likely to be most susceptible? Videotex systems seem especially problematic. What are the psychological roots of individual curiosity which seem to motivate computer hackers? Clearly, information on a competitor is advantageous, but other forms of invasion seem to be based more on pure curiosity. Why do some cultures, such as the Japanese, seem less concerned about privacy? How can invasion of privacy be defined in a way that will stand up in court?

Another area where research is especially lacking is privacy legislation. Few scholars have attempted to explain Congress' lack of interest in privacy issues related to interactive cable and videotex. Thus far, privacy legislation is limited to one privacy provision within the Cable Telecommunications Act of 1985.

INFORMATION MISUSE

Information misuse, or what Pelton (1981) refers to as dysfunctional byproducts of new telecommunications, involves illegal or unethical use of computers and telecommunication systems. For purposes of clarity, I have categorized four types of misuse. First is misuse of communications technology for material gain. Entry into electronic fund transfer systems and illegally transferring funds to a new account has resulted in the loss of approximately $150 million per year in the United States alone (Burnham, 1983). This figure is no doubt a very conservative estimate as most experts agree that only 10% of all computer crimes are reported (Ball, 1982). U.S. Trust Co. of New York and Security Pacific National Bank in Los Angeles have lost $397 million and $10 million, respectively (Pasztor, 1982).

A second type of misuse is electronic plagiarism. Documents are downloaded from large data bases such as NewsNet or Knowledge Index and submitted for publication under a new name, or information on a particular invention is obtained in order to gain a competitive edge. Both electronic plagiarism and theft of industrial and/or technological information are becoming significant problems.

Manipulation of information, (e.g., work records, credit information, financial statements, etc.) is a third type of misuse. Hackers have gained illegal access to major computer systems across the country.

A fourth type of information misuse is information sabotage. Thus far, information sabotage has primarily been perpetrated by student hackers. A student at Carnegie-Mellon University halted operations of the mainframe computer at Columbia University by sending a message through the Department of Defense's Advance Research Projects Agency computer network (ARPANET). The cost to the university was $25,000 for repairing the damage. There is the potential, however, of political activists and foreign government agencies sabotaging data bases and operating systems. The ease at which sabotage through computers and telecommunications systems can be perpetrated was dramatically seen in the summer of 1983 when teen-agers in Minneapolis successfully altered records in numerous data bases across the country, including Los Alamos and a cancer research center.

Research

Misusing communications technology is basically a crime involving communication with a machine. Traditionally, communication scholars have limited their studies to human communication or mass media communication. Thus, it is not surprising that there are few if any studies of information misuse by communication scholars.

The major studies have been written by computer security consultants and computer scientists. Logsdon (1980), and Parker (1983) have examined key ethical issues and have provided insight into the nature of computer crime. Parker lists seven types of computer criminals: amateur, deranged, system hacker, organizations, career, extreme advocate, and government. The majority of reported computer crimes are perpetrated by amateurs.

Pelton (1983) has raised the issue of information sabotage and notes:

> Embezzlement, credit card and magnetic card forgeries, destruction of vital records, covert acquisition of secrets, and falsification of data to incriminate or exonerate key officials, destruction or immobilization of transportation systems, weapon systems, communication systems, credit and banking systems—indeed any system dependent upon telecommunication—are potentially vulnerable to an adept saboteur. (p. 62)

Hiltz and Turoff (1978) offer the most penetrating study of human use of computer communications in a study that will no doubt set the standard for future research in this area. Computer communication involves at least four features: messages, conferences, notebooks (e.g., drafts of coauthors), and bulletin boards (containing newsletters). What is of primary interest to Hiltz and Turoff are the social and psychological aspects of using these services. To give one example, the authors note that "computerized conferencing is much less intimate and self-exposing than oral modes of communication in the sense that only your words (which can be carefully considered and edited) are transmitted" (p. 27). If correct, this may partly account for the fact that many individuals, who are ordinarily shy and respectful in face-to-face communication, are not reluctant to enter the files of others and leave obscene messages. Other conclusions offered by Hiltz and Turoff could serve as a basis for future studies dealing with computer communication.

Technical answers to questions of how communications systems can be made more secure are best left for professionals. Communication scholars, however, have much to contribute to the study of the nature of human to machine communication, the psychology of anonymous computer-mediated communication, and the motivation behind hacking and mediated communication patterns. Turkle (1984) has established an excellent methodology in her study of hackers. Major questions relative to information seeking abound. Why do hackers enthusiastically roam through another's computer file and why do they feel compelled to leave evidence of their intrusion? Is the fact that information is intangible and the intruder invisible a crucial factor? Thus far, few if any hypotheses have evolved. When they do, experimental research that controls key variables might lend support to one or more theories.

On a macrolevel, what kind of communication patterns can we expect in a society where the elite are tied into vast communications networks and the less affluent continue to use traditional forms of mass communication? Is the increase in misuse of communications technology tied to the perception of information as power?

Numerous policy questions also remain. To what degree would stringent government regulations on communications technology be desirable? At what point would a strong regulatory agency monitoring the use of communications technology represent a greater threat than public misuse?

INFORMATION INEQUITY

Prior to 1982, there was some debate over the hypothesis that communications technology would lead to information haves and information have-nots. The inequity theory, however, received considerable support when AT&T was deregulated. The effect of the 1984 divestiture and deregulation of AT&T, the world's largest corporation, is higher "local" telephone rates. The theory that deregulation and marketplace competition would keep cost down is unsupportable, at least temporarily. Rates are scheduled to rise substantially, and services are scheduled to decline. Typically, the new regional Bell operating companies (RBOCs) are asking public utility commissions to permit rate increases ranging from 100 to 300%. For example, in June of 1983, Southwestern Bell Telephone proposed a $1.7 billion statewide rate increase in Texas, which would triple the cost of telephone service (Sanders, 1983).

In addition to the issue of telephone rates the spectre of inequity involves access to computers, videotex, software, interactive cable systems and information data bases.

Research

Research on information inequity has been carried out using various approaches. In light of the FCC's trend toward deregulation, some scholars have asked whether deregulation benefits the consumer. Rose (1983) observes that the FCC's intention to deregulate telecommunications is based on encouraging diversity, yet historically, diversity has never taken place.

A second line of research is to examine the ability of state and local municipalities to monitor the cost of communications technology and to assure that the public is receiving adequate access to it. Cable television is fertile grounds for research on inequity. Whether the public is being offered an outdated 12-channel cable system or a system with 120 channels, videotex, and health care services at a cost that the majority of the population can afford is left to the city council because they award cable franchises. Garay (1983) studied the cable franchising system in Houston and found that the city council lacked an understanding of the importance of cable technology. Moreover, the franchise process in Houston involved improper procedures. More studies at a microlevel are needed in order to ascertain the ability of local municipalities to make decisions on cable communications.

A third line of research focuses on how communications technology is used by various social groups. Danowski (1980a) has researched the use of communications technology and the aging process and has raised some research questions germane to the equity issue. Danowski (1980a) notes that it is important to study adult life-course changes with respect to established media and to study change over time in communication behaviors relative to the effects of period, cohort, and aging factors.

An especially relevant approach to the information inequity problem is the development and refinement of propositions, theoretical models, and taxonomies. Katzman (1974) posits six propositions on information inequity. Proposition three notes that it is an almost universal empirical phenomenon that communications technology raises the information level of all individuals and widens the gap between the information-rich and information-poor in society. Empirical studies conducted on more traditional forms of communications technology might be applicable here.

Probably the most difficult type of research on inequity, due to a lack of funding, is behavioral research on communities where some individuals do have access to communications technology. Since 1978, millions of dollars have been spent on the study of consumer use of teletext, videotex, video conferencing, video disc, video cassette recorders, interactive cable, and electronic mail. These studies are generally corporate sponsored and could provide valuable insight into the inequity problem. The majority, however, are proprietary. In certain cases, where an extensive research project did study community use of communications technology, the results have provided significant data that can be used in inequity research.

Elton and Carey (1983) conducted a 2-1/2 year program of empirical research on teletext. The findings were based upon meter records of approximately 5,000 user sessions and 100 in-home interviews in 40 households with teletext. The results of the study offer insight into the types of people who are willing to experiment with teletext and the degree to which individuals will use a public system. Elton and Carey (1983) report that when a public terminal is located at a library or civic center, there is a positive indication that the public will use it. In this case, a terminal was located at the Smithsonian Institution and at local community libraries, and each terminal was used by approximately 50 people each day.

Another question is how many individuals will pay for teletext. Elton and Carey's survey suggests that 40% of the household respondents and 50% of the public site users would pay a premium over the normal cost of a TV to receive teletext in their homes. Interestingly enough, at public sites willingness to pay was higher among blacks and blue-collar workers. These findings may indicate that teletext will appeal in its early phases more to the current population of heavy television viewers than to those who now rely strongly on newspapers, magazines, and other forms of print for information. Other explanations are also plausible.

Another empirical research project involved the Green Thumb videotex system sponsored by the U.S. government. The University of Kentucky's report (Warner & Clearfield, 1982) showed that farmers with more than 1,000 acres used the information more than those with less acreage. On the other hand, the "top farm sales category" ($100,000 and over) actually had the lowest percentage of high users. More high users were found among farmers with a high school education or less than among farmers with college training. Interestingly enough, heaviest users were not farmers with a high family income. Rather, use was inverse to income. "The lowest income category (under $15,000) had the greatest percentage of 'high' users and this percentage declined as income increased" (p. 29). Further analysis of Warner and Clearfield's study is required.

A survey by CompuServe, the most widely used videotex network (150,000–200,000 subscribers) in the United States, offers conflicting data. The CompuServe survey of 2,009 customers indicated that 96.4% of the respondents were male and were from upper-income brackets. According to CompuServe, 52% reported incomes of $30,000 or more a year, with 27.5% coming from the executive and managerial professions. Are the differences reported by these two studies attributable to the kind of use or the kind of equipment needed?

Knight-Ridder has invested more than $25 million into its Viewtron system, which many experts believe to be the prototype of future systems in the United States. Knight-Ridder's system requires the consumer to purchase a $600 terminal and pay $12 per month and $1 per hour of use. If Viewtron is typical of future information systems, inequity may be more of a problem than previously thought.

Two major research questions stand out. Does increased communications technology mean that information will be available to all? If not, what is the effect of not being able to access information? Ultimately, these questions revolve around the nature of how individuals use communications technology. We know much about how the public uses traditional television, but very little is known about how individuals use information-retrieval systems, computers, and narrowcast programming.

Teletext systems will be less expensive than two-way videotex systems. This could mean that those with the resources will utilize videotex, whereas those with lower incomes will utilize teletext. What will be the difference in terms of economic and educational benefits? Will deregulation, especially as it affects rate increases, be in the best interest of the public? This issue has drawn considerable attention (Dizzard, 1982; Haight, 1979; D. Schiller, 1982; H. Schiller, 1981). Will information retrieval become more important than communication in an information society? As more colleges turn to telecourses to solve transportation problems, cable and/or videotex services may eventually become a social necessity rather than a cultural enhancement. If this is the case, will our educational system exhibit the kinds of inequity problems seen in the entertainment area?

ADDITIONAL RESEARCH AREAS

In addition to privacy, misuse, and inequity, other salient issues need to be researched. A critical area for future research revolves around the race between the United States and Japan and, to a lesser extent, between these two countries and Europe for dominance in the communications technology field. A growing body of literature in the popular press attests to the race for dominance in supercomputers, artificial intelligence, and advanced telecommunication systems. Numerous economists have bemoaned the United States' laissez-faire approach to technology and some have called for the creation of a ministry of Technology. Is dominance in communications technology clearly of benefit to the public or simply a compelling argument by industry for government subsidies?

Related to this race is the potential for a new communications agency, which some believe should replace an impotent National Telecommunications and Information Administration (NTIA) and a languishing FCC. The implications of a new central agency, which would have the power and authority of Japan's Ministry of Posts and Telecommunications (MPT) or Europe's Post Telegraph and Telephone agencies (PTTS), would be significant. An earlier attempt at an agency for policy planning was the Office of Telecommunications Policy (OTP). Miller (1982) provides some insight into why that particular agency was abolished. However, there is a paucity of research on the pros and cons of the NTIA, which replaced the OTP.

The number of joint ventures between Japan and the United States and the United States and West Germany grows daily. Is the information industry becoming a multinational industry, and if so, what are the social and economic consequences?

As the United States continues to deregulate the communications industry, scholars have become increasingly aware of potential problems that may result in a purely competitive atmosphere (Cole & Oettinger, 1978; Nelson, 1983; Wiley & Neustad, 1982). Deregulation will clearly affect privacy, misuse, inequity, and unemployment, but the problem that most scholars cite as a consequence of deregulation is *information monopoly*. Bagdikian (1980, 1983), and others have examined media concentration and its effects to some degree, though little has been done in the evolving areas of DBS, direct broadcast satellite, low-power television, interactive cable, and videotex.

Information overload will increasingly be viewed as a major problem. As information increases in one's own specialized field, there is less time to stay abreast of broader social issues. This raises the possibility that more individuals will opt to entrust public issues to professionals. Blumler (1980) and Klapp (1982) have discussed information overload in greater detail.

A potential social problem that has received little attention is the possibility that communications technology will be used for social control. Electronic ankle bracelets for monitoring the movement of parolees, computer chip dog tags for the Army, and electronic sensors buried in the ground for surveillance of traffic movement in Hong Kong are some of the Orwellian devices now in the testing stage. When introduced, many of these devices are touted as being beneficial to society. For example, closed circuit cameras allow security guards to monitor parking lots and department stores. Yet, when cameras are placed behind one-way mirrors in department store dressing rooms, one wonders whether the benefits to the store outweigh the invasion of privacy to the public. This raises the question of whether the public perceives the potential threat to their civil liberties that new communications technologies represent. If correctly perceived, can public policy be developed in time to circumvent the misuse of this technology?

Elliott and Elliott (1976) have concluded that professional specialists with the intent of designing technology for human good find that there are powerful pressures which inevitably place them in a "servant of power role," thus reenforcing the existing ideology. Schiller (1983) has also argued that ideological forces control media use. Slack and Fejes (1984) have examined this phenomenon in greater detail in *The Ideology of the Information Society* (cf. Heath & Nelson, 1983).

Much more needs to be known about information itself. Dervin, Jacobson, and Nilan (1982) point out that the term information has never been adequately defined and that, as a consequence, mistaken research assumptions often result. Conjointly with research on information is the need for research on the nature of information societies. Bowes (1981) and Edelstein (1979) are among those who have examined the Japanese approach to the study of information societies.

Possibly the most serious problem that has received only perfunctory attention is the control of information. The Reagan administration has imposed strict regulations on access to CIA files, has censored materials imported from Cuba, and has authorized CIA surveillance of researchers traveling abroad. Fortunately, journalists have not let this issue go unnoticed (cf. Abrams, 1983; American Civil Liberties Union, 1983; Taylor, 1983).

An area of research that will continue to demand attention is the role of communications technology in the Third World. Transborder information flow, inequity, and transfer of technology are just three areas researchers have focused on. Fortunately, the many studies on this subject are too numerous to list. (cf. Smith, 1980)

By 1990, Japan and the United States will have spent more than a billion dollars researching supercomputers and attempting to develop artificially intelligent computers. Artificially intelligent computers are almost certain to have an adverse effect on employment. More interesting are the social implications of the cybernetic relationship between humans and intelligent computers (see Weizenbaum, 1976) which will evolve. It is already known that individuals are inclined to imbue computers and robots with more intelligence than they possess. More than a decade ago Weizenbaum invented Eliza, a computer program that simulated human thought. An individual would type in a question or statement, and Eliza would respond in a manner very similar to a human therapist. Eliza's responses were so well programmed that it was easy to interpret the program's remarks as though they came from a therapist. Although this did not surprise Weizenbaum, he was astounded and disappointed to learn that psychiatrists were interested in using a computer game for patients they didn't have time to see. It then became apparent to Weizenbaum that even sophisticated members of the general public did not understand the nature of computer programming and the difference between an electronic computer simulating a human response and true intelligence.

By 1990, home robots will be in many homes. The more expensive models will have some artificial intelligence capabilities, whereas Eliza was only mimicking intelligence. Voice recognition and voice synthesis will be common. How will individuals react to advice and to companionship from a robot with these human capabilities? To what degree will they develop emotional attachments, learn to trust, and confide in semi-intelligent robots? Cybernetics makes it clear that feedback from an experience changes the user. In what ways will we change as a result of interacting to greater degrees with personal robots? Though it still seems more science fiction than social science, robotics and cybernetics will become increasingly significant.

One major question remains unanswered. Are communication scholars up to the task of doing information society research? On the surface, this is a strange and self-effacing question. However, upon examination of the citations in this chapter, it becomes clear that the vast majority of information society research has not been conducted by communication scholars. And as pointed out earlier, only one American communication journal consistently publishes studies dealing with the information society. The quest to base studies on empirical data could discourage communication scholars from pursuing theoretical questions. The issues discussed in this chapter need to be studied from a variety of perspectives (e.g., Ellul, 1983), which at some point should come together. Behavioral research on communications technology could be integrated with archival studies and theoretical essays. Only by combining empirical findings with qualitative research will a theoretical foundation evolve for the study of the information society.

ACKNOWLEDGMENT

The author would like to acknowledge the invaluable help provided by R. A. Nelson in the preparation of this paper.

REFERENCES

Abrams, F. (1983, September 25). The new effort to control information. *The New York Times Magazine*, p. 14, 22.

American Civil Liberties Union. (1983). *Free Speech, 1984: The rise of government controls on information, debate and association* (Public Policy Report). New York: Author.

Bagdikian, B. H. (1980). Conglomeration, concentration, and the media. *Journal of Communication, 30*, 59–64.

Bagdikian, B. H. (1983). *The media monopoly*. Boston: Beacon.

Ball, L. D. (1982). Computer crime. *Technology Review, 21*, pp. 21–30.

Bamford, J. (1982). *The puzzle palace*. Boston: Houghton Mifflin.

Blackhall, K. (1979). Affordable privacy. *Telecommunications International Edition, 10*, 96–104.

Blumler, J. G. (1980). Information overload: Is there a problem? In Witte (Ed.), *Human aspects of telecommunications* (pp. 77–95). New York: Springer-Verlag.

Bowes, J. E. (1981). Japan's approach to an information society: A critical perspective. In C. G. Wilhoit & H. deBock (Eds.), *Mass communication review yearbook* (Vol. 2, pp. 699–716). Beverly Hills, CA: Sage.

Breckenridge, A. C. (1970). *The right to privacy*. Lincoln: University of Nebraska Press.

A Buck Rogers' type of concept: Electronic parolee surveillance, brain implants for criminals suggested. (1982, October 26). *The Houston Post*, pp. 11A. 1982.

Burgoon, J. (1982). Privacy and communication. In M. Burgoon (Ed.), *Communication yearbook 6* (pp. 206–249). Beverly Hills, CA: Sage.

Burnham, D. (1983). *The rise of the computer state*. New York: Random House.

Burnham, D. (1983, October 27). Computer fraud in 12 U.S. agencies put far above 172 cases. *The New York Times*, pp. 4.

Cole, B., & Oettinger M., *Reluctant regulators: The FCC and the broadcast audience* (1978) Reading, MA: Addison-Wesley.

Danowski, J. A. (1980a). *Adult life-course socialization to communication technologies: Aging, cohort and period effects*. Paper presented at the Mass Communication Division, annual meeting of the International Communication Association, Minneapolis, MN.

Danowski, J. (1980b). Group attitude uniformity and connectivity of organizational communication networks for production, innovation, and maintenance content. *Human Communication Research, 6*, 299–308.

Dervin, B., Jacobson, T. L., & Nilan, M. S. (1982). Measuring aspects of information seeking: A test of a quantitative/qualitative methodology. In M. Burgoon (Ed.), *Communication Yearbook 6.* Beverly Hills, CA: Sage.

Diebold, J. (1973). *The world of the computer.* New York: Random House.

Dizard, W. (1982). *The information era. New York: Longman/Annenberg.*

Donner, F. (1981). The age of surveillance: The aims and methods of America's political intelligence system. New York: Vintage.

Edelstein, A. S., Bowes, J. E., & Harsel, S. M. (Eds.). (1979). *Information societies: Comparing the Japanese and American experiences.* Seattle: University of Washington Press.

Elliott, D., & Elliott, R. (1976). *The control of technology.* London: Wykeham, 1976.

Ellul, J. (1983). *The technological system* (J. Neugroschel, Trans.). New York: Continuum.

Elton, M., & Carey, J. (1983). Computerizing information: Consumer reactions to teletext. *Journal of Communication, 33,* 162–173.

Faber, J. P. (1983, July 25). Drug abuse in workplace costs employers billions. *Houston Chronicle,* pp. 7a.

Gabor, D. (1973). Social control through communications. In G. Gerbner, L. Gross, & W. H. Melody (Eds.), *Communications technology and social policy: Understanding the new cultural revolution* (pp. 83–97). New York: Wiley.

Garay, R. (1983). Cable television in Houston, Texas: A case study in the politics of cable franchising. In R. Bostrom. (Ed.), *Communication Yearbook VII.* Beverly Hills, CA: Sage.

Garfield, E. (1979). 2001: An information society? *Journal of Information Science, 1,* 209–215.

Gerbner, G., Gross, L. P., & Melody, W. H. (1973). *Communications technology and social policy.* New York: Wiley.

Haight, T. R. (Ed.). (1979). *Telecommunications policy and the citizen.* New York: Praeger Special Studies.

Heath, R. L., & Nelson, R. A. (1983). Image issue advertising tap rules: Understanding corporate rights. *Public Affairs Review, 4,* 94–101, 104–105.

Hiltz, S. R., & Turoff, M. (1978). *The network nation.* Reading, MA: Addison-Wesley.

Hiramatsu, T. (1983). Privacy law in Japan. *Transnational Data Report, 6,* 43–44.

Homet, R. S., Jr. (1983). Monopoly versus competition: Social effects of media convergence. In J. L. Salvaggio (Ed.), *Telecommunications: Issues and choices for society* (pp. 78–84). York: Longman/Annenberg.

Hong Kong to test electronic road pricing to ease traffic chaos. (1983, April 23). *the Houston Post,* pp. 16a.

How a Carnegie-Mellon student may have crashed a computer at Columbia University. (1983, July 27). *The Chronicle of Higher Education,* pp. 18.

Huxley, A. (1946). *Brave new world.* New York: Harper & Row. (Originally published 1932).

Katzman, N. (1974). The impact of communication technology: Promise and prospects. *Journal of Communication, 24,* 47–58.

Klapp, O. E. (1982). Meaning lag in the information society. *Journal of Communication, 32,* 56–66.

Lasswell, H. D., Lerner, D., & Speier, H. (Eds.). (1980). *Propaganda and communication in world history.* Honolulu: East-West Center.

Linowes, D. F. (1978, June 26). The privacy crisis. *Newsweek,* p. 19.

Logsdon, T. (1980). *Computers & social controversy.* Potomac, MD: Computer Science Press.

Marchand, D. A. (1980). *The politics of privacy, computers, and criminal justice records.* Arlington, VA: Information Resources Press.

McLuhan, M., & Powers, B. (1981). Electronic banking and the death of privacy. *Journal of Communication, 31,* 164–169.

Miller, J. (1982). Policy planning and technocratic power: The significance of OTP. *Journal of Communication, 32,* 53–61.

Moses, J. (1981). The computer in the home. In M. L. Dertouzos & J. Moses (Eds.), *The computer age: A twenty-year view* (pp. 3–20). Cambridge, MA: MIT Press.

Muller, H. J. (1972). *The children of Frankenstein: A primer on modern technology and human values.* Bloomington: Indiana University Press.

Nelson, R. A. (1983). Entering a brave new world: The impact of the new information and tele-communications technologies. *Journal of the University Film and Video Association, 35,* 23–3.

Nilsen, S. E. (1979). The use of computer technology in some developing countries. *International Social Science Journal, 31,* 513–528.

Orwell, G. (1961). *1984.* New York: New American Library.

Parker, D. B. (1983). *Fighting computer crime.* New York: Scribner's.

Pasztor, A. (1982, May 28). Expert fights fraudulent use of computers. *The Wall Street Journal.*

Pelton, J. N. (1981a). The future of telecommunications. *Journal of Communication, 31,* 177–189.

Pelton, J. N. (1981b). *Global talk.* The Netherlands: Sijthoff & Noordhoff.

Pelton, J. N. (1983). Life in the information society. In J. L. Salvaggio (Ed.), *Telecommunications: Issues and choices for society* (pp. 51–68). New York: Longman/Annenberg.

Personal privacy in an information society (The Report of the Privacy Protection Study Commission). (1977). Washington, DC: U.S. Government Printing Office.

Pool, I. S. (1976). International aspects of computer communications. *Telecommunications Policy,* 33–51.

Pool, I. S. (1983). *Technologies of freedom.* Cambridge, MA: Harvard University Press.

Porat, M. U. (1978). Communication policy in an information society. In G. O. Robinson (Ed.), *Communications for tomorrow: Policy perspectives for the 1980's* (pp. 3–123). New York: Praeger.

Porat, M. U. (1978). Global implications of the information society. *Journal of Communication, 28,* 70–79.

Rose, E. (1983). Moral and ethical dilemmas inherent in an information society. In J. L. Salvaggio (Ed.), *Telecommunications: Issues and choices for society* (pp. 9–23). New York: Longman/Annenberg.

Salvaggio, J. L. (1982). An assessment of Japan as an information society in the 1980's. In H. F. Didsbury (Ed.), *Communications and the future* (pp. 88–95). Bethesda, MD: World Future Society.

Salvaggio, J. L. (1983a). Information societies and social problems: The Japanese and American experience. *Telecommunications Policy, 7,* 228–242.

Salvaggio, J. L. (Ed.). (1983b). *Telecommunications: Issues and choices for society.* New York: Longman/Annenberg.

Salvaggio, J. L. (1985). From technological adoption to social problems: Four models of the process. *Information and behavior, 1.*

Salvaggio, J. L., & Trettivik, S. (1981, May). *Information inequity in an information society.* Paper presented at the International Communication Association, Minneapolis, Minnesota.

Sanders, M. (1983, July 3). The new bell: Rate boost only one among many changes proposed. *The Houston Post.*

Schiller, D. (1982). *Telematics and government.* Norwood, NJ: Ablex.

Schiller, H. I. (1978). Computer systems: Power for whom and for what? *Journal of Communication, 28,* 184–193.

Schiller, H. I. (1981). *Who knows: Information in the age of Fortune 500.* Norwood, NJ: Ablex.

Schiller, H. I. (1983). Information for what kind of society? In J. L. Salvaggio (Ed.), *Telecommunications: Issues and choices for society* (pp. 24–33). New York: Longman/Annenberg.

Schramm, W. (1980). The effects of mass media in an information era. In H. D. Lasswell, D. Lerner, & H. Speier (Eds.), *Propaganda and communication in world history* (pp. 295–345). Honolulu: East-West Center.

Simon, H. A. (1982). What computers mean for man and society. In T. Forrester (Ed.), *The microe-lectronics revolution* (pp. 419–433). Cambridge, MA: MIT Press.

Slack, J., & Fejes, F. (1985). *The ideology of the information society*. Norwood, NJ: Ablex.

Smith, A. (1980). *The Geopolitics of Information*. New York: Oxford University Press.

Taylor, R. E. (1983, August 16). Debate grows over access to U.S. files. *The Wall Street Journal*, pp.   ).

Teich, A. H. (Ed.). (1977). *Technology and man's future*. New York: St. Martin's Press.

Turkle, S. (1984). *The second self: Computers and the human spirit*. New York: Simon and Schuster.

Warner, P. D., & Clearfield, F. (1982). *An evaluation of a computer-based videotext information delivery system for farmers: The green thumb project*. University of Kentucky, Department of Sociology, Lexington. (Unpublished manuscript)

Washburn, P. (1979). Electronic journalism: Computers and privacy. *Journal of information science, 1*.

Weizenbaum, J. (1976). *Computer power and human reason: From judgment to calculation*. San Francisco: Freeman.

Westin, A. F., & Baker, M. A. (1972). *Databanks in a free society: Computers, record-keeping and privacy*. New York: Quadrangle/New York Times.

Who is watching you? (1982, July 12). *U.S. News & World Report*, pp. 35–37.

Wigand, R. F. (1982). Direct satellite broadcasting: Selected social implications. In M. Burgoon (Ed.), *Communication Yearbook 6* (pp.   ). Beverly Hills, CA: Sage.

Wiley, R., & Neustadt, R. M. (1982). U.S. communications policy in the new decade. *Journal of Communication, 32*, 22–32.

Author Index

Page numbers in *italics* show where complete bibliographic references are given.

Subject Index